W9-CAE-827

WITHDRAWN

Guide to American Literature

Guide to
AMERICAN LITERATURE

VALMAI KIRKHAM FENSTER

LIBRARIES UNLIMITED, INC.

Littleton, Colorado
1983

84-334

LIBRARIES UNLIMITED, INC.
P. O. Box 263
Littleton, Colorado 80160-0263

Library of Congress Cataloging in Publication Data

Fenster, Valmai Kirkham.
    Guide to American literature.

    Includes indexes.
    1. American literature--Bibliography. 2. Literary
research. I. Title.
Z1225.F46   1983   [PS88]   016.81   82-23985
ISBN 0-87287-373-0

Libraries Unlimited books are bound with Type II nonwoven material that meets and
exceeds National Association of State Textbook Administrators' Type II nonwoven
material specifications Class A through E.

Table of Contents

PART II

CHAPTER EIGHT: GUIDES TO 100 INDIVIDUAL AUTHORS (cont'd)

CHAPTER EIGHT: GUIDES TO 100 INDIVIDUAL AUTHORS (cont'd)

Introduction

This guide to library materials in American literature that have been published through May 1982 is intended for undergraduate and graduate students who are engaged in academic study to assist in locating important titles in their field. Because the titles selected are those considered essential for the support of serious literary study, librarians who are responsible for collection building and reference services will also find it helpful. Brief descriptive annotations characterize the titles.

The guide is organized so that general survey tools that cover a number of authors are treated first. Seven chapters give help on how to use the library, its card catalog, bibliographic guides and indexes; reference tools; literary surveys; criticism; political, social, and intellectual history; language; and anthologies and series that have been found useful for study and teaching.

The second part, Chapter Eight, which comprises the major portion of the guide, gives bibliographic assistance for 100 exceptional literary authors who are frequently studied in American literature, black studies, and women's studies courses. Other important names that have been omitted because of space limitations may be located by referring to appropriate bibliographic tools described in the first seven chapters. For each author there is a list of primary sources, which includes separate works chronologically by date of their first publication and important collected editions. Such listing enables a handy historical overview that quickly allows the reader to gain perspective on the author's contributions. Secondary sources are selected and categorized as biography, criticism, bibliographies, and reference works.

With the exception of a few items, titles are in English. Dissertations, journal articles, and nonbook materials are normally excluded. Though some of the titles mentioned are no longer in print, most of them will be available in established college and university libraries.

The compiler takes responsibility for the judgments on titles included, realizing that other choices may be equally valid. Special thanks is given for the generous advice given from colleagues at the University of Wisconsin-Madison, especially William M. Gibson, Walter B. Rideout, Merton M. Sealts, Jr., Jack A. Clarke, and Yvonne Schofer.

Part I

1

How to Use the Library

BEGINNING A LITERATURE SEARCH

Students of literature go to the library wanting two types of information:

1) They may be seeking PRIMARY SOURCES, which include manuscripts, printed editions, sound recordings or videotapes of an author's imaginative work, as well as transcribed interviews, letters, and diaries that will illuminate the author's life or craft of writing.

2) Students may also need to use SECONDARY SOURCES, which include biographical accounts and criticism written by somebody other than the author whose work they are studying. They may want to verify factual information in reference sources, or to consult the catalog, bibliographies, and indexes, for access to further sources.

These primary and secondary sources are in many formats, including books, periodicals, government publications, dissertations, microforms, slides, films, video disks, phonograph recordings, sound tapes, and computer data bases. In order to find these resources it is necessary to use a variety of bibliographic tools.

The following sections of this chapter are intended to guide you as you begin a literature search. You will be introduced to the card catalog and to published guides, bibliographies, and indexes that should be available in the reference section of your library to help you gain access to materials in the collection.

THE CARD CATALOG

Author, Title, and Subject Approaches

In many cases, the best starting point for finding which primary and secondary sources are owned by the library is the catalog. Some catalogs are bound as books, or computer printouts, while others are available as microforms or through cathode ray tubes. A typical catalog is on 3x5 cards, alphabetically arranged, with three types of access provided. AUTHOR cards tell which works the library owns by a given writer, whose name appears on the top line, under surname. TITLE cards list works by title. SUBJECT cards list the subject of the work on the top line, and several different subject cards may be provided for a work. Depending on the library you are using, the cards for these three types of approach may be integrated in one sequence or they may be filed in separate catalogs. Each record will indicate where the work is shelved, usually by means of a call number located in the upper left-hand corner that matches the numbers printed on a work's spine.

How to Approach Primary Sources

Many works can be located if you have an author, title, or subject citation. However, in the field of BELLES LETTRES, the primary sources of an individual author, such as Sherwood Anderson, are not usually assigned subject headings because they are imaginative works. Neither are they assigned headings that reflect their genre, such as AMERICAN FICTION. Indeed, it is assumed that users will search for a work they know of, either by the author's name (Anderson, Sherwood) or by the work's title (*Winesburg, Ohio*).

When more than three authors have contributed to a collection, a subject heading is assigned, so that for an anthology of short stories by several writers the catalog should have three approaches: the title (*Major American Short Stories*), the editor (Litz, A. Walton), and a heading that reflects the genre represented by the collection (SHORT STORIES, AMERICAN). The lack of headings for each author and title represented in an anthology is a serious disadvantage when searching for items such as poems or short stories that are gathered in collections containing the primary sources of more than three authors.

How to Approach Secondary Sources

For an individual author, the secondary sources, or works about that author, may be sought by subject in one of two ways: If you want a general critical study about Sherwood Anderson's works, you should look for a subject card under his specific name (ANDERSON, SHERWOOD). There may also be additional entries subfiled under narrower aspects (ANDERSON, SHERWOOD–BIOGRAPHY; ANDERSON, SHERWOOD–CRITICISM AND INTERPRETATION). Should you want a work devoted specifically to Anderson's **Winesburg, Ohio**, you must search under a heading that narrows to the author and the title of the work about which you need a critical study (ANDERSON, SHERWOOD. WINESBURG, OHIO).

It is a good idea to search through the entire subject file of your author when seeking criticism because you may find that relevant aspects for your consideration are filed under subdivisions of the author that you have not considered. It is more difficult to find criticism of individual authors contained in general surveys because the catalog does not normally give access by the topics contained merely in sections of the work. For example, a chapter on "Sherwood Anderson," by Walter B. Rideout, in **Fifteen Modern American Authors: A Survey of Research and Criticism**, ed. Jackson R. Bryer, will have no access by either the author of the essay (Rideout, Walter B.), or by the title (Sherwood Anderson). For this work, there will be cards at the title of the collection (Fifteen Modern American Authors), the editor (Bryer, Jackson R.), and at a subject heading (AMERICAN LITERATURE–20th CENTURY–HISTORY AND CRITICISM). These three approaches give access to the anthology as an entity, but not to the fifteen essays on different authors by many scholars. In later sections of this chapter are citations to bibliographic indexes that will help you to find such individual essays contained in collections and periodicals.

Information on the Catalog Record

Beneath the record's heading is a description of the work for which it stands. Other information indicates the work's subtitle, additional authors, illustrators, translators and editors, the particular edition, the place of publication, the publisher and the date of publication, the number of pages or volumes, the categories of illustrations, and the size of the book. Further notes indicate if the work is in a series, the different titles under which it has appeared, or the presence of bibliographies.

Locating the Work

Before setting out to locate the work, copy down the call number, the author's names, and a few words of the title. Next consult the library's floor plan to find the shelf location so that you can match the classification from the work at the shelves with the call number that you copied. If you are unable to locate the work, there remain several steps that you can take. Always look about the shelf to see that the work has not been misshelved. Decide if you could usefully select a substitute. Recheck that you copied the call number correctly from the catalog. If you still need the original work, ask at the circulation desk whether someone has checked it out. The librarian may be able to recall the work for you. If the book is lost, you may want to try another local library or ask the interlibrary loan office for help.

It may be that the work you need is not listed in the catalog. Remember that the catalog does not usually list individual magazine articles, lectures, or essays in anthologies. Before giving up your search, ask a librarian where to look next. Your item may be listed in a specialized bibliographic index to which the librarian can direct you. (See also the following sections in this chapter.) Finally, if the work is unavailable and you decide to buy it, you should search in two closely related annual bibliographies to find out if it is still current: **Books in Print** (New York: Bowker, 1948-) and **Subject Guide to Books in Print** (Bowker, 1957-).

LITERATURE GUIDES

Literature guides list the histories, bibliographies, collections of explication and criticism, dictionaries, handbooks, encyclopedias, periodicals, and other sources considered most helpful for the study of the field. Usually located in the reference section of the library, they present information in a variety of ways. Some are formatted as lists; others are formal essays. Use of the following guides, especially those that are thoughtfully annotated, will help you to choose the appropriate material to look for in the library catalog.

—Altick, Richard D., and Andrew Wright. **Selective Bibliography for the Study of English and American Literature.** 6th ed. (New York: Macmillan, 1978). Selects about 600 reference works and bibliographies. Includes a glossary of terms used in literary research and a list of "Some Books Every Student of Literature Should Read."

—**A Bibliographical Guide to the Study of Southern Literature: With an Appendix Containing Sixty-Eight Additional Writers of the Colonial South,** ed. Louis D. Rubin (Baton Rouge: Louisiana State Univ. Press, 1969). Items by specialists on southern literature from colonial times to the present, under such topics as "Ante-Bellum Southern Writers" and "Local Color." Includes bibliographies of individual writers.

—Callow, James T., and Robert J. Reilly. **Guide to American Literature from Emily Dickinson to the Present** (New York: Barnes & Noble, 1977). Twelve chapters are devoted to overviews of literary movements and major individual authors. In a second section, there are a general bibliography and separate bibliographies for the authors in the first section that include both major editions of their collected works and secondary sources. A short chapter containing those bibliographic tools most useful for updating a personal bibliography is included.

—Callow, James T., and Robert J. Reilly. **Guide to American Literature from the Beginnings through Walt Whitman** (New York: Barnes & Noble, 1967). On a similar plan to the preceding volume.

—Gohdes, Clarence. **Bibliographical Guide to the Study of the Literature of the U.S.A.** 4th ed. (Durham, NC: Duke Univ. Press, 1976). Lists and annotates thirty-five broad categories of items under such headings as "Book Trade" and "Poetry." Includes titles on methods of research and covers related fields such as theatre, history, and folklore.

—Kennedy, Arthur, and Donald Sands. **A Concise Bibliography for Students of English**. 5th ed., rev. by William E. Colburn (Stanford, CA: Stanford Univ. Press, 1972). Gives unannotated approaches by broad historical periods. Includes Dewey and Library of Congress classification numbers.

—Kolb, Harold H., Jr. **A Field Guide to the Study of American Literature** (Charlottesville: Univ. Press of Virginia, 1976). Six chapters cover broad topics such as "Journals" and "Reference Works." Helpful for its lists on literary history and criticism.

—Koster, Donald N. **American Literature and Language: A Guide to Information Sources** (Detroit: Gale, 1982). A helpful guide with thoughtfully annotated entries, covering 149 general aids and 135 authors with biographical, critical, and bibliographical sources, emphasizing works since 1950.

—Leary, Lewis, with the collaboration of John Auchard. **American Literature: A Study and Research Guide** (New York: St. Martin's Press, 1976). Succinct evaluations in essay format of literary histories, genre studies, works on foreign influence, language, schools of criticism, and bibliographical guides. Includes bibliographic essays on twenty-eight major authors and advice on writing a research paper, as well as an essay on the history of the study and teaching of American literature.

—Patterson, Margaret. **Literary Research Guide** (Detroit: Gale, 1976). Contains over 15,000 critical annotated entries, organized by national literature with subcategories on genres and issues.

—Schweik, Robert C., and Dieter Riesner. **Reference Sources in English and American Literature: An Annotated Bibliography** (New York: Norton, 1977). Annotated lists covering approaches to the bibliography of American literature under such topics as indexes, handbooks, literary theory and criticism, textual history, analytical bibliography and editing, reference materials, general and national bibliography, media, dissertations, serials, reviews, myth, folklore, dictionaries, catalogs, and guides to libraries.

BIBLIOGRAPHIES

Most bibliographies contain systematic descriptions that include author, title, edition statement, and publication data. For a historical account of the development of bibliographies in American literature, see Vito Joseph Brenni, **The Bibliographic Control of American Literature, 1920-1975** (Metuchen, NJ: Scarecrow, 1979); and for a comprehensive guide to the field of American publishing and its history, see G. Thomas Tanselle, **Guide to the Study of United States Imprints.** 2v. (Cambridge: Harvard Univ. Press, 1971).

Bibliographies of Bibliographies

—Havlice, Patricia P. **Index to American Author Bibliographies** (Metuchen, NJ: Scarecrow, 1971). Index to bibliographies of American writers which have been published in periodicals. Includes writers from other countries who were professionally active in the United States. Supplements Nilon.

—Nilon, Charles H. **Bibliography of Bibliographies in American Literature** (New York: Bowker, 1970). Lists bibliographies for literature, publishing, printing history, newspapers, and other aspects of American culture.

General Bibliographies of American Literature

—Blanck, Jacob N. **Bibliography of American Literature** (New Haven, CT: Yale Univ. Press, 1955-). In progress. When finished, Blanck will be the most comprehensive bibliography of American literature. Lists works in book form of about 300 authors, beginning in the Federal period. Excludes authors who died after 1930, or whose writings are not classed as belles-lettres. Each author's works are arranged chronologically to include extensive pamphlets which contain the first appearance of any work, reprints containing changes, and a selected list of secondary sources. Excludes later editions, translations, and newspaper or periodical literature.

—**Eight American Authors: A Review of Research and Criticism.** rev. ed., ed. James Woodress (New York: Norton, 1971). Evaluative bibliographic essays on Poe, Thoreau, Emerson, Hawthorne, Melville, Whitman, Mark Twain, and Henry James.

—**Fifteen American Authors before 1900: Bibliographic Essays on Research and Criticism,** eds. Robert A. Rees and Earl N. Harbert (Madison: Univ. of Wisconsin Press, 1971). Essays on the primary and secondary sources of Adams, Bryant, Cooper, Crane, Dickinson, Edwards, Franklin, Holmes, Howells, Irving, Longfellow, Lowell, Norris, Taylor, and Whittier. Includes essays on the literature of the "Old South" and the "New South."

—**Goldentree Bibliographies** (New York: Appleton-Century-Crofts, 1966-). This ongoing series includes many excellent guides to primary and secondary materials such as Richard Beale Davis. **American Literature through Bryant, 1585-1830** (1969); Harry Hayden Clark. **American Literature: Poe through Garland** (1971); C. Hugh Holman. **The American Novel through Henry James** (1966); and Charles Altieri. **Modern Poetry** (1979).

–Leary, Lewis G. **Articles on American Literature, 1900-1950** (Durham, NC: Duke Univ. Press, 1954); **1950-1967** (Duke Univ. Press, 1970); **1968-1975** (Duke Univ. Press, 1979). Unannotated bibliography of English-language articles and significant reviews in periodicals, based on quarterly checklists in **American Literature.**

–**Literary History of the United States.** 4th ed., rev., ed. Robert Spiller, et al. 2v. (New York: Macmillan, 1974). Volume 2 contains evaluative bibliographic essays on literature to 1970. Covers guides to resources, bibliographies on culture, periods, language, movements, regionalism, and local color. In addition, there are extensive scholarly assessments on individual authors, alphabetically arranged, that cover both primary and secondary sources.

–**Literary Writings in America: A Bibliography.** 8v. (Millwood, NY: KTO Press, 1977). Lists creative American literature, 1850-1940.

–**Sixteen Modern American Authors: A Survey of Research and Criticism.** rev. and enl. ed., ed. Jackson Bryer (Durham, NC: Duke Univ. Press, 1974). Evaluative bibliographic essays on primary and secondary sources of Anderson, Cather, Hart Crane, Dreiser, Eliot, Faulkner, Fitzgerald, Frost, Hemingway, O'Neill, Pound, Robinson, Steinbeck, Stevens, William Carlos Williams, and Wolfe.

–Yannella, Donald, and John H. Roch. **American Prose to 1820: A Guide to Information Sources** (Detroit: Gale, 1979). Annotates nearly 3,000 items which are the work of 139 authors, and contains a useful general section.

Selected Continuing Bibliographies

–**American Literary Realism, 1870-1910** (Arlington: Univ. of Texas, 1967-). 2 times a year. An important review of trends and areas needing research. Usually lags about a year behind the period covered.

–**American Literary Scholarship** (Durham, NC: Duke Univ. Press, 1963-). Annual review of scholarship in the form of bibliographic essays by leading specialists, who review and evaluate the published work of the year, covering important literary figures and research trends. The publication lags behind the literature by about a year.

–**American Literature** (Durham, NC: Duke Univ. Press, 1929-). 4 times a year. Each issue provides bibliographic updating, with reviews and lists of "Articles on American Literature Appearing in Current Periodicals."

–**M.L.A. International Bibliography of Books and Articles on the Modern Languages and Literatures** (New York: Modern Language Association of America, 1921-). The most comprehensive annual bibliography, covering Western-language literature of all periods, with a separate section for American literature. Lists books, journal articles, and dissertations by period and then by literary figure. This bibliography is also available as a computerized data base.

–**Resources for American Literary Study** (College Park, MD: Virginia Commonwealth Univ. & Univ. of Maryland, 1971-). Semiannual issues include annotated checklists of criticism and bibliography as well as evaluative essays on major figures and scholarly trends, notable editions, and library collections.

PERIODICALS

Guides to Periodicals

—Gerstenberger, Donna, and George Hendrick. **Fourth Directory of Periodicals Publishing Articles in English and American Literature and Language** (Chicago: Swallow Press, 1974). International directory of over 600 scholarly journals giving for each title the major fields covered, manuscript information, and subscription. Arrangement by periodical title and subject index.

—Mackesy, Eileen M., and Karen Mateyak, with the assistance of Nancy B. Hoover. **MLA Directory of Periodicals: A Guide to Journals and Series in Languages and Literatures.** 1980-81 ed. (New York: Modern Language Association of America, 1981). Over 3,000 journals indexed in the **MLA International Bibliography** are arranged by title, and information is provided on acronyms, international standard serial numbers, ordering facts, including addresses and subscriptions, and details on preparation and submission of manuscripts.

—Patterson, Margaret C. **Author Newsletters and Journals** (Detroit: Gale, 1979). International guide to 1,087 serial publications on the lives and works of 420 authors from over twenty-five countries.

Indexes

To find the individual articles in periodicals it is necessary to consult specialized indexes under the author, title, or subject of the articles required. Because each index covers a specified group of periodicals, which is usually listed in the front, it may be necessary to search in several indexes to find appropriate material. When you have located a citation to the article needed, copy the volume number, date, and page number of the periodical that contains it and go to the catalog to find the call number.

The following sections are devoted to: 1) continuing periodical indexes that will provide access to current items; 2) eighteenth- and nineteenth-century periodical indexes that have ceased publication; and 3) indexes to little magazines.

CONTINUING PERIODICALS

—**Humanities Index** (New York: H. W. Wilson, 1974-). Quarterly, with annual cumulations. Part 1 is an author and subject index to 260 humanities periodicals. Part 2 is a list of reviews under the names of the book's authors. Subject approaches are provided for such topics as Literature—Themes; Motifs; Individual Authors; and Folk Lore. For 1920-1965, consult the **International Index to Periodicals**.

—**Readers' Guide to Periodical Literature** (New York: H. W. Wilson, 1901-). Semimonthly, with frequent cumulations. An author, subject, and title index to about 160 general and popular American periodicals.

EIGHTEENTH- AND NINETEENTH-CENTURY PERIODICALS

—Cameron, Kenneth W. **Research Keys to the American Renaissance** (Hartford, CT: Transcendental Books, 1967). Reprints indexes of the mid-nineteenth-century American periodicals: **Christian Examiner; North American Review;** and the **New Jerusalem Magazine.**

—**Early American Periodicals Index to 1850** (New York: Readex Microprint, 1960). Index on opaque microcards of 340 American periodicals published from 1730 to 1860.

—**Nineteenth Century Readers' Guide to Periodical Literature, 1890-1899, with Supplementary Indexing, 1900-1922,** eds. Helen Grant Cushing and Adah V. Morris, 2v. (New York: H. W. Wilson, 1944). Index of subjects, authors, and illustrators in fifty-one general and literary periodicals, giving access to poems, short stories, and novels. Unfinished.

—Poole, William F., and William I. Fletcher. **Index to Periodical Literature, 1802-1881.** rev. ed. 2v. (Boston: Houghton Mifflin, 1891); **Supplement, 1882-1907.** 5v. (Houghton Mifflin, 1887-1908). Subject index covering articles published over 105 years in 479 American and English periodicals with reviews of novels under authors' names. Errors have been published in the **Bulletin of Bibliography,** v.1-4. Access to names of authors in the **Index** is in C. Edward Wall, **Cumulative Author Index for Poole's Index to Periodical Literature, 1802-1906** (Ann Arbor, MI: Pierian Press, 1971).

—**The Wellesley Index to Victorian Periodicals, 1824-1900,** ed. Walter E. Houghton (Toronto: Univ. of Toronto Press, 1966-). In progress. Provides access to authors, subjects, and reviews in Victorian periodicals. Arrangement is by journal name with chronological subarrangement of the separate issues. A table of contents for each issue lists authors and contributions.

LITTLE MAGAZINES

The approaches to materials in little magazines are most unsatisfactory, and there is need for continuing indexes to cover current titles.

—**Access: The Supplementary Index to Periodicals** (Evanston, IL: John Gordon Burke, 1975-). 3 times a year. Indexes periodicals, including regional and city magazines, that are not indexed in **Readers' Guide to Periodical Literature.** Two listings, by author and subject.

—Sader, Marion. **Comprehensive Index to English-Language Little Magazines, 1890-1970.** 8v. (Millwood, NY: Kraus-Thomson, 1976). Indexes only 100 titles by author, and although inadequate, remains the most complete index.

Selected Periodicals Important for Students of American Literature

For the following periodicals are given the full title, the acronym representing the customary abbreviation of the title, place of publication, publisher, and the year in which it began publication. For an exhaustive listing, see Eileen M. Mackesy and Karen Mateyak. **MLA Directory of Periodicals.**

—**Abstracts of English Studies** (AAS) (Champaign, IL: National Council of Teachers of English, 1958-). Screens articles on American, English, and Commonwealth literature in about 1,000 journals, stating the thesis, method, and implications.

—**American Literature: A Journal of Literary History, Criticism, and Bibliography** (AL) (Durham, NC: Duke Univ. Press, 1929-). 4 times a year. The most important journal on American literature. As well as scholarly articles, each issue includes the columns: "Articles on American Literature Appearing in Current Periodicals" and "Research in Progress." An index to earlier issues is Thomas F. Marshall. **An Analytical Index to "American Literature,"** volumes I-XXX, March 1929-January 1959 (Durham, NC: Duke Univ. Press, 1963).

—**American Literary Realism, 1870-1910** (ALR) (Arlington: Univ. of Texas, 1967-). 2 times a year. Serves as an important research tool for emphasis on "lesser literary figures" such as Adams, Alcott, Chesnutt, Chopin, Dreiser, Fuller, Freeman, and Garland, with primary and secondary bibliographies. A cumulative index is in each autumn issue.

—**American Quarterly** (AQ) (Philadelphia: Univ. of Pennsylvania, 1949-). 5 times a year. Focuses on "the culture of the United States, past and present," with a selective annotated list of interdisciplinary periodical articles in the annual summer supplement.

—**Contemporary Literature** (CL) (Madison: Univ. of Wisconsin Press, 1960-). 4 times a year. Concentrates on literature "since World War II, on both sides of the Atlantic," with focus on "younger authors. . .viewed against the background of the major concerns which inform contemporary writing." Special issues on topics such as Nabokov (1967) and H. D. (1969).

—**Early American Literature** (EAL) (Amherst: Univ. of Massachusetts, 1966-). 3 times a year. Covers seventeenth and eighteenth centuries, occasionally including editions and bibliographies.

—**Mississippi Quarterly: The Journal of Southern Culture** (MISS Q) (State College: Mississippi State Univ., 1948-). 4 times a year. Interdisciplinary focus on civilization and culture of the American South. Each summer issue is devoted to Faulkner, and each spring issue has an annotated bibliography on southern literature.

—**Modern Fiction Studies** (MFS) (Lafayette, IN: Purdue Univ., 1955-). 4 times a year. Focuses on scholarship, bibliography, and criticism of American, English, and European fiction since 1880, with special numbers devoted to individual authors.

—**New England Quarterly** (NEQ) (Brunswick, ME: Colonial Society of Massachusetts and New England, 1928-). 4 times a year. Contains articles, notes, and book reviews on literature, history, and culture of New England.

—**Publications of the Modern Language Association of America** (PMLA) (New York: Modern Language Association of America, 1885-). Contains articles that are of interest to the entire membership, employing a widely applicable methodology, treating major authors or works, or discussing minor authors in such a way as to bring insight to a major author, genre, work, period, or critical method.

—**Resources for American Literary Study** (RALS) (Richmond: Virginia Commonwealth Univ.; College Park: Univ. of Maryland, 1971-). 2 times a year. Publishes annotated checklists of criticism and bibliography on both major and minor authors and disseminates information on scholarly resources.

—**Studies in American Humor** (SAH) (San Marcos: Southwest Texas State Univ., 1974-). 3 times a year. Concentrates on humor in literature.

—**Twentieth Century Literature** (TCL) (Hempstead, NY: Hofstra Univ., 1955-). 4 times a year. Includes articles on all aspects of modern literature and contains a "Current Bibliography" which has been collected in David E. Pownall. **Articles on Twentieth Century Literature: An Annotated Bibliography, 1954 to 1970** (New York: Kraus-Thomson, 1973-).

—**Western American Literature** (WAL) (Logan: Utah State Univ. Press, 1966-). 4 times a year. Concentrates on literature of the western United States.

GENRE INDEXES TO PRIMARY MATERIALS, THEIR CRITICISM AND EXPLICATION

It is difficult to locate particular primary sources such as poems, plays, fiction, and essays because they are collected in comprehensive anthologies or periodicals. The search for explication and criticism can be similarly tedious. In the reference section of your library there are indexes to help you find these individual items contained in anthologies, periodicals, and other sources. To locate an appropriate subject index, look in the catalog under a subject heading which reflects the genre in which you are interested (e.g., POETRY—INDEXES). At the shelves, consult the index for the author, title, or subject of the item you need and copy its citation so that you can search again in the catalog to find the call number for the anthology in the library.

The following indexes will help you to locate the genres of poetry, drama, fiction, and essays, as well as criticism and explication.

Indexes to Poetry

PRIMARY MATERIALS

—Chicorel, Marietta. **Chicorel Index to Poetry in Anthologies and Collections in Print.** 1st ed. 4v. [i.e. v.5, 5A, 5B, 5C of **Chicorel Index**] (New York: Chicorel Library Pub. Corp., 1974).

—Congdon, Kirby. **Contemporary Poets in American Anthologies, 1960-1977** (Metuchen, NJ: Scarecrow, 1978). Lists 6,500 poets whose works are in about 400 anthologies published since 1960. Part 1 lists anthologies with names of poets contained in them. Part 2 lists poets with references to the anthology titles in Part 1.

—Davis, Lloyd, and Robert Irwin. **Contemporary American Poetry** (Metuchen, NJ: Scarecrow, 1975). Helpful guide to poetry of the 1950s and 1960s.

—**Granger's Index to Poetry.** 7th ed., eds. William J. Smith and William F. Bernhardt (New York: Columbia Univ. Press, 1982). Indexes over 40,000 poems in 248 anthologies of poetry published from 1970 through 1981, by author, title, subject, and first line. Asterisks designate those anthologies judged most valuable for small libraries. Although earlier editions incorporated many older anthologies from Granger's former compilations, the seventh edition concentrates on anthologies from 1970 only, so that earlier editions, especially the sixth, should also be consulted.

—**Index of American Periodical Verse,** 1971- (Metuchen, NJ: Scarecrow, 1973-). Annual. Indexes poetry in over 150 magazines.

CRITICISM AND EXPLICATION

—Cline, Gloria S., and Jeffrey A. Baker. **An Index to Criticisms of British and American Poetry** (Metuchen, NJ: Scarecrow, 1973). Gives approaches to criticism of about 285 poets that was written between 1960 and 1970 and includes a list of the books and journals which have been indexed.

—Kuntz, Joseph M. **Poetry Explication: A Checklist of Interpretation Since 1925 of British and American Poems Past and Present.** 3rd ed. (Boston: G. K. Hall, 1980). Arranged by author with citations to criticism on individual poems not over 500 lines in length that appeared in books and periodicals.

—Library of Congress. Poetry Office. **Literary Recordings: A Checklist of the Archive of Recorded Poetry and Literature in the Library of Congress.** rev., enl. ed., comp. Jennifer Whittington (Washington, DC: Library of Congress; for sale by the Superintendent of Documents, 1981).

—Tate, Allen. **Sixty American Poets, 1896-1944.** rev. ed. (Washington, DC: Library of Congress, 1954). Brief bibliographies of significant poets. Includes works, recordings, bibliography, criticism, and location of important collections.

Indexes to Drama

PRIMARY MATERIALS

—Chicorel, Marietta. **Chicorel Theater Index to Plays in Periodicals.** 1st ed. [i.e. v.8 of **Chicorel Index**] (New York: Chicorel Library Pub. Corp., 1973). Provides access to plays in nineteenth- and twentieth-century periodicals by author, title, and subject of play.

—Keller, Dean H. **Index to Plays in Periodicals** (Metuchen, NJ: Scarecrow, 1971); **Supplement** (Scarecrow, 1973). Indexes plays in 103 periodicals by author and title, with references from adapters. Each entry contains a description of the play.

—Meserve, Walter J. **American Drama to 1900: A Guide to Information Sources** (Detroit: Gale, 1980). A general guide which covers a range of sources including indexes.

—Ottemiller, John H. **Ottemiller's Index to Plays in Collections: An Author and Title Index to Plays Appearing in Collections Published Between 1900 and Mid-1970.** 5th ed., rev. and enl. by John M. Connor and Billie M. Connor (Metuchen, NJ: Scarecrow, 1971). Gives author and title approaches to plays by over 1,600 authors in 1,047 collections.

CRITICISM AND EXPLICATION

—Adelman, Irving, and Rita Dworkin. **Modern Drama: A Checklist of Critical Literature on the 20th Century Plays** (Metuchen, NJ: Scarecrow, 1967). Index to critical articles and important reviews on twentieth-century drama appearing in books and periodicals.

—Breed, Paul F., and Florence M. Sniderman. **Dramatic Criticism Index: A Bibliography of Commentaries on Playwrights from Ibsen to the Avant-Garde** (Detroit: Gale, 1972). Cites about 12,000 critical studies of twentieth-century playwrights in 200 journals and 630 books, with approaches by authors, titles, and critics.

—Coleman, Arthur, and Gary R. Tyler. **Drama Criticism: A Checklist of Interpretation Since 1940** (Denver: A. Swallow, 1966). Cites criticism in 1,500 books and 1,050 periodicals, 1940-1964, under author of play, with subarrangement by title. Section 1 is devoted to authors other than Shakespeare.

—Salem, James M. **A Guide to Critical Reviews.** 2nd ed. (Metuchen, NJ: Scarecrow, 1973-). Gives citations to reviews mainly in the New York **Times** and general magazines. Part I. American Drama, 1909-1969; Part II. The Musical, 1909-1974. Other parts are devoted to non-American plays and screenplays.

—Samples, Gordon. **How to Locate Reviews of Plays and Films: A Bibliography of Criticism from the Beginnings to the Present** (Metuchen, NJ: Scarecrow, 1976). Should be used to supplement approaches of indexes that were published earlier.

Indexes to Fiction

PRIMARY MATERIALS

—Chicorel, Marietta. **Chicorel Index to Short Stories in Anthologies and Collections.** 1st ed. [i.e. v.12, 12A, 12B, 12C of **Chicorel Index**] (New York: Chicorel Library Pub. Corp., 1974). Some 1,300 anthologies and collections of individual authors are indexed with over 60,000 short stories listed under author, title, and title of collection, with a subject approach in volume 12C.

—**Short Story Index**, ed. Dorothy Elizabeth Cook (New York: H. W. Wilson, 1953). Indexes texts of 60,000 stories in 4,320 collections, by author, title, and subject, with supplements to cover further collections.

—Woodress, James. **American Fiction, 1900-1950: A Guide to Information Sources** (Detroit: Gale, 1974). As well as a general bibliography, there are fifty-four individual essays.

—Wright, Lyle H. **American Fiction, 1774-1850: A Contribution Toward a Bibliography.** 2nd rev. ed. (San Marino, CA: Huntington Library, 1957; repr. with additions and corrections, 1965); **1851-1875** (Huntington Library, 1965); **1876-1900** (Huntington Library, 1966). Bibliography of fiction of all types, arranged by author, with a title index. Excludes juvenile fiction and periodicals and includes contents of collections when the title is unclear.

CRITICISM AND EXPLICATION

—Adelman, Irving, and Rita Dworkin. **The Contemporary Novel: A Checklist of Critical Literature on the British and American Novel Since 1945** (Metuchen, NJ: Scarecrow, 1972). Bibliography of critical studies on writers producing major work after 1945. Includes citations to items in journals and books up to 1969.

—Gerstenberger, Donna, and George Hendrick. **The American Novel, 1789-1959: A Checklist of Twentieth Century Criticism** (Denver: A. Swallow, 1961).

—Gerstenberger, Donna, and George Hendrick. **The American Novel: A Checklist of Twentieth Century Criticism on Novels Written Since 1789. Criticism Written 1961-1968.** 2v. (Denver: A. Swallow, 1961-70). Selective bibliography of general studies and criticism on individual authors.

—**Studies in Short Fiction** (Newberry, SC: Newberry College, 1963-). 4 times a year. Contains an international "Annual Bibliography of Short Fiction" written during the year in books and periodicals.

—**Studies in the Novel** (Denton: North Texas State Univ., 1969-). 4 times a year. Contains many bibliographic citations on individual novelists and more general topics.

—Thurston, Jarvis A., et al. **Short Fiction Criticism: A Checklist of Interpretation Since 1925 of Stories and Novelettes (American, British, Continental) 1800-1958** (Denver: A. Swallow, 1960). Gives approaches to criticism of short fiction in 200 periodicals and many books, by author of the work criticized.

—Walker, Warren S. **Twentieth Century Short Story Explication: Interpretations, 1900-1966, of Short Fiction Since 1800.** 2nd ed. (Hamden, CT: Shoe String Press, 1967); **Supplement, 1967-1969** (Shoe String Press, 1970); **Supplement, 1970-1972** (Shoe String Press, 1973). Gives access to explication on international short stories, which are listed beneath each author's name, with citations for criticism of each title.

Indexes to Essays

—**Essay and General Literature Index** (New York: H. W. Wilson, 1934-). Index to essays and critical writings appearing in collections of essays on literature, collective biographies, or books treating several subjects. The main list is by author, title, and subject, with a separate listing of the books analyzed. A cumulative index is available for works indexed from 1900 to 1969 (H. W. Wilson, 1972).

INDEXES TO BOOK REVIEWS

Book reviews describe or evaluate works so that a reader can decide whether or not to read them. Reviews appear in a variety of sources, such as newspapers, magazines, and scholarly or professional journals. Access to them is facilitated by using indexes such as the following:

—**Book Review Digest** (Minneapolis: H. W. Wilson, 1906-). Monthly, with cumulations. Provides citations or excerpts from reviews in about eighty general periodicals and a few scholarly journals. Arranged by authors of the books reviewed, with subject and title indexes. Limited to books published in the United States.

—**Book Review Index** (Detroit: Gale, 1965-). Monthly, with cumulations. Provides access to reviews by author of the book, in over 200 journals, covering more scholarly titles than **Book Review Digest**, but containing no abstracts.

—**Cumulative Book Review Index, 1905-1974** (Princeton, NJ: National Library Service Co., 1975). An author, title index to reviews that appeared between 1905 and 1974 in **Book Review Digest**, **Library Journal**, and **Saturday Review**.

—**Current Book Review Citations** (New York: H. W. Wilson, 1976-). A monthly index to reviews appearing in over 1,200 journals, by author and title of work reviewed.

—Eichelberger, Clayton L., et al. **A Guide to Critical Reviews of United States Fiction, 1870-1910** (Metuchen, NJ: Scarecrow, 1971); **Supplement** (Scarecrow, 1974). Selects reviews of fiction, 1870-1910, that appeared in about thirty contemporary journals. It is extremely valuable for minor figures. Arranged alphabetically by author, with a title index. About 9,000 additional citations are in the **Supplement**.

—Gray, Richard A. **A Guide to Book Review Citations: A Bibliography of Sources** (Columbus: Ohio State Univ. Press, 1968). A bibliography of books, journals, and other sources that cite book reviews. Arranged by broad subject.

—**An Index to Book Reviews in the Humanities** (Detroit: P. Thomson, 1960-). Annual index to reviews appearing in about 400 scholarly journals and general periodicals. Approach is by author of the book reviewed.

BIBLIOGRAPHIES OF DISSERTATIONS

—**Datrix II Service** (Ann Arbor, MI: Xerox Univ. Microfilms, 1974-). A computerized data base of doctoral dissertations which can be searched by key words from titles. It also provides a printout, citing title, author, and a reference to **Dissertation Abstracts International** if the dissertation is contained therein. Covers dissertations accepted in the United States since 1861. Order forms from Xerox University Microfilms provide instructions for use.

—**Dissertation Abstracts International** (Ann Arbor, MI: Xerox Univ. Microfilms, 1969-). Monthly abstracts of dissertations submitted to Xerox University Microfilms by about 350 universities in the United States and Canada. Since 1966, Section A is devoted to the humanities. **A Retrospective Index**. 9v. (Xerox Univ. Microfilms,

1970) provides a key word subject index and an author index for volumes 1-29. Continues **Dissertation Abstracts, 1952-69**, which was **Microfilm Abstracts, 1938-1951**.

—McNamee, Lawrence F. **Dissertations in English and American Literature: Theses Accepted by American, British and German Universities, 1865-1964** (New York: Bowker, 1968); **Supplement One, 1964-1968** (Bowker, 1969); **Supplement Two, 1969-1973** (Bowker, 1974). A classified subject list of doctoral dissertations, with chronological subarrangement. Supplementary volumes include dissertations from British Commonwealth universities.

—Woodress, James Leslie. **Dissertations in American Literature, 1891-1966**. newly rev. and enl. with the assistance of Marian Kunitz (Durham, NC: Duke Univ. Press, 1968). Lists 4,700 international dissertations under subjects of individual authors and general topics, with an index by authors of dissertations.

GUIDES TO MANUSCRIPTS

—**American Literary Manuscripts: A Checklist of Holdings in Academic, Historical and Public Libraries, Museums, and Authors' Homes in the United States**. 2nd ed., ed. Albert Robbins, et al. (Athens: Univ. of Georgia Press, 1977). Published under the auspices of the American Literature Group of the Modern Language Association of America. A list of the manuscripts of over 2,000 American authors in all types of libraries. Arranged alphabetically by author, with indication of the types of materials available.

—Hamer, Philip M. **A Guide to Archives and Manuscripts in the United States** (New Haven, CT: Yale Univ. Press for the National Historical Publications Commission, 1961). A guide to manuscript collections arranged by state, city, and name of depository. Entries describe the nature of collections, and citations are provided for published guides to the individual collections. Detailed indexes of personal names and subjects.

—**The National Union Catalog of Manuscript Collections** (Ann Arbor, MI: J. W. Edwards, 1962; Hamden, CT: Scarecrow, 1963; Washington, DC: Library of Congress, 1964-). Lists over 200,000 manuscript collections in the United States that have been reported to the Library of Congress. Describes contents of collections, such as personal papers, and indicates if an inventory is available. Indexes by names, places, subjects, and historical periods.

Reference Tools

Although almost any work in a library can be used as a reference source, the following titles will probably be in the reference department of your library because they have proved to be authoritative sources of information, easily consulted without reading the entire book. In using such sources, you will find that the table of contents and the index are important access points which complement the approaches made possible by a tool's general arrangement.

To help you find the names of other reference books not listed here, see Eugene P. Sheehy. **Guide to Reference Books**, 9th ed. (Chicago: American Library Association, 1976) and its supplements. In addition, for valuable leads to subsequent reference works and critical assessment of them, see **American Reference Books Annual**, ed. Bohdan S. Wynar (Littleton, CO: Libraries Unlimited, 1970-). This provides an annual cumulation of over 1,600 reviews of American reference books from all disciplines, including American literature. Citations are provided to other reviews for the reference work being considered, and comparisons are made with works of similar scope. For reference works on American literature published in the current year, there are approximately forty reviews of bibliographies, handbooks, indexes, library catalogs, and collected biography as well as reference tools that are devoted to individual American authors. Cumulative indexes are available for all previous annuals. To make the reader aware of retrospective reference titles, the reviews for those works judged to be the most valuable in the preceding decade are republished in **Best Reference Books 1970-1980: Titles of Lasting Value Selected from American Reference Books Annual**, eds. Susan Holte and Bohdan S. Wynar (Littleton, CO: Libraries Unlimited, 1981).

DICTIONARIES AND GLOSSARIES

Dictionaries not only define the meanings of words, but they may also allow you to check spelling, pronunciation, word division, abbreviations, and the history of words. For a classified guide to dictionaries in all languages, covering both general and technical subjects, see Robert L. Collison. **Dictionaries of English and Foreign Languages**. 2nd ed. (New York: Hafner, 1971).

Modern English Dictionaries Published in the United States
(See also Chapter Six, American English)

—**Funk & Wagnalls Comprehensive Standard International Dictionary**. Bicentennial ed. (Chicago: J. G. Ferguson Pub. Co., 1974). Modern English is emphasized, and obsolete and archaic words are included.

—**Random House Dictionary of the English Language**. Unabridged ed., eds. Jess Stein and Laurence Urdang (New York: Random House, 1973). In addition to information such as that in **Webster's** there are many appendices that include concise dictionaries of French, Spanish, Italian, and German; signs and symbols; a style manual; and an atlas and gazetteer.

—**Webster's Third New International Dictionary of the English Language Unabridged**, ed. Philip Babcock Gove (Springfield, MA: G. & C. Merriam, 1976). Concentrates on words in use after 1775, excluding names of people and places. Each entry supplies American spelling, pronunciation, part of speech, inflection, capitalization, etymology, status if archaic or slang, definitions in historical order, cross-references, and synonyms.

Dictionaries and Glossaries of Literary Terms

—Abrams, M. H. **A Glossary of Literary Terms**. 3rd ed. (New York: Holt, Rinehart & Winston, 1971). Essays define general topics such as Allegory, Irony, New Criticism, Realism, and Naturalism, with narrower aspects of these also explained. Includes citations to further explanations.

—Beckson, Karl, and Arthur Ganz. **Literary Terms: A Dictionary**. rev. and enl. ed. (New York: Farrar, Straus, & Giroux, 1975). Definitions of terms used in literary research, which are frequently supplemented by citations to further discussions.

—Fowler, Roger. **A Dictionary of Modern Critical Terms** (Boston: Routledge & Kegan Paul, 1973). Definitions are provided for critical terms, and citations are given for further reading on the terms.

—Holman, C. Hugh. **A Handbook to Literature Based on the Original Edition by William Flint Thrall and Addison Hibbard**. 4th ed. (Indianapolis: Bobbs-Merrill, 1980). Defines terms used in English and American literary history and criticism, such as "metaphor," "realism," and "Oxford Movement," and includes many extended discussions and a parallel outline of English and American literature.

—Shipley, Joseph T. **Dictionary of World Literary Terms: Forms, Technique, Criticism**. completely rev. and enl. ed. (Boston: The Writer, Inc., 1970). Three parts contain definitions of literary terms, forms, techniques, essays surveying the history of critical theory in various countries, and lists of critical writings by country.

LITERARY HANDBOOKS AND ENCYCLOPEDIAS

—Benét, William Rose. **The Reader's Encyclopedia**. 2nd ed. (New York: Crowell, 1965). Combines in a single list plot summaries, literary terms of all nations and time periods, and brief articles on writers, scientists, and philosophers.

—**Cassell's Encyclopedia of World Literature**. rev. and enl. ed., ed. J. Buchanan-Brown. 3v. (New York: W. Morrow, 1973). Volume 1 contains signed articles on world literary history and broad topics. Volumes 2-3 contain about 9,000 critical biographies of writers, with bibliographies.

—Freeman, William. **Everyman's Dictionary of Fictional Characters**. 3rd ed., rev. by Fred Urquhart (London: Dent, 1969). Identifies characters from the literature of British, American, and Commonwealth authors.

—Hart, James David. **The Oxford Companion to American Literature**. 4th ed. (New York: Oxford Univ. Press, 1965). Short articles arranged alphabetically to cover the period 1577-1965. Includes biographies of authors, primary bibliographies, fictional characters, titles, place names, summaries of novels, literary societies, awards, and literary movements. A chronological index gives parallel approaches to major social and literary events.

—**Princeton Encyclopedia of Poetry and Poetics**. enl. ed., ed. Alex Preminger (Princeton, NJ: Princeton Univ. Press, 1974). Signed articles on poetry, poetics, history, technique, and criticism. Some bibliographies are included, but there are no entries for individual poets.

—**The Reader's Encyclopedia of American Literature**, by Max J. Herzberg, et al. (New York: Crowell, 1962). This dictionary of Canadian and American literature includes authors and many portraits, literary movements, characters, and plot summaries, with signed articles for some subjects. Less scholarly than the **Oxford Companion**, but more inclusive.

—Spender, Stephen, and Donald Hall. **The Concise Encyclopedia of English and American Poets and Poetry**. 2nd ed. (London: Hutchinson, 1970). Short evaluative articles on poetry and poets, with brief biographies.

BIOGRAPHICAL SOURCES

Guides, Bibliographies, and Indexes

—**Author Biographies Master Index**, ed. Dennis La Beau. 2v. (Detroit: Gale, 1977). Indexes nearly 150 standard biographical reference works with emphasis on English and American literature.

—**Biographical Dictionaries Master Index**, eds. Dennis La Beau and Gary C. Tarbert. (Detroit: Gale, 1975-). A biennial guide to over 800,000 names in more than fifty current collections of biography. International in scope.

—**Biography and Genealogy Master Index**. 2nd ed., eds. Miranda C. Herbert and Barbara McNeil (Detroit: Gale, 1980-). "A consolidated index to more than 3,200,000 biographical sketches in over 350 current and retrospective biographical dictionaries."

—**Biography Index** (New York: H. W. Wilson, 1947-). Quarterly index with annual and triennial cumulations. Covers current biographical material, including obituaries, in English-language books and periodicals indexed by the Wilson Company. Indexes by profession.

—Chicorel, Marietta. **Chicorel Index to Biographies.** 2v. [i.e. v.15 and 15A **Chicorel Index**] (New York: Chicorel Library Pub. Corp., 1974). Groups over 21,000 biographies by occupation and indexes by name and subject.

—Kaplan, Louis, et al. **A Bibliography of American Autobiography** (Madison: Univ. of Wisconsin Press, 1961). Indexes over 6,000 autobiographies.

Collections of Biography

Of particular importance to students of American literature who need an introduction to an author's life are two series of biographies written by noted authorities. Twayne's United States Author's Series (New York: Twayne, 1961-) is an ongoing series that covers over 300 American authors. The University of Minnesota Pamphlets on American Writers (Minneapolis: Univ. of Minnesota Press, 1959-) has produced excellent bio-critical pamphlets which have also been collected in **American Writers: A Collection of Literary Biographies,** ed. Leonard Unger. 4v. (New York: Scribner, 1974) and **Supplement,** 2v. (Scribner, 1979). The easiest way to locate the works in these series is under a catalog entry for the name of the series, or by looking under a subject card for the name of the author for whom you require a biography.

—**Appleton's Cyclopedia of American Biography,** eds. J. G. Wilson and John Fiske. 7v. (New York: Appleton, 1887-1900); **Supplementary Edition,** 6v. (Appleton, 1926-31). Although largely superseded by the **Dictionary of American Biography,** this encyclopedia is still useful for names not listed in the latter. Includes portraits and facsimiles of autographs.

—Burke, W. J., and Will D. Howe. **American Authors and Books, 1640 to the Present Day.** 3rd ed., rev. by Irving Weiss and Anne Weiss (New York: Crown, 1972). Provides brief factual identification for American authors, publishers, periodicals, and literary works, with biographical entries predominating. Useful for identifying minor figures.

—**Contemporary Authors: A Bio-Bibliographical Guide to Current Authors and Their Works** (Detroit: Gale, 1967-). Lists basic biographical data for international authors and primary and secondary bibliographies which include work in progress. For deceased authors, or those no longer publishing, see reprinted biographies in **Contemporary Authors: Permanent Series,** (Gale, 1975-).

—**Contemporary Poets of the English Language.** 2nd ed., ed. J. Vinson (New York: St. Martin's Press, 1975). Brief biographies of 1,100 poets from all countries. Includes addresses, lists of works and editorship, excerpts from criticism, or brief comments by the poets about their life and work. Indicates anthologies in which the poets' works are collected.

—**Current Biography** (New York: H. W. Wilson, 1940-). Biographical articles include notable persons of all nationalities. Monthly issues are cumulated annually and every decade. Thirty years are indexed in **Current Biography: Cumulative Index, 1940-1970** (H. W. Wilson, 1973).

—**Dictionary of American Biography,** eds. Alden Johnson and Dumas Malone. 20v. and index. (New York: Scribner, 1928-37); **Supplement One** [to Dec. 31, 1935, 1944;

repr. in 22v. with corrigenda in v.1, 1946]; **Supplement Two** [to Dec. 31, 1940, 1955]; **Supplement** [to Dec. 31, 1945, 1973]. Contains signed biographical articles on deceased prominent Americans in many fields, with bibliographies of sources. There are six indexes to the original set, by name of biographee, contributor, state, school or college, occupation, topics and subjects, that include titles of literary works.

—**Directory of American Scholars: A Biographical Directory.** 7th ed., 4v. (New York: Bowker, 1974). Brief biographies of recognized American scholars in the humanities, giving educational background, positions held, and society memberships. Useful for determining backgrounds of current scholars. Earlier volumes cover years to 1942. Vol. 2: English, Speech, Drama; Vol. 3: Linguistics and Philology.

—Duyckinck, Evert A., and George L. Duyckinck. **Cyclopedia of American Literature** (New York: Scribner, 1855). Useful for biographical material on writers from the earliest period to the mid-nineteenth century. Many statements of the later period were written or revised by the authors themselves.

—Garraty, John A., and Jerome L. Sternstein. **Encyclopedia of American Biography** (New York: Harper & Row, 1974). Over 1,000 signed biographies of living and deceased Americans, which include brief factual details and citations to further sources.

—Kunitz, Stanley J., and Howard Haycraft. **American Authors, 1600-1900: A Biographical Dictionary of American Literature** (New York: H. W. Wilson, 1938). Contains biographical sketches of 1,300 major and minor American authors, including some not generally regarded as "literary" but who are important in the development of early national literature. Excludes authors living at the time of compilation.

—Kunitz, Stanley J., and Howard Haycraft. **Twentieth Century Authors: A Biographical Dictionary of Modern Literature** (New York: H. W. Wilson, 1942); **First Supplement,** by Stanley J. Kunitz and Vineta Colby (H. W. Wilson, 1955). Biographies of 1,850 prominent twentieth-century British and American authors with 1,700 portraits. A supplement adds 700 biographies and revises some from the earlier volume. Valuable for minor authors.

—Myerson, Joel. **The American Renaissance in New England** (Detroit: Gale, 1978). Contains biographies and bibliographies of primary and secondary sources for ninety-eight New England authors, 1830-1860. (For other similar works see Chapter Seven: Series, **Dictionary of Literary Biography.**)

—**National Cyclopedia of American Biography** (New York: J. T. White, 1893-1919); Index (J. T. White, 1971). In two series. Permanent Series are numbered and contain biographies of deceased Americans from colonial times, chronologically arranged, with an alphabetical index. Though shorter than articles in the **Dictionary of American Biography,** more names are included. Current Series contains Americans living at time of publication, with fuller biographies than those in **Who's Who in America.** Since there is no systematic arrangement, the index volume is crucial for providing access by name and subject to both Permanent and Current series.

—**Who Was Who in America** (Chicago: A. N. Marquis, 1942-). An ongoing dictionary arrangement of biographies of deceased Americans who were in earlier editions of **Who's Who in America**. For retrospective information consult volumes for 1607-1896 and 1897-1942.

—**Who's Who in America** (Chicago: A. N. Marquis, 1899-). Current biographical dictionary of living Americans who are noted for their "meritorious achievement."

3

Literary Surveys

Literary surveys are useful when you are beginning study in a new area. They sketch the milieu and main trends with which you need to be familiar in order to place particular literary contributions in context. The following titles are highly selective. They encompass both general historical surveys and more specific approaches by genre, region, ethnic background, and contributions of women. In many cases, where good bibliographies are available, these are listed as a help for locating further information.

HISTORICAL SURVEYS

General

—The Cambridge History of American Literature, ed. William Peterfield Trent, et al. 4v. (New York: Putnam, 1917-21). Attempts a comprehensive history of American literature and literary milieus with chapters by eminent scholars. Unfortunately the bibliographies are now dated, but coverage of colonial and revolutionary periods remains important.

—Literary History of the United States. 4th ed., rev., ed. Robert E. Spiller, et al. 2v. (New York: Macmillan, 1974). Often referred to as Spiller or LHUS. The most definitive survey of American literature. Volume 1 is a survey containing critical and evaluative chapters by sixty scholars. It covers authors, and cultural and historical backgrounds from colonial times to the mid-twentieth century. Volume 2, which is available separately, contains detailed bibliographies covering movements and influences as well as the primary and secondary sources of major individual authors. A supplement adds sixteen notable authors for the period 1958-1970.

Period

The following selected surveys are arranged chronologically to cover periods from colonial times to the present.

—Tyler, Moses Coit. A History of American Literature During the Colonial Period. rev. ed. 2v. (New York: G. P. Putnam, 1897). This work remains the classic history of the period.

—Tyler, Moses Coit. **The Literary History of the American Revolution**. 2v. (New York: G. P. Putnam, 1897). Taken together with the previous title, this provides a detailed standard history covering colonial American literature.

—Leary, Lewis. **Soundings: Some Early American Writers** (Athens: Univ. of Georgia Press, 1975). Contains fourteen essays on writers from Franklin to Cooper and Irving.

—**Major Writers of Early American Literature**, ed. Everett Emerson (Madison: Univ. of Wisconsin Press, 1972). Collects essays on writers such as William Bradford and Charles Brockden Brown.

—Matthiessen, F. O. **American Renaissance: Art and Expression in the Age of Emerson and Whitman** (New York: Oxford Univ. Press, 1941). A seminal study that analyzes the work of Emerson, Thoreau, Hawthorne, Melville, and Whitman, between 1800 and 1855. Establishes the milieu, interrelationships and patterns that influenced their writing.

—**The Transcendentalists: An Anthology**, ed. Perry Miller (Cambridge: Harvard Univ. Press, 1950). Reprints philosophical statements and definitions made by the transcendentalists.

—Koster, Donald N. **Transcendentalism in America** (Boston: Twayne, 1975). Brings the history of transcendentalism forward from its beginnings to the present.

—**Studies in the American Renaissance**, ed. Joel Myerson (Boston: G. K. Hall, 1977-). An annual publication devoted to original research into the lives and works of authors, 1830-1860. Covers biography, unpublished letters, journals, calendars of manuscripts, accounts of publishing, and primary and secondary bibliographies.

—Wilson, Edmund. **Patriotic Gore: Studies in the Literature of the American Civil War** (New York: Oxford Univ. Press, 1962). An influential study of popular writers from the Civil War period.

—Martin, Jay. **Harvests of Change: American Literature, 1865-1914** (Englewood Cliffs, NJ: Prentice-Hall, 1967). Covers the period between the Civil War and World War I in which industry and technology caused important changes that were reflected in literature.

—Jones, Howard Mumford. **The Age of Energy: Varieties of American Experience, 1865-1915** (New York: Viking, 1971). A survey of American intellectual and cultural history. Earlier periods are covered in **O Strange New World: American Culture: The Formative Years** (Viking, 1964) and **Revolution & Romanticism** (Cambridge: Harvard Univ. Press, 1974).

—Jones, Howard Mumford, and Richard M. Ludwig. **Guide to American Literature and Its Backgrounds Since 1890**. 4th ed., rev. and enl. (Cambridge: Harvard Univ. Press, 1972). An outline and selected bibliography on American literature from 1870 to 1971. The first section presents bibliographies which cover the intellectual, social, and cultural context; and the second section contains fifty-two reading lists of titles covering important trends in American literature 1890-1919 and 1920-1972.

—**Harvard Guide to Contemporary American Writing**, with essays by Leo Braudy, et al., ed. Daniel Hoffman (Cambridge: Harvard Univ. Press, 1979). Critically surveys significant writing from the end of World War II through the 1970s, with essays on Intellectual Background; Literary Criticism; Realists, Naturalists, and Novelists of Manners; Southern Fiction; Jewish Writers; Experimental Film; Black Literature; Women's Literature; Drama; Poetry; After Modernism; Poetry: Schools of Dissidents; Poetry: Dissidents from Schools.

GENRE SURVEYS

Folklore

BIBLIOGRAPHIES AND INDEXES

—Diehl, Katharine. **Religions, Mythologies, Folklores: An Annotated Bibliography.** 2nd ed. (New York: Scarecrow, 1962). Annotated bibliography under broad subjects with an author-title index. Covers books and periodicals.

—Haywood, Charles. **A Bibliography of North American Folklore and Folksong.** 2nd rev. ed., 2v. (New York: Dover, 1961). Annotates both primary and secondary materials, including coverage of American and Canadian Indians.

—Thompson, Stith. **Motif-Index of Folk-Literature: A Classification of Narrative Elements in Folktales, Ballads, Myths, Fables, Medieval Romances, Exempla, Fabliaux, Jest-Books and Local Legends.** rev. and enl. ed. 6v. (Bloomington: Indiana Univ. Press, 1955-58). The fullest source of themes and motifs. Includes brief definitions and citations to primary sources of motifs.

SURVEYS

—Brunvand, Jan Harold. **The Study of American Folklore: An Introduction** (New York: Norton, 1968). Links the English-language folklore of the United States with its traditions.

—Dorson, Richard M. **American Folklore: With Revised Bibliographical Notes** Chicago: Univ. of Chicago Press, 1977). Traces the development of folk traditions in the United States.

—**Funk and Wagnalls' Standard Dictionary of Folklore, Mythology, and Legend**, ed. Maria Leach. 2v. (New York: Crowell, 1972). Covers all countries and times in short signed articles that summarize themes and give definitions. Longer articles, on topics such as ballads, include bibliographies.

Poetry

—Bogan, Louise. **Achievement in American Poetry, 1900-1950** (Chicago: Regnery, 1951). A brief but useful survey which contains selections from twentieth-century poets.

—Dembo, L. S. **Conceptions of Reality in Modern American Poetry** (Berkeley: Univ. of California Press, 1966). Focuses on Fletcher, H. D., Amy Lowell, William Carlos Williams, Wallace Stevens, Marianne Moore, E. E. Cummings, Hart Crane, Ezra Pound, and T. S. Eliot.

—Gregory, Horace, and Marya Zaturenska. **A History of American Poetry, 1900-1940** (New York: Harcourt Brace, 1946). An excellent study by two poets that covers the period from Moody to Robinson, the influence of Harriet Monroe and the "Poetic Renaissance," the 1930s, from Benét to Crane, and more recent poetry of Jarrell, Rexroth, and others.

—Mazzaro, Jerome. **Postmodern American Poetry** (Urbana: Univ. of Illinois Press, 1980). Seven significant essays on W. H. Auden, Randall Jarrell, Theodore Roethke, David Ignatow, John Berryman, Sylvia Plath, and Elizabeth Bishop.

—Pearce, Roy Harvey. **The Continuity of American Poetry** (Princeton: Princeton Univ. Press, 1961). Pearce traces the influence of Walt Whitman on modern poetry.

—Waggoner, Hyatt H. **American Poets from the Puritans to the Present** (Boston: Houghton Mifflin, 1968). Discusses fifty-two poets from Bradstreet to Robert Kelly, and the influence of Ralph Waldo Emerson on the development of American poetry.

Drama

—Bogard, Travis, Richard Moody, and Walter J. Meserve. **American Drama** (New York: Methuen, 1977). Useful overview with extensive chronologies and bibliography.

—Krutch, Joseph Wood. **The American Drama Since 1918: An Informal History.** rev. ed. (New York: Braziller, 1957). Treats the most significant playwrights, defining differences and tracing trends up to 1956.

—Meserve, Walter J. **American Drama to 1900: A Guide to Information Sources** (Detroit: Gale, 1980). Focuses on drama as literature from the colonial period to the rise of realism. Includes thirty-four individual dramatists.

—Quinn, Arthur Hobson. **A History of the American Drama from the Beginning to the Civil War.** 2nd ed. (New York: F. S. Crofts, 1943). This is the standard history of the early American drama. It contains a chronological list of plays from 1665 to 1860.

—Quinn, Arthur Hobson. **A History of the American Drama from the Civil War to the Present Day.** rev. ed. (New York: Appleton-Century-Crofts, 1964). Brings Quinn's history forward to about 1936, including Lillian Hellman.

Fiction

BIBLIOGRAPHIES

—Helterman, Jeffrey, and Richard Layman. **American Novelists Since World War II** (Detroit: Gale, 1978). Covers eighty novelists since 1945 with full lists of primary and secondary sources.

—Kirby, David K. **American Fiction to 1900** (Detroit: Gale, 1975). Describes general sources and gives bio-bibliographical information on forty-one prominent authors.

—Woodress, James Leslie. **American Fiction, 1900-1950** (Detroit: Gale, 1974). Contains bio-bibliographical facts for forty-four significant twentieth-century authors.

SURVEYS

—Chase, Richard. **The American Novel and Its Tradition** (Garden City, NY: Doubleday, 1957). A chronological study from Charles Brockden Brown to Faulkner that demonstrates how the American novel employs the romance as a vehicle for moral and intellectual ideas.

—Cowie, Alexander. **The Rise of the American Novel** (New York: American Book Co., 1948). Scholarly study of the novel's history to 1940.

—Fiedler, Leslie A. **Love and Death in the American Novel.** rev. ed. (New York: Stein & Day, 1966). Delightfully outrageous, provoking many interesting questions.

—Kazin, Alfred. **Bright Book of Life: American Novelists and Story Tellers from Hemingway to Mailer** (Boston: Little, Brown, 1973). Focuses on fiction in the United States since World War II, including Salinger, Sontag, Cheever, Capote, and others.

—Kazin, Alfred. **On Native Grounds: An Interpretation of Modern American Prose Literature** (New York: Harcourt Brace, 1942). Covers three periods: 1. The Search for Reality, 1890-1917; 2. The Great Liberation, 1918-1929; 3. The Literature of Crisis, 1930-1940.

—Petter, Henri. **The Early American Novel** (Columbus: Ohio State Univ. Press, 1971). A complete survey of the beginnings of American fiction to 1820, with summaries of eighty-two novels.

—Rideout, Walter B. **The Radical Novel in the United States, 1900-1954: Some Interpretations of Literature and Society** (Cambridge: Harvard Univ. Press, 1956). Concentrates on writers of the 1930s and 1940s who sought to change the system.

—Tanner, Tony. **City of Words: American Fiction, 1950-1970** (New York: Harper & Row, 1971). Examines the themes of twenty-five novelists and the "ambiguous relationship of the self" to social, psychological, and linguistic patterns.

—Voss, Arthur. **The American Short Story: A Critical Study** (Norman: Univ. of Oklahoma Press, 1973). A survey that comes forward to Roth and Updike, with many plot summaries.

Humor

—Blair, Walter. **Native American Humor, 1800-1900** (New York: American Book Co., 1937). With this work, the significance of humor in the nineteenth century was established.

—**The Comic Imagination in American Literature**, ed. Louis D. Rubin, Jr. (New Brunswick, NJ: Rutgers Univ. Press, 1973). Thirty-one essays by twenty-five scholars on humor from colonial times to the present.

—**The Frontier Humorists: Critical Views**, ed. M. Thomas Inge (Hamden, CT: Archon Books, 1975). This anthology of criticism on the Southwest humorists includes a good bibliography.

—Gibson, William M. **Theodore Roosevelt among the Humorists: W. D. Howells, Mark Twain and Mr. Dooley** (Knoxville: Univ. of Tennessee Press, 1980). Indicates Roosevelt's relationship with Howells, Mark Twain, and "Mr. Dooley." Based on three lectures, with a useful selected bibliography.

—Hoffman, Daniel G. **Form and Fable in American Fiction** (New York: Oxford Univ. Press, 1961). Ten works by Irving, Hawthorne, Melville, and Mark Twain are examined and their themes discussed.

—Rourke, Constance M. **American Humor: A Study of the National Character** (New York: Harcourt Brace, 1931). Pioneering study of homespun sources that reveals the importance of the tradition of a distinctively American humor.

—Wallace, Ronald. **The Last Laugh: Form and Affirmation in the Contemporary American Comic Novel** (Columbia: Univ. of Missouri Press, 1979). Reflects the form, themes, and techniques of earlier comic literature and reaffirms the value of life and self in an irrational and often destructive world. Detailed analyses of five contemporary American novels by Barth, Hawkes, Nabokov, Kesey, and Coover.

—Yates, Norris Y. **The American Humorist: Conscience of the Twentieth Century** (Ames: Iowa State Univ. Press, 1964). A fine survey of humor in the period from "Mr. Dooley" to Perelman and Thurber.

REGIONAL SURVEYS

New England and Middle Atlantic States

BIBLIOGRAPHIES

—**New England Quarterly** (Brunswick, ME: Colonial Society of Massachusetts and New England, 1928-). 4 times a year. Contains an annual "Bibliography of New England."

SURVEYS

—Westbrook, Perry D. **Acres of Flint: Writers of Rural New England, 1870-1900** (Washington, DC: Scarecrow, 1951). Covers some local colorists who are seldom considered in general surveys.

The South

BIBLIOGRAPHIES

—**Mississippi Quarterly** (State College: Mississippi State Univ., 1948-). Contains annual bibliographical checklists.

—Rubin, Louis D., Jr. **A Bibliographical Guide to the Study of Southern Literature** (Baton Rouge: Louisiana State Univ. Press, 1969). Part I: general topics, such as Civil War. Part II: checklists for 135 southern writers. An appendix contains checklists for 68 writers of the colonial South.

SURVEYS

—Hoffman, Frederick J. **The Art of Southern Fiction** (Carbondale: Southern Illinois Univ. Press, 1968). Examines the work of Eudora Welty, Carson McCullers, James Agee, Flannery O'Connor, Truman Capote, William Goyen, Walker Percy, Reynolds Price, and William Styron.

—Hubbell, Jay B. **The South in American Literature, 1607-1900** (Durham, NC: Duke Univ. Press, 1954). Detailed, authoritative account of history and biography, with summaries and analyses of major themes of the period and the conditions from which they emerged.

—Payne, Ladell. **Black Novelists and the Southern Literary Tradition** (Athens: Univ. of Georgia, 1981). Examines themes and narrative forms in the works of Chesnutt, Johnson, Toomer, Wright, and Ellison.

—Rubin, Louis D., Jr. **The Faraway Country: Writers of the Modern South** (Seattle: Univ. of Washington Press, 1963). Considers southern writers, Cable, Faulkner, Wolfe, Welty, Tate, and others.

The West—General

BIBLIOGRAPHIES

—Etulain, Richard W. **Western American Literature: A Bibliography of Interpretative Books and Articles** (Vermillion, SD: Dakota Press, 1972). Contains lists on 225 individual authors.

SURVEYS

—**Critical Essays on the Western American Novel**, ed. William T. Pilkington (Boston: Twayne, 1980). Contains twenty-four essays on major writers of western themes.

—Fussell, Edwin. **Frontier: American Literature and the American West** (Princeton, NJ: Princeton Univ. Press, 1965). Examines the concept of the West in the writings of Cooper, Hawthorne, Poe, Thoreau, Melville, and Whitman.

—Milton, John R. **The Novel of the American West** (Lincoln: Univ. of Nebraska Press, 1980). Indicates the contributions of Vardis Fisher, A. B. Guthrie, Jr., Frederick Manfred, Walter Van Tilburg Clark, Harvey Fergusson, and Frank Waters.

—Smith, Henry Nash. **Virgin Land; The American West As Symbol and Myth** (Cambridge: Harvard Univ. Press, 1950). Indicates how conceptions of the West have influenced American literature in fact and symbol.

—**The Western: A Collection of Critical Essays** (Englewood Cliffs, NJ: Prentice-Hall, 1979). A valuable collection of criticism on the genre.

The Southwest

BIBLIOGRAPHIES

—Anderson, John Q., et al. **Southwestern American Literature: A Bibliography** (Chicago: Swallow Press, 1980).

—Major, Mabel, and T. M. Pearse. **Southwest Heritage: A Literary History with Bibliography**. 3rd ed. (Albuquerque: Univ. of New Mexico Press, 1972). The first part lists titles on general and literary topics, and the second lists authors, many quite obscure, with both primary and secondary listings.

The Northwest

—**Northwest Perspectives: Essays on the Culture of the Pacific Northwest**, eds. Edwin R. Bingham and Glen A. Love (Seattle: Univ. of Washington Press, 1979). Includes sections on Oregon Indian literature, Northwest regional folklore, and a Pacific Northwest bibliography.

The West Coast

—Walker, Franklin. **San Francisco's Literary Frontier** (New York: Knopf, 1939). Examines the period from 1848 to 1875.

The Midwest

BIBLIOGRAPHIES

—Nemanic, Gerald. **A Bibliographical Guide to Midwestern Literature** (Iowa City: Univ. of Iowa Press, 1981). Lists of primary and secondary sources are included broadly. Part 1: subject bibliographies for States, History and Society, Folklore, Personal Narratives, Architecture, Black Literature, Indians, and many other topics. Part 2: separate author bibliographies, both primary and secondary.

SURVEYS

–Dondore, Dorothy. **The Prairie and the Making of Middle America** (Cedar Rapids, IA: Torch, 1926). Traces the history of literature in the Middle West.

–Rusk, Leslie. **The Literature of the Middle Western Frontier.** 2v. (New York: Columbia Univ. Press, 1925). The standard literary history to 1840.

SELECTED ETHNIC BIBLIOGRAPHIES AND SURVEYS

Although the United States is pluralistic, until recently the study of literature was based on an ethnocentric and homogeneous set of values that reflected the dominant group. The nation's rich multiethnic traditions had often been absent from anthologies and courses in literature. However, as attention began to be given to the study of minorities by departments of ethnic studies, curriculum development specialists, and literary scholars and critics, a need arose for access to primary sources and to works about this long-neglected literature. In response, anthologies, critical surveys, and bibliographies have begun to appear, with some groups more adequately represented than others. Helpful historical background on the many ethnic groups is available in the **Harvard Encyclopedia of American Ethnic Groups**, ed. Stephen Thernstrom (Cambridge: Harvard Univ. Press, 1980).

When approaching the imaginative literature of various ethnic minorities and its criticism, there is a variety of potential sources. Anthologies presenting an overview of different genres and groups often represent the most fruitful sources for any literature which is not yet widely published and for which little criticism is yet available. Although anthologies that do not contain secondary material are beyond the scope of this guide, they may be found in the library catalog under the heading AMERICAN LITERATURE–MINORITY AUTHORS. Two reliable anthologies that gather a variety of genres and contain introductions to authors from many backgrounds are Lillian Faderman and Barbara Bradshaw, **Speaking for Ourselves: American Ethnic Writing** (Glenview, IL: Scott Foresman, 1969), and Gerald W. Haslam, **Forgotten Pages of American Literature** (Boston: Houghton Mifflin, 1970). Periodicals are another rich source of ethnic literature and studies about it. **MELUS** (Los Angeles: Society for the Study of Multi-Ethnic Literature of the United States, 1974-) is a quarterly with issues devoted to criticism and reviews on themes such as the "Ethnic American Dream" and "Literature and Cultural Nationalism." An important publisher of relevant bibliographies is the National Council of Teachers of English, 508 South Sixth Street, Champaign, IL 61820.

The following sections are intended to help in locating bibliographies and surveys on those ethnic minority groups that are widely studied in literature departments. Since a broad inclusion of all ethnic groups is beyond the present scope of American literature students, a brief listing of works that encompass general coverage of ethnic literature is included first, to point the user towards reliable guides that will expand coverage. This section is followed by bibliographies and surveys of the Asian American, Black American, Mexican American, and Native American groups.

General Ethnic Literature

BIBLIOGRAPHIES

—Inglehart, Babette F., and Anthony R. Mangione. **The Image of Pluralism in American Literature: An Annotated Bibliography on the American Experience of European Ethnic Groups** (New York: Institute of Pluralism and Group Identity of the American Jewish Committee, 1974). An annotated bibliography of work in English prepared for the Conference on Multi-Ethnic Literature, Chicago State University, 1974, which was planned for teachers of English and social studies in high schools. Chapters cover anthologies dealing with the white ethnic experience and the literature of Armenians, Dutch, German, Greek, Hungarian, Irish, Italian, Jewish, Polish, Scandinavian, and Slavic groups, as well as history, autobiography, and criticism.

—Miller, Wayne Charles, and Faye Nell Vowell, et al. **A Comprehensive Bibliography for the Study of American Minorities.** 2v. (New York: New York Univ. Press, 1976). Includes 29,300 entries that provide comprehensive interdisciplinary coverage on all aspects of American minority groups under the headings: From Africa and the Middle East; From Europe; From Eastern Europe and the Balkans; From Asia; From the Islands; and Native American. Each chapter contains a historical review and an introduction that cites the sources most useful for beginning students. A classed and annotated bibliography follows that includes separate listings under Bibliographies, Periodicals, Biography and Autobiography, Literary History and Criticism, Fiction, Ballads, Songs, and Comic Strips. Includes literature by and about each group, citing monographs and full-length studies with some pamphlets and articles for less prolific groups. Contains extensive author and title indexes.

—Miller, Wayne Charles. **A Handbook of American Minorities** (New York: New York Univ. Press, 1976). Makes available the same excellent overview essays for each minority group as the previous title, but omits the bibliographies.

SURVEYS

—Comparative Literature Symposium, 9th, Texas Tech University, 1976. **Ethnic Literatures Since 1776: The Many Voices of America**, eds. Wolodymyr T. Zyla and Wendell M. Aycock (Lubbock: Interdepartmental Committee on Comparative Literature, Texas Tech Univ., 1978). Proceedings focus on the following ethnic groups and their literatures: Afro-Americans, Czech, Chinese, Chicano, Estonian, French, German, Native American, Irish, Italian, Japanese, Lithuanian, Latvian, Dutch, Norwegian, Polish, Portuguese, Puerto Rican, Russian, Ukrainian, Yiddish, and Yugoslav.

—**Minority Language and Literature: Retrospective and Perspective**, ed. Dexter Fisher (New York: Modern Language Association of America, 1977). A collection of papers presented at a 1976 symposium in New York City that presents the state of the art of studies in minority language and literature. Includes papers such as David Dorsey, "Minority Literature in the Service of Cultural Pluralism," Raymund A. Paredes, "The Promise of Chicano Literature," Stephen D. Chennault, "Black Dialect: A Cultural Shock," Michel Benamou, "The Concept of Marginality in Ethnopoetics," and Walter J. Ong, "Oral Culture and the Literate Mind."

Asian American

There are few separately published works currently available about Chinese, Filipino, and Japanese contributions to American literature. Searches for recent publications should be made in the catalog under the subject AMERICAN LITERATURE–ASIAN AMERICAN AUTHORS and the subdivisions of that heading.

BIBLIOGRAPHIES

There are no separately published bibliographies solely devoted to Asian American literature. Miller, **A Comprehensive Bibliography for the Study of American Minorities** (above) lists works in separate sections devoted to Chinese, Filipino, and Japanese groups. Japanese authors are well represented, but many of the primary sources cited in the Chinese American section deal with the image of the Chinese in literature rather than with works by Chinese American authors.

SURVEYS

There are no separately published critical surveys, and the best readily available comment is contained in the following important anthologies:

—**Aiiieeeee!: An Anthology of Asian-American Writers**, ed. Frank Chin, et al. (Washington, DC: Howard Univ. Press, 1974). The selections in this anthology are preceded by an excellent critical essay that places the works in context.

—**Asian American Authors**, eds. Kai-yu Hsu and Helen Pablubinskas (Boston: Houghton Mifflin, 1972). This anthology gathers shorter literary works of Chinese, Filipino, and Japanese writers who have lived extensively in America. For each culture, there are an introductory essay and a brief chronology of the major legislation and milestones that have affected the group. Each author's contribution is preceded by a portrait and a biographical sketch.

Black American

Annual updates on scholarship and criticism appear in the **MLA International Bibliography** and in **American Literary Scholarship**, under sections devoted to black literature. An important periodical containing comment and bibliographies is **Black American Literature Forum** (Terre Haute: School of Education, Indiana State Univ., 1976-), which continues **Negro American Literature Forum**. Recent publications should be searched for in the library catalog under the subject AMERICAN LITERATURE–AFRO-AMERICAN AUTHORS and its subdivisions. Some catalogs may use an earlier term, AMERICAN LITERATURE–NEGRO AUTHORS. Specific genres may also be approached, e.g., AMERICAN POETRY–AFRO-AMERICAN AUTHORS. See also the following individual authors in Chapter Eight: Baldwin, Baraka, Brooks, Chesnutt, Cullen, DuBois, Ellison, Hughes, Reed, Toomer, Wheatley, and Wright.

BIBLIOGRAPHIES

—**Afro-American Poetry and Drama, 1760-1975: A Guide to Information Sources** (Detroit: Gale, 1979). Poetry section is by William P. French, Amritjit Singh, and

Michel J. Fabre. Drama section is by Genevieve E. Fabre. Covers critical, historical, and biographical studies of individual authors, including items in periodicals. Few annotations.

—Arata, Esther Spring, and Nicholas John Rotoli. **Black American Playwrights, 1800 to the Present: A Bibliography** (Metuchen, NJ: Scarecrow, 1976). Contains citations to criticism and reviews of plays and musicals.

—**Black American Writers: Bibliographical Essays**, eds. M. Thomas Inge, Maurice Duke, Jackson R. Bryer. 2v. (New York: St. Martin's Press, 1978). Contains critical essays on "America's seminal black writers," giving an overview of scholarship and identifying major editions, sources of manuscripts, and secondary sources. Volume 1 covers eighteenth-century writers, slave narratives, early modern writers, the Harlem Renaissance, and Langston Hughes. Volume 2 covers Richard Wright, Ralph Ellison, James Baldwin, and Amiri Baraka.

—Fairbanks, Carol, and Eugene A. Engeldinger. **Black American Fiction: A Bibliography** (Metuchen, NJ: Scarecrow, 1978). Bibliographic listings of primary and secondary sources for individual black authors, arranged alphabetically by author, with categories subarranged for forms such as novels, short fiction, biography, and criticism. Includes literature in periodicals. Unannotated.

—Hatch, James V., and Omanii Abdullah. **Black Playwrights: 1823-1977: An Annotated Bibliography of Plays** (New York: Bowker, 1977). Gives brief annotations for 2,700 plays of about 900 black authors. Includes bibliographies of criticism, anthologies, dissertations, and taped interviews, as well as awards and current addresses.

—Kallenback, Jessamine A. **Index to Black American Literary Anthologies** (Boston: G. K. Hall, 1979). Indexes 142 collections through the mid 1970s, with author access and a title index.

—Margolies, Edward, and David Bakish. **Afro-American Fiction, 1853-1976** (Detroit: Gale, 1979). Contains: 1) checklist of novels, 2) short story collections, 3) secondary sources for fifteen major black novelists, 4) bibliographies and general studies.

—Page, James Allen. **Selected Black American Authors: An Illustrated Bio-Bibliography** (Boston: G. K. Hall, 1977). A ready-reference alphabetical listing of authors from a variety of disciplines.

—Peavy, Charles D. **Afro-American Literature and Culture Since World War II: A Guide to Information Sources** (Detroit: Gale, 1979). An annotated guide to subjects and fifty-six individual authors.

—Turner, Darwin T. **Afro-American Writers** (New York: Appleton-Century-Crofts, 1970). This Goldentree bibliography lists: 1) aids to research such as bibliographies, collections, reference works, periodicals, 2) backgrounds, including autobiographies, collections of essays, slave narratives, and folklore, 3) literary history and criticism by genre, 4) 135 writers, their works, and criticism of them.

SURVEYS

—Baker, Houston A. **The Journey Back: Issues in Black Literature and Criticism** (Chicago: Univ. of Chicago Press, 1980). By examining literature from the eighteenth century to the present, Baker seeks to explain how black narrative texts, written in English, preserve and communicate culturally unique meanings.

—**The Black Aesthetic**, ed. Addison Gale (Garden City, NY: Doubleday, 1971). An anthology of radical criticism.

—Bone, Robert A. **The Negro Novel in America**. rev. ed. (New Haven, CT: Yale Univ. Press, 1965). The most comprehensive survey of fiction by blacks, 1850-1962. Establishes each work of art in its own right before viewing it as part of the cultural process.

—Christian, Barbara. **Black Women Novelists: The Development of a Tradition, 1892-1976** (Westport, CT: Greenwood, 1980). Discusses the major themes of black women's novels, comparing them with those of black men. The first part is the history of the black heroine in literature, and the second examines novels of Paule Marshall, Toni Morrison, and Alice Walker.

—**Five Black Writers**, ed. Donald B. Gibson (New York: New York Univ. Press, 1970). An important collection of critical essays on Wright, Ellison, Baldwin, Hughes, and Baraka.

—Huggins, Nathan Irvin. **Harlem Renaissance** (New York: Oxford Univ. Press, 1971). A history of the movement, with useful discussions of the novels of Carl Van Vechten and Wallace Thurman included.

—Jackson, Blyden. **The Waiting Years: Essays on American Negro Literature** (Baton Rouge: Louisiana State Univ. Press, 1976). Essays of Jackson on general topics such as "The Case for American Negro Literature," "Harlem Renaissance," and "A Survey Course in Negro Literature," as well as individual authors Jean Toomer and Richard Wright.

—Wagner, Jean. **Black Poets of the United States: From Laurence Dunbar to Langston Hughes** (Chicago: Univ. of Illinois Press, 1973). A study of religious and racist sentiment between 1890 and 1940.

—Whitlow, Roger. **Black American Literature: A Critical History** (Chicago: Nelson Hall, 1973). Includes a bibliography of over 1,500 primary and secondary sources.

Mexican American and Chicano

Among important periodicals that include short literature are **Chicano Literary Prize** (Irvine: Dept. of Spanish and Portuguese, Univ. of California, Irvine, 1974/75-); **El Grito** (Berkeley, CA: Quinto Sol Publications, v.1, 1967- v.7, 1974); **Grito Del Sol** (Berkeley, CA: Tonatiuh International, 1976-); and **Revista Chicano-Riqueña** (Houston: Univ. of Houston, 1973-). An important index to selected Chicano periodicals, 1967-1978, is **Chicano Periodical Index** (Boston: G. K. Hall, 1981). Further works may be sought in the library catalog under the subject heading AMERICAN

LITERATURE–MEXICAN AMERICAN AUTHORS and its subdivisions. This heading includes works on Chicano authors.

BIBLIOGRAPHIES

–Lomelí, Francisco A., and Donaldo W. Urioste. **Chicano Perspectives in Literature: A Critical and Annotated Bibliography** (Albuquerque, NM: Pajarito Publications, 1976). An annotated bibliography of poetry, novels, short fiction, theatre, anthologies, literary criticism, oral tradition, journals, and literatura chicanesca, which will be valuable for identifying primary sources.

–Tatum, Charles. **A Selected and Annotated Bibliography of Chicano Studies**. 2nd ed. (Lincoln, NE: Society of Spanish and Spanish American Studies, 1979). Includes creative and critical publications by Chicanos who have evaluated and analyzed their own experiences and that of La Raza. The section on literature contains anthologies, bibliographies, criticism, drama, the novel, poetry, and short fiction.

SURVEYS

–Bruce-Novoa, Juan D. **Chicano Authors: Inquiry by Interviews** (Austin: Univ. of Texas Press, 1980). Following the general introduction and a chronology of Chicano literature by genre, 1959-1979, fourteen Chicano authors are interviewed about their perceptions on the literary, linguistic, and social cultural significance of Chicano literature. A selected bibliography helpfully identifies primary and secondary sources, including important anthologies.

–**Modern Chicano Writers: A Collection of Critical Essays**, eds. Joseph Sommers and Tomás Ybarra-Frausto (Englewood Cliffs, NJ: Prentice-Hall, 1979). Essays cover social, cultural, linguistic, and structural aspects, as well as historical perspectives and folklore. Helpful techniques for the analysis of Chicano literature are suggested.

–**New Directions in Chicano Scholarship**, eds. Ricardo Romo and Raymund Paredes (La Jolla: Chicano Studies Program, Univ. of California, San Diego, 1978). Essays that appeared originally in the **New Scholar**, 1977, include literary criticism by Joseph Sommers, Tomás Ybarra-Frausto, Doris Meyer, and Rafael Jesus Gonzalez.

–Robinson, Cecil. **Mexico and the Hispanic Southwest in American Literature: Revised from "With the Ears of Strangers."** 1977 ed. (Tucson: Univ. of Arizona Press, 1977). Surveys the history of the regional literature that was inspired by contact between Mexico and the Southwest United States. A chapter documents the vitality of the "double vision" that has resulted from the emergence of Chicano literature.

Native American

As scholarly contributions appear, bibliographic updates will be found in **American Literary Scholarship** under the chapter "Themes, Topics, Criticism." Many literary works are published in tribal magazines and in periodicals such as **Suntracks** (Tucson, AZ: Suntracks, 1971- , quarterly; 1978- annual). For further works see the library catalog under the subject AMERICAN LITERATURE–INDIAN AUTHORS and its subdivisions.

BIBLIOGRAPHIES

—Hirschfelder, Arlene B. **American Indian and Eskimo Authors: A Comprehensive Bibliography** (New York: Association on American Indian Affairs, 1973). Contains almost 400 titles from many disciplines written or narrated by nearly 300 Indian and Eskimo authors, representing more than 100 tribes. Includes a tribal index, listing names of individual authors under their tribal names. It is necessary to read each of the descriptive annotations to discover the genre of the material.

—Jacobson, Angeline. **Contemporary Native American Literature: A Selected & Partially Annotated Bibliography** (Metuchen, NJ: Scarecrow, 1977). Index to works published, 1960-1976. Includes Eskimo, Canadian, and Mexican tribal writers. There are indexes by title and first line, and a list of the analyzed periodicals is included.

—Littlefield, Daniel F., and James W. Parins. **A Bio-Bibliography of Native American Writers, 1772-1924** (Metuchen, NJ: Scarecrow, 1981). Lists 4,000 articles and books by hundreds of Native Americans, with brief bibliographies of writers and indexes by subject and tribe. No continuation of this index has been planned.

SURVEYS

—**American Indian Authors**, ed. Natachee Scott Momaday (Boston: Houghton Mifflin, 1971). An anthology containing literature of Chief Joseph, D. Chief Eagle, Black Elk, Charles A. Eastman, Thomas S. Whitecloud, and others. In addition, there are portraits, brief biographies, maps, and a classification of tribes by state.

—Hymes, Dell H. **"In Vain I Tried to Tell You": Essays in Native American Ethnopoetics** (Philadelphia: Univ. of Pennsylvania Press, 1981). The first in a series, Studies in Native American Literature, covering criticism of poetry and legends.

—Larson, Charles R. **American Indian Fiction** (Albuquerque: Univ. of New Mexico Press, 1978). A critical survey of novels published in English by American Indians from the work of Chief Simon Pokagon in 1899 to the contemporary period. The authors, identified as genuine American Indians on tribal rolls, include: Denton R. Bedford, Dallas Chief Eagle, John Joseph Mathews, D'Arcy McNickle, N. Scott Momaday, Roger Russell Nasnaga, John M. Oskison, Chief George Pierre, Chief Simon Pokagon, Leslie Marmon Silko, Hyemeyohsts Storm, and James Welch. Because of some doubt regarding authenticity, two works are discussed separately in appendices. **Co-ge-we-a, The Half Blood,** by Hum-Ishu-Ma, may have been written with the aid of an amanuensis, and **The Wokosani Road,** by Jon Mockingbird, has not been authentically identified as Indian in origin. Valuable lists of all known Indian fiction and secondary sources for it are included.

—**Literature of the American Indian: Views and Interpretations: A Gathering of Indian Memories, Symbolic Contents, and Literary Criticism,** ed. Abraham Chapman (New York: New American Library, 1975). An excellent selection from Indian works which also includes interpretative essays by both Indians and non-Indians.

—Stensland, Anna Lee. **Literature by and about the American Indian: An Annotated Bibliography for Junior and Senior High School Students** (Urbana, IL: National Council of Teachers of English, 1973). Although the titles in this general bibliography are for high school students, the annotations indicate that many will be useful for adults. Especially helpful as primary sources are the collections of myths, legends, oratory, and poetry. The titles listed under the sections on bibliography and auto-biography and the capsule biographies of twenty-five prolific American Indian scholars, writers, novelists, poets, editors, and compilers will provide leads for further searching.

—Velie, Alan R. **Four American Literary Masters: N. Scott Momaday, James Welch, Leslie Marmon Silko, and Gerald Vizenor.** 1st ed. (Norman: Univ. of Oklahoma Press, 1982). Modern Indian literature in English is the focus of this work, which arose from Professor Velie's teaching. Velie shows how contemporary Indian writers have drawn on their tribal heritage and how they have been affected by modern American and European literary movements. Includes a selected bibliography of critical items on each of the four authors.

WOMEN AND FEMINISM

BIBLIOGRAPHIES

—Myers, Carol Fairbanks. **Women in Literature: Criticism of the Seventies** (Metuchen, NJ: Scarecrow, 1976). Secondary materials on women authors and literary characters. Useful for finding criticism on particular women.

—Reardon, Joan, and Kristine A. Thorsen. **Poetry by American Women, 1900-1975: A Bibliography** (Metuchen, NJ: Scarecrow, 1979). Lists work of 5,500 poets.

—Schwartz, Narda Lacey. **Articles on Women Writers: A Bibliography** (Santa Barbara, CA: ABC-Clio, 1977). Lists articles on over 600 women writers, medieval to modern, from English-speaking countries, that were published in scholarly and popular period-icals from 1960 to 1975, alphabetically by author.

—Terris, Virginia R. **Woman in America: A Guide to Information Sources** (Detroit: Gale, 1980). Includes a section on women in literature.

—White, Barbara A. **American Women Writers: An Annotated Bibliography of Criticism** (New York: Garland, 1977). Annotates criticism that covers groups of women in fiction, poetry, and drama. Arranges in categories such as minorities or lesbians; special topics; literary history of women's contributions; contemporary assessments; feminine sensibility; problems; phallic criticism; feminist literary criti-cism; and miscellaneous other topics.

—**Women and Literature: An Annotated Bibliography of Women Writers** (Cambridge, MA: Cambridge-Goddard Graduate School, 1972). Gives access to prose fiction of individual women authors.

SURVEYS

—**American Women Writers: A Critical Reference Guide from Colonial Times to the Present**, eds. Lina Mainiero and Langdon Lynne Faust. 4v. (New York: Ungar, 1979-1982). The most comprehensive reference tool, covering about 1,500 known and little known women writers and therefore a good starting place. Contains brief biographies and interpretations of the most representative novels as well as a list of primary and secondary sources for each entry.

—Auchincloss, Louis. **Pioneers and Caretakers: A Study of Nine American Women Novelists** (Minneapolis: Univ. of Minnesota Press, 1965). An important study concentrating on twentieth-century women writers.

—Flexner, Eleanor. **Century of Struggle: The Woman's Rights Movement in the United States** (Cambridge: Harvard Univ. Press, 1959). Scholarly account of the movement.

—Olauson, Judith. **The American Woman Playwright: A View of Criticism and Characterization** (Troy, NY: Whitston, 1981). Survey of representative plays that center on women, by women dramatists from 1930 to 1970. Sees a trend "which indicates a change of characterization from the simple, passive, socially subjugated women characters of earlier plays to complicated active women who attempt . . . to become autonomous beings."

—**Seven American Women Writers: An Introduction**, ed. Maureen Howard (Minneapolis: Univ. of Minnesota Press, 1977). Gathers essays on Glasgow, Cather, Porter, Welty, McCarthy, McCullers, and O'Connor, which were first published as introductions in the series, University of Minnesota Pamphlets on American Writers.

—Wasserstrom, William. **Heiress of All the Ages: Sex and Sentiment in the Genteel Tradition** (Minneapolis: Univ. of Minnesota Press, 1959). A social and literary analysis of the genteel tradition from 1830 to World War I. Although fictional heroines and readers are the subject, there is also useful material for understanding women authors.

—Watts, Emily Stipes. **The Poetry of American Women from 1632 to 1945** (Austin: Univ. of Texas Press, 1977). Surveys women poets from Anne Bradstreet to Muriel Rukeyser, claiming that "American women poets have developed their own themes, prosodic techniques, types of poems, and particular images."

4

Criticism

GENERAL SURVEYS

—The Achievement of American Criticism: Representative Selections from Three Hundred Years of American Criticism, ed. Clarence Arthur Brown (New York: Ronald Press Co., 1954). An anthology containing sixty-five critical statements chronologically arranged to represent four historical periods. Includes a useful selective bibliography of primary and secondary works.

—The Development of American Literary Criticism, by Harry H. Clark, et al., ed. Floyd Stovall (Chapel Hill: Univ. of North Carolina Press, 1955). A study for the American Literature Group of the Modern Language Association of America, which contains essays by leading scholars.

—Hyman, Stanley Edgar. The Armed Vision: A Study in the Methods of Modern Literary Criticism. rev. [i.e. 2nd] ed., abridged (New York: Vintage Books, 1955). Analyzes the first fifty years of American literary criticism with individual chapters on leading critics such as Van Wyck Brooks, T. S. Eliot, Constance Rourke, and R. P. Blackmur.

—Lentricchia, Frank. After the New Criticism (Chicago: Chicago Univ. Press, 1980). An account of critical movements since the publication of Northrop Frye's Anatomy of Criticism, 1957. Covers such movements as existentialist criticism, phenomonology, hermeneutics, structuralism, and post-structuralism.

—Pritchard, John Paul. Criticism in America: An Account of the Development of Critical Techniques from the Early Period of the Republic to the Middle Years of the Twentieth Century (Norman: Univ. of Oklahoma Press, 1956). Surveys the development of criticism from 1800 through to Edmund Wilson, Van Wyck Brooks, and the Chicago Critics.

—Rathbun, John Wilbert. American Literary Criticism. 3v. (Boston: G. K. Hall, 1979). Volume 1, 1800-1860, discusses continental influences on the developing national literature and critical approaches. Volume 2, 1860-1905, by Rathbun and Harry H. Clark, concentrates on critical idealism, realism, and individualism. Volume 3, 1905-1965, by Rathbun and Arnold L. Goldsmith, treats topics such as new humanism, Marxism, new criticism, and mythic criticism.

—Webster, Grant. **The Republic of Letters: A History of Postwar American Literary Opinion** (Baltimore: Johns Hopkins Univ. Press, 1979). Places contemporary criticism in context, outlining the contributions of significant critics and providing useful bibliographic citations.

INDIVIDUAL CRITICAL SCHOOLS
AND APPROACHES

—**Art and Error: Modern Textual Editing**, eds. Ronald Gottesman and Scott Bennett (Bloomington: Univ. of Indiana Press, 1970). Textual criticism. Essays on the problems of reconstructing authoritative texts.

—Baxandall, Lee. **Marxism and Aesthetics: A Selective Annotated Bibliography: Books and Articles in the English Language** (New York: Humanities Press, 1968). Lists articles on Marxist aesthetics, under such topics as Cinema, Literature, Theater, etc.

—**Bibliography and Textual Criticism: English and American Literature, 1700 to the Present**, eds. O. M. Brack, Jr., and Warner Barnes (Chicago: Univ. of Chicago Press, 1969). Textual criticism. Includes essays by scholars such as Fredson Bowers.

—**Directions for Criticism: Structuralism and Its Alternatives**, eds. Murray Krieger and L. S. Dembo (Madison: Univ. of Wisconsin Press, 1977). Contains five important essays by members of the School of Criticism and Theory, University of California, Irvine. Traces the main concerns of continental criticism as well as American trends.

—Farber, Marvin. **The Aims of Phenomenology: The Motives, Methods and Impact of Husserl's Thought** (New York: Harper & Row, 1966). Introduction to the theory of phenomenological criticism expounded by Edmund Husserl, which is an attempt to describe objects exactly as they are.

—Finkelstein, Sidney. **Existentialism and Alienation in American Literature** (New York: International Publishers, 1960). Traces the European origins of existentialist criticism and the view that the individual is isolated in an indifferent world.

—Foster, Richard. **The New Romantics: A Reappraisal of the New Criticism** (Bloomington: Indiana Univ. Press, 1962). Gives perspectives on the New Criticism.

—Fraiberg, Louis. **Psychoanalysis & American Literary Criticism** (Detroit: Wayne State Univ. Press, 1960). Examination of the application of the principles of modern psychology to literary analysis.

—Frye, Northrop. **Anatomy of Criticism** (Princeton, NJ: Princeton Univ. Press, 1957). Four essays examine critical theories of mode, symbol, myth, and genre.

—Hoffman, Frederick J. **Freudianism and the Literary Mind.** 2nd ed. (Baton Rouge: Louisiana State Univ. Press, 1957). Analysis of the impact of Freud's theories of motivation in the unconscious and conscious mind and their influence on literature.

—Lukács, Georg. **Realism in Our Time: Literature and the Class Struggle** (New York: Harper & Row, 1964). This Marxist approach examines modern literature that reveals social conflict from which arises a new state.

—Scholes, Robert. **Structuralism in Literature: An Introduction** (New Haven, CT: Yale Univ. Press, 1974). Analysis of structuralist methods, which attempt to seek principles by which literature can be accepted as a coherent work of art.

—Spiller, Robert E. "Literary History," in **The Aims and Methods of Scholarship in Modern Languages and Literature**, ed. James Thorpe (New York: Modern Language Association of America, 1970). Defends the central aim of historical criticism which attempts to interpret the significance of a work for the cultural and historical milieu in which it was originally written.

—Thorpe, James. **Principles of Textual Criticism** (San Marino, CA: Huntington Library, 1972). Discussion of the principles of modern textual editing.

Political, Social, and Intellectual History

AMERICAN PHILOSOPHERS:
SELECTED CSE EDITIONS

In addition to the critical accounts annotated below, you may wish to consult some important primary sources of American philosophers which have been published under the aegis of the Center for Scholarly Editions (CSE), or its predecessor, the Center for Editions of American Authors (CEAA), such as:

—Dewey, John. **The Early Works of John Dewey**, ed. Jo Ann Boydston. 5v. (Carbondale: Southern Illinois Univ. Press, 1967-72); and **The Middle Works of John Dewey**, ed. Jo Ann Boydston. 8v. (Southern Illinois Univ. Press, 1976-).

—James, William. **The Works of William James**, ed. Fredson Bowers. (Cambridge: Harvard Univ. Press, 1975-).

GENERAL

—Ahlstrom, Sydney E. **A Religious History of the American People** (New Haven, CT: Yale Univ. Press, 1972). Relates religion in America to the nation's social movements.

—Cargill, Oscar. **Intellectual America: Ideas on the March** (New York: Macmillan, 1941). Traces successive movements between the 1890s and World War II: French naturalism and decadence, German absolutism, English liberalism, the naturalists, the decadents, the primitivists, the intelligentsia, and the Freudians.

—Cassara, Ernest. **History of the United States of America: A Guide to Information Sources** (Detroit: Gale, 1977). Annotates 2,000 items from the general field of history.

—Curti, Merle. **The Growth of American Thought**. 2nd ed. (New York: Harper, 1951). A scholarly history of intellectual movements.

—Freidel, Frank Burt, with the assistance of Richard K. Showman. **Harvard Guide to American History**. rev. ed., 2v. (Cambridge: Harvard Univ. Press, 1974). Six sections give access to unannotated titles that cover: 1) Status, Methods, and Presentation, 2) Materials and Tools, 3) Colonial History and the Revolutions, 1492-1788, 4) National Growth, 1789-1865, 5) The Rise of Modern America, 1865-1900, 6) America in the Twentieth Century.

—Horton, Rod W., and Herbert W. Edwards. **Backgrounds of American Literary Thought**. 3rd ed. (Englewood Cliffs, NJ: Prentice-Hall, 1974). Covers the political, social, and intellectual backgrounds to American literature and examines movements such as transcendentalism, naturalism, and existentialism.

—Jones, Howard Mumford. **O Strange New World: American Culture: The Formative Years** (New York: Viking, 1964). Traces the development of American culture during the colonial era.

—Library of Congress. General Reference and Bibliography Division. **A Guide to the Study of the United States of America** (Washington, DC: Library of Congress, 1960); **Supplement, 1956-1965**. Usefully annotated titles on all aspects of American culture and civilization.

—Marx, Leo. **The Machine in the Garden: Technology and the Pastoral Ideal in America** (New York: Oxford Univ. Press, 1964). Traces the response of literature to the effects of machine technology.

—Matthiessen, F. O. **American Renaissance: Art and Expression in the Age of Emerson and Whitman** (New York: Oxford Univ. Press, 1941). Examines the ideals of Emerson, Thoreau, Hawthorne, Melville, and Whitman regarding the function of literature in a democracy.

—Nye, Russel Blaine. **Society and Culture in America, 1830-1860** (New York: Harper Torchbooks, 1974). Demonstrates that during the period from Jackson to the Civil War, the forces of romanticism, which were rooted in the Old World, gained new expression in the culture of the United States.

—Sandeen, Ernest R., and Frederick Hale. **American Religion and Philosophy: A Guide to Information Sources** (Detroit: Gale, 1978). Lists both primary and secondary sources that relate religion and philosophy to American culture.

—Tyler, Alice Felt. **Freedom's Ferment: Phases of American Social History from the Colonial Period to the Outbreak of the Civil War** (New York: Harper Torchbooks, 1962, c1944). Examines religious, social, cultural, and humanitarian forces, and provides insights into the reform movement in the United States.

6

American English: Language Studies and Dictionaries

INTRODUCTION

For access to further studies and dictionaries, see Vito J. Brenni, **American English: A Bibliography** (Philadelphia: Univ. of Pennsylvania Press, 1964), which is an annotated bibliography covering books and articles published through 1961 in sections devoted to topics such as pronunciation, usage, dialects, slang, and dictionaries.

—Burkett, Eva M. **American English Dialects in Literature** (Metuchen, NJ: Scarecrow, 1978). Demonstrates the use of dialect as a literary vehicle and shows the relationship of American English to history and culture, providing lists that give examples of the dialects.

—Craigie, Sir William A., and James R. Hulbert. **A Dictionary of American English on Historical Principles.** 4v. (Chicago: Univ. of Chicago Press, 1938-44). The standard work, which distinguishes differences between the English language in the United States and elsewhere, from colonial times until the end of the nineteenth century. Illustrates changes in meaning by quotations.

—Dillard, J. L. **Black English: Its History and Usage in the United States** (New York: Random House, 1972). Traces black English back to the slave trade, examining syntax and noting its influence on standard American speech.

—Ehrlich, Eugene, et al. **Oxford American Dictionary** (New York: Oxford Univ. Press, 1980). A guide to contemporary American English with very brief definitions.

—Follett, Wilson. **Modern American Usage: A Guide**, eds. Jacques Barzun, Carlos Baker, et al. (New York: Hill & Wang, 1966). A reliable guide, similar to Fowler's **Dictionary of Modern English Usage.**

—Krapp, George Philip. **The English Language in America.** 2v. (New York: Modern Language Association of America, 1925; repr. New York: Ungar, 1960). A standard study on English as spoken and written in the United States. Pronunciation and bibliography are emphasized in volume 2.

—Laird, Charlton. **Language in America.** 2v. (New York: World, 1970). A straight-forward and reliable description of the development of language in the United States.

—Marckwardt, Albert H. **American English** (New York: Oxford Univ. Press, 1958). A lucid account of the "interaction between linguistic and cultural factors in the growth of American English," presented as a series of topical essays with titles such as "Frontier Spirit" and "The Genteel Tradition."

—Mathews, Mitford M. **A Dictionary of Americanisms on Historical Principles.** 2v. (Chicago: Univ. of Chicago Press, 1951). Contains 50,000 words contributed to the English language in the United States, with dated examples.

—Mencken, H. L. **The American Language: An Inquiry into the Development of English in the United States.** 4th ed., corr., enl., and rev. (New York: Knopf, 1960); **Supplement I** (Knopf, 1945); **Supplement II** (Knopf, 1948). Highly readable and scholarly account of the development of American English, stressing differences from British English and covering pronunciation, spelling, slang, and proper names.

—Wentworth, Harold. **American Dialect Dictionary** (New York: Crowell, 1944). Examines variations in vocabulary, morphology, phonology, and semantics as they occur in different regions. When published, F. Cassidy, **Dictionary of American Regional English** will be the definitive work on regional variations.

—Wentworth, Harold, and Stuart B. Flexner. **Dictionary of American Slang, with a Supplement** (New York: Crowell, 1967). The standard reference work on slang as used by the general American public, with examples and dates of usage.

—Williamson, Juanita V., and Virginia M. Burke. **A Various Language: Perspectives on American Dialects** (New York: Holt, Rinehart & Winston, 1971). Essays by linguists on topics such as "Inherited Features," "Literary Representations of American English Dialects," and "Urban Dialects."

7

Anthologies and Series Used in Study and Teaching

ANTHOLOGIES

Listed here are a few anthologies of literature that have been useful as central volumes in survey courses and that can be supplemented by a combination of available paperbacks.

General

—**American Literature: A Period Anthology**. rev. ed. ed. Oscar Cargill. 4v. (New York: Macmillan, 1949). Volume 1. **The Roots of National Culture: American Literature to 1830**, eds. Robert E. Spiller and Harold W. Blodgett; Volume 2. **The Romantic Triumph: American Literature from 1830-1860**, ed. Tremaine McDowell; Volume 3, **The Rise of Realism: American Literature from 1860 to 1900**, ed. Louis Wann; Volume 4. **Contemporary Trends: American Literature since 1900**, eds. John H. Nelson and Oscar Cargill.

—**American Literature: The Makers and the Making**, eds. Cleanth Brooks, R. W. B. Lewis, Robert Penn Warren. 2v. (New York: St. Martin's Press, 1973). Chronologically arranged selections that include less notable works in order to throw light on the taste of a period and the significant development of an author. Perceptive critical introductions are included for the authors.

—**The Norton Anthology of American Literature**, ed. Ronald Gottesman, et al. 2v. (New York: Norton, 1979). Volume 1. Early American Literature, 1620-1820; American Literature, 1820-1865. Volume 2. American Literature, 1865-1914; American Literature between the Wars, 1914-1945; Contemporary American Prose, 1954- ; Contemporary American Poetry, 1945- . Excellent selections which include twenty-nine women writers and many authors who have not been adequately represented previously. Selected bibliographies are included at the end of each volume, and reliable texts have been employed, giving excellent selections overall.

Poetry

—**American Poetry**, eds. Gay Wilson Allen, Walter B. Rideout, James K. Robinson (New York: Harper & Row, 1965). Selects fifty poets for their literary excellence, twenty of whom wrote before 1930. They are presented in chronological sequence from Anne Bradstreet to Wendell Berry, with accurate texts. Brief biographical sketches, helpful notes, and lists of standard editions and helpful criticism are included.

—**Fifteen Modern American Poets**, ed. George P. Elliott (New York: Holt, Rinehart & Winston, 1956). Poets represented are Elizabeth Bishop, Richard Eberhart, Randall Jarrell, Robert Lowell, Josephine Miles, Howard Nemerov, Hyam Plutzik, Theodore Roethke, Muriel Rukeyser, James Schevill, Delmore Schwartz, Winfield Townley Scott, Karl Shapiro, Robert Penn Warren, and Richard Wilbur.

—**The Norton Anthology of Modern Poetry**, eds. Richard Ellmann and Robert O'Claire (New York: Norton, 1973). Collects 158 British and American twentieth-century poets along with Whitman and Dickinson, and provides introductions and bibliographies.

—**Seventeenth-Century American Poetry**, ed. Harrison T. Meserole (Garden City, NY: Anchor Books, 1968). Includes works by Edward Taylor, Anne Bradstreet, Michael Wigglesworth, and fourteen less well known poets, together with representative selections of about 100 other poets who wrote before 1725. Includes anonymous verse and selections from the Bay Psalm Book.

Short Story

—**Major American Short Stories**, ed. A. Walton Litz (New York: Oxford Univ. Press, 1975). A historical perspective results from the chronological arrangement of fiction writers from Irving to Cheever under the topics Regionalism and Realism, A National Art Form, and The Short Story Today.

Humor

—**Humor of the Old Southwest**. 2nd ed., eds. Hennig Cohen and William B. Dillingham (Athens: Univ. of Georgia Press, 1975). Collects the work of twenty-four authors, including August B. Longstreet, William Tappan Thompson, George Washington Harris, Johnson Jones Hoover, T. B. Thorpe, and Mark Twain.

—**Native American Humor**, ed. Walter Blair (New York: American Book Co., 1937; repr. San Francisco: Chandler, 1960). A notable anthology with an important introduction and useful bibliography. Organization is by topics such as "Down East Humor, 1830-1867," "Humor of the Old Southwest," "Local Colorists," and "Twentieth-Century Humorists."

SERIES

A number of publishers have devoted reliable series to aspects of American literature. In many libraries, you will be able to gain access to individual titles through entries in the catalog under the names of these series. In the following section are listed guides to series, and titles of series that publish editions of major works, biography, criticism, and bibliographies.

Guides to Series

—Baer, Eleanora A. **Titles in Series: A Handbook for Librarians and Students**. 3rd ed. 4v. (Metuchen, NJ: Scarecrow, 1978). Includes books in series published in America and foreign countries prior to January 1975, with approaches also by author and title.

–**Books in Series.** 3rd ed. (New York: Bowker, 1980-). Lists "original, reprinted, in-print, and out-of-print books, published or distributed in the U.S. in popular, scholarly, and professional series."

–**Library of Congress Catalogs: Monographic Series, 1974-** (Washington, DC: Library of Congress, 1976-). Three issues yearly, with annual cumulations. Prints records of all monographs in series cataloged by the Library of Congress, under the name of the series.

Series That Publish Editions of Major Works

–**Center for Scholarly Editions,** or its predecessor, the **Center for Editions of American Authors** (New York: Modern Language Association of America). This is not strictly a series disseminated by a given publisher, and different titles meeting the standard of the Center are published by different presses. The Center for Scholarly Editions (CSE), which is administered by the Committee on Scholarly Editions of the Modern Language Association, was officially established in 1976. At that time, a grant, under which the MLA Center for Editions of American Authors (CEAA) had been operating, ended. The CEAA had overseen a large number of editions of American Authors, and in so doing had increased the awareness of editorial problems broadly in the scholarly environment. With the founding of the CSE, therefore, the scope of the editions undertaken has changed and services of the CSE may be sought in the editing of any document, not necessarily literary, from any country. Funds for the editing of editions are sought directly from the National Endowment for the Humanities. Specifically, the CSE is concerned with the following functions: 1) to serve as a clearinghouse for information about scholarly editing and editorial projects; 2) to offer advice and consultation to editors who wish to avail themselves of this service; 3) to call attention to excellence in editing by awarding emblems to volumes that meet their standards; and 4) to promote dissemination of the most reliable texts into classrooms and among general readers.
Current lists of editions which have met the approval of the CSE are available from the Coordinator, Center for Scholarly Editions, Modern Language Association, 62 Fifth Avenue, New York, NY 10011.

–**Chandler Facsimile Editions in American Literature** (San Francisco: Chandler Publishing). Reprints first editions of major works, preceding each by a critical introduction, brief biography, textual note, and a bibliography. Includes Stephen Crane, **Maggie, A Girl of the Streets,** Walt Whitman, **Leaves of Grass,** Nathaniel Hawthorne, **The Scarlet Letter,** and Herman Melville, **The Confidence Man.**

–**The Library of America** (New York: Viking; available by subscription from Time-Life Books). A nonprofit publishing program supported by the National Endowment for the Humanities and the Ford Foundation, which plans to publish collected works of major American authors in a reliable uniform series of hardcover editions in large type on lightweight, durable paper. To date, the series includes some works of **Herman Melville,** ed. G. Thomas Tanselle; **Harriet Beecher Stowe,** ed. Kathryn Kish Sklar; **Walt Whitman,** ed. Justin Kaplan; and **Nathaniel Hawthorne,** ed. Roy Harvey Pearce.

–**Norton Critical Editions** (New York: Norton). Authoritative texts printed with accompanying source materials and a few of the most important critical essays. Includes Samuel Langhorne Clemens, **Adventures of Huckleberry Finn,** ed. Sculley

Bradley, et al; Stephen Crane, **The Red Badge of Courage**, ed. Sculley Bradley; Nathaniel Hawthorne, **The Scarlet Letter**, ed. Sculley Bradley, et al.; **Adrienne Rich's Poetry**, ed. Barbara Charlesworth Gelpi; and Kate Chopin, **The Awakening**, ed. Margaret Culley.

—**Riverside Editions** (Boston: Houghton Mifflin). Important paperback teaching editions which contain short critical introductions by notable scholars and selected bibliographies, with notes on the text employed. Includes authors such as Cooper, Stephen Crane, Hawthorne, Howells, James, Melville, Norris, and Mark Twain.

—**Viking Portable Library** (New York: Penguin Books). Includes writings of major and minor American authors, with fiction, letters, essays, and autobiography. Among authors represented are Arthur Miller, Faulkner, and Veblen.

Series That Publish Biography and Criticism

—**Boise State University Western Writers Series** (Boise, ID: Boise State Univ., Dept. of English). Pamphlet-length introductions to the lives and works of significant authors from the western United States, such as Bret Harte, Frederick Manfred, Hamlin Garland, Owen Wister, N. Scott Momaday, and Jack Kerouac.

—**Columbia Introduction to Twentieth Century American Poetry** (New York: Columbia Univ. Press). Focuses on the way the poetry of the writer under study has evolved by including themes and placing the writer in an intellectual and literary milieu. Includes volumes on writers such as Hart Crane, Langston Hughes, Marianne Moore, Ezra Pound, and Theodore Roethke.

—**Critical Essays in English and American Literature** (Pittsburgh: Univ. of Pittsburgh Press). Includes work on George W. Cable, Margaret Fuller, Henry James, and Katherine Anne Porter.

—**Critical Essays on American Literature** (Boston: G. K. Hall). Noted scholars have contributed papers on such writers as Bellow, Cable, Edwards, Fuller, Oates, and Stowe.

—**Crosscurrents/Modern Critiques** (Carbondale: Southern Illinois Univ. Press). Harry T. Moore introduces critical monographs on writers such as Isaac Singer, E. E. Cummings, and Wallace Stevens. Also treats more general topics such as Oscar Cargill, **Toward a Pluralistic Criticism**.

—**Dictionary of Literary Biography** (Detroit: Gale). Each volume is devoted to a specific genre, region, or time period, with entries supplementing and updating information from the **Dictionary of American Biography** and **Contemporary Authors** in signed articles. Each volume contains about 100 entries, with biographical sketches, overviews of critical reception, bibliographic checklists of primary and secondary sources, and portraits. Volumes include: 1. **The American Renaissance in New England**, ed. Joel Myerson; 2. **American Novelists since World War II**, eds. Jeffrey Helterman and Richard Layman; 3. **Antebellum Writers in New York and the South**, ed. Joel Myerson; 4. **American Writers in Paris**, ed. Karen Lane Rood; 5. **American Poets Since World War II**, ed. Donald J. Grand.

—**Penguin Critical Anthologies** (Harmondsworth, England: Penguin Books). Excellent collections of important critical essays for authors, including Ezra Pound, Walt Whitman, and William Carlos Williams.

—**Twayne's United States Authors Series** (New Haven, CT: College and Univ. Press). Bio-critical introductions, which vary in quality, for over 350 authors.

—**Twentieth Century Interpretations** (Englewood Cliffs, NJ: Prentice-Hall). Collections of critical essays on individual works, such as Henry James, **Portrait of a Lady**, and Arthur Miller, **The Crucible**. A companion series is **Twentieth Century Views**, which collects short critical essays on individual authors that are useful introductory reading.

—**University of Minnesota Pamphlets on American Writers** (Minneapolis: Univ. of Minnesota Press). Provides 103 reliable short introductions to authors from the seventeenth century to the present day, by notable scholars. Each contains an account of the life, a discussion of style and literary contributions, and a bibliography of primary and secondary sources. These accounts have been reprinted in **American Writers: A Collection of Literary Biographies**, ed. Leonard Unger, 6v. (New York: Scribner, 1974-81). In this set, two volumes supplement the original essays, so that altogether 126 articles are available on writers such as Bradstreet, Hughes, Hellman, Plath, and Thurber.

Series That Publish Bibliographies

—**Calendars of American Literary Manuscripts** (Columbus: Ohio State Univ. Press). Publishes the "results of specialized searches for all of the available pre- and post-publication inscriptions of individual authors," in an effort to prevent duplication of research effort. Calendars are available for Hart Crane, Upton Sinclair, and Henry David Thoreau.

—**Charles E. Merrill Checklists** (Columbus, OH: Merrill). Brief checklists of primary and secondary works, divided into books and separate publications, editions, letters, bibliographies, biographies, scholarship, and criticism.

—**G. K. Hall Reference Guides** (Boston: G. K. Hall). Bibliographies of secondary sources, usually chronologically arranged. Titles vary in quality.

—**Gale Research. Modern Authors Checklist Series** (Detroit: Gale). Bibliographical descriptions of primary sources of twentieth-century authors, including James Dickey, Kurt Vonnegut, Jr., and Robert Lowell.

—**Goldentree Bibliographies** (New York: Appleton-Century-Crofts). Reliable, inexpensive guides covering both primary and secondary sources.

—**Pittsburgh Series in Bibliography** (Pittsburgh: Pittsburgh Univ. Press). Important descriptive bibliographies of primary sources for authors such as Hart Crane, Scott Fitzgerald, Wallace Stevens, Eugene O'Neill, Marianne Moore, and Margaret Fuller.

—**Scarecrow Author Bibliographies** (Metuchen, NJ: Scarecrow). Bibliographies cover materials by and about authors, usually taking a genre approach.

—**Serif Series: Bibliographies and Checklists** (Kent, OH: Kent State Univ. Press). Covers primary and secondary bibliography for authors and genres.

Part II

Guides to 100 Individual Authors

The 100 authors listed in this section have been chosen because they are frequently studied in courses by undergraduates and graduate students. Care has been taken to include women and black authors who have made leading contributions to belles lettres.

For each author, the general plan is an arrangement of PRIMARY AND SECONDARY sources.

Under PRIMARY sources are listed: 1) Separate Works, using short titles, in chronological order, to enable an overview of the author's literary development; 2) Collected Works and Edited Texts, citing editions of belles lettres, correspondence, diaries, and autobiographies that are considered important, with works published in periodicals and anthologies normally excluded; 3) Other Source Materials, which are the important collections of authors' papers or manuscripts which may be available for research or on display in special collections to which the student has access.

Under SECONDARY sources, an attempt has been made to list titles in chronological order, so that critical development in a field can be traced. Where it is thought to be helpful, as in the case of some more specialized studies, these are grouped in subcategories. Materials included as secondary sources are: 1) Biography; 2) Criticism, with emphasis on monographs that are general studies but including some specialized studies considered important (citations to collections of criticism by several authors follow the listing of monographs by individual critics); 3) Bibliographies, including the most important primary and secondary bibliographies; 4) Reference Works, including concordances, newsletters, and other tools that are generally considered to be ready reference in scope.

HENRY (BROOKS) ADAMS, 1838-1918

PRIMARY SOURCES

Separate Works

Chapters of Erie, and Other Essays, with Charles Francis Adams, Jr. (1871); Essays in Anglo-Saxon Law (1876); Documents Relating to New England Federalism (1800-15, 1877); Democracy: An American Novel (1879); The Life of Albert Gallatin (1879); The Writings of Albert Gallatin (1879); John Randolph (1882); Esther: A Novel (1884); History of the United States of America during the Administration of Thomas Jefferson (1884-85); History of the United States of America during the Administration of James Madison (1888-89); Historical Essays (1891); Memoirs of Marau Taaroa (1893); Mont-Saint-Michel and Chartres (1904); The Education of Henry Adams: An Autobiography (1907); The Life of George Cabot Lodge (1911); The Degradation of the Democratic Dogma (1919).

Collected Works and Edited Texts

There is no authoritative collection of Adams' writings. The Education, Riverside ed., edited by Ernest Samuels (Boston: Houghton Mifflin, 1974) is the best edition available and makes use of Adams' own annotations and comments. Vandersee and Harbert (see Bibliography) have commented on editions and reprints of other works. Some of Adams' letters are collected in four volumes as A Cycle of Adams Letters, 1861-1865, 2v.; Letters of Henry Adams, 1858-1891; and Letters of Henry Adams, 1892-1918, ed. Worthington C. Ford (Boston: Houghton Mifflin, 1920-38). A six-volume edition is projected by Harvard University Press.

Other Source Materials

The major collection of Adams papers is at the Massachusetts Historical Society, Boston, which issued a thirty-six-reel microfilm edition of the Papers in 1979.

SECONDARY SOURCES

Biography

The standard biography to draw upon the Adams papers is the trilogy of Ernest Samuels, The Young Henry Adams; Henry Adams: The Middle Years; and Henry Adams: The Major Phase (Cambridge: Harvard Univ. Press, 1948-64). Elizabeth Stevenson, Henry Adams: A Biography (New York: Macmillan, 1956) is a shorter account that shows the relation of Adams to The Education.

Criticism

A clear introductory chapter on each of the main works is in George Hochfield, Henry Adams: An Introduction and Interpretation (New York: Barnes & Noble, 1962). A short introductory pamphlet is Louis Auchincloss, Henry Adams (Minneapolis: Univ. of Minnesota Press, 1971). Most important is J. C. Levenson, The Mind and Art of Henry Adams (Boston: Houghton Mifflin, 1957). Other studies of value are Max I. Baym, The French Education of Henry Adams (New York: Columbia Univ. Press, 1951); John J. Conder, A Formula of His Own: Henry Adams's Literary Experiment (Chicago: Univ. of Chicago Press, 1970), which concentrates on form and technique of *Chartres* and *The Education*; William H. Jordy, *Henry Adams: Scientific Historian* (New Haven, CT: Yale Univ. Press, 1952); Ernest Scheyer, *The Circle of Henry Adams: Art and Artists* (Detroit: Wayne State Univ. Press, 1970); and a treatment of Adams' humor is Vern Wagner, *The Suspension of Henry Adams* (Wayne State Univ. Press, 1969). Earl N. Harbert, *The Force So Much Closer Home: Henry Adams and the Adams Family* (New York: New York Univ. Press, 1977) follows the thesis that ideas in Adams' writings were largely shaped by principles passed on from his forebears. A collection of *Critical Essays on Henry Adams*, ed. Earl N. Harbert (Boston: G. K. Hall, 1981) brings together important shorter criticism of Adams.

Bibliography

Most useful are the essay by Earl N. Harbert, "Henry Adams," in *Fifteen American Authors Before 1900*, ed. Robert A. Rees and Earl N. Harbert (Madison: Univ. of Wisconsin Press, 1971), pp.3-36; and a review by Charles Vandersee, "Henry Adams, 1838-1918," in *American Literary Realism* 2 (1969): 89-120. Earl N. Harbert, *Henry Adams: A Reference Guide* (Boston: G. K. Hall, 1978) is a briefly annotated bibliography which lists major writing of Adams and selects secondary works about him that appeared between 1879 and 1975.

LOUISA MAY ALCOTT, 1832-1888
Pseuds: A. M. Barnard; Flora Fairfield; L. M. A.

PRIMARY SOURCES

Separate Works

Flower Fables (1855); *Hospital Sketches* (1863); *On Picket Duty and Other Tales* (1864); *The Rose Family* (1864); *Moods* (1865); *The Mysterious Key and What It Opened* (1867); *Morning-Glories, and Other Stories* (1868); *Kitty's Class Day* (1868); *Aunt Kipp* (1868); *Nelly's Hospital* (1868); *Psyche's Art* (1868); *Little Women; Or, Meg, Jo, Beth, and Amy* (1868); *Little Women; Or, Meg, Jo, Beth, and Amy: Part Second* (1869); *An Old-Fashioned Girl* (1870); *Little Men: Life at Plumfield with Jo's Boys* (1871); *Aunt Jo's Scrap-Bag*, 6v. (1872-82); *Work* (1873); *Eight Cousins; Or, The Aunt-Hill* (1875); *Silver Pitchers: And Independence, a Centennial Love Story* (1876); *Rose in Bloom: A Sequel to "Eight Cousins"* (1876); *A Modern Mephistopholes* (1877); *Under the Lilacs* (1878); *Meadow Blossoms* (1879); *Sparkles for Bright Eyes* (1879); *Water Cresses* (1879); *Jack and Jill: A Village Story* (1880); *Proverb Stories* (1882); *Spinning-Wheel Stories* (1884); *Jo's Boys and How They Turned Out: A Sequel to "Little Men"* (1886); *A Garland for Girls* (1888); *A Modern Mephistopholes and a Whisper in the Dark* (1889); *Diana and Persis* [written 1879; published 1977].

Collected Works and Edited Texts

There is no complete collection of Alcott's works. Two editions of her letters are *Louisa May Alcott: Her Life, Letters and Journals*, ed. Ednah D. Cheney (Boston: Roberts, 1889); and *Little Women Letters from the House of Alcott*, ed. Jessie Bonstelle and Marion DeForest (Boston: Little, Brown, 1914). Two important collections of recently discovered gothic tales published under the pseudonym A. M.

Barnard are *Behind a Mask: The Unknown Thrillers of Louisa May Alcott*, ed. Madeleine Stern (New York: Morrow, 1975); and *Plots and Counterplots: More Unknown Thrillers of Louisa May Alcott*, ed. Madeleine Stern (Morrow, 1976). A recent reprinting is *Work: A Story of Experience* (Boston: Roberts, 1873; repr. New York: Schocken, 1977, ed. Sarah Elbert). Short fiction is collected in *Glimpses of Louisa: A Centennial Sampling of the Best Short Stories*, ed. Cornelia Meigs (Boston: Little, Brown, 1968).

Other Source Materials

A major collection of Alcott's letters is at Harvard University.

SECONDARY SOURCES

Biography and Criticism

The full-length works on Alcott have combined biography and criticism. Two early memoirs are Clara Gowing, *The Alcotts As I Knew Them* (Boston: Clark, 1909); and Caroline Ticknor, *May Alcott: A Memoir* (Boston: Little, Brown, 1929). A reliable biography for young adults, useful as an introduction, is Cornelia L. Meigs, *The Struggle of the Author of Little Women: Invincible Louisa* (Little, Brown, 1933). An early psychological study was Katharine Anthony, *Louisa May Alcott* (New York: Knopf, 1938). The best full-length critical biography, based on primary sources and with an excellent bibliography, is Madeleine B. Stern, *Louisa May Alcott*, 2nd ed. (Norman: Univ. of Oklahoma Press, 1971). Other studies to consult are Marjorie Worthington, *Miss Alcott of Concord* (New York: Doubleday, 1958); Martha Saxton, *Louisa May: A Modern Biography of Louisa May Alcott* (Boston: Houghton Mifflin, 1977); and Sarah Elbert, *Louisa May Alcott and the Woman Problem* (Little, Brown, 1978).

Bibliographies

Lucile Gulliver, *Louisa May Alcott: A Bibliography* (Boston: Little, Brown, 1932) is a descriptive bibliography of Alcott's editions. Judith C. Ullom, *Louisa May Alcott: A Centennial for Little Women* (Washington, DC: Library of Congress, 1969) served as an exhibition catalog and contains illustrations from editions and extracts from prefaces and reviews. Alma J. Payne, *Louisa May Alcott: A Reference Guide* (Boston: G. K. Hall, 1980) contains lists of books, short fiction, and nonfiction by Alcott, and a chronologically arranged, annotated bibliography of secondary sources, 1854-1979.

SHERWOOD ANDERSON, 1876-1941

PRIMARY SOURCES

Separate Works

Windy McPherson's Son (1916); *Marching Men* (1917); *Mid-American Chants* (1918); *Winesburg, Ohio* (1919); *Poor White* (1920); *The Triumph of the Egg* (1921); *Many Marriages* (1923); *Horses and Men* (1923); *A Story Teller's Story* (1924); *Dark*

Laughter (1925); *The Modern Writer* (1925); *Sherwood Anderson's Notebook* (1926); *Tar: A Midwest Childhood* (1926); *A New Testament* (1927); *Alice and the Lost Novel* (1929); *Hello Towns!* (1929); *Nearer the Grass Roots* (1929); *The American County Fair* (1930); *Perhaps Women* (1931); *Beyond Desire* (1932); *Death in the Woods* (1933); *No Swank* (1934); *Puzzled America* (1935); *Kit Brandon: A Portrait* (1936); *Plays, Winesburg and Others* (1937); *Home Town* (1940); *Sherwood Anderson's Memoirs* (1942); *The Writer's Book* (1975); *Paris Notebook, 1921* (1976).

Collected Works and Edited Texts

Anderson's works are not available in a collected edition. Major editions containing selections are *The Sherwood Anderson Reader*, ed. Paul Rosenfeld (Boston: Houghton Mifflin, 1947); and *The Portable Sherwood Anderson*, rev. ed., ed. Horace Gregory (New York: Viking-Penguin, 1977). Ray Lewis White has edited a series of critical texts for the Press of Case Western Reserve University, titled *Major Fiction of Sherwood Anderson*; and John H. Ferres edited a teaching edition of *Winesburg, Ohio: Text and Criticism* (New York: Penguin Books, 1977). Two editions of Anderson's newspaper writing are *Return to Winesburg: Selections from Four Years of Writing for a Country Newspaper*, ed. Ray Lewis White (Chapel Hill: Univ. of North Carolina Press, 1967); and *The Buck Fever Papers*, ed. Welford Dunaway Taylor (Charlottesville: Univ. Press of Virginia, 1971), which is a collection of essays originally published in the *Smyth County News* and the *Marion Democrat, 1927-31*. Several of Anderson's autobiographical works have been edited in critical editions by Ray Lewis White. These include a text based on the Newberry Library's typescript of *A Story Teller's Story* (Cleveland: Press of Case Western Reserve Univ., 1968), illustrated with photographs; *Tar* (Press of Case Western Reserve Univ., 1969); and White's annotated transcription from the original manuscripts of Sherwood Anderson's *Memoirs* (Chapel Hill: Univ. of North Carolina Press, 1969). The *"Writer's Book,"* ed. Martha Mulroy Curry (Metuchen, NJ: Scarecrow, 1975) makes available Anderson's unfinished project of seven essays and stories addressed to fellow writers, with his ideas on the difference between a short story and a novel, and the telling of a story as well as a description of the processes by which the story is shaped. *France and Sherwood Anderson: Paris Notebook*, 1921, ed. Michael Fanning (Baton Rouge: Louisiana State Univ. Press, 1976) is from a fragmentary manuscript at the Newberry Library which includes observations of Paris, impressionistic story outlines, and remarks on aesthetics.

There are several collections of correspondence, the standard being *Letters of Sherwood Anderson*, eds. Howard Mumford Jones and Walter B. Rideout (Boston: Little, Brown, 1953), which publishes letters in the Newberry collection. *Sherwood Anderson/Gertrude Stein: Correspondence and Personal Essays*, ed. Ray Lewis White (Chapel Hill: Univ. of North Carolina Press, 1972) is an absorbing presentation of the extant correspondence between these two writers. Further letters of Anderson and other writers which have been published in journals or collections are listed in the bibliographies of Rogers and White (*see* Bibliographies).

Other Source Materials

Over 16,700 items deposited at the Newberry Library, Chicago, include letters, works, art work, dust jackets, photographs, and manuscripts of *Winesburg, Ohio*, *Beyond Desire*, *Many Marriages*, and *Marching Men*, as well as the texts of two unfinished novels, *Talbot Wittingham* and *Mary Cochran*. In addition, there are over sixty items of correspondence, photographs, and manuscripts in the Barrett Library, University of Virginia, Charlottesville.

SECONDARY SOURCES

Biography

There is not yet a definitive biography of Anderson, and the most helpful accounts available are those of his third wife, Elizabeth Anderson, and Gerald R. Kelly, *Miss Elizabeth: A Memoir* (Boston: Little, Brown, 1969). Margaret Anderson, *My Thirty Years' War* (New York: Covici, Friede, 1930) is a revealing memoir by the editor of *The Little Review*; and another author's account is in August Derleth, *Three Literary Men: A Memoir of Sinclair Lewis, Sherwood Anderson, Edgar Lee Masters* (New York: Candlelight Press, 1963).

Criticism

There are several useful introductions to Anderson. Irving Howe, *Sherwood Anderson* (New York: Sloane, 1951) has some mistakes in the biographical accounts, but criticism on the short stories is helpful. Brom Weber, *Sherwood Anderson* (Minneapolis: Univ. of Minnesota Press, 1964) is a thoughtful pamphlet, while a longer study is David D. Anderson, *Sherwood Anderson: An Introduction and Interpretation* (New York: Holt, Rinehart, and Winston, 1967). A shrewd discussion including the influence of the post-impressionists and Gertrude Stein on *Winesburg* is provided by Rex Burbank, *Sherwood Anderson* (New York: Twayne, 1964); and Welford Dunaway Taylor, *Sherwood Anderson* (New York: Ungar, 1977) is a first-rate introduction to the most significant aspects of Anderson's work and career.

Among the anthologies which were generated by Anderson's centenary in 1976 are *Sherwood Anderson: Dimensions of His Literary Art: A Collection of Critical Essays*, ed. David D. Anderson (East Lansing: Michigan State Univ. Press, 1976); and *Sherwood Anderson: Centennial Studies*, eds. Hilbert H. Campbell and Charles E. Modlin (Troy, NY: Whitston, 1976). The three most valuable collections of critical writing are *The Achievement of Sherwood Anderson*, ed. Ray Lewis White (Chapel Hill: Univ. of North Carolina Press, 1966); the fine introduction and judicious selection in *Sherwood Anderson: A Collection of Critical Essays*, ed. Walter B. Rideout (Englewood Cliffs, NJ: Prentice-Hall, 1974); and Sherwood Anderson, *Winesburg, Ohio: Text and Criticism*, rev. ed., ed. John H. Ferres (New York: Penguin Books, 1977).

Bibliographies

An efficient guide, which focuses selectively on English and American editions and criticism, is Douglas G. Rogers, *Sherwood Anderson: A Selective Annotated Bibliography* (Metuchen, NJ: Scarecrow, 1976). Ray Lewis White, *Sherwood Anderson: A Reference Guide* (Boston: G. K. Hall, 1977) is a massive work of scholarship, arranged by year to provide a definitive bibliography with more than 2,550 entries, including works in foreign languages and newspaper clippings. Of lasting value is an interpretative bibliographical essay by Walter B. Rideout, "Sherwood Anderson," in *Fifteen Modern American Authors*, ed. Jackson R. Bryer (Durham, NC: Duke Univ. Press, 1969), pp.3-22.

Reference Works

The *Winesburg Eagle*, newsletter of the Sherwood Anderson Society, began at the University of Virginia in 1975 and should be consulted for current bibliography, articles, and reviews.

JAMES BALDWIN, 1924-

PRIMARY SOURCES

Separate Works

Go Tell It on the Mountain (1953); *Notes of a Native Son* [essays] (1955); *Giovanni's Room* (1956); *Nobody Knows My Name* [essays] (1961); *This Morning, This Evening, So Soon* (1962); *Another Country* (1962); *The Fire Next Time* [essays] (1963); *Nothing Personal* [with Richard Avedon] (1964); *Blues for Mister Charlie* [play] (1964); *Going to Meet the Man* [short stories] (1965); *Tell Me How Long the Train's Been Gone* (1968); *The Amen Corner* [play] (1968); *A Rap on Race* [conversation with Margaret Mead] (1971); *A Dialogue* [conversation with Nikki Giovanni] (1971); *No Name in the Street* [essays] (1972); *One Day When I Was Lost* [scenario based on *The Autobiography of Malcolm X]* (1973); *If Beale Street Could Talk* (1974); *The Devil Finds Work* [essay] (1976); *Little Man, Little Man: A Story of Childhood* (1976); *Just Above My Head* (1979).

Collected Works and Edited Texts

Going to Meet the Man (New York: Dial, 1965) is a collection of many of Baldwin's short stories.

Other Source Materials

Citations for many of Baldwin's essays, interviews, and discussions, which are widely dispersed in periodicals, may be found in Fred L. Standley and Nancy V. Standley (*see* Bibliographies).

SECONDARY SOURCES

Biography

The book-length biography, Fern Eckman, *The Furious Passage of James Baldwin* (New York: M. Evans; distr. Philadelphia: Lippincott, 1966) is based on interviews and Baldwin's own autobiographical works. William J. Weatherby, *Squaring Off: Mailer Versus Baldwin* (New York: Mason/Charter, 1977) shows Mailer and Baldwin as representative figures of the sixties.

Criticism

An introduction to the short stories, novels, and plays is Louis H. Pratt, *James Baldwin* (Boston: Twayne, 1978). Stanley Macebuh, *James Baldwin: A Critical Study* (New York: Third Press-Joseph Okpaku, 1973) is a full-length study which concentrates on the novels. *James Baldwin: A Collection of Critical Essays*, ed. Keneth Kinnamon (Englewood Cliffs, NJ: Prentice-Hall, 1974) contains a useful short biography and discussion of themes, in addition to thirteen previously published essays; and *James Baldwin: A Critical Evaluation*, ed. Therman B. O'Daniel (Washington, DC: Howard Univ. Press, 1977) is another collection of criticism which contains a reliable bibliography of primary and secondary sources.

Bibliographies

A helpful bibliographic essay is Daryl Dance, "James Baldwin," in *Black American Writers: Bibliographical Essays*, 2v., eds. M. Thomas Inge, Maurice Duke, Jackson R. Bryer (New York: St. Martin's Press, 1978), v.2, pp.73-120. A more recent bibliography is Fred L. Standley and Nancy V. Standley, *James Baldwin: A Reference Guide* (Boston: G. K. Hall, 1980), which contains a checklist of Baldwin's works and an annotated chronological listing of secondary sources appearing 1946-1978.

(IMAMU) AMIRI BARAKA, 1934-
Earlier name: LeRoi Jones

PRIMARY SOURCES

Separate Works

Preface to a Twenty Volume Suicide Note (1961); *Blues People: Negro Music in White America* (1963); *Dutchman* and *The Slave* [plays] (1964); *The Dead Lecturer* (1964); *The System of Dante's Hell* [novel] (1965); *Home: Social Essays* (1966); *Slave Ship* (1967); *The Baptism* and *The Toilet* [plays] (1967); *Arm Yrself or Harm Yrself* [play] (1967); *Tales* (1967); *Black Music* [music criticism] (1967); *Black Magic: Poetry, 1961-1967* (1969); *Four Black Revolutionary Plays* (1969); *Jello* [play] (1970); *It's Nation Time* (1970); *In Our Terribleness* (1970); *Raise Race Rays Raze: Essays since 1965* (1971); *Strategy and Tactics of a Panafrican Nationalist Party* (1971); *Spirit Beach* (1972); *Crisis in Boston* [essays] (1974); *Hard Facts* [poems] (1975); *The Motion of History and Other Plays* (1978).

Collected Works and Edited Texts

Three Books by Imamu Amiri Baraka (LeRoi Jones) (New York: Grove Press, 1975) contains *The System of Dante's Hell*, *Tales*, and *The Dead Lecturer*. Two useful collections are *Selected Poetry* (New York: Morrow, 1979) and *Selected Plays and Prose* (Morrow, 1979). Most of Baraka's separate works, whose publisher is Jihad, are in print; however, assistance in tracking down fugitive items may be gained from Dace's essay (*see* Bibliographies) and from the bibliography in Sollors (*see* Biography and Criticism).

Other Source Materials

Significant collections of letters and manuscripts are in the libraries of Syracuse University, Indiana University, and Northwestern University.

SECONDARY SOURCES

Biography and Criticism

So far there has been no separate biography of Baraka, and his vast number of periodical contributions have usually been neglected by critics. Theodore R. Hudson, *From LeRoi Jones to Amiri Baraka: The Literary Works* (Durham, NC: Duke Univ. Press, 1973) combines biography with detailed analysis of fiction, drama, poetry, and nonfiction. Kimberly W. Benston, *Baraka: The Renegade and the Mask* (New Haven, CT: Yale Univ. Press, 1976) is useful for aesthetic analysis of the poetry and plays. Werner Sollors, *Amiri Baraka/LeRoi Jones: The Quest for a "Populist Modernism"* (New York: Columbia Univ. Press, 1978) considers the relation between Baraka's ideological development and his literary work; Lloyd W. Brown, *Amiri Baraka* (Boston: Twayne, 1980) provides a sound introduction to Baraka's life and work, concentrating on separately published books; and Henry C. Lacey, *To Raise, Destroy, and Create: The Poetry, Drama and Fiction of Imamu Amiri Baraka, LeRoi Jones* (Troy, NY: Whitston, 1981) examines Baraka's literary development. A collection that conveniently gathers important essays on Baraka by genre is *Imamu Amiri Baraka (LeRoi Jones): A Collection of Critical Essays*, ed. Kimberly W. Benston (Englewood Cliffs, NJ: Prentice-Hall, 1978).

Bibliographies

The most reliable bibliography is Letitia Dace, *LeRoi Jones (Imamu Amiri Baraka): A Checklist of Works by and about Him* (London: Nether Press, 1971), which covers a wide range of primary sources including his contributions to serials, films, and recordings, as well as works about him. A selected bibliography in Sollors (*see* Biography and Criticism) lists many of the uncollected writings. These, together with Dace's more recent essay on scholarship and criticism, "Amiri Baraka (LeRoi Jones)" in *Black American Writers: Bibliographical Essays*, eds. M. Thomas Inge, Maurice Duke, Jackson R. Bryer, 2v. (New York: St. Martin's Press, 1978), v.2, pp.121-78, provide bibliographical guidance.

JOHN BARTH, 1930-

PRIMARY SOURCES

Separate Works

The Floating Opera (1956; rev. 1967); *The End of the Road* (1958; rev. 1967); *The Sot-Weed Factor* (1960; rev. 1967); *Giles Goat-Boy: Or, The Revised New Syllabus* (1966); *Lost in the Funhouse: Fiction for Print, Tape, Live Voice* (1968); *Chimera* (1972); *Letters: A Novel* (1979); *Sabbatical: A Romance* (1982).

Other Source Materials

Barth's manuscripts and papers are deposited at the Library of Congress and in the libraries of Pennsylvania State University, Johns Hopkins University, and Washington University, St. Louis.

SECONDARY SOURCES

Biography

There is no book-length biography of Barth, but access to helpful information can be gained via the annotated list of biographical articles in Weixlmann (*see* Bibliographies).

Criticism

An introductory pamphlet, Gerhard Joseph, *John Barth* (Minnesota: Univ. of Minnesota Press, 1970), is a condensed analysis of the first five books. Jac Tharpe, *John Barth: The Comic Sublimity of Paradox* (Carbondale: Southern Illinois Univ. Press, 1974) was the first book-length critical work. For an excellent, straightforward chronological survey that also covers titles through *Lost in the Funhouse*, giving the genesis and development of each book, the reception by publishers and reviewers, and an analysis and interpretation, see David Morell, *John Barth: An Introduction* (University Park: Pennsylvania State Univ. Press, 1976).

Bibliographies

Two good annotated bibliographies that cover primary and secondary sources are Joseph Weixlmann, *John Barth: A Descriptive Primary and Annotated Secondary Bibliography, Including a Descriptive Catalog of Manuscript Holdings in United States Libraries* (New York: Garland, 1976); and Richard Allan Vine, *John Barth: An Annotated Bibliography* (Metuchen, NJ: Scarecrow, 1977). Another annotated chronological list of writings about Barth written between 1956 and 1973 is included in Thomas P. Walsh and Cameron Northouse, *John Barth, Jerzy Kosinski and Thomas Pynchon: A Reference Guide* (Boston: G. K. Hall, 1977). Morell's work (*see* Criticism) also contains an extensive bibliography of primary and secondary sources through 1976.

SAUL BELLOW, 1915-

PRIMARY SOURCES

Separate Works

Dangling Man (1944); *The Victim* (1947); *The Adventures of Augie March* (1953); *The Wrecker* [play] (1954); *Seize the Day* (1956); *Henderson the Rain King* (1959); *Herzog* (1964); *The Last Analysis* [play] (produced 1964; rev. and published 1965); *Mosby's Memoirs and Other Stories* (1968); *Mr. Sammler's Planet* (1970); *Humboldt's Gift* (1975); *To Jerusalem and Back* [account of a visit to Israel] (1976); *The Dean's December* (1982).

Collected Works and Edited Texts

There is no uniform edition of Bellow's works.

Other Source Materials

Among the many lectures and articles on writing is "Some Notes on Recent American Fiction," *Encounter* 21 (November 1963): 22-29; repr. with minor changes as *Recent American Fiction: A Lecture Presented under the Auspices of the Gertrude Clarke Whittal Poetry and Literature Fund* (Washington, DC: Reference Dept., Library of Congress, 1963). Another important statement is "Saul Bellow: The Art of Fiction," an interview with Gordon L. Harper, *Paris Review* 37 (Winter 1965): 48-73. Bellow's *Nobel Lecture* (Stockholm: U.S. Information Service, 1976), delivered December 12, 1976, expresses his philosophy of the novel's role. Since 1963, an extensive collection of manuscripts, typescripts, galley proofs, correspondence, and published and unpublished works has been deposited in the Regenstein Library, University of Chicago. A minor collection of working materials is at the Humanities Research Center, University of Texas, Austin. Permission must be gained from Bellow to use either collection.

SECONDARY SOURCES

Biography

There is no definitive biography. Mark Harris, *Saul Bellow: Drumlin Woodchuck* (Athens: Univ. of Georgia Press, 1980) is a journalist's impressions of Bellow. Many short articles can be located through the bibliographies, below.

Criticism

A perceptive introductory pamphlet which discusses the theme of personality displacement is Earl Rovit, *Saul Bellow* (Minneapolis: Univ. of Minnesota Press, 1967). Two other introductory discussions, which devote a chapter to each novel through *Herzog*, are Tony Tanner, *Saul Bellow* (New York: Barnes & Noble, 1965); and Robert R. Dutton, *Saul Bellow* (New York: Twayne, 1971). Keith M. Opdahl, *The Novels of Saul Bellow: An Introduction* (University Park: Pennsylvania State Univ. Press, 1967) discusses the novels through *Herzog*, seeing opposition between the willful and the loving and the skeptical and believing as the unifying element. Irving Malin, *Saul Bellow's Fiction* (Carbondale: Southern Illinois Univ. Press, 1969) discusses how themes of moha, madness, time, masquerade, and Jewishness influence characters, imagery, and style. M. Gilbert Porter, *Whence the Power?: The Artistry and Humanity of Saul Bellow* (Columbia: Univ. of Missouri Press, 1974) devotes a chapter to each of the novels, seeing Bellow as a neo-transcendentalist. Bellow's use of the comic mode is explored in the works through *Mr. Sammler's Planet* by Sarah Blacher Cohen, *Saul Bellow's Enigmatic Laughter* (Urbana: Univ. of Illinois Press, 1974). Comedy is seen to bring "relief from the long prevalent mood of pessimism, discouragement and low-seriousness"; Chirantan Kulshrestha, *Saul Bellow: The Problem of Affirmation* (New Delhi: Arnold-Heinemann, 1978) analyzes fictional method through *Mr. Sammler's Planet*; and John J. Clayton, *Saul Bellow: In Defense of Man*, 2nd ed., enl. (Bloomington: Indiana Univ. Press, 1979) studies the theme of interrelated contradictions and psychic patterns in the fiction. Three anthologies of criticism are *Saul Bellow and the Critics*, ed. Irving Malin (New York: New York Univ. Press, 1967), a collection of twelve previously published essays, and Bellow's own "Where Do We Go from Here?: The Future of Fiction"; *Saul Bellow: A Collection of Critical Essays*, ed. Earl Rovit (Englewood Cliffs, NJ: Prentice-Hall, 1975), which represents a wide range of previously published critical perspectives and five original essays; and a similar collection, *Critical Essays on Saul Bellow*, ed. Stanley Trachtenberg (Boston: G. K. Hall, 1979), which contains insights based on recently analyzed documents.

Bibliographies

Marianne Nault, *Saul Bellow: His Works and His Critics, An Annotated International Bibliography* (New York: Garland, 1977) is the most comprehensive bibliography. It lists published works to 1977, a descriptive catalog of Bellow manuscripts at the University of Chicago and the University of Texas, a list of works in translation, a sampling of British and American reviews, interviews, and an annotated bibliography of all articles and books of criticism published in Britain and the United States. Foreign criticism is listed but not annotated, and a checklist of American and British dissertations is included. Robert G. Noreen, *Saul Bellow: A Reference Guide* (Boston: G. K. Hall, 1978) annotates Bellow criticism chronologically by year of publication, 1944-1976. Foreign criticism is representative.

ELIZABETH BISHOP, 1911-1979

PRIMARY SOURCES

Separate Works

North & South (1946); *Poems: North & South–A Cold Spring* (1955); *Poems* (1956); *The Diary of Helena Morley*, by Alice Dayrell Brant [translation] (1957); *Brazil* [with the editors of *Life*. Life World Library Series] (1962); *Questions of Travel* (1965); *The Ballad of the Burglar of Babylon* (1968); *The Complete Poems* (1969); *Poem* (1973); *Poems* (1976); *Geography III* (1976).

Collected Works and Edited Texts

Selected Poems (London: Chatto & Windus, 1967) contains the poetry through *Questions of Travel*. *The Complete Poems* (New York: Farrar, Straus, & Giroux, 1969) must be supplemented by subsequent work.

Other Source Materials

Correspondence between Bishop and the Houghton Mifflin Company is at the Houghton Library, Harvard University.

SECONDARY SOURCES

Biography

There is no full-scale biography, but a useful introduction with a selected bibliography is John Unterecker, "Elizabeth Bishop," in *American Writers: A Collection of Literary Biographies*, ed. Leonard Unger (New York: Scribner, 1979), Supplement I, Part 1, pp.72-97.

Criticism

The only book-length study to date is Anne Stevenson, *Elizabeth Bishop* (New York: Twayne, 1966). A collection of useful criticism is "Homage to Elizabeth Bishop, Our 1976 Laureate," *World Literature Today* 51 (Winter 1977): 4-52. Also valuable is "Elizabeth Bishop: Questions of Memory, Questions of Travel," in David

Kalstone, *Five Temperaments: Elizabeth Bishop, Robert Lowell, James Merrill, Adrienne Rich, and John Ashbery* (New York: Oxford Univ. Press, 1977), pp.12-40.

Bibliographies

Candace W. MacMahon, *Elizabeth Bishop: A Bibliography, 1927-1979* (Charlottesville: Published for the Bibliographical Society of the Univ. of Virginia, 1980) is an excellent bibliography of primary and secondary sources which will provide further access to interviews, reviews, and shorter criticism.

ANNE (DUDLEY) BRADSTREET, 1612?-1672

PRIMARY SOURCES

Collected Works and Edited Texts

Anne Bradstreet's writings have been published in several editions. *The Tenth Muse Lately Sprung Up in America* (London: Printed for Stephen Bowtell at the Sign of the Bible in Popes Head-Alley, 1650) was issued without her supervision. She corrected errors in a posthumously published revised and enlarged edition, *Several Poems Compiled with Great Variety of Wit and Learning* (Boston: J. Foster, 1678; reprinted in Boston in 1758). A nineteenth-century edition, with important biographical and critical notes as well as contents of the Bradstreet manuscripts, is *The Works of Anne Bradstreet in Prose and Verse*, ed. John H. Ellis (Charlestown, MA: A. E. Cutter, 1867; repr. Gloucester, MA: P. Smith, 1962). Another text is *The Poems of Mrs. Anne Bradstreet, Together with Her Prose Remains*, with an introduction by Charles Eliot Norton (New York: The Duodecimos, 1897). A facsimile edition is *The Tenth Muse (1650) and, from the Manuscripts: Meditations Divine and Morall Together with Letters and Occasional Pieces*, ed. Josephine K. Piercy (Gainesville, FL: Scholars' Facsimiles & Reprints, 1965). The standard edition is *The Works of Anne Bradstreet*, ed. Jeannine Hensley, with a foreword by Adrienne Rich (Cambridge: Harvard Univ. Press, 1967). It reproduces the Boston edition of 1678 owned by the Massachusetts Historical Society, and contains all the extant poetry and prose, published with modernized spelling and pronunciation. An appendix lists all the variations in every available copy of the book. *The Complete Works of Anne Bradstreet*, eds. Joseph R. McElrath, Jr., and Allan P. Robb (Boston: Twayne, 1981) is based on all of the known writings of Bradstreet and is accompanied by data which allow for reconstruction of the textual history. An inexpensive edition is *Poems of Anne Bradstreet*, ed. Robert Hutchinson (New York: Dover, 1969). Based on the Ellis text, it employs original spelling and pronunciation with corrections based on Hensley's study of the variant texts. Bradstreet's works are available in the Readex Microprint edition of Early American Imprints published by the American Antiquarian Society. A *Dialogue between Old England and New, and Other Poems* was issued in Old South Leaflets, General Series 7, no.159 (Boston: Directors of the Old South Work, 1905).

Other Source Materials

A ninety-eight page manuscript book kept by Bradstreet is in the Stevens Memorial Library, North Andover, Massachusetts. Bradstreet's papers are at the Houghton Library, Harvard University.

SECONDARY SOURCES

Biography

The definitive biography is Elizabeth Wade White, *Anne Bradstreet: "The Tenth Muse"* (New York: Oxford Univ. Press, 1971). An earlier account is Helen Stuart Campbell, *Anne Bradstreet and Her Time* (Boston: D. Lathrop, 1891). Bradstreet has also been the subject of a poem by John Berryman, *Homage to Mistress Bradstreet* (New York: Farrar, Straus, & Cudahy, 1956).

Criticism

Josephine K. Piercy, *Anne Bradstreet* (New York: Twayne, 1965) is the first full-length study of the poet and her career. Ann Stanford, *Anne Bradstreet: The Worldly Puritan* (New York: B. Franklin, 1975) follows the thesis that the author acted out the drama of Puritan tension between this world and the hope of the next. Useful appendices include a chronology and a list of books with which Bradstreet was acquainted.

Bibliographies

A list of scholarship and criticism, 1930-1974, is in Stanford (*see* Criticism). A bibliography which includes both scholarly and general sources is in Anne Stanford, "Anne Bradstreet: An Annotated Checklist," *Bulletin of Bibliography* 27 (1970): 34-37.

GWENDOLYN BROOKS, 1917-

PRIMARY SOURCES

Separate Works

A Street in Bronzeville (1945); *Annie Allen* (1949); *Maud Martha* (1953); *Bronzeville Boys and Girls* (1956); *The Bean Eaters* (1960); *Selected Poems* (1963); *In the Mecca* (1968); *Riot* (1970); *Aloneness* (1971); *A Broadside Treasury* (1971); *Family Pictures* (1971); *Jump Bad* (1971); *Report from Part One* [autobiography] (1972); *The Tiger Who Wore White Gloves* (1974); *Beckonings* (1975).

Collected Works

The World of Gwendolyn Brooks (New York: Harper & Row, 1971) comprises *A Street in Bronzeville*, *Annie Allen*, *Maud Martha*, *The Bean Eaters*, and *In the Mecca*.

SECONDARY SOURCES

Biography and Criticism

No full-length biography or criticism is yet available, and studies about Brooks must be sought among journal articles and dissertations.

Bibliographies

R. Baxter Miller, *Langston Hughes and Gwendolyn Brooks: A Reference Guide* (Boston: G. K. Hall, 1978) contains a chronological annotated list of writings about Brooks written 1944 to 1977.

WILLIAM CULLEN BRYANT, 1794-1878

PRIMARY SOURCES

Separate Works

The Embargo; Or, Sketches of the Times: A Satire (1808); The Embargo and Other Poems (1809); An Oration Delivered at Stockbridge (1820); Poems (1821); Poems (1832); Poems (1834); Poems (1836); Poems (1839); Popular Considerations on Homoeopathia (1841); The Fountain and Other Poems (1842); An Address to the People of the United States in Behalf of the American Copyright Club (1843); The White-Footed Deer and Other Poems (1844); Letters of a Traveller; Or Notes of Things Seen in Europe and America (1850); Reminiscences of the Evening Post (1851); A Discourse on the Life and Genius of James Fenimore Cooper (1852); Poems (1854); Letters of a Traveller; Second Series (1859); A Discourse on the Life, Character, and Genius of Washington Irving (1860); Thirty Poems (1864); Hymns (1864); Hymns (1869); Some Notices of the Life and Writings of Fitz-Greene Halleck (1869); Letters from the East (1869); A Discourse on the Life, Character, and Writings of Gulian Crommelin Verplanck (1870); The Iliad of Homer, Translated into English Blank Verse (1870); Poems (1871); The Odyssey of Homer (1871-72); Poems (1875); The Flood of Years (1878).

Collected Works and Edited Texts

There is no modern critical edition of Bryant's poetry. *The Poetical Works of William Cullen Bryant* (New York: Appleton, 1876) is the last the poet himself supervised, and reprintings such as *The Poetical Works*, Roslyn ed. (New York: Arno Press, 1969), which reprints the 1903 edition of H. C. Sturges and R. H. Stoddard, must be relied upon. Recently available are *The Letters of William Cullen Bryant*, ed. William Cullen Bryant, II, and Thomas G. Voss. 2v. (New York: Fordham Univ. Press, 1975-77).

Other Source Materials

Collections of Bryant manuscripts are in the New York Public Library, Huntington Library, Massachusetts Historical Society Library, and Harvard University Library. Manuscripts are described in Rocks' bibliographic essay (*see* Bibliographies).

SECONDARY SOURCES

Biography

No definitive biography is available, and the standard work, which includes autobiographical materials, is by Bryant's son-in-law, Parke Godwin, *A Biography of William Cullen Bryant with Extracts from His Private Correspondence*, 2v. (New York:

Appleton, 1883; repr. 1967). To date, the best biography is Charles H. Brown, *William Cullen Bryant* (New York: Scribner, 1971). Allen Nevins, *The Evening Post: A Century of Journalism* (New York: Boni and Liveright, 1922) contains an extensive account of Bryant as editor.

Criticism

The best introduction is a synthesis of Albert F. McLean Jr., *William Cullen Bryant* (New York: Twayne, 1964). A collection of critical views is *William Cullen Bryant: Representative Selections*, ed. Tremaine McDowell (New York: American Book Co., 1935). McDowell's introduction assesses Bryant as poet, critic, and editor.

Bibliographies

James E. Rocks, "William Cullen Bryant," in *Fifteen American Authors Before 1900*, eds. Robert A. Rees and Earl N. Harbert (Madison: Univ. of Wisconsin Press, 1971), pp.37-62, is an indispensable guide. Jacob Blanck, *Bibliography of American Literature* (New Haven, CT: Yale Univ. Press, 1955) lists Bryant's works which are difficult to date. Secondary materials are in the Goldentree Bibliography of Richard Beale Davis, *American Literature through Bryant, 1585-1830* (New York: Appleton-Century-Crofts, 1969); and Judith Turner Phair, *A Bibliography of William Cullen Bryant and His Critics, 1808-1872* (Troy, NY: Whitston, 1975) annotates books, periodicals, and book reviews about Bryant.

ABRAHAM CAHAN, 1860-1951

PRIMARY SOURCES

Separate Works

Cahan's Yiddish works are not included. *Yekl: A Tale of the New York Ghetto* (1896); *The Imported Bridegroom and Other Stories of the New York Ghetto* (1898); *The White Terror and the Red: A Novel of Revolutionary Russia* (1905); *The Rise of David Levinsky* (1917).

Reprints

No authorized editions of Cahan's works exist, but the following reprints have been issued: *Yekl, and the Imported Bridegroom and Other Stories of the New York Ghetto* (New York: Dover, 1970); *The Imported Bridegroom and Other Stories of the New York Ghetto* (New York: Garrett, 1968); *The White Terror and the Red* (New York: Arno Press, 1975); *The Rise of David Levinsky* (New York: P. Smith, 1951).

Other Source Materials

Two volumes of Cahan's autobiography, *Bleter Fun Mein Leben*, 5v. (New York: Forward Association, 1926-31) have been translated into English as *The Education of Abraham Cahan*, tr. by Leon Stein, Abrahan P. Conan, and Lynn Davison (Philadelphia: Jewish Publication Society of America, 1969).

SECONDARY SOURCES

Biography

There is as yet no full authoritative biography, and the major source is his *Bleter Fun Mein Leben*. Ronald Sanders, *The Downtown Jews: Portrait of an Immigrant Generation* (New York: Harper & Row, 1969) draws heavily on the autobiography.

Criticism

The only book-length study to date is Jules Chametzky, *From the Ghetto: The Fiction of Abraham Cahan* (Amherst: Univ. of Massachusetts Press, 1977), which concentrates on the 1890-1917 period. Critical essays and reminiscences in Yiddish are collected in *Festschrift for Abraham Cahan's 50th Birthday* (New York: Jubilee Committee, 1910).

Bibliographies

The most extensive bibliographies are Ephim Jeshurin, *Abraham Cahan Bibliography* (New York: United Vilner Relief Committee, 1941), which lists works in Russian, Yiddish, and English; and Sanford E. Marovitz and Lewis Fried, "Abraham Cahan, 1860-1951: An Annotated Bibliography," *American Literary Realism, 1870-1910* 3 (1970): 197-243.

WILLA (SIBERT) CATHER, 1873-1947
Pseuds: Helen Delay, Elizabeth L. Seymour,
Henry Nicklemann, and many others

PRIMARY SOURCES

Separate Works

April Twilights (1903); *The Troll Garden* (1905); *Alexander's Bridge* (1912); *O Pioneers!* (1913); *My Autobiography* [by S. S. McClure ghost-written by Cather] (1914); *The Song of the Lark* (1915); *My Ántonia* (1918); *Youth and the Bright Medusa* (1920); *One of Ours* (1922); *A Lost Lady* (1923); *The Professor's House* (1925); *My Mortal Enemy* (1926); *Death Comes for the Archbishop* (1927); *Shadows on the Rock* (1931); *Obscure Destinies* (1932); *Lucy Gayheart* (1935); *Not under Forty* (1936); *Sapphira and the Slave Girl* (1940); *The Old Beauty and Others* (1948); *Willa Cather on Writing* (1949).

Collected Works and Edited Texts

The Novels and Stories, library ed., 13v. (Boston: Houghton Mifflin, 1937-41) was intended as the definitive selection and authorized text, approved by Cather, but much published writing was omitted and further work has been posthumously identified, so that subsequently editions of former uncollected writings have appeared. *Early Short Stories*, ed. Mildred Bennett (New York: Dodd, Mead, 1957) reprints some little-known short stories and others more recently discovered, but the edition suffers from inaccuracy which is corrected in *Collected Short Fiction, 1892-1912*, ed. Virginia Faulkner (Lincoln: Univ. of Nebraska Press, 1965; rev. 1970). Faulkner includes a further nine previously unpublished stories. *Five Stories* (New York: Vintage Books, 1956) contains an essay by George N. Kates, "Willa Cather's Unfinished Avignon Story," which Cather did not complete and ordered destroyed. *Uncle Valentine and Other Stories*, ed. Bernice Slote (Lincoln: Univ. of Nebraska Press, 1973) is an edition of formerly uncollected short fiction from 1915 to 1929. As Cather made many changes between editions of her novels, there is much work to be done on authoritative editions. One reprint which contains a useful introduction is *Alexander's Bridge*, ed. Bernice Slote (Univ. of Nebraska Press, 1977). *April Twilights* (1903), ed. Bernice Slote (Univ. of Nebraska Press, 1962; rev. 1968) is the complete text of Cather's first book of poems and also includes several others, previously uncollected. Cather's journalistic writings are contained in several important editions. *Writings from Willa Cather's Campus Years*, ed. James R. Shively (Univ. of Nebraska Press, 1950) is a collection of Cather's work in Lincoln newspapers and University of Nebraska periodicals. A series of travel columns from the *Nebraska State Journal, 1902*, is in *Willa Cather in Europe* (New York: Knopf, 1956). The University of Nebraska Press' multivolume project has made most of Cather's early journalism available in two fine scholarly editions. *The Kingdom of Art*, ed. Bernice Slote (Univ. of Nebraska Press, 1967) is a selection of columns and reviews Cather wrote from 1893 to 1896 and her first published newspaper articles from 1891. Slote has contributed a valuable introduction to these selections. Another collection of journalistic material written between 1893 and 1903 in *The World and the Parish*, 2v., ed. William M. Curtin (Univ. of Nebraska Press, 1970) includes the letters of *Willa Cather in Europe* in an accurate version.

Other Source Materials

Unfortunately Cather's will specifies that her correspondence may not be published. Materials may be examined at the Willa Cather Pioneer Memorial, Red Cloud, Nebraska, the Nebraska State Historical Society, Lincoln, and the University of Nebraska, Lincoln. In Margaret Anne O'Connor, "A Guide to the Letters of Willa Cather," *Resources for American Literary Study* 4 (1974): 145-72, 900 letters in forty-three locations are briefly noted for their scope. The published newspaper and periodical articles are important primary sources for autobiographical and critical information.

SECONDARY SOURCES

Biography

Early biographical articles on Cather are unauthoritative. Not until Mildred R. Bennett, *The World of Willa Cather*, new ed. (Lincoln: Univ. of Nebraska Press, 1961) was there a coherent picture of her early youth. E. K. Brown, *Willa Cather: A Critical Biography*, completed by Leon Edel (New York: Knopf, 1953) is indispensable because it draws on memories of those who knew Cather well. The views of close friends are contained in Edith Lewis, *Willa Cather Living* (Knopf, 1953); and a 1953 account reissued as A Bison Book, by Elizabeth Shepley Sergeant, *Willa Cather: A Memoir* (Univ. of Nebraska Press, 1963). An essay, "Writer in Nebraska," in Slote's *Kingdom of Art* (*see* Collected Works), documents Cather's early years in Nebraska and corrects many former misconceptions. The scholarly activity at the University of Nebraska has made it possible to employ new evidence in James Woodress, *Willa Cather: Her Life and Art* (New York: Pegasus, 1970).

Criticism

Well-founded and lucid introductions are in David Daiches, *Willa Cather: A Critical Introduction* (Ithaca, NY: Cornell Univ. Press, 1951), who provides a good overview of Cather's work; and in a pamphlet by Dorothy Van Ghent, *Willa Cather* (Minneapolis: Univ. of Minnesota Press, 1964). More recent is Philip L. Gerber, *Willa Cather* (New York: Twayne, 1975), who discusses works, life, and artistic principles as he traces Cather's growing reputation. Fresh observations based on recent scholarship are in David Stouck, *Willa Cather's Imagination* (Lincoln: Univ. of Nebraska Press, 1975). Criticism is collected in *Willa Cather and Her Critics*, ed. James Schroeter (Ithaca, NY: Cornell Univ. Press, 1967), which provides editorial notes and thirty-four critical and biographical accounts. The observance of Cather's centenary by symposia in 1973 resulted in two valuable collections. *The Art of Willa Cather*, eds. Bernice Slote and Virginia Faulkner (Univ. of Nebraska Press, 1974) contains interviews, discussion, and notes accompanying the essays. *Five Essays on Willa Cather: The Merrimack Symposium*, ed. John J. Murphy (North Andover, MA: Merrimack College, 1974) contains thoughtful essays by Cather scholars.

Bibliographies

There is no definitive Cather bibliography, and as further writings are still being found, such a work is not yet foreseen. The most complete compilation is by JoAnna Lathrop, *Willa Cather: A Checklist of Her Published Writings* (Lincoln: Univ. of Nebraska Press, 1975). This lists the 776 items of Cather's writings which were identified to that date, as well as reprints and editions published in the United States. An excellent bibliographical essay by Bernice Slote, "Willa Cather," in *Sixteen Modern American Authors: A Survey of Research and Criticism*, ed. Jackson R. Bryer (Durham, NC: Duke Univ. Press, 1974) is useful for its evaluation of trends and scholarship.

Reference Works

Newly discovered items since 1972 are reprinted in the *Newsletter* of the Willa Cather Pioneer Museum, Red Cloud, Nebraska.

JOHN CHEEVER, 1912-1982

PRIMARY SOURCES

Separate Works

The Way Some People Live (1943); *Town House* [play adapted by Gertrude Tonkonogy, same title] (1948); *The Enormous Radio and Other Stories* (1953); *Stories* (1956); *The Wapshot Chronicle* (1957); *The Housebreaker of Shady Hill and Other Stories* (1958); *Some People, Places and Things That Will Not Appear in My Next Novel* (1961); *The Wapshot Scandal* (1964); *The Brigadier and the Golf Widow* (1964); *The Swimmer* [screenplay adapted by Eleanor Perry, same title] (1966); *Homage to Shakespeare* (1968); *Bullet Park* (1969); *The World of Apples* (1973); *Children* [play adapted by A. R. Gurney, Jr., same title] (1976); *Falconer* (1977); *Stories of John Cheever* (1978); *O Youth and Beauty* [teleplay adapted by A. R. Gurney, same title] (1979); *The Five Forty-Eight* [teleplay adapted by Terrence

McNally, same title] (1979); *The Sorrows of Gin* [teleplay adapted by Wendy Wasserstein] (1979); *The Shady Hill Kidnapping* [teleplay] (1982); *Oh What a Paradise It Seems* (1982).

Collected Works and Edited Texts

The Stories of John Cheever, 1st ed. (New York: Knopf, 1978) collects stories published 1946-1975.

SECONDARY SOURCES

Biography

There is no full-length biography of Cheever, but biographical articles are listed with annotations in Bosha's bibliography (*see* Bibliographies), and the works by Coale and Waldeland (*see* Criticism) contain biographical data in introductions.

Criticism

Samuel Coale, *John Cheever* (New York: Ungar, 1977) is an introduction to Cheever's four novels; and Lynne Waldeland, *John Cheever* (Boston: Twayne, 1979) is a survey of the work through *Falconer*.

Bibliographies

Francis J. Bosha, *John Cheever: A Reference Guide* (Boston: G. K. Hall, 1981) contains a primary bibliography including periodical articles and an annotated chronological list of secondary sources covering 1943 through 1979.

CHARLES W(ADDELL) CHESNUTT, 1858-1932

PRIMARY SOURCES

Separate Works

The Conjure Woman (1899); *The Wife of His Youth* (1899); *Frederick Douglass* (1899); *The House Behind the Cedars* (1900); *The Marrow of Tradition* (1901); *The Colonel's Dream* (1905).

Collected Works and Edited Texts

There is no authoritative edition of Chesnutt's works, and readers must rely on reprints, some of which appeared in the late sixties with new critical introductions. *The Short Fiction of Charles W. Chesnutt*, ed. Sylvia Lyons Render (Washington, DC: Howard Univ. Press, 1974) is a major anthology with an important critical introduction. Many of Chesnutt's books have been reprinted most recently by Scholarly Press, St. Clair Shores, Michigan.

Other Source Materials

Chesnutt's scrapbooks are in the Fisk University Library's Chesnutt Collection, which is described in two guides, Mildred Freeney and Mary T. Henry, *List of*

Manuscripts, Published Works and Related Items in the Charles Waddell Chesnutt Collection (Nashville: Fiske Univ. Library, 1954); and Beth M. Howse, *Charles W. Chesnutt Collection* (Fiske Univ. Library, 1973). Another important collection of manuscripts is listed in Olivia J. Martin, *Guide to the Microfilm Edition of the Charles Waddell Chesnutt Papers in the Library of the Western Reserve Historical Society* (Cleveland: Ohio Historical Society Library, 1972).

SECONDARY SOURCES

Biography

The first book-length biography is by his daughter, Helen M. Chesnutt, *Charles Waddell Chesnutt: Pioneer of the Color Line* (Chapel Hill: Univ. of North Carolina Press, 1952). The best biography, which includes discussion of his writing, is J. Noel Heermance, *Charles W. Chesnutt: America's First Great Black Novelist* (Hamden, CT: Archon Books, 1974). Francis Richardson Keller, *An American Crusade: The Life of Charles Waddell Chesnutt* (Provo, UT: Brigham Young Univ. Press, 1978) is less useful.

Criticism

The major critical contribution to date is William L. Andrews, *The Literary Career of Charles W. Chesnutt* (Baton Rouge: Louisiana State Univ. Press, 1980), which traces Chesnutt's role as an innovator in the Afro-American fictional tradition, as regionalist, and as social realist. Other important contributions have been made in doctoral dissertations, journal articles, and anthologies of Afro-American materials.

Bibliographies

William L. Andrews, "Charles Waddell Chesnutt: An Essay in Bibliography," *Resources for American Literary Study* 6 (1976): 3-22 is an excellent bibliographical essay which covers editions, manuscripts, letters, biography, criticism, and bibliographies. In addition, Andrews has a checklist, including books, short fiction, poems, essays, and articles, in "The Works of Charles W. Chesnutt," *Bulletin of Bibliography* 34 (1976): 4-52, which is also available in his critical study *The Literary Career of Charles W. Chesnutt* (*see* Criticism), pp.279-92. Curtis W. Ellison and Eugene W. Metcalf, Jr., *Charles W. Chesnutt: A Reference Guide* (Boston: G. K. Hall, 1977) contains an annotated bibliography of secondary sources, chronologically arranged, which is the best source of access to articles in journals, anthologies, newspapers, and dissertations.

KATE (O'FLAHERTY) CHOPIN, 1851-1904

PRIMARY SOURCES

Separate Works

At Fault (1890); *Young Dr. Gosse* (1891); *Bayou Folk* (1894); *An Embarrassing Position* [one-act comedy] (1895); *A Night in Acadie* (1897); *The Awakening* (1899).

Collected Works and Edited Texts

The Complete Works of Kate Chopin, ed. Per Seyersted. 2v. (Baton Rouge: Louisiana State Univ. Press, 1969) is an anthology of the final versions of Chopin's writings, which Seyersted defines as the "book version of the stories included in her two collections, and the magazine or newspaper version of the stories she published only in this way." Included is everything Chopin wrote except three unfinished children's stories and twenty poems, mostly occasional. An extensive appendix provides bibliographical information about all the writings included.

A Norton critical edition is available of *The Awakening*, 1st ed., ed. Margaret Culley (New York: Norton, 1976). As no manuscript of the novel exists, Culley has presented the text of the first edition as it appeared in 1899. It is accompanied by a selection of material by Dorothy Dix, Charlotte Perkins Gilman, and Thorstein Veblen "in order to establish the context in which the novel appeared," and thus to account for its hostile reception. Eleven reviews and fifteen critical essays are included.

Other Source Materials

Manuscripts of twenty stories, forty poems, and numerous letters and papers are at the Missouri Historical Society, St. Louis. Other papers are at New York Public Library, West Virginia University Library, Morgantown, and Harvard University Library.

SECONDARY SOURCES

Biography

The most important full-length study is by Per Seyersted, *Kate Chopin: A Critical Biography* (Baton Rouge: Univ. of Louisiana Press, 1969). This work contains photographs and useful notes. Seyersted acknowledges the earlier work of Daniel Rankin, *Kate Chopin and Her Creole Stories* (Philadelphia: Univ. of Pennsylvania Press, 1932), which, though out of date and inadequate by modern standards, drew upon interviews with those who had known Chopin. Rankin concentrated on regional and local color aspects rather than on the artistic portrayal of the characters.

Criticism

Seyersted's critical biography is the most important full study to date. A special issue of *Louisiana Studies* 14 (1975) was devoted to Chopin. Other criticism of value is contained in journals and can be located by consulting Springer's guide (*see* Bibliographies) and the annual volumes of *American Literary Scholarship*.

Bibliographies

A checklist of Chopin's own writings, in order of composition, is in Seyersted's biography. The most recent secondary bibliography is Marlene Springer, *Edith Wharton and Kate Chopin: A Reference Guide* (Boston: G. K. Hall, 1976). This chronological list annotates scholarship, criticism, and reviews that were published between 1890 and 1973.

Reference Works

The *Kate Chopin Newsletter*, spring 1975-winter 1976/77, which ran for a few issues, has been continued as *Regionalism and the Female Imagination*. It now includes items on other women besides Chopin.

SAMUEL L(ANGHORNE) CLEMENS, 1835-1910
Pseud: Mark Twain

PRIMARY SOURCES

Separate Works

The Celebrated Jumping Frog of Calaveras County and Other Sketches (1867); *The Innocents Abroad* (1869); *Mark Twain's Burlesque Autobiography* (1871); *Roughing It* (1872); *The Gilded Age* [with Charles Dudley Warner] (1873); *Mark Twain's Sketches: New and Old* (1875); *The Adventures of Tom Sawyer* (1876); *A True Story* (1877); *Punch, Brothers, Punch!* (1878); *A Tramp Abroad* (1880); *The Prince and the Pauper* (1882); *The Stolen White Elephant, Etc.* (1882); *Life on the Mississippi* (1883); *The Adventures of Huckleberry Finn* (1885); *A Connecticut Yankee in King Arthur's Court* (1889); *The American Claimant* (1892); *Merry Tales* (1892); *The £1,000,000 Bank-Note* (1893); *Tom Sawyer Abroad* (1894); *The Tragedy of Pudd'nhead Wilson* (1894); *Personal Recollections of Joan of Arc* (1896); *Tom Sawyer Abroad, Tom Sawyer Detective, and Other Stories* (1896); *Following the Equator* (1897); *How to Tell a Story and Other Essays* (1897); *The Man That Corrupted Hadleyburg and Other Stories and Essays* (1900); *A Double Barrelled Detective Story* (1902); *My Début As a Literary Person* (1903); *A Dog's Tale* (1904); *Extracts from Adam's Diary* (1904); *King Leopold's Soliloquy* (1905); *What Is Man?* (1906); *The $30,000 Bequest* (1906); *Eve's Diary* (1906); *Christian Science* (1907); *A Horse's Tale* (1907); *Is Shakespeare Dead?* (1909); *Extract from Captain Stormfield's Visit to Heaven* (1909); *The Mysterious Stranger* (1916); *What Is Man? and Other Essays* (1917); *The Curious Republic of Gondour* (1919); *The Mysterious Stranger and Other Stories* (1922); *Europe and Elsewhere* (1923).

Collected Works and Edited Texts

The Works of Mark Twain, ed. Frederick Anderson (Berkeley: Published for the Iowa Center for Textual Studies by the Univ. of California Press, 1972-), and *The Mark Twain Papers*, ed. Frederick Anderson (Berkeley: Univ. of California Press, 1966-), both produced by the University of Iowa and the University of California, will be the definitive edition, replacing *The Writings of Mark Twain*, ed. Albert Bigelow Paine. 37v., (New York: G. Wells, 1922-25). Two volumes of letters have been published in the *Papers*, and another indispensable edition is the *Mark Twain-Howells Letters: The Correspondence of Samuel L. Clemens and William Dean Howells, 1872-1910*, eds. Henry Nash Smith and William M. Gibson. 2v. (Cambridge: Harvard Univ. Press, 1960). *Mark Twain's Autobiography*, 2v. (New York: Harper, 1924) is introduced by Albert Bigelow Paine.

Among important critical editions are *Selected Shorter Writings of Mark Twain*, ed. Walter Blair (Boston: Houghton Mifflin, 1962); *The Adventures of Huckleberry Finn: An Annotated Text, Background and Sources, Essays in Criticism*, ed. Sculley

Bradley (New York: Norton, 1962); *The Art of Huckleberry Finn: Texts, Sources, Criticism*, eds. Hamlin Hill and Walter Blair (San Francisco: Chandler, 1969), which contains a facsimile of the first illustrated edition; *Mark Twain's Mysterious Stranger Manuscripts*, ed. William M. Gibson (Berkeley: Univ. of California Press, 1969), which makes available the three versions of this text; and *Pudd'nhead Wilson and Those Extraordinary Twins*, 1st ed., ed. Sidney Berger (New York: Norton, 1980), which provides authoritative texts, tables of variants, and criticism.

Other Source Materials

The most extensive collection of papers is in the Bancroft Library, University of California, Berkeley.

SECONDARY SOURCES

Biography

There are several lives of Mark Twain, of which the most reliable is De Lancey Ferguson, *Mark Twain: Man and Legend* (Indianapolis: Bobbs-Merrill, 1943). The early account of Albert Bigelow Paine, *Mark Twain: A Biography: The Personal and Literary Life of Samuel Langhorne Clemens*, 3v. (New York: Harper, 1912), though not entirely reliable, remains important. Also valuable are Edward Wagenknecht, *Mark Twain: The Man and His Work*, rev. ed. (Norman: Univ. of Oklahoma Press, 1961); the reliable introductory pamphlet of Lewis Leary, *Mark Twain* (Minneapolis: Univ. of Minnesota Press, 1960); and Frank Baldanza, *Mark Twain: An Introduction and Interpretation* (New York: Barnes & Noble, 1961). The difficult final decade of Mark Twain's life is documented in Hamlin Hill, *Mark Twain: God's Fool* (New York: Harper & Row, 1973). A useful tool, containing sections devoted to biography, Hannibal, the West, and Twain's literary stature, is E. H. Long, *Mark Twain Handbook* (New York: Hendricks House, 1957).

Criticism

Among the most distinguished critical contributions are E. M. Branch, *The Literary Apprenticeship of Mark Twain* (Urbana: Univ. of Illinois Press, 1950), which analyzes the writings to 1867; G. C. Bellamy, *Mark Twain as a Literary Artist* (Norman: Univ. of Oklahoma Press, 1950), which demonstrates Twain's literary craftsmanship and the dilemma surrounding responsible free will and determinism; Albert E. Stone, *The Innocent Eye: Childhood in Mark Twain's Imagination* (New Haven, CT: Yale Univ. Press, 1961), which treats many of the child characters; a provocative study by Henry Nash Smith, *Mark Twain: The Development of a Writer* (Cambridge: Harvard Univ. Press, 1962), which addresses style, structure, and vernacular language in nine works; and a thorough analysis of literary technique by William M. Gibson, *The Art of Mark Twain* (New York: Oxford Univ. Press, 1976). For a study of relationships between writers, see *Turn West, Turn East: Mark Twain and Henry James* (Boston: Houghton Mifflin, 1951).

Among the most important studies which focus on Huckleberry Finn are Walter Blair, *Mark Twain & Huck Finn* (Berkeley: Univ. of California Press, 1960); and James M. Cox, *Mark Twain: The Fate of Humor* (Princeton, NJ: Princeton Univ. Press, 1966). Collections which trace changing critical concerns are *Mark Twain: A Collection of Critical Essays*, ed. Henry Nash Smith (Englewood Cliffs, NJ: Prentice-Hall, 1963); *Critics on Mark Twain*, ed. David B. Kesterson (Coral Gables, FL: Univ.

of Miami Press, 1973); and *Mark Twain: A Collection of Criticism*, ed. Dean Morgan Schmitter (New York: McGraw-Hill, 1974).

Bibliographies

For an introductory bibliographic essay, see Harry Hayden Clark, "Mark Twain," in *Eight American Authors*, rev. ed., ed. James Woodress (New York: Norton, 1971), pp.273-320. Volume 24 of the Iowa/California edition will be devoted to a bibliography of Twain's works. Thomas Asa Tenney, *Mark Twain: A Reference Guide* (Boston: G. K. Hall, 1977) is a meticulous bibliography of secondary literature, which annotates books, reviews, and articles about Twain from 1858 through 1974. It is updated annually in *American Literary Realism*. A checklist of newspaper and magazine interviews with Twain is in Louis J. Budd, *Interviews with Samuel L. Clemens 1874-1910* (Arlington: Univ. of Texas at Arlington, 1977).

Reference Works

Robert L. Gale, *Plots and Characters in the Works of Mark Twain*, 2v. (Hamden, CT: Archon Books, 1973) summarizes notebook and autobiographical material, and identifies over 7,000 characters. Robert L. Ramsay and Frances G. Emberson, *A Mark Twain Lexicon* (New York: Russell & Russell, 1963) is a dictionary of Twain's usage. Alan Gribben, *Mark Twain's Library: A Reconstruction*, 2v. (Boston: G. K. Hall, 1980) provides full bibliographic descriptions for each title and notes inscriptions and marginalia. Three journals devoted to Twain are *Mark Twain Journal*, v.1, 1936- , which is a quarterly published by the International Mark Twain Society; *Twainian*, 1941- , journal of the Mark Twain Association of America, which is published every other month; and the *Bulletin of the Mark Twain Society of Elmira, New York*, 1978- .

JAMES FENIMORE COOPER, 1789-1851

PRIMARY SOURCES

Separate Works

Precaution: A Novel (1820); *The Spy: A Tale of Neutral Ground* (1821); *The Pioneers; Or, The Sources of the Susquehanna: A Descriptive Tale* (1823); *Tales for Fifteen* (1823); *The Pilot: A Tale of the Sea* (1823); *Lionel Lincoln; Or, The Leaguer of Boston* (1825); *The Last of the Mohicans: A Narrative of 1757* (1826); *The Prairie: A Tale* (1827); *The Red Rover: A Tale* (1828); *Notions of the Americans, Picked up by a Travelling Bachelor* (1828); *The Wept of Wish-Ton-Wish: A Tale* (1829); *The Water-Witch; Or, The Skimmer of the Seas* (1831); *The Bravo: A Tale* (1831); *The Heidenmauer; Or, The Benedictines: A Legend of the Rhine* (1832); *The Headsman; Or, The Abbaye Des Vignerons: A Tale* (1833); *A Letter to His Countrymen* (1834); *The Monikins* (1835); *Sketches of Switzerland* (1836); *Sketches of Switzerland: Part Second* (1836); *Gleanings in Europe: France* (1837); *Gleanings in Europe: England* (1837); *Gleanings in Europe: Italy* (1838); *The American Democrat* (1838); *Homeward Bound; Or, The Chase: A Tale of the Sea* (1838); *Home as Found* (1838); *The History of the Navy of the United States of America* (1839); *The Pathfinder; Or, The Inland Sea* (1840); *Mercedes of Castile; Or, The Voyage to Cathay* (1840); *The Deerslayer; Or, The First War-Path* (1841); *The Two Admirals: A Tale* (1842); *The*

Wing-and Wing; Or, Le Feu-Follet: A Tale (1842); Le Mouchoir: An Autobiographical Romance (1843); Wyandotté; Or, The Hutted Knoll: A Tale (1843); Ned Myers; Or, A Life before the Mast (1843); Afloat and Ashore; Or, The Adventures of Miles Wallingford [two series] (1844); Satanstoe; Or, The Littlepage Manuscripts: A Tale of the Colony (1845); The Chainbearer; Or, The Littlepage Manuscripts (1845); Lives of Distinguished American Naval Officers (1846); The Redskins; Or, Indian and Injun: Being the Conclusion of the Littlepage Manuscripts (1846); The Crater; Or, Vulcan's Peak: A Tale of the Pacific (1847); Jack Tier; Or, The Florida Reef (1848); The Oak Openings; Or, The Bee-Hunter (1848); The Sea Lions; Or, The Lost Sealers (1849); The Ways of the Hour: A Tale (1850).

Collected Works and Editions

The long-planned critical edition of *The Writings of James Fenimore Cooper*, eds. James Franklin Beard and James P. Elliott (Albany: State Univ. of New York Press, 1980-) has begun to appear, with the following titles: *Gleanings in Europe: Italy, Switzerland; The Pathfinder;* and *The Pioneers.* Two early editions are *Cooper's Novels,* author's rev. ed., 32v. (New York: W. A. Townsend, 1859-61) and *The Works,* Mohawk ed., 33v. (New York: G. P. Putnam, 1895-96). Numerous reprints of individual tales are cited in Beard's bibliographic essay (*see* Bibliographies). Biographical documentation has been chronologically gathered and annotated in *The Letters and Journals of James Fenimore Cooper,* ed. J. F. Beard. 6v. (Cambridge: Harvard Univ. Press, 1960-68).

Other Source Materials

The largest collections of papers are with the Fenimore Cooper family, the Clifton Waller Barrett Library at the University of Virginia, the New York Public Library, and the Library of Yale University.

SECONDARY SOURCES

Biography

The first useful biography was W. B. Shubrick Clymer, *James Fenimore Cooper* (Boston: Small, Maynard, 1900; repr. St. Clair Shores, MI: Scholarly Press, 1968). Robert E. Spiller, *Fenimore Cooper: Critic of His Times* (New York: Minton, Balch, 1931) is an influential work which views Cooper grappling through his art with significant issues of the time. Other important studies are Henry W. Boynton, *James Fenimore Cooper* (New York: Appleton-Century, 1931); Marc Clavel, *Fenimore Cooper: Sa Vie Et Son Oeuvre* (Aix-en-Provence: E. Fourcine, 1938); and James Grossman, *James Fenimore Cooper* (New York: Sloane, 1949). J. F. Beard is engaged in a critical biography that draws on documentation contained in the *Letters and Journals.*

Criticism

A fine introduction is Donald A. Ringe, *James Fenimore Cooper* (New York: Twayne, 1961). Another, indicating the social background of Cooper's fiction, is Kay S. House, *Cooper's Americans* (Columbus: Ohio State Univ. Press, 1965). Works which trace Cooper's reception are Marc Clavel, *Fenimore Cooper and His Critics: American, British and French Criticisms of the Novelist's Early Work* (Aix-en-Provence:

E. Fourcine, 1938); and several collections, *James Fenimore Cooper: A Re-Appraisal*, ed. Mary E. Cunningham (Cooperstown: New York State Historical Association, 1954); *Fenimore Cooper: The Critical Heritage*, eds. George Dekker and John P. McWilliams (Boston: Routledge and Kegan Paul, 1973); and *James Fenimore Cooper: A Collection of Critical Essays*, ed. Wayne Fields (Englewood Cliffs, NJ: Prentice-Hall, 1979). Studies which deal with Cooper's relation to the environment are Blake Nevius, *Cooper's Landscapes: An Essay on the Picturesque Vision* (Berkeley: Univ. of California Press, 1976); and H. Daniel Peck, *A World by Itself: The Pastoral Moment in Cooper's Fiction* (New Haven, CT: Yale Univ. Press, 1977). Thomas L. Philbrick, *James Fenimore Cooper and the Development of American Sea Fiction* (Cambridge: Harvard Univ. Press, 1961) sees Cooper as the father of the American sea story.

Bibliographies

A helpful bibliographic essay by James Franklin Beard, "James Fenimore Cooper," is in *Fifteen American Authors before 1900*, eds. Robert A. Rees and Earl N. Harbert (Madison: Univ. of Wisconsin Press, 1971), pp.63-96. Robert E. Spiller and Philip C. Blackburn, *A Descriptive Bibliography of the Writings of James Fenimore Cooper* (New York: Bowker, 1934) remains the most useful account of Cooper's publishing practices.

Reference Works

Warren S. Walker, *Plots and Characters in the Fiction of James Fenimore Cooper* (Hamden, CT: Archon Books, 1978) is a handy reference guide.

(HAROLD) HART CRANE, 1899-1932

PRIMARY SOURCES

Separate Works

White Buildings: Poems (1926); *The Bridge: A Poem* (1930).

Collected Works and Edited Texts

The Collected Poems of Hart Crane, ed. with an intro. by Waldo Frank (New York: Liveright, 1933) includes Crane's essay "Modern Poetry." It was published again under a new title: *The Complete Poems of Hart Crane*, ed. Waldo Frank (Garden City, NY: Doubleday Anchor Books, 1958). Because some inaccuracies had appeared in the 1933 edition and some previously uncollected poems had come to light, another collection was published as *The Complete Poems and Selected Letters and Prose of Hart Crane*, ed. Brom Weber (Garden City, NY: Anchor Books, 1966). Weber excludes all fragments, preliminary drafts, and unfinished poems, and corrects textual errors of Frank's edition, presenting the arrangement chronologically. *The Letters of Hart Crane, 1916-1932*, ed. Brom Weber (New York: Hermitage House, 1952); repr. Berkeley: Univ. of California Press, 1965) contains a comprehensive selection of over 400 letters, both literary and personal, with many deletions for editorial brevity. Several other selections supplement Weber's edition. *Robber Rocks: Letters and Memories of Hart Crane, 1923-1932*, ed. Susan Jenkins Brown (Middletown, CT: Wesleyan Univ. Press, 1969) presents an interesting memoir and 39 letters to some of

Crane's most intimate friends. *Letters of Hart Crane and His Family*, ed. Thomas S. W. Lewis (New York: Columbia Univ. Press, 1974) are useful for biographical details rather than for poetic concerns. *Hart Crane and Yvor Winters: Their Literary Correspondence*, ed. Thomas Parkinson (Berkeley: Univ. of California Press, 1978) documents a literary friendship covering the years 1926-1930.

Seven Lyrics, ed. Kenneth A. Lohf (Cambridge, MA: Ibex Press, 1966) was published before *Complete Poems* (1966), drawing on manuscripts enclosed in a 1918 letter sent to Charles C. Bubb. Brom Weber's bibliographical essay (*see* Bibliographies) points out that several items are variants of published pieces and that some are not wholly reliable texts because they are not based on authentic Crane manuscripts. Similarly, *Ten Unpublished Poems* (New York: Gotham Book Mart, 1972) represents unfinished work, which the edition does not adequately describe.

Other Source Materials

An invaluable guide to 278 manuscripts in sixteen libraries and two private collections of Crane materials is in the series Calendars of American Literary Manuscripts, Kenneth A. Lohf, *The Literary Manuscripts of Hart Crane* (Columbus: Ohio State Univ. Press, 1967). It is collated with the Frank edition (1933). There is also a facsimile with notes of six previously unpublished prose manuscripts, Kenneth A. Lohf, "The Prose Manuscripts of Hart Crane: An Editorial Portfolio," *Proof* 2 (1970): 1-60.

SECONDARY SOURCES

Biography

There are three major biographies. Philip Horton, *Hart Crane: The Life of an American Poet* (New York: Norton, 1937; New York: Viking, 1957) is based on Crane's correspondence and material from his literary associates. Brom Weber, *Hart Crane: A Biographical and Critical Study*, rev. ed. (New York: Russell & Russell, 1970) concentrates on aspects of the life which illuminate the poetry. John Unterecker, *Voyager: A Life of Hart Crane* (New York: Farrar, Straus, & Giroux, 1969) adds much detail to previous accounts, using interviews which are now in the Crane Collection at Columbia University. Unfortunately, the work lacks focus, details of reminiscences differ, and footnotes are not included. Personal reminiscences of Crane's close friend are in Samuel Loveman, *Hart Crane: A Conversation with Samuel Loveman*, eds. Jay Socin and Kirby Congdon (New York: Interim Books, 1964).

Criticism

A clearly written pamphlet is Monroe K. Spears, *Hart Crane* (Minneapolis: Univ. of Minnesota Press, 1965). Samuel Hazo, *Hart Crane: An Introduction and Interpretation* (New York: Barnes & Noble, 1963) is a longer, introductory commentary on all the poems. More selective and more comprehensive is the introduction of Vincent Quinn, *Hart Crane* (New York: Twayne, 1963). L. S. Dembo, *Hart Crane's Sanskrit Charge: A Study of "The Bridge"* (Ithaca, NY: Cornell Univ. Press, 1960) is an in-depth interpretation of the poem as a picture of man's struggle to come to terms with himself in his world. It analyzes the meaning, form, and language of the poem in a detailed explication. R. W. B. Lewis, *The Poetry of Hart Crane: A Critical Study* (Princeton, NJ: Princeton Univ. Press, 1967; repr. Westport, CT: Greenwood Press, 1978) sees Crane as a "religious poet" concerned with transforming the world through poetry. An analysis which concentrates on the imagery, diction, verse form, and structure of the shorter poetry to show how Crane achieved meaning is Herbert A. Leibowitz, *Hart Crane: An Introduction to the Poetry* (New York: Columbia Univ. Press, 1968). Hunce Voelcker, *The Hart Crane Voyages* (New York: Brownstone Press, 1968) attempts to recreate the composition process of the *Voyages*. A full-scale examination of Crane's development in relation to biographical, social, and psychological factors is R. W. Butterfield, *The Broken Arc: A Study of Hart Crane* (Edinburgh: Oliver & Boyd, 1969). Sherman Paul, *Hart's Bridge* (Urbana: Univ. of Illinois Press, 1972) analyzes all Crane's poetry in detail for individual poems. It is more useful for consultation than for reading as a whole, since it lacks major focus. M. D. Uroff, *Hart Crane: The Patterns of His Poetry* (Urbana: Univ. of Illinois Press, 1974) examines the patterns which recur in both the shorter poems and *The Bridge*, finding continuity of image and meaning.

Bibliographies

The best bibliographical introduction is an essay by Brom Weber, "Hart Crane," in *Sixteen Modern American Authors*, ed. Jackson R. Bryer (Durham, NC: Duke Univ. Press, 1974), pp.75-122. Joseph Schwartz, *Hart Crane: An Annotated Critical Bibliography* (New York: D. Lewis, 1970) aims to include all critical items published in any language between 1921 and 1968. For primary sources see Joseph Schwartz and Robert C. Schweik, *Hart Crane: A Descriptive Bibliography* (Pittsburgh: Univ. of Pittsburgh Press, 1972), which gives an accurate description of all Crane's separate publications, including drawings, translations, adaptations, and doubtful attributions, together with chronologies of Crane's life and works and a listing of periodicals in which his work first appeared. Some items which are represented as finished poems are actually fragments of variant versions. Kenneth A. Lohf, *The Library of Hart Crane* (Columbia: Univ. of South Carolina Press, 1973) is a descriptive catalog of the books Crane owned.

Reference Works

Two concordances to Crane's poems, both based on Brom Weber's edition of *Complete Poems* (1966), are Gary Lane, *A Concordance to the Poems of Hart Crane* (New York: Haskell House, 1972); and Hilton Landry and Elaine Landry, *A Concordance to the Poems of Hart Crane*, rev. by Robert DeMott (Metuchen, NJ: Scarecrow, 1973).

STEPHEN CRANE, 1871-1900

PRIMARY SOURCES

Separate Works

Maggie: A Girl of the Streets (1892); *The Black Riders and Other Lines* [poems] (1895); *The Red Badge of Courage* (1895); *A Souvenir and a Medley* (1896); *The Little Regiment* (1896); *George's Mother* (1896); *The Third Violet* (1897); *The Open Boat and Other Tales of Adventure* (1898); *Active Service* (1899); *War Is Kind* [poems] (1899); *The Monster and Other Stories* (1899); *Wounds in the Rain* (1900);

Whilomville Stories (1900); *Great Battles of the World* (1901); *Last Words* (1902); *The O'Ruddy* [with Robert Barr] (1903); *A Battle in Greece* (1936); *Notebook* (1969).

Collected Works and Edited Texts

The Works of Stephen Crane, ed. Fredson Bowers. 10v. (Charlottesville: Univ. of Virginia Press, 1969-76) contains everything, published and unpublished, except Crane's letters. Controversial points in Bowers' editing are summarized by David J. Nordloh, "On Crane Now Edited: The University of Virginia Edition of The Works of Stephen Crane," *Studies in the Novel* 10 (1978): 103-119. On account of the controversy, other editions, such as *The Blue Hotel*, ed. Joseph Katz (Columbus, OH: Merrill Pub. Co., 1969), remain important. *The Red Badge of Courage* is to be published by Norton in 1982, with 5,000 words that were omitted from earlier editions. The standard edition of correspondence is *Stephen Crane: Letters*, eds. R. W. Stallman and Lillian Gilkes (New York: New York Univ. Press, 1960); and evidence for Crane's methods of composition is in *The Notebook of Stephen Crane*, eds. Donald Greiner and Ellen B. Greiner (Charlottesville: Univ. Press of Virginia, 1969).

Other Source Materials

Collections of Crane are at the New York Public Library, Columbia University, and the University of Virginia.

SECONDARY SOURCES

Biography

R. W. Stallman, *Stephen Crane: A Biography* (New York: G. Braziller, 1968) has been the major biographical account, although scholars such as Katz and Pizer have reservations (*see* Bibliographies). New biographies will be able to draw on additional evidence brought to light with the Virginia edition. Corwin K. Linson, *My Stephen Crane*, ed. Edwin H. Cady (Syracuse, NY: Syracuse Univ. Press, 1958) is a memoir by a friend.

Criticism

An excellent introduction is Edwin H. Cady, *Stephen Crane*, rev. ed. (Boston: Twayne, 1980), and the introductory essays in the Virginia edition will also be important. For critical response to Crane, three works are outstanding. Richard M. Weatherford, *Stephen Crane: The Critical Heritage* (Boston: Routledge & Kegan Paul, 1973) reprints significant contemporary reviews and surveys the response of the 1890s. *Stephen Crane in Transition: Centenary Essays*, ed. Joseph Katz (DeKalb: Northern Illinois Univ. Press, 1972) contains nine original essays on Crane by James B. Colvert, Jean Cazemajou, Max Westbrook, and others; and *Stephen Crane's Career: Perspectives and Evaluations*, ed. Thomas A. Gullason (New York: New York Univ. Press, 1972) brings together Crane criticism published since 1950. More specialized studies are Eric Solomon, *Stephen Crane: From Parody to Realism* (Cambridge: Harvard Univ. Press, 1966), which examines social irony in Crane's short stories and novels; and Daniel G. Hoffman, *The Poetry of Stephen Crane* (New York: Columbia Univ. Press, 1957), which treats major themes in the poetry. An important work, in French, is Jean Cazemajou, *Stephen Crane, 1871-1900: Écrivain Journaliste* (Paris: Didier, 1969). Cazemajou has also written a useful introduction, *Stephen Crane* (Minneapolis:

Univ. of Minnesota Press, 1969). Marston LaFrance, *A Reading of Stephen Crane* (Oxford: Clarendon Press, 1971) is a study which sees Crane's irony directed against those who refuse to accept responsibility for their actions and beliefs. Frank Bergon, *Stephen Crane's Artistry* (New York: Columbia Univ. Press, 1975) seeks to identify Crane's attitude towards life in his technique of rendering the complexity and ambiguity of immediate experience.

Bibliographies

Crane scholarship to 1970 is surveyed by Donald Pizer, "Stephen Crane," in *Fifteen American Authors before 1900*, eds. Robert A. Rees and Earl N. Harbert (Madison: Univ. of Wisconsin Press, 1971) pp.97-137; and updated through 1975 in his "Stephen Crane: A Review of Scholarship and Criticism since 1969," *Studies in the Novel* 10 (1978): 120-45. Also giving excellent guidance is Joseph Katz, "Afterword: Resources for the Study of Stephen Crane," in *Stephen Crane in Transition: Centenary Essays*, ed. J. Katz (DeKalb: Northern Illinois Univ. Press, 1972). A history of all printings for each item is in *Stephen Crane: A Bibliography* (Glendale, CA: J. Valentine, 1948). Two catalogs of Matthew J. Bruccoli's notable collection are also important: *Stephen Crane, 1871-1900: An Exhibition from the Collection of Matthew J. Bruccoli* (Dept. of English, Univ. of South Carolina, Bibliographical Series, no.6, 1971); and *The Stephen Crane Collection from the Library of Prof. Matthew J. Bruccoli* (New York: Swann Galleries, 1974). For secondary sources, an extensive, usefully annotated secondary bibliography of books and articles through 1978, by Stanley Wertheim, is in Theodore L. Gross and Stanley Wertheim, *Hawthorne, Melville, Stephen Crane: A Critical Biography* (New York: Free Press, 1971). R. W. Stallman, *Stephen Crane: A Critical Biography* (Ames: Iowa State Univ. Press, 1972) contains a list of all Crane's titles and their printing history, as well as a major secondary bibliography, annotated in a somewhat contentious manner.

Reference Works

The Stephen Crane Newsletter, 1966-1970, acted as a clearinghouse for bibliographical and textual notes on Crane. *Thoth*, Syracuse University, is now the major current bibliography offering help on items not found in PMLA listings.

Two concordances are available. Herman Baron, *A Concordance to the Poems of Stephen Crane* (Boston: G. K. Hall, 1974) gives access to *The Poems of Stephen Crane: A Critical Edition*, rev. by Joseph Katz (New York: Cooper Square Publishers, 1972). Andrew T. Crosland, *A Concordance to the Complete Poetry of Stephen Crane* (Detroit: Gale, 1975) is the first concordance to be made for a CEAA edition, *Poems and Literary Remains*, ed. Fredson Bowers (Charlottesville: Univ. of Virginia Press, 1975).

COUNTEE (PORTER) CULLEN, 1903-1946

PRIMARY SOURCES

Separate Works

Color (1925); *Caroling Dusk* (1927); *Copper Sun* (1927); *The Ballad of the Brown Girl* (1927); *The Black Christ* (1929); *One Way to Heaven* (1932); *The Medea and Some Poems* (1935); *The Lost Zoo* (1940); *My Lives and How I Lost Them*

(1942); *St. Louis Woman* [with Arna Bontemps, musical dramatization of Bontemps' novel *God Sends Sunday*] (1946); *The Third Fourth of July* [one-act play] (1946); *On These I Stand* (1947).

Collected Works and Edited Texts

There is no collected edition of Cullen's works, and no important editions are available. Reprintings have been made of *Color* (New York: Arno Press, 1969) and *One Way to Heaven* (New York: AMS Press, 1975).

Other Source Materials

Letters and manuscripts are in the libraries of Yale University, Atlanta University, Fisk University, the University of Chicago, and at the New York Public Library.

SECONDARY SOURCES

Biography

The only book-length biography is Blanche E. Ferguson, *Countee Cullen and the Negro Renaissance* (New York: Dodd, Mead, 1966); but Margaret Perry, *A Bio-Bibliography of Countee P. Cullen* (*see* Bibliographies) has a lengthy biographical introduction. Further accounts of value are contained in more general works such as Darwin T. Turner, "Countee Cullen: The Lost Ariel," in *In a Minor Chord: Three Afro-American Writers and Their Search for Identity* (Carbondale: Southern Illinois Univ. Press, 1971); Stephen H. Bronz, *Roots of Negro Racial Consciousness, The 1920's: Three Harlem Renaissance Authors* (New York: Libra, 1964); and Jean Wagner, *Black Poets of the United States: From Paul Laurence Dunbar to Langston Hughes* (Chicago: Univ. of Illinois Press, 1973).

Criticism

For a reliable introduction to Cullen's poetry, see Houston A. Baker, Jr., *A Many-Colored Coat of Dreams: The Poetry of Countee Cullen* (Detroit: Broadside Press, 1974). Other criticism contained in more general accounts and journals is discussed in *Black American Writers: Bibliographical Essays* (*see* Bibliographies).

Bibliographies

A helpful introduction to the scholarship is a bibliographic essay by Ruth Miller and Peter J. Katopes, "The Harlem Renaissance," in *Black American Writers: Bibliographical Essays*, eds. M. Thomas Inge, Maurice Duke, Jackson R. Bryer. 2v. (New York: St. Martin's Press, 1978), v.1, pp.161-86. Margaret Perry, *A Bio-Bibliography of Countee P. Cullen, 1903-1946* (Westport, CT: Greenwood, 1971) contains a complete list of primary sources, including unpublished works, as well as over 200 citations to critical and biographical items. In addition, about seventy collections are cited in which Cullen's poetry appears. Other selective listings of criticism are in *Modern Black Poets: A Collection of Critical Essays*, ed. Donald B. Gibson (Englewood Cliffs, NJ: Prentice-Hall, 1973); *Afro-American Poetry and Drama, 1760-1975: A Guide to Information Sources*, ed. William P. French, et al. (Detroit: Gale, 1979); and Carol Fairbanks and Eugene A. Engeldinger, *Black American Fiction: A Bibliography* (Metuchen, NJ: Scarecrow, 1978). For citations to criticism and reviews of plays and musicals, see Esther Spring Arata and Nicholas John Rotoli, *Black American Playwrights, 1800 to the Present: A Bibliography* (Scarecrow, 1976).

E(DWARD) E(STLIN) CUMMINGS, 1894-1962

PRIMARY SOURCES

Separate Works

Eight Harvard Poets (1917); *The Enormous Room* (1922); *Tulips and Chimneys* (1923 & 1925); *XLI Poems* (1925); *Is 5* (1926); *Him* (1927); *Christmas Tree* (1928); [no title] (1930); *CIOPW* (1931); *VV: Viva Seventy New Poems* (1931); *EIMI* (1933); *Tom: A Ballet* (1935); *No Thanks* (1935); *1/20: One over Twenty: Poems* (1936); *50 Poems* (1940); *I x I* (1944); *Anthropos: The Future of Art* (1945); *Santa Claus: A Morality* (1946); *Xaîpe* (1950); *i: Six Nonlectures* (1953); *Poems, 1923-1954* (1954); *95 Poems* (1958); *100 Selected Poems* (1959); *Selected Poems, 1923-1958* (1960); *Adventures in Value* [photographs by Marion Morehouse, text by Cummings] (1962); *73 Poems* (1963); *Fairy Tales* [for children] (1965); *Hist Whist & Other Poems for Children* [with George J. Firmage] (1981).

Collected Works and Edited Texts

The most inclusive collection of poetry is *Complete Poems, 1910-1962* (St. Albans, England: Granada, 1981). Another important edition is *Complete Poems, 1913-1962* (New York: Harcourt Brace Jovanovich, 1972). *E. E. Cummings: A Miscellany Revised*, ed. George J. Firmage (London: Owen, 1966) gathers previously uncollected prose. *Three Plays and a Ballet*, ed. George J. Firmage (New York: October House, 1967) gathers *Him, Anthropos, Santa Claus*, and *Tom*. Correspondence is in *Selected Letters of E. E. Cummings*, eds. F. W. Dupee and George Stade (New York: Harcourt, Brace & World, 1969). George J. Firmage has reedited the following for the Cummings Typescript Editions, *Tulips & Chimneys* (New York: Liveright, 1976); *No Thanks* (Liveright, 1978); *The Enormous Room* (Liveright, 1978); *Viva* (Liveright, 1979); and *Xaipe* (Liveright, 1979).

Other Source Materials

The most important collection of source materials is at the Houghton Library, Harvard University.

SECONDARY SOURCES

Biography

An early study of Cummings' background and milieu, Charles Norman, *The Magic-Maker: E. E. Cummings* (New York: Duell, Sloan & Pearce, 1958), was updated in 1967 following Cummings' death. Nancy Cummings De Forêt, *Charon's Daughter: A Passion of Identity* (New York: Liveright, 1977) is a memoir by his daughter, which includes nine previously unpublished poems. The authoritative critical biography, based on the Cummings papers at Harvard, is Richard S. Kennedy, *Dreams in the Mirror* (Liveright, 1980).

Criticism

Two pamphlets combining biography and introductions to the poetry are Eve Triem, *E. E. Cummings* (Minneapolis: Univ. of Minnesota Press, 1960); and Wilton Eckley, *Merrill Guide to E. E. Cummings* (Columbus, OH: Charles E. Merrill, 1970). A straightforward explication of the major poems, helpful for new students of Cummings, is Rushworth M. Kidder, *E. E. Cummings: An Introduction to the Poetry* (New York: Columbia Univ. Press, 1979). Two influential studies are Norman Friedman, *E. E. Cummings: The Art of His Poetry* (Baltimore, MD: Johns Hopkins Univ. Press, 1960), which analyzes language, techniques, and themes; and Friedman's *E. E. Cummings: The Growth of a Writer* (Carbondale: Southern Illinois Univ. Press, 1964), which demonstrates Cummings' poetic developments chronologically. Other studies to consult are Barry A. Marks, *E. E. Cummings* (New York: Twayne, 1964); Robert E. Wegner, *The Poetry and Prose of E. E. Cummings* (New York: Harcourt, Brace & World, 1965); Bethany K. Dumas, *E. E. Cummings: A Remembrance of Miracles* (London: Vision, 1974); and Gary Lane, *I Am: A Study of E. E. Cummings' Poems* (Lawrence: Univ. of Kansas, 1976), which is a thoughtful analysis of Cummings' "dialectic of love, death, and growth," in twenty-five poems.

Two collections of critical essays are Σοτί : *EEC: E. E. Cummings and the Critics*, ed. S. V. Baum (East Lansing: Michigan State Univ. Press, 1962); and *E. E. Cummings: A Collection of Critical Essays*, ed. Norman Friedman (Englewood Cliffs, NJ: Prentice-Hall, 1972), which reprints fourteen important essays, written over the previous thirty years, and provides useful primary and secondary bibliographies.

Bibliographies

George J. Firmage, *E. E. Cummings: A Bibliography* (Middletown, CT: Wesleyan Univ. Press, 1960) is a descriptive bibliography of primary works, including contributions to periodicals, recordings, and reproductions of Cummings' art. Paul Lauter, *E. E. Cummings: Index to First Lines and Bibliography of Works by and about the Poet* (Denver: A. Swallow, 1955; repr. Norwood, PA: Norwood Editions, 1976) is a working bibliography which gives access to the range of Cummings' work. An excellent overview of the scholarship and bibliography is the introductory essay in Guy L. Rotella, *E. E. Cummings: A Reference Guide* (Boston: G. K. Hall, 1979), which is an annotated bibliography of secondary sources.

EMILY DICKINSON, 1830-1886

PRIMARY SOURCES

Collected Works and Edited Texts

The authoritative text of Dickinson's 1,775 known poems with their variants is *The Poems of Emily Dickinson*, ed. Thomas H. Johnson. 3v. (Cambridge: Harvard Univ. Press, 1955), and 1,150 letters are chronologically collected in *The Letters of Emily Dickinson*, eds. Thomas H. Johnson and Theodora Ward. 3v. (Harvard Univ. Press, 1958).

Thomas H. Johnson, *The Complete Poems of Emily Dickinson* (Boston: Little, Brown, 1960) contains a single version of all the poems; and his *Final Harvest* (Little, Brown, 1961) selects 575 representative poems. He has also edited a selection of the correspondence as *Emily Dickinson: Selected Letters* (Harvard Univ. Press, 1971).

The Manuscript Books of Emily Dickinson: A Facsimile Edition, ed. R. W. Franklin. 2v. (Harvard Univ. Press, 1981) reproduces 1,447 poems in Dickinson's hand, with alternate readings and pencilled revisions, keeping Dickinson's original sequence.

Other Source Materials

The Years and Hours of Emily Dickinson, ed. Jay Leyda, 2v. (New Haven, CT: Yale Univ. Press, 1960) contains biographical documents, chronologically arranged. Most of the Dickinson manuscripts, described in R. W. Franklin, *The Editing of Emily Dickinson* (Madison: Univ. of Wisconsin Press, 1967), are available at the Houghton Library of Harvard University and the Amherst College Library. A further collection at Princeton is described in Robert Fraser, *The Margaret Jane Pershing Collection of Emily Dickinson* (Princeton, NJ: Princeton Univ. Press, 1969).

SECONDARY SOURCES

Biography

The first reliable biography was George Whicher, *This Was a Poet: A Critical Biography* (New York: Scribner, 1938; repr. Hamden, CT: Archon Books, 1980). An objective study is Richard B. Sewall, *The Life of Emily Dickinson*, 2v. (New York: Farrar, Straus & Giroux, 1974). Thomas H. Johnson, *Emily Dickinson: An Interpretative Biography* (Cambridge: Harvard Univ. Press, 1955) shows the relation of Dickinson's inner life to her poetry. Theodora Ward, *The Capsule of the Mind* (Harvard Univ. Press, 1961) carefully interprets the life through the poems and manuscripts. David Higgins, *Portrait of Emily Dickinson: The Poet and Her Prose* (New Brunswick, NJ: Rutgers Univ. Press, 1967); and Ruth Miller, *The Poetry of Emily Dickinson* (Middletown, CT: Weslyan Univ. Press, 1968) argue that Samuel Bowles was the object of Dickinson's love. Jack L. Capps, *Emily Dickinson's Reading, 1836-1886* (Cambridge: Harvard Univ. Press, 1966) indicates influences from literature that Dickinson read. Two good biographical introductions are John B. Pickard, *Emily Dickinson: An Introduction and Interpretation* (New York: Barnes & Noble, 1967); and Denis Donoghue, *Emily Dickinson* (Minneapolis: Univ. of Minnesota Press, 1969).

Criticism

Klaus Lubbers, *Emily Dickinson: The Critical Revolution* (Ann Arbor: Univ. of Michigan Press, 1968) traces critical reaction to Dickinson since 1862. *The Recognition of Emily Dickinson*, eds. Caesar R. Blake and Carlton F. Wells (Ann Arbor: Univ. of Michigan Press, 1964) documents reception to 1930. A later period is covered in *Emily Dickinson: A Collection of Critical Essays*, ed. Richard B. Sewall (Englewood Cliffs, NJ: Prentice-Hall, 1963); and *Critics on Emily Dickinson*, ed. Richard H. Rupp (Coral Gables: Univ. of Miami Press, 1972). A good general introduction, which explicates major poems clearly, is Paul J. Ferlazzo, *Emily Dickinson* (Boston: Twayne, 1976). Among the most important full-length critical studies are Richard Chase, *Emily Dickinson* (New York: Sloane, 1951); and Charles Anderson, *Emily Dickinson's Poetry: Stairway of Surprise* (New York: Holt, Rinehart & Winston, 1960), who analyzes 103 poems, establishing his own readings. Existential views are in Clark Griffith, *The Long Shadow: Emily Dickinson's Tragic Poetry* (Princeton, NJ: Princeton Univ. Press, 1964). David G. Porter, *The Art of Emily Dickinson's Early Poems* (Cambridge: Harvard Univ. Press, 1966) concentrates on 301 poems written prior to

1862; Albert J. Gelpi, *Emily Dickinson: The Mind of the Poet* (Harvard Univ. Press, 1965) examines Dickinson's mind and its relation to her poetry. Brita Lindberg-Seyersted, *The Voice of the Poet: Aspects of Style in the Poetry of Emily Dickinson* (Harvard Univ. Press, 1968) examines colloquial patterns, "slantness," and privateness in the diction, metrics, and syntax. Robert Weibuch, *Emily Dickinson's Poetry* (Chicago: Univ. of Chicago Press, 1975) demonstrates the multiple meanings Dickinson achieved from "archetypal" situations, and Rebecca Patterson, *Emily Dickinson's Imagery*, ed. Margaret H. Freeman (Amherst: Univ. of Massachusetts Press, 1979) links Dickinson's imagery to the theme of erotic love transforming into erotic death. Two studies of Dickinson as a nineteenth-century woman poet are Sandra Gilbert, *The Mad Woman in the Attic* (New Haven, CT: Yale Univ. Press, 1979); and Margaret Homans, *Women Writers and Poetic Identity: Dorothy Wordsworth, Emily Brontë and Emily Dickinson* (Princeton, NJ: Princeton Univ. Press, 1980).

Bibliographies

James Woodress, "Emily Dickinson," in *Fifteen American Authors before 1900*, eds. Robert A. Rees and Earl N. Harbert (Madison: Univ. of Wisconsin Press, 1971), pp.139-68, is an introductory bibliographic essay which includes a succinct history of Dickinson's editions. Willis J. Buckingham, *Emily Dickinson: An Annotated Bibliography: Writings, Scholarship, Criticism and Ana, 1830-1968* (Bloomington: Indiana Univ. Press, 1970) is the most extensive bibliography. Also valuable for its organization and annotations is Sheilah T. Clendenning, *Emily Dickinson: A Bibliography, 1850-1966* (Kent, OH: Kent State Univ. Press, 1968). Joseph Duchac, *The Poems of Emily Dickinson* (Boston: G. K. Hall, 1979) is an annotated guide to criticism in English, 1890-1977.

Reference Works

The Emily Dickinson Bulletin 1 (1968)-33 (1978), which is continued by *Dickinson Studies*, is a quarterly newsletter that acts as a clearinghouse for short articles and bibliographic updating. S. P. Rosenbaum, *A Concordance to the Poems of Emily Dickinson* (Ithaca, NY: Cornell Univ. Press, 1964) gives words in context and first lines of poems as access points which are keyed to Johnson's 1955 edition.

HILDA DOOLITTLE (ALDINGTON), 1886-1961
Pseud: "H. D."

PRIMARY SOURCES

Separate Works

Sea Garden (1916); *Hymen* (1921); *Heliodora and Other Poems* (1924); *Collected Poems of H. D.* (1925); *Palimpsest* (1926); *H. D.* (1926); *Hippolytus Temporizes* [play] (1927); *Hedylus* (1928); *Red Roses for Bronze* (1929); *The Hedgehog* (1936); *Ion of Euripides* [translation] (1937); *The Walls Do Not Fall* (1944); *Tribute to the Angels* (1945); *The Flowering of the Rod* (1946); *By Avon River* (1949); *Tribute to Freud: With Unpublished Letters by Freud to the Author* (1956); *Selected Poems of H. D.* (1957); *Bid Me to Live* (1960); *Helen in Egypt* (1961); *Hermetic Definition* (1972); *The Poet & the Dancer* (1975; poem originally appeared in 1935); *End to Torment: A Memoir of Ezra Pound* (1979).

Collected Works and Edited Texts

There is no definitive collection of H. D.'s work. *Trilogy* (New York: New Directions, 1975) collects *The Walls Do Not Fall* and *Tribute to the Angels*; and *The Flowering of the Rod Hedylus* (Redding Ridge, CT: Black Swan Books, 1980) has reset the text of this imagist novel following the author's original galley markings and comments as well as including a memoir by H. D.'s daughter and a list of textual notes from a 1951-1953 notebook.

Other Source Materials

Manuscripts of H. D. are at the libraries of Harvard University, the University of Chicago, and the University of Buffalo.

SECONDARY SOURCES

Biography

Of value for biographical information is the autobiography of her closest friend, Bryher (Winifred Ellerman), *The Heart to Artemis* (New York: Harcourt, Brace & World, 1962); and her 1958 journal-memoir, *End to Torment: A Memoir of Ezra Pound*, ed. Michael King (New York: New Directions, 1979), which also contains his previously unpublished poems of "Hilda's Book." Janice S. Robinson, *H. D.: The Life and Work of an American Poet* (Boston: Houghton Mifflin, 1982) recounts H. D.'s relationships with Pound, Lawrence, Bryher, and others, relating her essentially autobiographical work to her life experiences.

Criticism

There are few full-length studies. Thomas Barnett Swann, *The Classical World of H. D.* (Lincoln: Univ. of Nebraska Press, 1962) treats only the work on classical subjects, while Vincent Quinn, *Hilda Doolittle (H. D.)* (New York: Twayne, 1967) is a useful introduction to the life and works. A special issue of *Contemporary Literature* 10 (1969) contains articles, letters, and selections of her poetry, prose, and letters. Norman H. Holland, *Poems in Person* (New York: Norton, 1973) studies H. D.'s relation with Freud in order to understand her use of myth; and Susan Stanford Friedman, *Psyche Reborn: The Emergence of H. D.* (Bloomington: Indiana Univ. Press, 1981) draws on previously unavailable papers to examine ways in which interest in psychoanalysis and the occult influenced H. D.'s imagist work.

Bibliographies

A preliminary checklist, Jackson R. Bryer and Pamela Roblyer, "H. D.: A Preliminary Checklist," *Contemporary Literature* 10 (1969): 632-75 is the best bibliography of primary sources.

JOHN (RODERIGO) DOS PASSOS, 1896-1970

PRIMARY SOURCES

Separate Works

One Man's Initiation–1917 (1920); Three Soldiers (1921); Rosinante to the Road Again (1922); A Pushcart at the Curb (1922); Streets of Night (1923); Manhattan Transfer (1925); The Garbarge Man (1926); Orient Express (1927); Airways, Inc. (1928); The 42nd Parallel (1930); 1919 (1932); In All Countries (1934); Three Plays (1934); The Big Money (1936); Journeys between Wars (1938); Adventures of a Young Man (1939); The Ground We Stand On (1941); Number One: A Novel (1943); State of the Nation (1944); Tour of Duty (1946); The Grand Design (1949); The Prospect before Us (1950); Chosen Country (1951); Most Likely to Succeed (1954); The Head and Heart of Thomas Jefferson (1954); The Theme Is Freedom (1956); The Men Who Made the Nation (1957); The Great Days (1958); Prospects of a Golden Age (1959); Midcentury (1961); Mr. Wilson's War (1962); Brazil on the Move (1963); Occasions and Protests (1964); Thomas Jefferson: The Making of a President (1964); The Best Times: An Informal Memoir (1966); The Shackles of Power: Three Jeffersonian Decades (1966); The Portugal Story: Three Centuries of Exploration and Discovery (1969); Easter Island: Island of Enigmas (1971); Century's Ebb: Thirteenth Chronicle (1975).

Collected Works and Edited Texts

Neither collected works nor authorized editions are yet available, but there are numerous reprints. *The Fourteenth Chronicle: Letters and Diaries of John Dos Passos*, ed. Townsend Ludington (Boston: Gambit, 1973) quotes from the letters and diaries selectively, covering the period from 1910 until two months before Dos Passos' death. Ludington's literary narrative presents a kind of autobiography by filling gaps and clarifying references.

Other Source Materials

The largest collection of Dos Passos' papers is at the University of Virginia Library, Charlottesville, which also contains about 340 first editions and foreign editions, many in original book jackets. Many editions from this collection are described and annotated in Anne Freudenberg and Elizabeth Fake, *John Dos Passos, Writer and Artist, 1896-1970: A Guide to the Exhibition at the University of Virginia Library, 1975* (Charlottesville: Univ. of Virginia Library, 1975). *An Interview with John Dos Passos*, ed. Frank Gado (published in the *Idol*, literary quarterly of Union College, Schenectady, New York. special issue, v.45, 1969) includes a reprinting of "A Humble Protest," which Dos Passos published in *Harvard Monthly* during his senior year.

SECONDARY SOURCES

Biography

Townsend Ludington, *John Dos Passos: A Twentieth Century Odyssey* (New York: Dutton, 1980) is by the editor of the letters and diaries. Melvin Landsberg, *Dos Passos' Path to "U.S.A.": A Political Biography, 1912-1936* (Boulder: Colorado

Associated Univ. Press, 1972) deals with Dos Passos' involvement in public affairs as a preparation for his writing. Assessment of the plays and essays and accounts of his connections with the theatre are incomplete.

Criticism

As yet, no major critical study does justice to this neglected modernist, but among the useful works available are those of George-Albert Astre, *Thèmes Et Structures Dans L'Oeuvre De John Dos Passos*, 2v. (Paris: Minard, 1956-58); John H. Wrenn, *John Dos Passos* (New Haven, CT: Twayne, 1961); Robert Gorham Davis, *John Dos Passos* (Minneapolis: Univ. of Minnesota Press, 1962), a pamphlet; and Linda W. Wagner, *Dos Passos: Artist as American* (Austin: Univ. of Texas Press, 1979), which treats the *District of Columbia Trilogy* and *Midcentury*. Robert C. Rosen, *John Dos Passos: Politics and the Writer* (Lincoln: Univ. of Nebraska Press, 1981) draws on diaries and journalism to provide background on Dos Passos' political involvement in order to interpret his fiction. Two anthologies which draw together important critical essays are *Dos Passos: The Critics and the Writer's Intention*, ed. Allen Belkind (Carbondale and Edwardsville: Southern Illinois Univ. Press, 1971); and *Dos Passos: A Collection of Critical Essays*, ed. Andrew Hook (Englewood Cliffs, NJ: Prentice-Hall, 1974). "John Dos Passos" is a special issue of *Modern Fiction Studies* 26 (1980).

Bibliographies

The fullest primary bibliography is Jack Potter, *A Bibliography of John Dos Passos* (Chicago: Normandie House, 1950). It is supplemented by Virginia S. Reinhart, "John Dos Passos Bibliography: 1950-1966," *Twentieth-Century Literature* 13 (1967): 167-78. Wagner (*see* Criticism) contains chronological lists of Dos Passos' books and his selected essays, as well as a selection of secondary sources. A selected secondary bibliography is John Rohrkemper, "Criticism of John Dos Passos: A Selected Checklist," *Modern Fiction Studies* 26 (Fall 1980): 417-30; and John Rohrhkemper, *John Dos Passos: A Reference Guide* (Boston: G. K. Hall, 1980) is a full-scale annotated secondary bibliography.

THEODORE (HERMAN ALBERT) DREISER, 1871-1945

PRIMARY SOURCES

Separate Works

Sister Carrie (1900); *Jennie Gerhardt* (1911); *The Financier* (1912); *A Traveller at Forty* (1913); *The Titan* (1914); *The "Genius"* (1915); *Plays of the Natural and the Supernatural* (1916); *A Hoosier Holiday* (1916); *Free and Other Stories* (1918); *The Hand of the Potter* (1918); *Twelve Men* (1919); *Hey Rub-Adub-Dub* (1920); *A Book about Myself* (1922); *The Color of a Great City* (1923); *An American Tragedy* (1925); *Moods, Cadenced and Declaimed* (1926); *Chains* (1927); *Dreiser Looks at Russia* (1928); *A Gallery of Women* (1929); *The Aspirant* (1929); *My City* (1929); *Epitaph* (1929); *Fine Furniture* (1930); *Dawn* (1931); *Tragic America* (1931); *America Is Worth Saving* (1941); *The Bulwark* (1946); *The Stoic* (1947); *Notes on Life* (1974).

Collected Works and Edited Texts

Although no uniform edition of Dreiser's works is yet available, a definitive edition is underway at the University of Pennsylvania. *Sister Carrie*, ed. James L. West, III, et al. (Philadelphia: Univ. of Pennsylvania, 1981) includes the controversial last chapter, together with maps, illustrations, and historical notes. Most of Dreiser's novels and short stories are in print, and there are some selections of letters and poems. Among the Charles E. Merrill series of standard editions is a reprint of the 1900 first edition of *Sister Carrie*, introduction by Louis Auchincloss (Columbus, OH: C. E. Merrill, 1969). *Sister Carrie: An Authoritative Text, Backgrounds and Sources Criticism*, ed. Donald Pizer (New York: Norton, 1970) annotates the same edition and also republishes newspaper articles, autobiographical excerpts, exchanges of correspondence, and fourteen critical essays. *Theodore Dreiser: A Selection of Uncollected Prose*, ed. Donald Pizer (Detroit: Wayne State Univ. Press, 1977) selects nonfiction prose to reveal "major moments in the history of Dreiser's thought" and to display "the range of his ideas," so as to provide material "to confront the vexing problem of consistency and coherence" in Dreiser's beliefs. No complete edition of poems has been attempted because many are buried under pseudonyms in magazines, but *Selected Poems (from Moods)*, introduction and notes by Robert Palmer Saalbach (New York: Exposition Press, 1969, c1935) presents 160 poems roughly chronologically. *Notes on Life*, eds. Marguerite Tjader and John J. McAleer (University: Univ. of Alabama Press, 1974) is a representative selection from Dreiser's notes about the universe that he had hoped to formalize as a collection of philosophical essays. Dreiser's letters to his literary assistant, from 1917 to 1945, are in *Letters to Louise*, ed. Louise Campbell (Philadelphia: Univ. of Pennsylvania Press, 1959). *Letters of Theodore Dreiser*, ed. Robert H. Elias, 3v. (Univ. of Pennsylvania Press, 1959) is a selection chosen to illuminate Dreiser as writer and to indicate his relationships with H. L. Mencken and others.

Other Source Materials

Among Dreiser's works which reveal much about himself are *Hey-Rub-A-Dub-Dub*, *A Book about Myself* (also published as *Newspaper Days*), and the travel books, *A Hoosier Holiday*, *A Traveller at Forty*, and *Dreiser Looks at Russia*. The major repository of Dreiser's papers is the Charles Patterson Van Pelt Library, University of Pennsylvania. A catalog interpreting materials in this collection is *Theodore Dreiser Centenary Exhibition* (Philadelphia: Univ. of Pennsylvania Library, 1971). Other important collections are in the New York Public Library and the Clifton Waller Barrett Collection at the University of Virginia. Further sources are listed in *American Literary Manuscripts*, ed. Joseph Jones, et al. (Austin: Univ. of Texas Press, 1960).

SECONDARY SOURCES

Biography

The first serious estimate of Dreiser was by H. L. Mencken in *A Book of Prefaces* (New York: Knopf, 1917), pp. 67-148. The standard critical biography, Robert A. Elias, *Theodore Dreiser: Apostle of Nature*, emended ed. (Ithaca, NY: Cornell Univ. Press, 1970), carefully documents Dreiser's life to illuminate the writings. W. A. Swanberg, *Dreiser* (New York: Scribner, 1965) is a massive accumulation of biographical information drawing on interviews and much previously unpublished correspondence, but attempting no in-depth literary criticism. It is supplemented by

Marguerite Tjader, *Theodore Dreiser: A New Dimension* (Norwalk, CT: Silvermine Publishers, 1965). Tjader, who was Dreiser's amanuensis, focuses on the spiritual and philosophical probings of Dreiser's later years, quoting extensively from drafts of *The Bulwark*. Ellen Moers, *Two Dreisers* (New York: Viking, 1969) uses Dreiser's letters, including those to "Jug," his first wife, those with psychologists and biologists, and with Stieglitz, Stephen Crane, Howells, and others, to document the backgrounds for *Sister Carrie* and *An American Tragedy*. Helen Dreiser, *My Life with Dreiser* (Cleveland, OH: World Pub. Co., 1951) is an account of his activities between 1919 and 1945 and includes previously unpublished correspondence with his second wife. Vera Dreiser, with Brett Howard, *My Uncle Theodore* (New York: Nash Pub. Co., 1976) presents an "intimate family portrait." Although not a scholarly work, it is useful for including previously unpublished correspondence and extracts from diaries of Dreiser's niece, a psychologist, who interprets the artist as a "functioning schizophrenic."

Criticism

Charles Shapiro, *Theodore Dreiser: Our Bitter Patriot* (Carbondale: Southern Illinois Univ. Press, 1962) analyzes the destructive influence of the American dream on all aspects of life. F. O. Matthiessen, *Theodore Dreiser* (New York: Sloane, 1951; Westport, CT: Greenwood Press, 1973) examines the images, structure, symbols, and language of the novels. A critical introduction which contains chapter-length analyses of the novels and interprets Dreiser's life as it bears on his writing is Philip L. Gerber, *Theodore Dreiser* (New York: Twayne, 1964). John J. McAleer, *Theodore Dreiser: An Introduction and Interpretation* (New York: Holt, Rinehart & Winston, 1968) emphasizes the conflict between nature and the American dream; and Richard Lehan, *Theodore Dreiser: His World and His Novels* (Carbondale: Southern Illinois Univ. Press, 1969) emphasizes the evolution of the artist and his themes. The ambitions, frustrations, and ambivalence of Dreiser are indicated in Robert Penn Warren, *Homage to Theodore Dreiser, August 27, 1871-December 28, 1945, on the Centennial of His Birth* (New York: Random House, 1971). An introductory pamphlet, W. M. Frohock, *Theodore Dreiser* (Minneapolis: Univ. of Minnesota Press, 1972) focuses on Dreiser's grim interpretation of American life. James Lundquist, *Theodore Dreiser* (New York: Ungar, 1974) is a survey introduction, for nonspecialists, of the major events of Dreiser's life as they bear on his works. Donald Pizer, *The Novels of Theodore Dreiser: A Critical Study* (Minneapolis: Univ. of Minnesota Press, 1976) establishes the facts, sources, and composition of each of the novels and studies themes and forms. Dreiser's reputation in the review media is traced in *Theodore Dreiser: The Critical Reception*, ed. Jack Salzman (New York: D. Lewis, 1972). Several anthologies gather much important Dreiser criticism. *The Stature of Theodore Dreiser*, eds. Alfred Kazin and Charles Shapiro (Bloomington: Indiana Univ. Press, 1955) contains thirty-four articles, including essays, personal reminiscences, and statements which represent various viewpoints on naturalism, by Sherwood Anderson, H. L. Mencken, and others. *Dreiser: A Collection of Critical Essays*, ed. John Lyndenberg (Englewood Cliffs, NJ: Prentice-Hall, 1971) republishes fifteen essays written from 1915 to 1964, which represent the controversy over Dreiser's work. Five reviews by Sherwood Anderson, Clarence Darrow, Joseph Wood Krutch, H. L. Mencken, and Stuart Sherman, together with eight critical studies by F. O. Matthiessen and others, are gathered in *The Merrill Studies in an American Tragedy*, ed. Jack Salzman (Columbis, OH: Merrill, 1971); and a more recent collection covering eighty years of the most influential criticism is *Critical Essays on Theodore Dreiser*, ed. Donald Pizer (Boston: G. K. Hall, 1981).

Bibliographies

A valuable bibliographical essay providing the best scholarly perspective is Robert W. Elias, "Theodore Dreiser," in *Sixteen Modern American Authors* (Durham, NC: Duke Univ. Press, 1974), pp.123-79. Donald Pizer, Richard W. Dowell, and Frederic E. Rusch, eds., *Theodore Dreiser: A Primary and Secondary Bibliography* (Boston: G. K. Hall, 1975) list works by and about Dreiser, including careful descriptions of the textual variants in successive editions, contributions to periodicals, speeches, and interviews.

Reference Works

The Dreiser Newsletter, v.1 (Spring 1970)- is a semi-annual publication which coordinates and reports on Dreiser scholarship and includes new editions, translations, and bibliographies.

Philip L. Gerber, *Plots and Characters in the Fiction of Theodore Dreiser* (Hamden, CT: Archon Books, 1977) contains a chronology, which is not entirely accurate, useful plot synopses, including summaries of the revised versions, and an alphabetical list of about 1,000 characters and their aliases.

W(ILLIAM) E(DWARD) B(URGHARDT) DUBOIS, 1868-1963

PRIMARY SOURCES

Separate Works

The Souls of Black Folk: Essays and Sketches (1903); *The Quest of the Silver Fleece* (1911); *Darkwater: Voices from within the Veil* [short stories] (1921); *Dark Princess* (1928); *The Black Flame* [a trilogy which includes *The Ordeal of Mansart*] (1957); *Mansart Builds a School* (1959); *Worlds of Color* (1961); *Selected Poems* (1964).

Collected Works and Edited Texts

There is no collected edition of DuBois, but a microfilm makes available a substantial body of his shorter works, such as *W. E. B. DuBois, 1883-1922: The First Four Decades of His Published Writings*, ed. Paul G. Partington, 1 reel (Los Angeles: Microfilm Co. of California, 1979). Other collections are *W. E. B. DuBois Speaks: Speeches and Addresses*, ed. Philip S. Foner. 2v. (New York: Pathfinder Press, 1970); *A W. E. B. DuBois Reader*, ed. Andrew G. Paschal (New York: Macmillan, 1971); and *The Emerging Thought of W. E. B. DuBois: Essays and Editorials from the "Crisis,"* ed. Henry Lee Moon (New York: Simon & Schuster, 1972). A reprint of his 1940 *Dusk of Dawn: An Essay toward an Autobiography of a Race Concept* (Millwood, NY: Kraus-Thomson, 1975) has an introduction by Herbert Aptheker. DuBois' letters are collected as *The Correspondence of W. E. B. DuBois*, ed. Herbert Aptheker. 3v. (Amherst: Univ. of Massachusetts Press, 1973-78). Available in microform are *The Papers of W. E. B. DuBois, 1877-1963, 1803*, 79 microfilm reels (Sanford, NC: Microfilming Corp. of America, 1980).

Other Source Materials

A guide to DuBois' papers at the University of Massachusetts, Amherst, is Robert W. McDowell, *The Papers of W. E. B. DuBois, 1803* (1877-1963) 1979 (Sanford, NC: Microfilming Corp. of America, 1981).

SECONDARY SOURCES

Biography

Two book-length biographies are Leslie A. Lacey, *Cheer the Lonesome Traveller* (New York: Dial Press, 1970); and the memoir by Shirley Graham DuBois, *His Day Is Marching on* (Philadelphia: Lippincott, 1971). Essays on his role as a black leader are collected in *W. E. B. DuBois: A Profile*, ed. Rayford W. Logan (New York: Hill & Wang, 1971).

Criticism

Arnold Rampersad, *The Art and Imagination of W. E. B. DuBois* (Cambridge: Harvard Univ. Press, 1976) is an important examination of form and content, including both social and aesthetic qualities of the fiction. Works on his social contribution are Francis L. Broderick, *W. E. B. DuBois: Negro Leader in a Time of Crisis* (Stanford, CA: Stanford Univ. Press, 1959); and Elliott M. Rudwick, *W. E. B. DuBois: Propagandist of the Negro Protest* (New York: Atheneum, 1969).

Bibliographies

Among primary bibliographies are an extensively annotated guide by Herbert Aptheker, *Annotated Bibliography of the Published Writings of W. E. B. DuBois* (Millwood, NY: Kraus-Thomson, 1973); Paul G. Partington, *W. E. B. DuBois: A Bibliography of His Published Writings* (Whittier, CA: Partington, 1977); and Partington's "A Checklist of the Creative Writings of W. E. B. DuBois," *Black American Literature Forum* 13 (1979): 110-11, which conveniently lists books, poems, short fiction, and plays. For secondary sources, see an extensive listing by Dan S. Green, "Bibliography of Writing about W. E. B. DuBois," *College Language Association Journal* 20 (1977): 410-21.

JONATHAN EDWARDS, 1703-1758

PRIMARY SOURCES

Separate Works

God Glorified in the Work of Redemption (1731); *A Divine and Supernatural Light* (1734); *A Faithful Narrative* (1737); *Discourses on Various Important Subjects* (1738); *The Distinguishing Marks of a Work of the Spirit of God* (1741); *Sinners in the Hands of an Angry God* (1741); *Some Thoughts Concerning the Present Revival of Religion in New England* (1742); *A Treatise Concerning Religious Affections* (1746); *An Humble Attempt to Promote Explicit Agreement* (1747); *An Account of the Life of the Late Reverend Mr. David Brainerd* (1749); *An Humble Inquiry into the Rules* of the Word of God Concerning. . .Communion (1749); *A Farewell Sermon Preached at the First Precinct in Northampton* (1751); *True Grace* (1753); *A Careful and Strict Enquiry into. . .Freedom of Will. . .* (1754); *The Great Christian Doctrine of Original Sin Defended* (1758); *Two Dissertations: I. Concerning the End for Which God Created the World; II. The Nature of True Virtue* (1765); *Charity and Its Fruits* (1852); *Selections from the Unpublished Writings* (1865); *Observations Concerning the Scripture Oeconomy* (1880); *An Unpublished Essay of Edwards on the Trinity* (1903).

Collected Works and Edited Texts

When completed, *The Works of Jonathan Edwards*, ed. Perry Miller (New Haven, CT: Yale Univ. Press, 1957-) will be the definitive edition. *Jonathan Edwards: Representative Selections.* rev. ed., eds. Clarence H. Faust and Thomas H. Johnson (New York: Hill & Wang, 1962) is an important anthology which is accompanied by helpful notes and a bibliography.

Other Sources

Yale University and Andover-Newton Theological Seminary contain the largest collections of Edwards' papers.

SECONDARY SOURCES

Biography

Samuel Hopkins, *Life and Character of the Late Rev. Mr. Jonathan Edwards* (1765) was the first biography, and it is reprinted in the collection *Jonathan Edwards: A Profile*, ed. David Levin (New York: Hill & Wang, 1969). Other important studies are Ola E. Winslow, *Jonathan Edwards, 1703-1758* (New York: Macmillan, 1940); Edward H. Davidson, *Jonathan Edwards: The Narrative of a Puritan Mind* (Cambridge: Harvard Univ. Press, 1968); and Patricia J. Tracy, *Jonathan Edwards: Religion and Society in Eighteenth Century Northampton* (New York: Hill & Wang, 1980), which examines Edwards as pastor.

Criticism

The best critical-biographical approach is Perry Miller, *Jonathan Edwards* (New York: Sloane, 1949). Other useful studies are Alfred Owen Aldridge, *Jonathan Edwards* (New York: Washington Square Press, 1964); and Conrad Cherry, *The Theology of Jonathan Edwards: A Reappraisal* (Garden City, NY: Anchor Books, 1966). For a convenient overview, see Edward M. Griffin, *Jonathan Edwards* (Minneapolis: Univ. of Minnesota Press, 1971). A collection of writings by and about Edwards is *Jonathan Edwards and the Enlightenment*, ed. John Opie (Lexington, MA: Heath, 1969), while *Jonathan Edwards: His Life and Influence*, ed. Charles Angoff (Rutherford, NJ: Fairleigh Dickinson Univ. Press, 1974) is a collection of papers by Cherry and others. William J. Scheick, *The Writings of Jonathan Edwards: Theme, Motif and Style* (College Station: Texas A&M Univ. Press, 1975) analyzes sermon imagery and rhetoric. An important collection of criticism covering biography, philosophy, theology, and literary aspects, and including Edwin H. Cady's influential essay "The Artistry of Jonathan Edwards," reprinted from *New England Quarterly* 22

(March 1949): 61-72 is in *Critical Essays on Jonathan Edwards*, ed. William J. Scheick (Boston: G. K. Hall, 1980).

Bibliographies

A bibliographic overview is Everett H. Emerson, "Jonathan Edwards," in *Fifteen American Authors before 1900*, eds. Robert A. Rees and Earl N. Harbert (Madison: Univ. of Wisconsin Press, 1971), pp.169-84. The "Selected Bibliography," revised by Stephen Webb, in the collection *Jonathan Edwards: Representative Selections (see Criticism)* is also useful. M. X. Lesser, *Jonathan Edwards: A Reference Guide* (Boston: G. K. Hall, 1981) is an annotated chronological bibliography of 1,800 items about Edwards that were published between 1729 and 1978.

T(HOMAS) S(TEARNS) ELIOT, 1888-1965

PRIMARY SOURCES

Separate Works

Prufrock and Other Observations (1917); *Ezra Pound: His Metric and Poetry* (1917); *Poems* (1919); *Poems* (1920); *The Sacred Wood: Essays on Poetry and Criticism* (1920); *The Waste Land* (1922); *Homage to John Dryden* (1924); *The Journey of the Magi* (1927); *Shakespeare and the Stoicism of Seneca* (1927); *A Song for Simeon* (1928); *For Lancelot Andrewes: Essays on Style and Order* (1928); *Animula* (1929); *Dante* (1929); *Ash-Wednesday* (1930); *Marina* (1930); *Charles Whibley: A Memoir* (1931); *Triumphal March* (1931); *Thoughts after Lambeth* (1931); *John Dryden the Poet, the Dramatist, the Critic* (1932); *Sweeney Agonistes* (1932); *The Use of Poetry and the Use of Criticism* (1933); *After Strange Gods* (1934); *The Rock: A Pageant Play* (1934); *Elizabethan Essays* (1934); *Murder in the Cathedral* (1935); *Essays, Ancient and Modern* (1936); *The Idea of a Christian Society* (1939); *The Family Reunion: A Play* (1939); *Old Possum's Book of Practical Cats* (1939); *The Music of Poetry* (1942); *The Classics and the Man of Letters* (1942); *Reunion by Destruction: Reflections on a Scheme for Church Union in South India* (1943); *Four Quartets* (1943), *Comprising: East Coker* (1940), *Burnt Norton* (1941), *The Dry Salvages* (1941), *and Little Gidding* (1942); *What Is a Classic?* (1945); *On Poetry* (1947); *A Practical Possum* (1947); *Milton* (1947); *Notes toward the Definition of Culture* (1948); *From Poe to Valéry* (1948); *A Sermon Preached in Magdalene College Chapel* (1948); *The Aims of Poetic Drama* (1949); *The Cocktail Party* (1950); *Talk on Dante* (1950); *Poetry and Drama* (1951); *The Value and Use of Cathedrals in England Today* (1951); *"Those Who Need Privacy and Those Whose Need Is Company"* (1951); *The Film of Murder in the Cathedral* [with George Hoellering] (1952); *The Three Voices of Poetry* (1953); *American Literature and the American Language* (1953); *The Confidential Clerk* (1954); *The Cultivation of Christmas Trees* (1954); *Religious Drama: Mediaeval and Modern* (1954); *The Literature of Politics* (1955); *The Frontiers of Criticism* (1956); *On Poetry and Poets* (1957); *The Elder Statesman* (1959); *Geoffrey Faber: 1889-1961* (1961); *George Herbert* (1962); *Knowledge and Experience in the Philosophy of F. H. Bradley* (1964); *To Criticize the Critic, and Other Writings* (1965); *Poems Written in Early Youth* (1967).

Collected Works and Edited Texts

There is no uniform edition of Eliot's works or his letters. His poetry has been gathered in *Collected Poems, 1909-1962* (New York: Harcourt, Brace & World, 1963); and *The Complete Poems and Plays of T. S. Eliot* (London: Faber & Faber, 1969), which includes his *Poems Written in Early Youth*. Two important facsimiles are *The Waste Land: A Facsimile Transcript of the Original Draft, Including the Annotations of Ezra Pound*, ed. Valerie Eliot (New York: Harcourt Brace Jovanovich, 1971), which allows observation of Eliot at work on revisions; and *Four Quartets* (London: Folio Society, 1968). Eliot's plays are available in *Collected Plays* (London: Faber & Faber, 1962); and *The Complete Plays*, 1st American ed. (New York: Harcourt, Brace & World, 1967). Although Eliot's prose has not been collected, much is gathered in *Selected Essays*, new ed. (New York: Harcourt Brace, 1950); and *Selected Prose of T. S. Eliot*, ed. Frank Kermode (New York: Harcourt Brace Jovanovich, 1975). *Milton: Two Studies* (London: Faber, 1968) is a paperback reprint of a 1936 essay and a 1947 lecture.

Other Source Materials

In addition to materials in private collections, the main body of manuscripts is in several research libraries. King's College, Cambridge, and Magdalene College and the Bodleian Library at Oxford have manuscripts, typescripts, and printed editions. The Houghton Library, Harvard University, contains letters from his family and a restricted collection of unpublished letters. Further collections are at the University of Virginia, Yale University, Princeton, the University of Chicago, and the University of Texas. The last collection is described using Gallup's numbering system [*see* Bibliographies] in Alexander Sackton, *The T. S. Eliot Collection of the University of Texas at Austin* (Austin: Humanities Research Center, Univ. of Texas at Austin, 1975). Many unpublished poems and the original manuscript of *The Waste Land* described in the *Times Literary Supplement*, Nov. 7, 1978, are in the Berg Collection of the New York Public Library.

SECONDARY SOURCES

Biography

T. S. Eliot: A Symposium, eds. Richard March and Thurairajah Tambimuttu (Chicago: H. Regnery, 1949) contains reminiscences by Conrad Aiken, Clive Bell, and Wyndham Lewis. Further reminiscences are in Herbert Howarth, *Notes on Some Figures behind T. S. Eliot* (New York: Houghton Mifflin, 1964); *T. S. Eliot: The Man and His Work*, ed. Allen Tate (New York: Delacorte Press, 1966); and *Affectionately, T. S. Eliot*, eds. William Turner Levy and Victor Scherle (New York: J. B. Lippincott, 1968). A full-length account is Robert Sencourt, *T. S. Eliot: A Memoir* (New York: Dodd, Mead, 1971). Because Eliot proscribed use of many central documents during this century, critical biography has been impeded. Two biographies which view the poetry as emerging from Eliot's consuming search for salvation are Bernard Bergonzi, *T. S. Eliot* (New York: Macmillan, 1972); and Lyndall Gordon, *Eliot's Early Years* (New York: Oxford Univ. Press, 1977).

Criticism

An excellent brief essay is the pamphlet Leonard Unger, *T. S. Eliot* (Minneapolis: Univ. of Minnesota Press, 1961). Among the many useful introductions are F. O. Matthiessen, *The Achievement of T. S. Eliot: An Essay on the Nature of Poetry*, 2nd ed. (New York: Oxford Univ. Press, 1947); Elizabeth Drew, *T. S. Eliot: The Design of His Poetry* (New York: Scribner, 1949); Helen Gardner, *The Art of T. S. Eliot* (London: Cresset, 1949); Grover Smith, *T. S. Eliot's Poetry and Plays: A Study of Sources and Meaning* (Chicago: Univ. of Chicago Press, 1956); Hugh Kenner, *The Invisible Poet* (New York: McDowell, Obolensky, 1959); Philip Headings, *T. S. Eliot* (New York: Twayne, 1964); John D. Margolis, *T. S. Eliot's Intellectual Development, 1922-1939* (Chicago: Univ. of Chicago Press, 1972); Elisabeth Schneider, *T. S. Eliot: The Pattern in the Carpet* (Berkeley: Univ. of California Press, 1975); A. D. Moody, *Thomas Stearns Eliot: Poet* (Cambridge: Cambridge Univ. Press, 1976); and Stephen Spender, *T. S. Eliot* (New York: Viking, 1976), which is an outstanding introduction by Eliot's friend of thirty-five years.

Among the best collections of essays about Eliot are *T. S. Eliot: A Collection of Critical Essays*, ed. Hugh Kenner (Englewood Cliffs, NJ: Prentice-Hall, 1962); and *Eliot in His Time*, ed. A. Walton Litz (Princeton, NJ: Princeton Univ. Press, 1973).

Criticism of major individual works is contained in Helen Gardner, *The Composition of Four Quartets* (London; Boston: Faber & Faber, 1978); Derek Traversi, *T. S. Eliot: The Longer Poems* (New York: Harcourt Brace Jovanovich, 1976), which is a good overview of *The Waste Land, Ash Wednesday*, and *Four Quartets*; *A Collection of Critical Essays on The Waste Land*, ed. Jay Martin (Englewood-Cliffs, NJ: Prentice-Hall, 1968), which contains essays by Tate, Kenner, and others; Derek Traversi, *T. S. Eliot: The Longer Poems* (New York: Harcourt Brace Jovanovich, 1976), which concentrates on *The Waste Land, Ash Wednesday*, and *Four Quartets*; *The Literary Criticism of T. S. Eliot: New Essays*, ed. David Newton-de Molina (London: Athlone Press, 1977); and *T. S. Eliot: A Collection of Criticism*, ed. Linda W. Wagner (New York: McGraw-Hill, 1979), which reprints nine essays by Unger, Berzoni, Gardner, and others.

Bibliographies

A bibliographical essay by Richard M. Ludwig, "T. S. Eliot," in *Sixteen Modern American Authors*, ed. Jackson R. Bryer (Durham, NC: Duke Univ. Press, 1974), pp.181-222, provides an excellent introduction to both primary and secondary sources. The standard primary bibliography, Donald C. Gallup, *T. S. Eliot: A Bibliography*, rev. and extended ed. (New York: Harcourt, Brace & World, 1969), is invaluable for its detailed information of Eliot's books, pamphlets, translations, and periodical contributions. A useful paperback listing works by Eliot and major critical studies of them is Bradley Gunter, *The Merrill Checklist of T. S. Eliot* (Columbus, OH: Merrill, 1970). Mildred Martin, *A Half Century of Eliot Criticism* (Lewisburg: Bucknell Univ. Press, 1972) is a chronologically arranged and annotated bibliography of books and articles about Eliot in English, published from 1919 to 1965. Beatrice Ricks, *T. S. Eliot: A Bibliography of Secondary Works* (Metuchen, NJ: Scarecrow, 1980) lists studies by genre, with indexes by topic and author and brief annotations.

Reference Works

Yeats Eliot Review, Dept. of English, Univ. of Alberta, v.5, no.1, Spring 1978- (formerly *T. S. Eliot Newsletter, 1974-75* and *T. S. Eliot Review, 1975-77*) is

published twice yearly as a clearinghouse for works in progress, dissertations, bibliographical updating, and brief research papers.

RALPH (WALDO) ELLISON, 1914-

PRIMARY SOURCES

Separate Works

Invisible Man (1952); Shadow and Act (1964).

SECONDARY SOURCES

Biography

There is no book-length biography, and reliance will be on such short accounts
as Ellison's own "That Same Pain, That Same Pleasure," "The Art of Fiction," and
"The World and the Jug," which are in Shadow and Act (New York: Random House,
1964), and an interview recorded in John Hersey's collection [see Criticism], in
magazine interviews listed in Joanne Giza's essay [see Bibliographies], and in the more
general biographical works, Contemporary Authors: A Bio-Bibliographical Guide to
Current Authors and Their Works, eds. James M. Ethridge and Barbara Kopala
(Detroit: Gale, 1965); and Current Biography Yearbook, ed. Charles Moritz (Bronx,
NY: H. W. Wilson, 1969).

Criticism

Among several collections of criticism devoted to The Invisible Man are Twen-
tieth Century Interpretations of "Invisible Man," ed. John M. Reilly (Englewood
Cliffs, NJ: Prentice-Hall, 1970); The Merrill Studies in "Invisible Man," ed. Ronald
Gottesman (Columbus, OH: Merrill, 1971); A Casebook on Ralph Ellison's "Invisible
Man," ed. Joseph Trimmer (New York: Crowell, 1972); and Ralph Ellison: A Collec-
tion of Critical Essays, ed. John Hersey (Englewood Cliffs, NJ: Prentice-Hall, 1973).
An analysis of Ellison's relation to the Black Left is in William Walling, "Art and
Protest: Ralph Ellison's Invisible Man, Twenty Years After," Phylon 34 (June 1973):
120-34.

Bibliographies

The best bibliographical introduction is an essay, Joanne Giza, "Ralph Ellison,"
in Black American Writers: Bibliographical Essays, eds. M. Thomas Inge, Maurice
Duke, Jackson R. Bryer. 2v. (New York: St. Martin's Press, 1978), pp.47-71. R. S.
Lillard, "A Ralph Waldo Ellison Bibliography (1914-1967)," American Book Collector
19 (November 1968): 18-22; and Carol Polsgrove, "Addenda. . . (1914-1968),"
American Book Collector 20 (November-December 1969): 11-12, list stories, reviews,
essays, interviews, and public addresses chronologically, providing reprints of hard-to-
find periodical items. Bernard Benoit and Michel Fabre, "A Bibliography of Ralph
Ellison's Published Writings," Studies in Black Literature 2 (Autumn 1971): 25-28

provides chronological listings by genre, with some errors and omissions. A bibliography of works about Ellison is Jacqueline Covo, *The Blinking Eye: Ralph Waldo Ellison and His American, French, German and Italian Critics, 1952-1971* (Metuchen, NJ: Scarecrow, 1974).

RALPH WALDO EMERSON, 1803-1882

PRIMARY SOURCES

Separate Works

Letter to the Second Church and Society (1832); *A Historical Discourse Delivered before the Citizens of Concord, 12th September, 1835* (1835); *Nature* (1836); *The American Scholar* (1837); *An Address Delivered before the Senior Class in Divinity College, Cambridge* (1838); *An Oration Delivered before the Literary Societies of Dartmouth College* (1838); *The Method of Nature* (1841); *Essays* (1841); *Man the Reformer* (1842); *The Young American* (1844); *Nature: An Essay, and Lectures of the Times* (1844); *An Address Delivered in Concord* (1844); *Orations, Lectures and Addresses* (1844); *Essays: Second Series* (1844); *Poems* (1847); *Representative Men: Seven Lectures* (1850); *English Traits* (1856); *The Conduct of Life* (1860); *May-Day and Other Pieces* (1867); *Society and Solitude* (1870); *Letters and Social Aims* (1876); *Selected Poems* (1876); *Fortune of the Republic* (1878); *The Preacher* (1880); *Lectures and Biographical Sketches* (1884); *The Senses and the Soul* (1884); *Natural History of the Intellect and Other Papers* (1893); *Two Unpublished Essays* (1896); *Tantalus* (1903).

Collected Works and Edited Texts

The standard text has been *Complete Works*, Centenary ed., ed. Edward Waldo Emerson. 12v. (Boston: Houghton Mifflin, 1903-1904). A new twelve-volume *Collected Works*, ed. Alfred R. Ferguson, et al. (Cambridge: Harvard Univ. Press, 1971-) is underway, and available to date are *Nature, Addresses and Lectures*, v.1, and *Essays: First Series*, v.2. *The Early Lectures*, eds. Stephen E. Whicher, Robert Spiller, and Wallace E. Williams. 3v. (Harvard Univ. Press, 1959-72) prints the lectures of 1833-1842, and an edition of later lectures is in preparation. A convenient sourcebook of important critical statements is *Emerson's Literary Criticism*, ed. Eric W. Carlson (Lincoln: Univ. of Nebraska Press, 1979). Most of Emerson's correspondence is collected in *Letters*, ed. Ralph L. Rusk. 6v. (New York: Columbia Univ. Press, 1939); and *The Correspondence of Emerson and Carlyle*, ed. Joseph Slater (Columbia Univ. Press, 1964). Supplementary volumes of letters are in preparation by Eleanor M. Tilton.

An outstanding collection is in *The Journals and Miscellaneous Notebooks*, ed. William H. Gilman, et al. 14v. (Cambridge: Harvard Univ. Press, 1960-78). For a brief compilation use *The Heart of Emerson's Journals*, ed. Bliss Perry (New York: Dover, 1926; repr. 1958). Emerson's poems are being edited by Carl Strauch.

Other Source Materials

The outstanding collection of Emerson's papers is at Harvard University's Houghton Library.

SECONDARY SOURCES

Biography

The standard biography, Ralph L. Rusk, *The Life of Ralph Waldo Emerson* (New York: Scribner, 1949), is factually reliable, but should be supplemented by Gay Wilson Allen, *Waldo Emerson: A Biography* (New York: Viking, 1981), a meticulous study which uses material that has appeared since Rusk's work. In addition, Stephen E. Whicher, *Freedom and Fate: An Inner Life of Ralph Waldo Emerson* (Philadelphia: Univ. of Pennsylvania Press, 1953) establishes important trends in Emersonian criticism; and Joel Porte, *Representative Man: Ralph Waldo Emerson in His Time* (New York: Oxford Univ. Press, 1979) focuses with sensitivity on Emerson in the act of thinking. A brief introduction is Josephine Miles, *Ralph Waldo Emerson* (Minneapolis: Univ. of Minnesota Press, 1964).

Criticism

Among the many noteworthy book-length studies are George E. Woodberry, *Ralph Waldo Emerson* (New York: Macmillan, 1926, c1907); Vivian C. Hopkins, *Spires of Form: A Study of Emerson's Aesthetic Theory* (Cambridge: Harvard Univ. Press, 1965, c1951); Sherman Paul, *Emerson's Angle of Vision* (Harvard Univ. Press, 1952); Jonathan Bishop, *Emerson on the Soul* (Harvard Univ. Press, 1964); Joel Porte, *Emerson and Thoreau: Transcendentalists in Conflict* (Middletown, CT: Wesleyan Univ. Press, 1966); and David T. Porter, *Emerson and Literary Change* (Harvard Univ. Press, 1978), which emphasizes Emerson's aesthetic, rather than his philosophical, influence on later writers.

Several convenient compilations of Emerson criticism include *The Recognition of Ralph Waldo Emerson*, ed. Milton R. Konvitz (Ann Arbor: Univ. of Michigan Press, 1972), which gathers criticism since 1837; *Emerson: A Collection of Critical Essays*, eds. Milton R. Konvitz and Stephen E. Whicher (Englewood Cliffs, NJ: Prentice-Hall, 1962; repr. Westport, CT: Greenwood Press, 1978); and *Ralph Waldo Emerson: A Profile*, ed. Carl Bode (New York: Hill & Wang, 1968). For secondary material on Emerson's first book, see *Emerson's "Nature": Origins, Growth, Meaning*, 2nd ed. enl., eds. Merton M. Sealts, Jr., and Alfred R. Ferguson (Carbondale: Southern Illinois Univ. Press, 1979), which contains a reprint of the 1836 edition of "Nature."

Bibliographies

The best general review of research and criticism on Emerson is Floyd Stovall, "Ralph Waldo Emerson," in *Eight American Authors*, rev. ed., ed. James Woodress (New York: Norton, 1971), pp.37-83. Later assessments are in the annual volumes of *American Literary Scholarship*. Also helpful are Frederick Ives Carpenter, *Emerson Handbook* (New York: Hendricks House, 1953); Jackson R. Bryer and Robert A. Rees, *A Checklist of Emerson Criticism, 1951-1961* (Hartford, CT: Transcendental Books, 1964); Alfred R. Ferguson, *The Merrill Checklist of Ralph Waldo Emerson* (Columbus, OH: Merrill, 1970). Jeanetta Boswell, *Ralph Waldo Emerson and the Critics* (Metuchen, NJ: Scarecrow, 1979) is a single alphabetical checklist of all works and articles about Emerson from 1900 to 1977.

Reference Works

George Shelton Hubbell, *A Concordance to the Poems of Ralph Waldo Emerson* (New York: H. W. Wilson, 1932) gives access to the Centenary Edition of Emerson's

Complete Works, v.10. Kenneth Walter Cameron, *An Emerson Index* (Hartford, CT: Transcendental Books, 1950) is based on selected materials from journals, manuscript blotting books, business and professional records, and indexes of topics that Emerson compiled. *ESQ*, formerly *Emerson Society Quarterly*, which began in 1955, contains current bibliographies and performs other clearinghouse functions.

WILLIAM FAULKNER, 1897-1962

PRIMARY SOURCES

Separate Works

The Marble Faun (1924); *Soldier's Pay* (1926); *Mosquitoes* (1927); *The Sound and the Fury* (1929); *Sartoris* (1929); *As I Lay Dying* (1930); *Sanctuary* (1931); *These 13* (1931); *Idyll in the Desert* (1931); *Salmagundi* (1932); *This Earth* (1932); *Miss Zilphia Gant* (1932); *Light in August* (1932); *A Green Bough* (1933); *Doctor Martino and Other Stories* (1934); *Pylon* (1935); *Absalom, Absalom!* (1936); *The Unvanquished* (1938); *The Wild Palms* (1939); *The Hamlet* (1940); *Go Down, Moses, and Other Stories* (1942); *Intruder in the Dust* (1948); *Knight's Gambit* (1949); *Collected Stories* (1950); *Requiem for a Nun* (1951); *A Fable* (1954); *Big Woods* (1955); *The Town* (1957); *Requiem for a Nun: A Play from the Novel* [with Ruth Ford] (1959); *The Mansion* (1959); *The Reivers* (1962); *Flags in the Dust* (1973); *The Marionettes* [play] (1978).

Collected Works and Edited Texts

There is no collected edition of Faulkner's works, and the numerous reissues of Random House are among the most reliable. *Uncollected Stories of William Faulkner*, ed. Joseph Blotner (New York: Random House, 1979) makes available many stories that are the originals of later revisions and some previously unpublished stories. Another important collection is *Essays, Speeches and Public Letters*, ed. James B. Meriwether (Random House, 1965). Faulkner's letters are available as *The Faulkner-Cowley File: Letters and Memories, 1944-1962*, ed. Malcolm Cowley (New York: Viking, 1966), which includes correspondence in connection with the editing of the *Portable Faulkner* (Viking, 1946); and as *Selected Letters of William Faulkner*, ed. Joseph L. Blotner (Random House, 1976). *The Marionettes* (Charlottesville: Univ. Press of Virginia, 1978) is a facsimile of a play, hand-lettered and hand-bound in 1920. Transcripts of interviews and discussions are in *Faulkner at Nagano*, ed. Robert A. Jelliffe (Tokyo: Kenkyusha, 1956); *Faulkner in the University: Class Conferences at the University of Virginia, 1957-1958*, eds. Frederick L. Gwynn and Joseph L. Blotner (Univ. Press of Virginia, 1959); *Faulkner at West Point*, eds. Joseph L. Fant and Robert Ashley (Random House, 1964); and in *The Lion in the Garden*, eds. James B. Meriwether and Michael Millgate (Random House, 1968), which records interviews between 1926 and 1962. *Mississippi Quarterly* annually prints previously unpublished works by Faulkner in a special Faulkner number.

Other Source Materials

The most extensive collections of Faulkner are at the universities of Virginia, Charlottesville, Texas at Austin, Princeton, Yale, and Tulane. Three valuable catalogs of the collections at Virginia and Tulane are Linton Reynolds Massey, *Man Working, 1919-1962: William Faulkner: A Catalogue of the William Faulkner Collections at the University of Virginia* (Charlottesville: Bibliographical Society of the Univ. of Virginia, 1968); Joan St. C. Crane and Anne E. H. Freudenberg, *Man Collecting: Manuscripts and Printed Works of William Faulkner in the University of Virginia Library* (Charlottesville: Univ. of Virginia, 1975); and Thomas Bonner, *William Faulkner: The William B. Wisdom Collection in the Howard-Tilton Memorial Library, Tulane University*, ed. Guillermo Nañez Falcón (New Orleans: Tulane Univ. Libraries, 1980).

SECONDARY SOURCES

Biography

Joseph L. Blotner, *Faulkner, A Biography*, 2v. (New York: Random House, 1974) was the first detailed life. A perceptive study which examines both life and works is David L. Minter, *William Faulkner: His Life and Work* (Baltimore: Johns Hopkins Univ. Press, 1980). For illuminating recollections by the designer of eight Faulkner books, see Evelyn Harter Glick, *The Making of William Faulkner's Books* (Columbia: Univ. of South Carolina, Southern Studies Program, 1979).

Criticism

Meriwether (*see* Bibliographies) warns that much Faulkner criticism is unreliable. A brief introduction to Faulkner's life and writing is by Michael Millgate, *William Faulkner*, rev. ed. (New York: Barnes & Noble, 1966). Millgate has also contributed the landmark *The Achievement of William Faulkner* (New York: Random House, 1966; repr. New York: Vintage, 1971) which combines biography and a full critical discussion of the novels and short stories. Cleanth Brooks, *William Faulkner: The Yoknapatawpha Country* (New Haven, CT: Yale Univ. Press, 1963) contains fourteen important essays about the complex rural life upon which Faulkner drew for his literary milieu. Studies of value which give focus to particular aspects of Faulkner's work are Warren Beck, *Man in Motion: Faulkner's Trilogy* (Madison: Univ. of Wisconsin Press, 1961), which is an examination of the Snopes trilogy as a study of "ubiquitous evil and its opposition"; and John W. Hunt, *William Faulkner: Art in Theological Tension* (Syracuse, NY: Syracuse Univ. Press, 1965), which sees tension between stoic and Christian values in *The Sound and the Fury, Absalom, Absalom!*, and "The Bear." André Bleikasten, *Faulkner's as I Lay Dying* (Bloomington: Indiana Univ. Press, 1973) and François Pitavy, *Faulkner's Light in August* (Indiana Univ. Press, 1973) are comprehensive scholarly and critical studies, translated from the French. Panthea Reid Broughton, *William Faulkner: The Abstract and the Actual* (Baton Rouge: Louisiana State Univ. Press, 1974) examines use of abstraction by Faulkner and his characters as a way of understanding reality. John T. Irwin, *Doubling and Incest: Repetition and Revenge* (Baltimore: Johns Hopkins Univ. Press, 1975) demonstrates recurring motifs in the novels. Irving Howe, *William Faulkner: A Critical Study*, 3rd ed. (Chicago: Univ. of Chicago Press, 1975) is a clear study of strengths and weaknesses in the fiction; Bruce Kawin, *Faulkner and Film* (New York: Ungar, 1977) examines the relation between cinematique technique and the works; Arthur F. Kinney, *Faulkner's Narrative Poetics: Style as Vision* (Amherst: Univ. of Massachusetts Press, 1978) interprets the relation between narrative viewpoint and form; and Cleanth Brooks, *William Faulkner: Toward Yoknapatawpha and Beyond* (New Haven,

CT: Yale Univ. Press, 1978) deals with the early poetry and the non-Yoknapatawpha works. An excellent collection of criticism is *Faulkner: A Collection of Critical Essays*, ed. Robert Penn Warren (Englewood Cliffs, NJ: Prentice-Hall, 1966).

Bibliographies

A lucid bibliographical overview of Faulkner's scholarship is James B. Meriwether, "William Faulkner," in *Sixteen Modern American Authors*, ed. Jackson R. Bryer (Durham, NC: Duke Univ. Press, 1974), pp.223-75. There is no definitive bibliography of primary sources, and the most important listing is James B. Meriwether, *William Faulkner: A Check List* (Princeton, NJ: Princeton Univ. Press, 1957) and its supplement, *The Literary Career of William Faulkner: A Bibliographical Study* (Princeton Univ. Press, 1961). Thomas L. McHaney, *William Faulkner: A Reference Guide* (Boston: G. K. Hall, 1976) is an invaluable chronologically arranged, helpfully annotated bibliography of Faulkner criticism that is more useful than Beatrice Ricks, *William Faulkner: A Bibliography of Secondary Works* (Metuchen, NJ: Scarecrow, 1981), with its primary grouping by genre and subarrangement by Faulkner's titles and critics' names.

Reference Works

A guide to Faulkner characters and places containing the fewest inaccuracies is Robert W. Kirk and Marvin Klotz, *Faulkner's People: A Complete Guide and Index* (Berkeley: Univ. of California Press, 1963). Calvin S. Brown, *Glossary of Faulkner's South* (New Haven, CT: Yale Univ. Press, 1976) glosses every southern phrase or reference, clearly explaining the basis of his decisions. *The Faulkner Concordances*, ed. Jack L. Capps (West Point: published by the Faulkner Concordance Advisory Board with the support of the Faculty Development and Research Fund, U.S. Military Academy; distr. by Univ. Microfilms International, Ann Arbor, MI, 1977-) is underway. *Faulkner Studies* 1 (1980)- is an annual compilation of research, criticism, and reviews, published from the University of Miami, Coral Gables.

F(RANCIS) SCOTT (KEY) FITZGERALD, 1896-1940

PRIMARY SOURCES

Separate Works

This Side of Paradise (1920); *Flappers and Philosophers* (1920); *Tales of the Jazz Age* (1922); *The Beautiful and the Damned* (1922); *The Vegetable; Or, From President to Postman* (1923); *The Great Gatsby* (1925); *All the Sad Young Men* (1926); *Tender Is the Night* (1934); *Taps at Reveille* (1935); *The Last Tycoon: An Unfinished Novel* (1941); *The Crack-Up* (1945); *Afternoon of an Author* (1957).

Collected Works and Edited Texts

There is no collected edition of Fitzgerald's works, and *The Bodley Head Scott Fitzgerald*, 6v. (London: Bodley Head, 1958-63), which collects all the novels and selected essays and short stories, is the most representative body of his work. Other important collections are *Afternoon of an Author*, ed. Arthur Mizener (Princeton, NJ: Princeton Univ. Library, 1957), which gathers previously uncollected stories and essays; *The Apprentice Fiction of F. Scott Fitzgerald, 1909-1917,* ed. John Kuehl (New Brunswick, NJ: Rutgers Univ. Press, 1965); and *F. Scott Fitzgerald in His Own Time: A Miscellany,* eds. Matthew J. Bruccoli and Jackson R. Bryer (Kent, OH: Kent State Univ. Press, 1971), which contains a selection of Fitzgerald's work, together with interviews, reviews, and essays by critics, characterizing the contemporary reception of his writing. For additional previously uncollected fiction, see *Bits of Paradise: 21 Uncollected Stories by F. Scott Fitzgerald and Zelda Fitzgerald,* selected by Scottie Fitzgerald Smith and Matthew J. Bruccoli (London: Bodley Head, 1973); *The Basil and Josephine Stories,* eds. Jackson R. Bryer and John Kuehl (New York: Scribner, 1973); and *The Price Was High,* ed. Matthew J. Bruccoli (New York: Harcourt Brace Jovanovich, 1979). *The Crack-Up,* ed. Edmund Wilson (Norfolk, CT: New Directions, 1945) collects unpublished letters, notebooks, and other writings; *The Romantic Egoists,* eds. Matthew J. Bruccoli, Scottie Fitzgerald Smith, and Joan P. Kerr (Scribner, 1974) is a chronologically arranged pictorial autobiography from the scrapbooks and albums of Scott and Zelda Fitzgerald, with helpful commentary interpolated. Four previously uncollected dramas are in *F. Scott Fitzgerald's St. Paul Plays, 1911-1914,* ed. Alan Margolies (Princeton, NJ: Princeton Univ. Library, 1978). *The Notebooks of F. Scott Fitzgerald,* ed. Matthew Bruccoli (Harcourt Brace Jovanovich/Bruccoli Clark, 1978) are topically arranged and include references to entries in the fiction.

Correspondence is collected in *The Letters of F. Scott Fitzgerald,* ed. Andrew Turnbull (Scribner, 1963); *Dear Scott/Dear Max: The Fitzgerald-Perkins Correspondence,* eds. John Kuehl and Jackson R. Bryer (Scribner, 1971); *As Ever, Scott Fitz: Letters between F. Scott Fitzgerald and His Literary Agent, Harold Ober,* eds. Matthew J. Bruccoli and Jennifer McCabe Atkinson (Philadelphia: Lippincott, 1972); and *Correspondence of F. Scott Fitzgerald,* eds. Matthew J. Bruccoli and Margaret M. Duggan (New York: Random House, 1980).

Other Source Materials

The most encompassing collection of papers and manuscripts is in Princeton University Library.

SECONDARY SOURCES

Biography

An extensively researched life is Matthew J. Bruccoli, *Some Sort of Epic Grandeur: The Life of F. Scott Fitzgerald* (New York: Harcourt Brace Jovanovich, 1981). Two other important biographies are Arthur Mizener, *The Far Side of Paradise* (Boston: Houghton Mifflin, 1951; rev. ed. 1965), a closely documented life and analysis of Fitzgerald's works; and Andrew W. Turnbull, *Scott Fitzgerald* (New York: Scribner, 1962), which focuses closely on Fitzgerald's personality. Sheila Graham and Gerold Frank, *Beloved Infidel* (New York: Holt, 1958) is important for its personal reminiscences of Fitzgerald during his last years in Hollywood; and Nancy Milford, *Zelda* (New York: Harper & Row, 1970) provides documentation, though little analysis, of Fitzgerald's relationship with his wife. *Scott and Ernest: The Authority of Failure and the Authority of Success,* ed. Matthew J. Bruccoli (New York: Random House, 1978) gathers letters, reminiscences, interviews, and published research to document the authors' complex relationship and also offers clarifying commentary.

Criticism

For reliable introductions, see the pamphlet Charles E. Shain, *F. Scott Fitzgerald* (Minneapolis: Univ. of Minnesota Press, 1961); Kenneth Eble, *F. Scott Fitzgerald*, rev. ed. (New York: Twayne, 1977); and Rose Adrienne Gallo, *F. Scott Fitzgerald* (New York: Ungar, 1978).

Full-length studies are William Goldhurst, *F. Scott Fitzgerald and His Contemporaries* (Cleveland, OH: World Pub. Co., 1963), which traces the influence of Edmund Wilson, H. L. Mencken, Ring Lardner, and Ernest Hemingway; James E. Miller, Jr., *F. Scott Fitzgerald: His Art and His Technique* (New York: New York Univ. Press, 1964), which analyzes literary influences in Fitzgerald's work; and Sergio Perosa, *The Art of F. Scott Fitzgerald* (Ann Arbor: Univ. of Michigan Press, 1965), which traces themes in the works. Richard D. Lehan, *F. Scott Fitzgerald and the Craft of Fiction* (Carbondale: Southern Illinois Univ. Press, 1966) and Robert Sklar, *F. Scott Fitzgerald: The Last Laocoön* (New York: Oxford Univ. Press, 1967) both examine Fitzgerald's work against the background of the romantic tradition. A more specialized study, which follows Fitzgerald's process of composition through various drafts, is Matthew J. Bruccoli, *The Composition of Tender Is the Night* (Pittsburgh: Univ. of Pittsburgh Press, 1963). Matthew J. Bruccoli, *"The Last of the Novelists": F. Scott Fitzgerald and the Last Tycoon* (Carbondale: Southern Illinois Univ. Press, 1977) points out that the working drafts were represented by Edmund Wilson as a finished novel.

Useful collections of criticism are *F. Scott Fitzgerald: The Man and His Work*, ed. Alfred Kazin (Cleveland, OH: World Pub. Co., 1951); *F. Scott Fitzgerald: A Collection of Critical Essays*, ed. Arthur Mizener (Englewood Cliffs, NJ: Prentice-Hall, 1963); *Profile of F. Scott Fitzgerald*, ed. Matthew J. Bruccoli (Columbus, OH: Merrill, 1971); *F. Scott Fitzgerald: A Collection of Criticism*, ed. Kenneth E. Eble (New York: McGraw-Hill, 1973); and *F. Scott Fitzgerald: The Critical Reception*, ed. Jackson R. Bryer (New York: B. Franklin, 1978).

Bibliographies

Fitzgerald's works are bibliographically recorded in Matthew J. Bruccoli, *F. Scott Fitzgerald: A Descriptive Bibliography* (Pittsburgh: Univ. of Pittsburgh Press, 1972) and its *Supplement* (Univ. of Pittsburgh Press, 1980). A lucid essay by Jackson R. Bryer, "F. Scott Fitzgerald," in *Sixteen Modern American Authors*, ed. Jackson R. Bryer (Durham, NC: Duke Univ. Press, 1974), pp.277-321, is the best bibliographic introduction to work published through 1973. For Fitzgerald's reputation abroad, see Linda Stanley, *The Foreign Critical Reception of F. Scott Fitzgerald: An Analysis and Annotated Bibliography* (Westport, CT: Greenwood, 1980).

Reference Works

Fitzgerald/Hemingway Annual, 1969-1979, until its suspension, provided current updating for critical, biographical, and bibliographical material. Andrew T. Crosland, *A Concordance to F. Scott Fitzgerald's "The Great Gatsby"* (Detroit: Bruccoli/Clark, Gale, 1975) is based on the first printing, 1925, and also keyed to the Scribner Library edition.

BENJAMIN FRANKLIN, 1706-1790

PRIMARY SOURCES

Separate Works

A listing of separate works is difficult because many important items were not separately printed. This list is based on that given in Spiller.

The *Dogood Papers* (1722); Preface to the *New England Courant* (1723); *A Dissertation on Liberty and Necessity* (1725); *Journal of a Voyage from London to Philadelphia* (1726); *Articles of Belief and Acts of Religion* (1728); *Rules for a Club* (1728); *Busybody Papers* (1728-29); *A Modest Enquiry into . . . Paper Currency* (1729); preface to *Pennsylvania Gazette* (1729); *A Dialogue between Philocles and Horatio* (1730); *A Second Dialogue* (1730); *A Witch Trial at Mount Holly* (1730); *An Apology for Printers* (1731; introduction to Logan's *Cato's Moral Distiches* (1735); *Essay on Human Vanity* (1735); *A Proposal for Promoting Useful Knowledge* (1743); *An Account of the New Invented Pennsylvania Fire-Places* (1744); preface to *Logan's Translation of Cicero's Cato Major* (1744); *Advice to a Young Man on Choosing a Mistress* (1745); *Reflections on Courtship and Marriage* (1746); *Plain Truth* (1747); *Proposals Relating to the Education of Youth in Pensilvania* (1749); *Experiments and Observations on Electricity* (1751-53); *Poor Richard's Almanack* (1732-64); *Idea of the English School* (1751); *Some Account of the Pennsylvania Hospital* (1754); *An Act for the Better Ordering and Regulating. . .for Military Purposes* (1755); *A Dialogue between X, Y, and Z* (1755); *Observations Concerning the Increase of Mankind* (1755); *Plan for Settling the Western Colonies* (1756?); *The Way to Wealth* (1757); *Some Account of. . .Small-Pox* (1759); *The Interest of Great Britain Considered* (1760); *Advice to a Young Tradesman* (1762); *A Parable against Persecution* (1764); *Cool Thoughts* (1764); *A Narrative of the Late Massacres* (1764); preface to *The Speech of Joseph Galloway, Esq.* (1764); *The Examination of Dr. Benjamin Franklin* (1766); *Physical and Meteorological Observations* (1766); *Remarks and Facts Concerning American Paper Money* (1767); *Causes of the American Discontent before 1768* (1768); preface to *Dickinson's Letters from a Farmer* (1768); *Art of Swimming* (1768); *A Scheme for a New Alphabet* (1768); *An Edict of the King of Prussia* (1773); *Rules by Which a Great Empire May Be Reduced to a Small One* (1773); notes to *Whatley's Principles of Trade* (1774); *Account of Negotiations in London* (1775); *Articles of Confederation* (1775); *The Ephemera* (1778); *The Morals of Chess* (1779); *The Whistle* (1779); *Dialogue between Franklin and the Gout* (1780); *The Handsome and the Deformed Leg* (1780); *Journal of the Negotiations for Peace* (1782); *Information to Those Who Would Remove to America* (1784); *Remarks Concerning the Savages of North America* (1784); *Maritime Observations* (1785); *Observations on the Causes and Cure of Smoky Chimneys* (1785); *Art of Procuring Pleasant Dreams* (1786); *Observations Relative. . .to the Academy in Philadelphia* (1789); *Autobiography* (1791-1868).

Collected Works

The *Papers of Benjamin Franklin*, ed. Leonard W. Labaree (New Haven, CT: Yale Univ. Press, 1959-) are being published. The definitive edition of Franklin's autobiography is available as *The Autobiography of Benjamin Franklin*, ed. Leonard W. Labaree, et al. (Yale Univ. Press, 1964). A text and facsimile of later essays printed on Franklin's own press is *The Bagatelles from Passy* (New York: Eakins, 1967). A reliable single-volume anthology is *Benjamin Franklin: Representative Selections*, rev. ed., eds. Chester E. Jorgenson and Frank Luther Mott (New York: Hill & Wang, 1962). *The Sayings of Poor Richard: The Prefaces, Proverbs and Poems*, ed. Paul Leicester Ford (New York: G. P. Putnam, 1890; repr. New York: Burt Franklin Reprints, 1975) were originally printed in *Poor Richard's Almanacs* for 1773-1758.

Other Source Materials

The major collections of manuscripts are at the American Philosophical Society, the Library of Congress, the University of Pennsylvania, and Yale University.

SECONDARY SOURCES

Biography

The standard biography is Carl Van Doren, *Benjamin Franklin* (New York: Viking, 1938). Two other carefully documented accounts are by Alfred Owen Aldridge, *Benjamin Franklin: Philosopher & Man* (Philadelphia: Lippincott, 1965); and his more specialized *Franklin and His French Contemporaries* (New York: New York Univ. Press, 1957).

Criticism

A clear and accurate introduction is Theodore Hornberger, *Benjamin Franklin* (Minneapolis: Univ. of Minnesota Press, 1962). Important critical views are in Bruce Granger, *Benjamin Franklin: An American Man of Letters* (Ithaca, NY: Cornell Univ. Press, 1964); and Lewis Leary, "Benjamin Franklin and the Requirements of Literature in America," in *Soundings: Some Early American Writers* (Athens: Univ. of Georgia Press, 1975). Alfred Owen Aldridge, *Benjamin Franklin and Nature's God* (Durham, NC: Duke Univ. Press, 1967) has considered Franklin's religious philosophy. A well-selected anthology of critical articles is *Benjamin Franklin: A Collection of Critical Essays*, ed. Brian M. Barbour (Englewood Cliffs, NJ: Prentice-Hall, 1979).

Bibliographies

The best bibliographical introduction is Bruce Granger, "Benjamin Franklin," in *Fifteen American Authors before 1900*, eds. Robert A. Rees and Earl N. Harbert (Madison: Univ. of Wisconsin Press, 1971), pp.185-206. The only other bibliography of note is Paul Leicester Ford, *Franklin Bibliography: A List of Books Written by, or Relating to Benjamin Franklin* (Brooklyn, NY: privately printed, 1889).

Reference Works

Frances M. Barbour, *A Concordance to the Sayings in Franklin's Poor Richard* (Detroit: Gale, 1974) provides access by key words to the *Almanacks, 1733-1758*.

MARY E(LEANOR) WILKINS FREEMAN, 1852-1930

PRIMARY SOURCES

Separate Works

Decorative Plaques (1883); The Adventures of Ann (1886); A Humble Romance (1887); A New England Nun and Other Stories (1891); The Pot of Gold and Other Stories (1892); Young Lucretia and Other Stories (1892); Giles Corey, Yeoman (1893); Jane Field (1893); Pembroke (1894); Comfort Pease and Her Gold Ring (1895); Madelon (1896); Jerome: A Poor Man (1897); Once upon a Time, and Other Child-Verses (1897); Silence and Other Stories (1898); The People of Our Neighborhood (1898); In Colonial Times (1899); The Jamesons (1899); The Heart's Highway (1900); The Love of Parson Lord and Other Stories (1900); Understudies (1901); The Portion of Labor (1901); Six Trees (1903); The Wind in the Rose-Bush (1903); The Givers (1904); The Debtor (1905); "Doc" Gordon (1906); By the Light of the Soul (1906); The Fair Lavinia (1907); The Shoulders of Atlas (1908); The Winning Lady (1909); The Green Door (1910); The Butterfly House (1912); The Yates Pride (1912); The Copy-Cat and Other Stories (1914); An Alabaster Box [with Florence M. Kingsley] (1917); Edgewater People (1918).

Collected Works and Edited Texts

Two collections are The Best Stories of Mary E. Wilkins, ed. Henry W. Lanier (New York: Harper, 1927); and A Humble Romance and Other Stories, ed. Clarence Gohdes (Richmond, VA: Garrett, 1969). A modernized text is Pembroke, ed. Perry D. Westbrook (New Haven, CT: College and Univ. Press, 1971).

SECONDARY SOURCES

Biography and Criticism

Two full-length studies combining biography and criticism are Edward Foster, Mary E. Wilkins Freeman (New York: Hendrick's House, 1956); and Perry D. Westbrook, Mary E. Wilkins Freeman (New York: Twayne, 1967).

Bibliographies

An extensive primary bibliography is in Jacob Blanck, Bibliography of American Literature, (New Haven, CT: Yale Univ. Press, 1959), v.3, pp.224-43. For material about Freeman, see the bibliographies in Foster and Westbrook (see Biography and Criticism) and the yearly reviews in American Literary Scholarship.

ROBERT (LEE) FROST, 1874-1963

PRIMARY SOURCES

Separate Works

A Boy's Will (1913); North of Boston (1914); Mountain Interval (1916); New Hampshire: A Poem with Notes and Grace Notes (1923); West-Running Brook (1928); A Way Out (1929); The Cow's in the Corn (1929); Two Letters Written on His Undergraduate Days at Dartmouth College in 1892 (1931); Three Poems (1935); A Further

Range (1936); *A Witness Tree* (1942); *A Masque of Reason* (1945); *Steeple Bush* (1947); *A Masque of Mercy* (1947).

Collected Works and Edited Texts

The Poetry of Robert Frost, ed. Edward Connery Lathem (New York: Holt, Rinehart & Sinston, 1969) is the most complete collection of Frost's poetry and incorporates *The Complete Poems* (New York: H. Holt, 1949); and his last volume, *In the Clearing* (Holt, Rinehart & Winston, 1962). Some versions, revised by Frost, are in *Selected Poems of Robert Frost* (Holt, Rinehart & Winston, 1963). Several noteworthy editions described in Cook's bibliographic essay (*see* Bibliographies) contain important prefatory essays by Frost.

Frost's prose has received attention in eleven of his early essays on farming, as *Robert Frost: Farm Poultryman*, eds. Edward Connery Lathem and Lawrance Thompson (Hanover, NH: Dartmouth Publications, 1963); and his critical essays are collected in *Selected Prose*, eds. Hyde Cox and Edward Connery Lathem (Holt, Rinehart & Winston, 1966).

Letters are gathered in several collections, *The Letters of Robert Frost to Louis Untermeyer*, ed. Louis Untermeyer (Holt, Rinehart & Winston, 1963); *Robert Frost and John Bartlett: The Record of a Friendship*, ed. Margaret Bartlett (Holt, Rinehart & Winston, 1963); *Selected Letters of Robert Frost*, ed. Lawrance Thompson (Holt, Rinehart & Winston, 1964); *Robert Frost and Sidney Cox: Forty Years of Friendship*, ed. William R. Evans (Hanover, NH: Univ. Press of New England, 1981); and *Family Letters of Robert Frost and Elinor Frost*, ed. Arnold Grade (Albany: State Univ. of New York Press, 1972).

Other Source Materials

Frost's manuscripts are widely scattered in many libraries which are conveniently listed in Cook's bibliographical essay (*see* Bibliographies). Interviews and conversations with Frost are collected in Daniel Smythe, *Robert Frost Speaks* (New York: Twayne, 1964); Louis Mertins, *Robert Frost: Life and Talks-Walking* (Norman: Univ. of Oklahoma Press, 1965); and Edward Connery Lathem, *Interviews with Robert Frost* (New York: Holt, Rinehart & Winston, 1966).

SECONDARY SOURCES

Biography

The authorized biography is Lawrance Thompson, *Robert Frost: The Early Years, 1874-1915* (New York: Holt, Rinehart & Winston, 1966); and *Robert Frost: The Years of Triumph, 1915-1938* (Holt, Rinehart & Winston, 1970). The third volume, completed from Thompson's materials after his death, by R. H. Winnick, is *Robert Frost: The Later Years, 1938-1963* (Holt, Rinehart & Winston, 1977). In addition, see a sympathetic tribute, Sidney Cox, *A Swinger of Birches: A Portrait of Robert Frost* (New York: New York Univ. Press, 1957); and two brief biographies, Philip L. Gerber, *Robert Frost* (New York: Twayne, 1966); and Lawrance Thompson, *Robert Frost*, rev. ed. (Minneapolis: Univ. of Minnesota Press, 1967).

Criticism

Two critical introductions are Lawrance Thompson, *Fire and Ice: The Art and Thought of Robert Frost* (New York: Holt, 1942); and James L. Potter, *Robert Frost*

Handbook (Union Park: Pennsylvania State Univ. Press, 1980), which draws on later scholarship. Other important estimates are Reginald Cook, *The Dimensions of Robert Frost* (New York: Rinehart, 1958); George W. Nitchie, *Human Values in the Poetry of Robert Frost* (Durham, NC: Duke Univ. Press, 1960), which takes an adverse stance; Radcliffe Squires, *The Major Themes of Robert Frost* (Ann Arbor: Univ. of Michigan Press, 1963); Reuben A. Brower, *The Poetry of Robert Frost: Constellations of Intention* (New York: Oxford Univ. Press, 1963); and Richard Poirier, *Robert Frost: The Work of Knowing* (Oxford Univ. Press, 1977), which indicates the influence of Emerson and William James.

Collections of criticism which should be consulted are *Recognition of Robert Frost*, ed. Richard Thornton (New York: Holt, 1937) for Frost's early reception; *Robert Frost: An Introduction*, eds. Robert A. Greenberg and James G. Hepburn (New York: Holt, Rinehart & Winston, 1961), which contains poetry, criticism, and reviews; and *Robert Frost: A Collection of Critical Essays*, ed. James M. Cox (Englewood Cliffs, NJ: Prentice-Hall, 1962): *Frost: Centennial Essays*, ed. Committee on the Frost Centennial of the Univ. of Mississippi (Jackson: Univ. Press of Mississippi, 1974) gathers forty important essays; *Frost Centennial Essays II*, ed. Jac Tharpe (Univ. Press of Mississippi, 1976) adds twenty-two essays; and *Frost Centennial Essays III*, ed. Jac Tharpe (Univ. Press of Mississippi, 1976) continues the series. *Robert Frost: The Critical Reception*, ed. Linda W. Wagner (New York: B. Franklin, 1977) is a repository of American reviews of Frost's major collections; and *Robert Frost: Studies of the Poetry*, ed. Kathryn Gibbs Harris (Boston: G. K. Hall, 1979) collects fifteen essays.

Bibliographies

The best survey of Frost scholarship is Reginald L. Cook, in *Sixteen Modern American Authors*, ed. Jackson R. Bryer (Durham, NC: Duke Univ. Press, 1974). Primary bibliographies are the somewhat dated W. B. Shubrick Clymer and Charles R. Green, *Robert Frost: A Bibliography* (Amherst, MA: Jones Library, 1937); and Uma Parameswaran, "Robert Frost: A Bibliography of Articles and Books, 1958-1964," *Bulletin of Bibliography* (January-April; May-August, 1967): 46-48; 58; 69, 72. Joan St. C. Crane, *Robert Frost: A Descriptive Catalog of Books and Manuscripts in the Clifton Waller Barrett Library, University of Virginia* (Charlottesville: Univ. Press of Virginia, 1974) is the most comprehensive primary bibliography. Donald J. Greiner, *Robert Frost: The Poet and His Critics* (Chicago: American Library Association, 1974) is a guide to sixty years of writing about Frost; and Frank Lentricchia and Melissa Christensen Lentricchia, *Robert Frost: A Bibliography, 1913-1974* (Metuchen, NJ: Scarecrow, 1976) adds to the earlier bibliographies of primary materials and also provides an important secondary bibliography.

Reference

A Robert Frost Newsletter, 1977- is published annually in November-December and acts as a clearinghouse for information on activities of Frost scholars. Edward Connery Lathem, *A Concordance to the Poetry of Robert Frost* (New York: Holt Information Systems, 1971) is based on Lathem's standard edition (1969).

(SARAH) MARGARET FULLER (OSSOLI), 1810-1850

PRIMARY SOURCES

Separate Works

Conversations with Goethe [translation from the German of Eckermann] (1939); *Günderode* [translation of Bettina Brentano's correspondence with Günderode] (1842); *Summer on the Lakes, in 1843* (1844); *Woman in the Nineteenth Century* (1845); *Papers on Literature and Art* (1846); *Memoirs* (1852); *At Home and Abroad* (1856); *Life without and Life within; Or, Reviews, Narratives, Essays, and Poems* (1860).

Collected Works and Edited Texts

Collections of Fuller's works are *Writings of Margaret Fuller*, ed. Mason Wade (New York: Viking, 1941), which includes *Summer on the Lakes, Woman in the Nineteenth Century*, critical essays from the *Dial* and the New York *Tribune, Tribune* letters, and twenty-five other letters; *Margaret Fuller, American Romantic: A Selection from Her Writings and Correspondence*, ed. Perry Miller (Garden City, NY: Doubleday, 1963); *The Woman and the Myth: Margaret Fuller's Life and Writings*, ed. Bell Gale Chevigny (Westbury, NY: Feminist Press, 1976), which is a selection of Fuller's writings linked by Chevigny's comments; and *Margaret Fuller: Essays on American Life and Letters*, ed. Joel Myerson (New Haven, CT: College and Univ. Press, 1978), which contains carefully edited selections from the writings, including reviews and an excellent biographical introduction. Caroline W. Healey Dall, *Margaret and Her Friends; Or, Ten Conversations with Margaret Fuller upon the Mythology of the Greeks and Its Expression in Art* (Boston: Roberts, 1895) is a report of discussions held at the house of the Rev. George Ripley, beginning March 1, 1841.

Robert N. Hudspeth is compiling a full edition of letters. Among available collections of correspondence are *Love Letters of Margaret Fuller, 1845-1846*, ed. Julia Ward Howe (New York: Appleton, 1903); and *The Letters of James Freeman Clarke to Margaret Fuller*, ed. John Wesley Thomas (Hamburg: Cram, de Gruyter, 1957). An edited and bowdlerized version of Fuller's letters and diaries is *The Memoirs of Margaret Fuller Ossoli*, eds. W. H. Channing, James Freeman Clarke, Ralph Waldo Emerson. 2v. (Boston: Phillips, Sampson, 1852). A facsimile edition with an introduction by Madeleine B. Stern and textual apparatus by Joel Myerson is available for *Woman in the Nineteenth Century* (Columbus: Univ. of South Carolina Press, 1980).

Other Source Materials

Other sources of Fuller's papers are collections at the Boston Public Library, Fruitlands Museum, and Harvard University.

SECONDARY SOURCES

Biography

Mason Wade, *Margaret Fuller: Whetstone of Genius* (New York: Viking, 1940) is a reliable introductory biography. An excellent general account of both the life and works is Arthur W. Brown, *Margaret Fuller* (New York: Twayne, 1964), and a carefully documented, fictionalized life is Madeleine B. Stern, *The Life of Margaret*

Fuller (New York: E. P. Dutton, 1942). Other works which are more popular and less carefully documented are Faith Chipperfield, *In Quest of Love: The Life and Death of Margaret Fuller* (New York: Coward, McCann, 1957); and Josephine Jay Deiss, *The Roman Years of Margaret Fuller* (New York: Crowell, 1969), which is an account of the Italian years based on her letters to the *Tribune.* Paula Blanchard, *Margaret Fuller: From Transcendentalism to Revolution* (New York: Delacorte Press/S. Lawrence, 1978); and Margaret Vanderhaar Allen, *The Achievement of Margaret Fuller* (University Park: Pennsylvania State Univ. Press, 1979) place Fuller in a milieu dominated by men such as Emerson and Thoreau.

Criticism

An outstanding collection of reprinted and new criticism that includes reviews from 1840 to the present is *Critical Essays on Margaret Fuller*, ed. Joel Myerson (Boston: G. K. Hall, 1980). Myerson's overview essay on scholarship and criticism is the best guide to criticism in dissertations and journals. A scholarly, book-length study of a single work is Marie Mitchell Oleson Urbanski, *Margaret Fuller's Woman in the Nineteenth Century: A Literary Study of Form and Content, of Sources and Influence* (Westport, CT: Greenwood, 1980).

Bibliographies

The two most scholarly bibliographies, both by Joel Myerson, are *Margaret Fuller: A Descriptive Bibliography* (Pittsburgh: Univ. of Pittsburgh Press, 1978), which employs analytical descriptions of the books and facsimiles of title pages and cites all known articles by Fuller in magazines, newspapers, and collections; and *Margaret Fuller: An Annotated Secondary Bibliography* (New York: Burt Franklin, 1977), which is a chronological listing that contains succinct evaluative annotations for criticism published between 1834 and 1975.

(HANNIBAL) HAMLIN GARLAND, 1860-1940

PRIMARY SOURCES

Separate Works

Under the Wheel: A Modern Play in Six Scenes (1890); *Main-Travelled Roads* (1891); *A Member of the Third House* (1892); *Jason Edwards: An Average Man* (1892); *A Little Norsk: Or, Ol' Pap's Flaxen* (1892); *A Spoil of Office* (1892); *Prairie Folks* (1893); *Prairie Songs* (1893); *Crumbling Idols* (1894); *Rose of Dutcher's Coolly* (1895); *Wayside Courtships* (1897); *Ulysses S. Grant: His Life and Character* (1898); *The Spirit of Sweetwater* (1898); *The Trail of the Goldseekers* (1899); *Boy Life on the Prairie* (1899); *The Eagle's Heart* (1900); *Her Mountain Lover* (1901); *The Captain of the Gray Horse Troop* (1902); *Hesper* (1903); *The Light of the Star* (1904); *The Tyranny of the Dark* (1905); *The Long Trail* (1907); *Money Magic* (1907); *The Shadow World* (1908); *The Moccasin Ranch* (1909); *Cavanagh, Forest Ranger* (1910); *Other Main-Travelled Roads* (1910); *Victor Ollnee's Discipline* (1911); *The Forester's Daughter* (1914); *They of the High Trails* (1916); *A Son of the Middle Border* (1917); *A Daughter of the Middle Border* (1921); *A Pioneer Mother* (1922); *The Book of the American Indian* (1923); *Trail-Makers of the Middle Border* (1926); *Memories of the*

Middle Border (1926); *The Westward March of American Settlement* (1927); *Back-Trailers from the Middle Border* (1928); *Roadside Meetings* (1930); *Companions on the Trail* (1931); *My Friendly Contemporaries* (1932); *Afternoon Neighbors* (1934); *Iowa, O Iowa!* (1935); *Forty Years of Psychic Research* (1936); *The Mystery of the Buried Crosses* (1939).

Collected Works and Edited Texts

Donald Pizer is editing Garland's works. Two useful compilations are the selections from journals at the Huntington Library in Garland's *Diaries*, ed. Donald Pizer (San Marino, CA: Huntington Library, 1968); and *Hamlin Garland's Observations on the American Indian, 1895-1905*, eds. Lonnie E. Underhill and Daniel F. Littlefield, Jr. (Tucson: Univ. of Arizona Press, 1976).

Other Source Materials

The University of Southern California, Los Angeles, contains the major collection of Garland's papers, which are described in Lloyd A. Arvidson, *Hamlin Garland: Centennial Tributes and a Checklist of the Hamlin Garland Papers in the University of Southern California Library* (Los Angeles: Univ. of Southern California Library Bulletin, no. 9, 1962).

SECONDARY SOURCES

Biography

The first full-length biography was Jean Holloway, *Hamlin Garland* (Austin: Univ. of Texas Press, 1960).

Criticism

A good introduction to the life and major work which also contains extensive primary and secondary bibliographies is Joseph B. McCullough, *Hamlin Garland* (Boston: Twayne, 1978). The most comprehensive bio-critical study, Robert Mane, *Hamlin Garland: L'homme et l'oeuvre, 1860-1940* (Paris: Didier, 1968), is in French. A study covering 1884-1895 is Donald Pizer, *Hamlin Garland's Early Work and Career* (Berkeley: Univ. of California Press, 1960); and a useful pamphlet on the writings of Garland's middle phase is Robert Gish, *Hamlin Garland: The Far West* (Boise, ID: Boise State Univ., 1976).

Bibliographies

For checklists of primary sources, consult Joseph B. McCullough's listing of books, articles, plays, poems, and short fiction (*see* Criticism), and Donald Pizer, "Hamlin Garland: A Bibliography of Newspaper and Periodical Publications, 1885-1895," *Bulletin of Bibliography* 22 (1957): 41-44. For secondary sources, Charles L. P. Silet, *Henry Blake Fuller and Hamlin Garland: A Reference Guide* (Boston: G. K. Hall, 1977) is not as reliable as Jackson R. Bryer, Eugene Harding, and Robert A. Rees, *Hamlin Garland and the Critics: An Annotated Bibliography* (Troy, NY: Whitston, 1973), which is the most extensive annotated secondary listing.

ELLEN (ANDERSON GHOLSON) GLASGOW, 1873-1945

PRIMARY SOURCES

Separate Works

The Descendant (1897); Phases of an Inferior Planet (1898); The Voice of the People (1900); The Battle-Ground (1902); The Freeman and Other Poems (1902); The Deliverance (1904); The Wheel of Life (1906); The Ancient Law (1908); The Romance of a Plain Man (1909); The Miller of Old Church (1911); Virginia (1913); Life and Gabriella (1916); The Builders (1919); One Man in His Time (1922); The Shadowy Third and Other Stories (1923); Barren Ground (1925); The Romantic Comedians (1926); They Stooped to Folly (1929); The Sheltered Life (1932); Vein of Iron (1935); In This Our Life (1941); A Certain Measure: An Interpretation of Prose Fiction (1943); The Woman Within [autobiography] (1954); Beyond Defeat [posthumously edited] (1966).

Collected Works and Edited Texts

The Old Dominion Edition of the Works of Ellen Glasgow (Garden City, NY: Doubleday, Doran, 1929-33), 8v.; and The Virginia Edition of the Works of Ellen Glasgow (New York: Scribner, 1938), 12v., are not complete. The Collected Stories of Ellen Glasgow, ed. Richard K. Meeker (Baton Rouge: Louisiana State Univ. Press, 1963) gathers all the short stories. There is no complete collection of Glasgow's correspondence, and Letters of Ellen Glasgow, ed. Blair Rouse (New York: Harcourt Brace, 1958) is a selection which may be supplemented by Glasgow's correspondence with her literary agent, "Agent and Author: Ellen Glasgow's Letters to Paul Revere Reynolds," Studies in Bibliography 14 (1961): 177-96; and Douglas Day, "Ellen Glasgow's Letters to the Saxtons," American Literature 35 (1963): 230-36.

Other Source Materials

Significant collections of Glasgow papers and manuscripts are at the University of Virginia and the University of Florida.

SECONDARY SOURCES

Biography

Because Glasgow's autobiography, The Woman Within (New York: Harcourt Brace, 1954), is filtered through her emotions, it is unreliable as fact. The most important bio-critical contribution is by French scholar Monique Parent Frazee, Ellen Glasgow: Romancière (Paris: A. G. Nizet, 1962). E. Stanly Godbold, Jr., Ellen Glasgow and the Woman Within (Baton Rouge: Louisiana State Univ. Press, 1972) is reliable in its treatment of her later life, but the earlier period is more accurately described by J. R. Raper, Without Shelter: The Early Career of Ellen Glasgow (Louisiana State Univ. Press, 1971).

Criticism

Glasgow's own A Certain Measure (New York: Harcourt Brace, 1943) is an outgrowth of the prefaces to her novels and valuable as a codification of her literary aims. For a brief and balanced introduction, see Louis Auchincloss, Ellen Glasgow

(Minneapolis: Univ. of Minnesota Press, 1964). Frederick P. W. McDowell, *Ellen Glasgow and the Ironic Art of Fiction* (Madison: Univ. of Wisconsin Press, 1960) is a useful account; Blair Rouse, *Ellen Glasgow* (New York: Twayne, 1962) provides a good overview of the life and work which is based on Rouse's previous editing of the *Letters*; and Joan Foster Santas, *Ellen Glasgow's American Dream* (Charlottesville: Univ. Press of Virginia, 1965) interprets Glasgow as a guardian of the "American dream." In a study of the fiction, 1916-1945, J. R. Raper, *From the Sunken Garden* (Baton Rouge: Louisiana State Univ. Press, 1980) examines Glasgow's fictional techniques. Barbro Eckman, *The End of a Legend: Ellen Glasgow's History of Southern Women* (Stockholm: Almquist & Wiksell, 1979) interprets Glasgow as a social observer. A collection of critical essays is *Ellen Glasgow: Centennial Essays*, ed. M. Thomas Inge (Charlottesville: Univ. Press of Virginia, 1976).

Bibliographies

A valuable overview of Glasgow studies, including journal articles and dissertations, is Edgar E. MacDonald, "An Essay in Bibliography," in *Ellen Glasgow: Centennial Essays* (*see* Criticism), pp.191-224. William W. Kelly, *Ellen Glasgow: A Bibliography*, ed. Oliver L. Steele (Charlottesville: published for the Bibliographical Society of Virginia by Univ. Press of Virginia, 1964) is the most comprehensive bibliography and lists primary sources as well as the location of Glasgow's papers and works about her. It will need to be updated by current listings in *American Literary Studies*.

Reference Works

The Ellen Glasgow Newsletter, vol. 1, 1974- is a semiannual clearinghouse for criticism, notes, reviews, and current bibliography.

(FRANCIS) BRET(T) HARTE, 1836-1902

PRIMARY SOURCES

Separate Works

The Lost Galleon and Other Tales (1867); *Condensed Novels* (1867); *The Luck of Roaring Camp* (1870); *Plain Language from Truthful James, the Heathen Chinee* (1870); *Poems* (1871); *East and West Poems* (1871); *Stories of the Sierras* (1872); *The Little Drummer* (1872); *Mrs. Skaggs's Husbands* (1873); *Tales of the Argonauts* (1875); *Echoes of the Foot-Hills* (1875); *Wan Lee: The Pagan* (1876); *Two Men of Sandy Bar* (1876); *Gabriel Conroy* (1875-76); *Thankful Blossom* (1877); *The Story of a Mine* (1878); *Drift from Two Shores* (1878); *The Twins of Table Mountain* (1879); *Poetical Works* (1880); *Flip and Found at Blazing Star* (1882); *In the Carquinez Woods* (1883); *On the Frontier* (1884); *By Shore and Sedge* (1885); *Maruja* (1885); *The Queen of the Pirate Isle* (1886); *Snow-Bound at Eagle's* (1886); *The Crusade of the Excelsior* (1887); *A Millionaire of Rough-and-Ready* (1887); *A Phyllis of the Sierras* (1888); *The Argonauts of North Liberty* (1888); *Cressy* (1889); *The Heritage of Dedlow Marsh* (1889); *A Ward of the Golden Gate* (1890); *A Waif of the Plains* (1890); *A Sappho of Green Springs* (1891); *A First Family of Tasajara* (1891); *Colonel Starbottle's Client* (1892); *Susy: A Story of the Plains* (1893); *Sally Dows* (1893); *A Protégée of Jack Hamlin's* (1894); *The Bell-Ringer of Angel's* (1894); *Clarence* (1895); *In a Hollow of the Hills* (1895); *Poetical Works of Bret Harte* (1896);

Barker's Luck and Other Stories (1896); *Three Partners* (1897); *Some Later Verses* (1898); *Tales of Trail and Town* (1898); *Stories in Lights and Shadow* (1898); *Mr. Jack Hamlin's Meditation* (1899); *From Sand Hill to Pine* (1900); *Under the Redwoods* (1901); *Condensed Novels: Second Series* (1902); *Sue: A Play in Three Acts* (1902); *Openings in the Old Trail* (1902); *Trent's Trust* (1903); *The Story of Enriquez* (1924).

Collected Works and Edited Texts

The Works of Bret Harte, Argonaut ed. 25v. (New York: P. F. Collier, 1914) includes items omitted from earlier editions. Poems are collected in *The Complete Poetical Works of Bret Harte* (Boston: Houghton Mifflin, 1899); and correspondence is gathered in *The Letters of Bret Harte,* ed. Geoffrey Bret Harte (Houghton Mifflin, 1926).

Other Source Materials

A major collection of papers is in the library of the University of California at Los Angeles.

SECONDARY SOURCES

Biography

The standard life is a balanced view by George R. Stewart, Jr., *Bret Harte: Argonaut and Exile* (Boston: Houghton Mifflin, 1931; repr. New York: AMS Press, 1979). A popular biography which lacks detailed documentation is Richard O'Connor, *Bret Harte: A Biography* (Boston: Little, Brown, 1966).

Criticism

A survey of Harte's contributions to the local color movement and as comic writer, critic, and editor is in the Western Writers Series pamphlet, Patrick Morrow, *Bret Harte* (Boise, ID: Boise State College, 1972). An extensive account of Harte's relationships in the San Francisco milieu is Franklin Walker, *San Francisco's Literary Frontier* (New York: Knopf, 1939; repr. Seattle: Univ. of Washington Press, 1969). Margaret Duckett, *Mark Twain and Bret Harte* (Norman: Univ. of Oklahoma Press, 1964) documents Harte's influence on Twain.

Bibliographies

Jacob Blanck, *Bibliography of American Literature* (New Haven, CT: Yale Univ. Press, 1959), v.3, pp.412-78, provides descriptions of primary sources. A list of Harte's contributions to seven periodicals, together with brief explanations of his connection with each, is George R. Stewart, Jr., "A Bibliography of the Writings of Bret Harte in the Magazines and Newspapers of California, 1857-1871," *University of California Publications in English* 3 (September 1933): 119-70; repr. Norwood, PA: Norwood Editions, 1977). For an annotated list of over 2,300 articles, books, and dissertations about Harte, written between 1865 and 1977, see Linda Diz Barnett, *Bret Harte: A Reference Guide* (Boston: G. K. Hall, 1980).

NATHANIEL HAWTHORNE, 1804-1864

PRIMARY SOURCES

Separate Works

Fanshawe: A Tale (1828); *Peter Parley's Universal History* (1837); *Twice-Told Tales* (1837); *Grandfather's Chair* (1841); *Famous Old People, Being the Second Epoch of Grandfather's Chair* (1841); *Liberty Tree, with the Last Words of Grandfather's Chair* (1841); *Biographical Stories for Children* (1842); *The Celestial Railroad* (1843); *Mosses from an Old Manse* (1846); *The Scarlet Letter* (1850); *True Stories from History and Biography* (1851); *The House of the Seven Gables* (1851); *A Wonder-Book for Girls and Boys* (1852); *The Snow-Image and Other Twice-Told Tales* (1852); *The Blithedale Romance* (1852); *Life of Franklin Pierce* (1852); *Tanglewood Tales for Girls and Boys* (1853); *The Marble Faun* (1860); *Our Old Home* (1863); *Pansie: A Fragment* (1864); *Septimius Felton; Or, The Elixir of Life* (1872); *The Dolliver Romance and Other Pieces* (1876); *Fanshawe and Other Pieces* (1876); *Dr. Grimshawe's Secret* (1883); *The Ghost of Doctor Harris* (1900).

Collected Works and Edited Texts

The Centenary Edition of the Works of Nathaniel Hawthorne, ed. Roy Harvey Pearce, et al. (Columbus: Ohio State Univ. Press, 1963-80) is the standard text. *Hawthorne's Lost Notebook, 1835-1841* (University Park: Pennsylvania State Univ. Press, 1978) reproduces on facing pages a facsimile of the manuscript and a transcription. A collection of the letters, edited by Smith and Woodson, is to be published, and until then letters must be sought through quotations in various biographies and the Centenary edition.

The Ohio State Centenary text was used in the Norton Critical Edition of *The Blithedale Romance*, eds. Seymour Gross and Rosalie Murphy (New York: Norton, 1978). Other reliable editions are *The House of the Seven Gables*, ed. Hyatt H. Waggoner (Boston: Houghton Mifflin, 1964); and a facsimile of the 1850 edition of *The Scarlet Letter*, eds. Hyatt H. Waggoner and George Monteiro (San Francisco: Chandler, 1968). *Nathaniel Hawthorne*, v.1. *Tales and Sketches*, ed. Roy Harvey Pearce (New York: Viking, 1982) has recently appeared in the series The Library of America.

Other Source Materials

Major manuscript collections are in the Boston Public Library, the Houghton Library, Harvard, and the Berg Collection of the New York Public Library.

SECONDARY SOURCES

Biography

Randall Stewart, *Nathaniel Hawthorne* (New Haven, CT: Yale Univ. Press, 1948) has been the major life, but with access to the letters, Arlin Turner, *Nathaniel Hawthorne, A Biography* (New York: Oxford Univ. Press, 1980) has been able to emphasize the biographical context of Hawthorne's fiction; and James R. Mellow, *Nathaniel Hawthorne in His Times* (Boston: Houghton Mifflin, 1980) places Hawthorne in his milieu. Documents cited in the following works will also be helpful: Julien Hawthorne,

Nathaniel Hawthorne and His Wife (Boston: J. R. Osgood, 1884; repr. Grosse Pointe, MI: Scholarly Press, 1968); Lawrence S. Hall, *Hawthorne: Critic of Society* (Yale Univ. Press, 1944); Robert Cantwell, *Nathaniel Hawthorne: The American Years* (New York: Rinehart, 1948); Louise H. Tharp, *The Peabody Sisters of Salem* (Boston: Little, Brown, 1950); and Vernon Loggins, *The Hawthornes: The Story of Seven Generations of an American Family* (New York: Columbia Univ. Press, 1951).

Criticism

Among the many important book-length studies are Roy R. Male, *Hawthorne's Tragic Vision* (Austin: Univ. of Texas Press, 1957); Hyatt H. Waggoner, *Hawthorne: A Critical Study*, rev. ed. (Cambridge: Harvard Univ. Press, 1963); eight of Waggoner's distinguished essays are collected in *The Presence of Hawthorne* (Baton Rouge: Louisiana State Univ. Press, 1979); Frederick C. Crews, *The Sins of the Fathers: Hawthorne's Psychological Themes* (New York: Oxford Univ. Press, 1966); John Caldwell Stubbs, *The Pursuit of Form: A Study of Hawthorne and the Romance* (Urbana: Univ. of Illinois Press, 1970); Neal Frank Doubleday, *Hawthorne's Early Tales: A Critical Study* (Durham, NC: Duke Univ. Press, 1972); Nina Baym, *The Shape of Hawthorne's Career* (Ithaca, NY: Cornell Univ. Press, 1976); Edgar A. Dryden, *Nathaniel Hawthorne: The Poetics of Enchantment* (Cornell Univ. Press, 1977), which explores the theme of enchantment and disenchantment throughout the works; Kenneth Dauber, *Rediscovering Hawthorne* (Princeton, NJ: Princeton Univ. Press, 1977), which examines the short stories and novels, seeking Hawthorne's theory of fiction; and Rita K. Gollin, *Nathaniel Hawthorne and the Truth of Dreams* (Baton Rouge: Louisiana State Univ. Press, 1979), which examines how the protagonists proceed in self exploration through their dreams.

Among the several surveys of Hawthorne's reputation are *Hawthorne Centenary Essays*, ed. Roy Harvey Pearce (Columbus: Ohio State Univ. Press, 1964); *Hawthorne: A Collection of Critical Essays*, ed. A. N. Kaul (Englewood Cliffs, NJ: Prentice-Hall, 1966); *Hawthorne among His Contemporaries*, ed. Kenneth W. Cameron (Hartford, CT: Transcendental Books, 1968); *The Recognition of Nathaniel Hawthorne*, ed. Bernard B. Cohen (Ann Arbor: Univ. of Michigan Press, 1969); *Hawthorne: The Critical Heritage*, ed. J. Donald Crowley (New York: Barnes & Noble, 1970); and *Nathaniel Hawthorne: A Collection of Criticism*, ed. J. Donald Crowley (New York: McGraw-Hill, 1975). For comment on *The Scarlet Letter*, see *The Scarlet Letter Handbook*, ed. Seymour Gross (Belmont, CA: Wadsworth, 1960); *The Scarlet Letter: Texts, Sources, Criticism*, ed. Kenneth S. Lynn (New York: Harcourt, 1961); *The Scarlet Letter: An Annotated Text, Background and Sources, Essays in Criticism*. 2nd ed., eds. Sculley Bradley, Richmond Croom Beatty, and E. Hudson Long (New York: Norton, 1978); *Twentieth Century Interpretations of the Scarlet Letter*, ed. John C. Gerber (Englewood Cliffs, NJ: Prentice-Hall, 1968); and Arlin Turner, *The Merrill Studies in the Scarlet Letter* (Columbus, OH: Merrill, 1970).

Bibliographies

An authoritative, chronological listing of all first appearance contributions to books, pamphlets, and newspapers is C. E. Frazer Clark, Jr., *Nathaniel Hawthorne: A Descriptive Bibliography* (Pittsburgh: Univ. of Pittsburgh Press, 1978). The best bibliographic introduction is the chapter by Walter Blair in *Eight American Authors*, rev. ed., ed. James Woodress (New York: Norton, 1971), pp.85-128. It should be updated with two further bibliographies, Beatrice Ricks, Joseph D. Adams, and Jack O. Hazlerig, *Nathaniel Hawthorne: A Reference Bibliography, 1900-1971*

(Boston: G. K. Hall, 1972); and Lea Bertani Vozar Newman, *Reader's Guide to the Short Stories of Nathaniel Hawthorne* (G. K. Hall, 1979), which devotes a separate chapter to each of the fifty-four stories, considering publication history, circumstances of composition, and significant scholarship.

Reference Works

Convenient indexes to Hawthorne are Evangeline M. O'Connor, *An Analytical Index to the Works of Nathaniel Hawthorne* (Boston: Houghton Mifflin, 1882; republished, Detroit: Gale, 1967); Kenneth Walter Cameron, *Hawthorne Index to Themes, Motifs, Topics, Archetypes, Sources and Key Words Dealt with in Recent Criticism* (Hartford, CT: Transcendental Books, 1968); and John R. Byers, Jr., and James J. Owen, *A Concordance to the Five Novels of Nathaniel Hawthorne*, 2v. (New York: Garland, 1979), which is based on Ohio State's Centennial Edition. Useful summaries are contained in Robert L. Gale, *Plots and Characters in the Fiction and Sketches of Nathaniel Hawthorne* (Hamden, CT: Archon Books, 1969). *Hawthorne Society Newsletter*, published spring and fall since 1975, contains current bibliography, notes, and queries, together with such topics as reviews of television and radio productions of *The Scarlet Letter*. *Nathaniel Hawthorne Journal* (NCR Microcard Editions) has been published annually since 1970.

LILLIAN HELLMAN, 1905-

PRIMARY SOURCES

Separate Works

The Children's Hour (1934); *Dark Angel* [screen play] (1935); *Days to Come* (1936); *These Three* [screen play] (1936); *Dead End* [screen play] (1937); *The Little Foxes* (1939; screen play, 1941); *Watch on the Rhine* (1941); *The North Star* [screen play] (1943); *The Searching Wind* (1944; screen play, 1946); *Another Part of the Forest* (1947); *Montserrat: Play in Two Acts* [adaptation of French play by Emmanuel Robles] (1950); *The Autumn Garden: A Play in Three Acts* (1951); *The Lark* [adaptation of French play by Jean Anouilh] (1956); *Candide* [comic operetta, based on Voltaire's satire, score by Leonard Bernstein, lyrics by Richard Wilbur] (1957); *Toys in the Attic* (1960); *My Mother, My Father and Me* [based on novel of Burt Blechman, *How Much?*] (1963); *An Unfinished Woman: A Memoir* (1969); *Pentimento* (1973); *Scoundrel Time* (1976); *Maybe: A Story* (1980).

Collected Works and Edited Texts

The Collected Plays (Boston: Little, Brown, 1972) is the most complete collection. *Six Plays* (New York: Modern Library, 1963; repr. New York: Vintage, 1979) includes *Children's Hour, Days to Come, Little Foxes, Watch on the Rhine, Another Part of the Forest*, and *The Autumn Garden*. For an edition that brings together Hellman's three autobiographical works, *An Unfinished Woman, Pentimento*, and *Scoundrel Time*, see *Three* (Little, Brown, 1979). A more recent supplement to these is *Maybe: A Story* (Little, Brown, 1980).

Other Source Materials

An important collection of Hellman's papers and supporting secondary materials is described in Manfred Triesch, *The Lillian Hellman Collection at the University of Texas* (Austin: Humanities Research Center, Univ. of Texas, 1966).

SECONDARY SOURCES

Biography

Richard Moody, *Lillian Hellman: Playwright* (New York: Pegasus, 1972) was the first biography. Another, which examines the many facets of Hellman's career as playwright and political liberal, is Doris V. Falk, *Lillian Hellman* (New York: Ungar, 1978).

Criticism

The first full-scale critical treatment, Katherine Lederer, *Lillian Hellman* (Boston: Twayne, 1979), examines irony in the dramatic works.

Bibliographies

Access to important writing about Hellman in categories such as biography, interviews, reviews, and scholarly writing is in Steven H. Bills, *An Annotated Bibliography of the Life and Works of Lillian Hellman* (New York: Garland, 1979). Mark W. Edstrin, *Lillian Hellman: Plays, Films, Memoirs: A Reference Guide* (Boston: G. K. Hall, 1980) provides an annotated chronological approach to work about Hellman, 1934-1974. Useful for its access to writings by Hellman as well as about her is Mary Marguerite Riordan, *Lillian Hellman, A Bibliography, 1926-1978* (Metuchen, NJ: Scarecrow, 1980).

ERNEST (MILLER) HEMINGWAY, 1899-1961

PRIMARY SOURCES

Separate Works

Three Stories and Ten Poems (1923); *in Our Time* (1924); *In Our Time* (1925); *The Torrents of Spring* (1926); *Today Is Friday* (1926); *The Sun Also Rises* (1926); *Men without Women* (1927); *A Farewell to Arms* (1929); *Death in the Afternoon* (1932); *God Rest You Merry Gentlemen* (1933); *Winner Take Nothing* (1933); *Green Hills of Africa* (1935); *To Have and Have Not* (1937); *The Spanish Earth* (1938); *The Fifth Column and the First Forty-Nine Stories* (1938); *For Whom the Bell Tolls* (1940); *Across the River and into the Trees* (1950); *The Old Man and the Sea* (1952); *A Moveable Feast* (1964); *"The Fifth Column" and Four Stories of the Spanish Civil War* (1969); *Islands in the Stream* (1970).

Collected Works and Edited Texts

There is no collected edition of Hemingway's works. His journalism is collected in *The Wild Years*, ed. Gene Z. Hanrahan (New York: Dell, 1962); *By-Line: Ernest Hemingway: Selected Articles and Dispatches of Four Decades*, ed. William White

(New York: Scribner, 1967); and Margaret Calien Lewis, "Ernest Hemingway's The Spanish War: Despatches from Spain, 1937-1938" (M.A. thesis, Univ. of Louisville, 1969; distr. Ann Arbor, MI: Univ. Microfilms International), which makes available the full texts of Hemingway's twenty-eight *NANA* despatches. Hemingway's complete correspondence is not to be published, but an important selection is *Ernest Hemingway: Selected Letters, 1917-1961*, ed. Carlos Baker (New York: Scribner, 1981). Many excerpts appear in Matthew J. Bruccoli and C. E. Frazer Clark, Jr., *Hemingway at Auction, 1930-1973* (Detroit: Gale, 1973). E. R. Hagemann, "A Preliminary Report on the State of Ernest Hemingway's Correspondence," *Literary Research Newsletter* 3 (1978): 163-72, provides groupings of the 594 available letters. A collection of the poetry is *Ernest Hemingway: 88 Poems*, ed. Nicholas Gerogiannis (New York: Harcourt Brace Jovanovich, 1979).

Other Source Materials

Many of Hemingway's unpublished materials are listed in Philip Young and Charles W. Mann, *The Hemingway Manuscripts: An Inventory* (University Park: Pennsylvania State Univ. Press, 1969). Major holdings of papers and manuscripts are in the John F. Kennedy Library.

SECONDARY SOURCES

Biography

Carlos Baker, *Ernest Hemingway: A Life Story* (New York: Scribner, 1969) is an authorized biography. There are many memoirs such as those by Marcelline Hemingway Sanford, *At the Hemingways: A Family Portrait* (Boston: Little, Brown, 1962); Leicester Hemingway, *My Brother, Ernest Hemingway* (Cleveland: World Pub. Co., 1962); Gregory H. Hemingway, *Papa* (Boston: Houghton Mifflin, 1976); and Hemingway's wife, Mary Welsh Hemingway, *How it Was* (New York: Knopf, 1976). Scott Donaldson, *By Force of Will: The Life and Art of Ernest Hemingway* (New York: Viking, 1977) draws on biographical information and the fiction to define Hemingway's attitudes. The literary friendship of Hemingway with F. Scott Fitzgerald is skillfully documented in a study by Matthew J. Bruccoli, *Scott and Ernest: The Authority of Failure and the Authority of Success* (New York: Random House, 1978).

Criticism

For critical introductions to Hemingway, see Philip Young, *Ernest Hemingway* (Minneapolis: Univ. of Minnesota Press, 1959); Earl Rovit, *Ernest Hemingway* (New York: Twayne, 1963); and Sheridan Baker, *Ernest Hemingway: An Introduction and Interpretation* (New York: Holt, Rinehart & Winston, 1967). Full-length studies are Philip Young, *Ernest Hemingway: A Reconsideration*, rev. ed. (University Park: Pennsylvania State Univ. Press, 1966); Robert O. Stephens, *Hemingway's Non Fiction: The Public Voice* (Chapel Hill: Univ. of North Carolina Press, 1968), which examines relationships between the journalism and the nonfiction; Jackson J. Benson, *Hemingway: The Writer's Art of Self Defense* (Minneapolis: Univ. of Minnesota Press, 1969); Emily Stipes Watts, *Ernest Hemingway and the Arts* (Urbana: Univ. of Illinois Press, 1971), which shows Hemingway's use of techniques borrowed from painters such as Cezanne; Carlos Baker, *Ernest Hemingway: The Writer as Artist*, 4th ed. (Princeton, NJ: Princeton Univ. Press, 1972); Arthur Waldhorn, *A Reader's Guide to Ernest*

Hemingway (New York: Farrar, Straus & Giroux, 1973), which analyzes style in the major works; and Scott Donaldson, *By Force of Will: The Life and Art of Ernest Hemingway* (New York: Viking, 1977).

There have been many collections of essays published, among which are *Ernest Hemingway: The Man and His Work*, ed. John K. M. McCaffery (Cleveland, OH: World, 1950; reissued New York: Cooper Square, 1969); *Hemingway and His Critics: An International Anthology*, ed. Carlos Baker (New York: Hill & Wang, 1961); *Ernest Hemingway: Critiques of Four Major Novels*, ed. Carlos Baker (New York: Scribner, 1962); *Hemingway: A Collection of Critical Essays*, ed. Robert P. Weeks (Englewood Cliffs, NJ: Prentice-Hall, 1962); *The Literary Reputation of Hemingway in Europe*, ed. Roger Asselineau (Paris: Minard, 1965); *Ernest Hemingway: A Collection of Criticism*, ed. Arthur Waldhorn (New York: McGraw-Hill, 1973); *Ernest Hemingway: Five Decades of Criticism*, ed. Linda Welshimer Wagner (East Lansing: Michigan State Univ. Press, 1974); *Hemingway in Our Time*, eds. Richard Astro and Jackson J. Benson (Corvallis: Oregon State Univ. Press, 1974); *The Short Stories of Ernest Hemingway: Critical Essays*, ed. Jackson J. Benson (Durham, NC: Duke Univ. Press, 1975); and *Ernest Hemingway: The Critical Reception*, ed. Robert O. Stephens (New York: B. Franklin, 1977). Further collections of essays on individual works are listed in Wagner's anthology (see above).

Bibliographies

For a fine introduction to Hemingway scholarship and bibliography, see Frederick J. Hoffman, "Ernest Hemingway," in *Sixteen Modern American Authors*, ed. Jackson R. Bryer (Durham, NC: Duke Univ. Press, 1974), pp.367-416. Audre Hanneman, *Ernest Hemingway: A Comprehensive Bibliography* (Princeton, NJ: Princeton Univ. Press, 1967) and Hanneman's *Supplement* (Princeton Univ. Press, 1975) are thorough, scholarly compilations of primary and secondary materials through 1973. Linda Welshimer Wagner, *Ernest Hemingway: A Reference Guide* (Boston: G. K. Hall, 1977) is a comprehensive annotated listing of English-language criticism from 1924 to 1975, arranged chronologically. It should be used alongside Hanneman, which it updates.

Reference Works

Appearing irregularly between 1969 and 1979, *Fitzgerald/Hemingway Annual*, eds. Matthew Bruccoli and Richard Layman, offered textual, bibliographic, and critical contributions of scholarly quality. *Hemingway Review, 1981- *, which was formerly *Hemingway Notes, 1971-1981*, provides a clearinghouse for Hemingway events, brief articles, reviews, and current bibliography.

OLIVER WENDELL HOLMES, 1809-1894

PRIMARY SOURCES

Separate Works

The Harbinger: A May-Gift (1833); *Poems* (1836); *Boylston Prize Dissertations for. . . 1836 and 1837* (1838); *Homoeopathy, and Its Kindred Delusions* (1842); *The Contagiousness of Puerperal Fever* (1843); *The Position and Prospects of the*

Medical Student (1844); *Urania: A Rhymed Lesson* (1846); *Poems* (1846); *Introductory Lecture, Delivered . . . Harvard University, Nov. 3, 1847* (1847); *Poems* (1849); *Astraea: The Balance of Illusions* (1850); *A Poem Delivered at . . . the Pittsfield Cemetery, Sept. 9, 1850* (1850); *The Benefactors of the Medical School of Harvard University* (1850); *The Poetical Works of Oliver Wendell Holmes* (1852); *Songs of the Class of MDCCCXXIX* (1854); *Oration Delivered before the New England Society* (1856); *Valedictory Address, Etc., March 10th, 1858* (1858); *The Autocrat of the Breakfast-Table* (1858); *Songs and Poems of the Class of 1829: Second Edition* (1859); *The Professor at the Breakfast-Table* (1860); *Currents and Counter-Currents in Medical Science* (1860); *Elsie Venner: A Romance of Destiny* (1861); *Songs in Many Keys* (1862); *The Poems of Oliver Wendell Holmes* (1862); *Border Lines of Knowledge in . . . Medical Science* (1862); *Oration . . . on the Fourth of July, 1863* (1863); *Soundings from the Atlantic* (1864); *Humorous Poems* (1865); *The Guardian Angel* (1867); *Teaching from the Chair and at the Bedside* (1867); *Songs and Poems of the Class of Eighteen Hundred and Twenty-Nine: Third Edition* (1868); *The Medical Profession in Massachusetts* (1869); *Mechanisim in Thought and Morals* (1871); *Valedictory Address . . . March 2, 1871* (1871); *The Claims of Dentistry* (1872); *The Poet at the Breakfast-Table* (1872); *Songs of Many Seasons, 1862-1874* (1875); *Poetical Works* (1877); *An Address Delivered at . . . the Boston Microscopical Society* (1877); *John Lothrop Motley: A Memoir* (1879); *The School-Boy* (1879); *The Iron Gate and Other Poems* (1880); *Address Delivered at . . . the Boston Medical Library Association, December 3, 1878* (1881); *The Medical Highways and By-Ways* (1882); *Farewell Address . . . to the Medical School of Harvard University, November 28, 1882* (1882); *Medical Essays 1842-1882* (1883); *Pages from an Old Volume of Life* (1883); *A Mortal Antipathy* (1885); *Ralph Waldo Emerson* (1885); *Illustrated Poems* (1885); *Our Hundred Days in Europe* (1887); *Before the Curfew and Other Poems* (1888); *Over the Teacups* (1891); *Memoir of Henry Jacob Bigelow* (1891); *A Dissertation on Acute Pericarditis* (1937).

Collected Works and Edited Texts

The standard edition is *The Writings of Oliver Wendell Holmes*, Riverside ed. 13v. (Boston: Houghton Mifflin, 1891). A collection of Holmes' literary reviews and essays which were not included in the Riverside edition is *The Autocrat's Miscellanies*, ed. Albert Mordell (New York: Twayne, 1959). The fullest collection of poetry is *The Complete Poetical Works of Oliver Wendell Holmes*, Cambridge ed., ed. Horace E. Scudder (Boston: Houghton Mifflin, 1895). An important single-volume anthology is *Oliver Wendell Holmes: Representative Selections*, eds. S. I. Hayakawa and Howard Mumford Jones (New York: American Book Co., 1939). There is no collected edition of Holmes' letters, but the best selection is *Life and Letters of Oliver Wendell Holmes*, ed. John T. Morse, Jr., 2v. (Boston: Houghton Mifflin, 1896).

Other Source Materials

The Houghton Library at Harvard University has the largest collection of manuscripts, but others are at the Library of Congress, the Huntington Library, and the New York Public Library.

SECONDARY SOURCES

Biography

Two reliable, balanced biographies are M. A. de Wolfe Howe, *Holmes of the Breakfast-Table* (New York: Oxford Univ. Press, 1939; repr. Mamaroneck, NY: Appel, 1972); and Edwin P. Hoyt, *The Improper Bostonian* (New York: W. Morrow, 1979). The definitive biography by Eleanor M. Tilton, *Amiable Autocrat: A Biography of Dr. Oliver Wendell Holmes* (New York: H. Schuman, 1947), includes a full portrait of Holmes as physician and writer. Thomas Wortham has a judicious essay on Holmes in *American Writers: A Collection of Literary Biographies*, ed. Leonard Unger (New York: Scribner, 1979), Supplement I, Part 1, pp.299-319.

Criticism

An excellent discussion on Holmes is in the introduction to *Oliver Wendell Holmes: Representative Selections* (*see* Collected Works). Also important are George Arms, *The Fields Were Green* (Stanford, CA: Stanford Univ. Press, 1953), which is a treatment of Holmes with other schoolroom poets; and a more recent overview of the life and works, David H. Burton, *Oliver Wendell Holmes, Jr.* (Boston: Twayne, 1980).

Bibliographies

The best introduction to scholarship and bibliography is Barry Menikoff, "Oliver Wendell Holmes," in *Fifteen American Authors before 1900*, eds. Robert A. Rees and Earl N. Harbert (Madison: Univ. of Wisconsin Press, 1971), pp.207-228. Thomas Franklin Currer, *A Bibliography of Oliver Wendell Holmes*, ed. Eleanor M. Tilton (New York: New York Univ. Press, 1953) is a bibliography of primary sources.

WILLIAM DEAN HOWELLS, 1837-1920

PRIMARY SOURCES

Separate Works

Poems of Two Friends [with John J. Piatt] (1860); *No Love Lost: A Romance of Travel* [poetry] (1869); *Their Wedding Journey* (1872); *Poems* (1873); *A Chance Acquaintance* (1873); *A Foregone Conclusion* (1875); *The Parlor Car* [play] (1876); *Out of the Question* [play] (1877); *A Counterfeit Presentment* [play] (1877); *The Lady of the Aroostook* (1879); *The Undiscovered Country* (1880); *Doctor Breen's Practice* (1881); *A Fearful Responsibility and Other Stories* (1881); *A Modern Instance* (1882); *A Woman's Reason* (1883); *The Sleeping Car* [play] (1883); *The Register* [play] (1884); *The Elevator* [play] (1885); *The Rise of Silas Lapham* (1885); *Indian Summer* (1886); *The Garroters* [play] (1886); *The Minister's Charge* (1887); *April Hopes* (1888); *Annie Kilburn* (1888); *A Sea-Change; Or, Love's Stowaway* [play] (1888); *The Mouse-Trap and Other Farces* [play] (1889); *A Hazard of New Fortunes* (1890); *The Shadow of a Dream* (1890); *An Imperative Duty* (1892); *The Quality of Mercy* (1892); *Christmas Every Day and Other Stories Told for Children* (1893); *The Albany Depot* [play] (1892); *A Letter of Introduction* [play] (1892); *The Unexpected Guests* [play] (1893); *Evening Dress* [play] (1893); *The World of Chance* (1893); *The Coast of Bohemia* (1893); *A Traveler from Altruria* (1894); *Stops of*

Various Quills [poetry] (1894); *A Likely Story* [play] (1894); *The Day of Their Wedding* (1896); *A Parting and a Meeting* (1896); *The Landlord at Lion's Head* (1897); *An Open-Eyed Conspiracy: An Idyl of Saratoga* (1897); *A Previous Engagement* [play] (1897); *The Story of a Play* (1898); *Ragged Lady* (1899); *Their Silver Wedding Journey* (1899); *Room Forty-Five* [play] (1900); *Bride Roses* [play] (1900); *The Smoking Car* [play] (1900); *An Indian Giver* [play] (1900); *A Pair of Patient Lovers* (1901); *The Kentons* (1902); *The Flight of Pony Baker* (1902); *Questionable Shapes* (1903); *Letters Home* (1903); *The Son of Royal Langbrith* (1904); *Miss Bellard's Inspiration* (1905); *Through the Eye of the Needle* (1907); *Between the Dark and Daylight* (1907); *Fennel and Rue* (1908); *The Mother and the Father: Dramatic Passages* [poetry] (1909); *Parting Friends* [play] (1911); *New Leaf Mills* (1913); *The Daughter of the Storage* (1916); *The Leatherwood God* (1916); *The Vacation of the Kelwyns* (1920); *Mrs. Farrell* (1921).

Travel, Criticism, Biography

Lives and Speeches of Abraham Lincoln and Hannibal Hamlin (1860); *Venetian Life* (1866); *Italian Journeys* (1867); *Suburban Sketches* (1871); *Sketch of the Life and Character of Rutherford B. Hayes, Etc.* (1876); *A Day's Pleasure and Other Sketches* (1876); *Three Villages* (1884); *A Little Girl among the Old Masters* (1884); *Niagra Revisited* (1884); *Tuscan Cities* (1886); *Modern Italian Poets* (1887); *A Boy's Town* (1890); *Criticism and Fiction* (1891); *A Little Swiss Sojourn* (1892); *My Year in a Log Cabin* (1893); *My Literary Passions* (1895); *Impressions and Experiences* (1896); *Stories of Ohio* (1897); *Literary Friends and Acquaintances* (1900); *Heroines of Fiction* (1901); *Literature and Life* (1902); *London Films* (1905); *Certain Delightful English Towns* (1906); *Roman Holidays and Others* (1908); *Seven English Cities* (1909); *Imaginary Interviews* (1910); *My Mark Twain* (1910); *Familiar Spanish Travels* (1913); *The Seen and the Unseen at Stratford-on-Avon* (1914); *Years of My Youth* (1916); *Eighty Years and After* (1921); *Life and Letters of William Dean Howells* (1928).

Collected Works and Edited Texts

The authoritative *A Selected Edition of W. D. Howells*, eds. Edwin H. Cady, Ronald Gottesman, David J. Nordloh (Bloomington: Indiana Univ. Press, 1968-) is being prepared as the most complete compilation of Howells. There are several important collections of Howells' letters, *Life in Letters of William Dean Howells*, ed. Mildred Howells, 2v. (New York: Doubleday, Doran, 1928; repr. New York: Russell & Russell, 1968); *Mark Twain-Howells Letters . . . 1872-1910*, eds. Henry Nash Smith and William M. Gibson (Cambridge: Harvard Univ. Press, 1960); *John Hay–Howells Letters*, eds. George Monteiro and Brenda Murphy (Boston: Twayne, 1980), which contains the correspondence of John Milton Hay and Howells between 1861 and 1905; and the University of Indiana edition of *Selected Letters*, ed. George Arms, et al. (Boston: Twayne, 1978-), which will be completed in six volumes.

Other Source Materials

The Howells Edition Center at Indiana University has copies of many manuscripts. Libraries holding major collections of manuscripts and letters are the Houghton Library at Harvard University and the University of Virginia's Barrett Library.

SECONDARY SOURCES

Biography

The best critical biography is by Edwin H. Cady, *The Road to Realism: The Early Years, 1837-1885, of William Dean Howells* (Syracuse, NY: Syracuse Univ. Press, 1956). Cady continues the later career in *The Realist at War: The Mature Years, 1885-1920* (Syracuse Univ. Press, 1958). A study of Howells and his contemporaries is Van Wyck Brooks, *Howells: His Life and World* (New York: Dutton, 1959); and Kenneth S. Lynn, *William Dean Howells: An American Life* (New York: Harcourt Brace Jovanovich, 1971) depicts Howells as a "man of modern sensibility, whose awareness of life was rooted in radical doubt and anxiety."

Criticism

For an excellent brief introduction, see William M. Gibson, *William D. Howells* (Minneapolis: Univ. of Minnesota Press, 1967). Another introduction is in *William Dean Howells: Representative Selections*, rev. ed., eds. Clara M. Kirk and Rudolf Kirk (New York: Hill & Wang, 1961). They have also collaborated on *William Dean Howells* (New York: Twayne, 1962). Other full-length studies are James L. Woodress, Jr., *Howells and Italy* (Durham, NC: Duke Univ. Press, 1952), which indicates Italian influences; Everett Carter, *Howells and the Age of Realism* (Philadelphia: Lippincott, 1954; repr. Hamden, CT: Archon Books, 1966), which shows Howells as a central figure among realists; and Olov W. Fryckstedt, *In Quest of America* (Cambridge: Harvard Univ. Press, 1958), which shows Howells' international importance. Robert L. Hough, *The Quiet Rebel* (Lincoln: Univ. of Nebraska Press, 1959) demonstrates Howells' influence on social reform through national magazines, while two works of George N. Bennett, *William Dean Howells: The Development of a Novelist* (Norman: Univ. of Oklahoma Press, 1959) and *The Realism of William Dean Howells, 1889-1920* (Nashville, TN: Vanderbilt Univ. Press, 1973) concentrate on his contribution as a novelist. Clara M. Kirk, *W. D. Howells and Art in His Time* (New Brunswick, NJ: Rutgers Univ. Press, 1965) shows the influence of painting and sculpture on Howells' philosophy of realism; George C. Carrington, *The Immense Complex Drama* (Columbus: Ohio State Univ. Press, 1966) deals with the theme of alienation in the artist; and Kermit Vanderbilt, *The Achievement of William Dean Howells* (Princeton, NJ: Princeton Univ. Press, 1968) is a thorough study of five novels. For Howells' writing on travel, see James L. Dean, *Howells' Travels toward Art* (Albuquerque: Univ. of New Mexico Press, 1970).

Collections of criticism are *The War of the Critics over William Dean Howells*, eds. Edwin H. Cady and David L. Frazier (Evanston, IL: Row, Peterson, 1962); and *Howells: A Century of Criticism*, ed. Kenneth Eble (Dallas, TX: Southern Methodist Univ. Press, 1962).

Bibliographies

A bibliographical essay, George Fortenberry, "William Dean Howells," in *Fifteen American Authors before 1900*, eds. Robert A. Rees and Earl N. Harbert (Madison: Univ. of Wisconsin Press, 1971), pp.229-44, provides a lucid overview. William M. Gibson and George Arms, *A Bibliography of William Dean Howells* (New York: New York Public Library, 1948; repr. 1971) describes books and periodical articles chronologically. It has been updated in Jacob N. Blanck, *Bibliography of American Literature* (New Haven, CT: Yale Univ. Press, 1963), v.4, pp.384-448. A definitive bibliography will be part of the completed Indiana Edition. Annotations of secondary sources are in James Woodress and Stanley P. Anderson, "A Bibliography of Writing about William Dean Howells," *American Literary Realism*, Special Issue (Arlington University of Texas, 1969), pp.1-139. A checklist of short stories, poems, novels, plays, travel writings, and criticism is in Vito J. Brenni, *William Dean Howells: A Bibliography* (Metuchen, NJ: Scarecrow, 1973), which also lists secondary sources. Clayton L. Eichelberger, *Published Comment on William Dean Howells through 1920: A Research Bibliography* (Boston: G. K. Hall, 1976) annotates secondary sources.

Reference Works

George C. Carrington, Jr., and Ildikó de Papp Carrington, *Plots and Characters in the Fiction of William Dean Howells* (Hamden, CT: Archon Books, 1976) provides a chronological list of Howells' novels, plot summaries, and character descriptions.

(JAMES) LANGSTON HUGHES, 1902-1967

PRIMARY SOURCES

Separate Works

The Weary Blues (1926); *Fine Clothes to the Jew* (1927); *Not without Laughter* [fiction] (1930); *Dear Lovely Death* (1931); *The Negro Mother* (1931); *Scottboro Limited* (1932); *The Dream Keeper* (1932); *Popo and Fifina* [for children] (1932); *The Ways of White Folks* [fiction] (1934); *A New Song* (1938); *The Big Sea* [autobiography] (1940); *Not without Laughter* [fiction] (1941); *Shakespeare in Harlem* (1942); *Freedom's Plow* (1943); *Fields of Wonder* (1947); *One Way Ticket* (1947); *Montage of a Dream Deferred* (1951); *Laughing to Keep from Crying* (1952); *I Wonder as I Wander* [autobiography] (1956); *Selected Poems* (1959); *Ask Your Mama: 12 Moods for Jazz* (1961); *The Best of Simple* [fiction] (1961); *Something in Common and Other Stories* (1964); *Simple's Uncle Sam* (1965); *The Panther and the Lash: Poems of Our Times* (1967); *Don't You Turn Back* (1969).

Collected Works and Edited Texts

Five Plays, ed. Webster Smalley (Bloomington: Indiana Univ. Press, 1963) reprints *Mulatto, Soul Gone Home, Little Ham, Simply Heavenly*, and *Tambourines to Glory. Good Morning Revolution*, ed. Faith Berry (New York: Lawrence Hill, 1973) contains previously uncollected writings of social protest. Selected correspondence is available in *Arna Bontemps-Langston Hughes Letters, 1925-1967*, ed. Charles H. Nichols (New York: Dodd, Mead, 1980).

Other Source Materials

Collections of manuscripts and correspondence are in the libraries of Yale University, Lincoln University, Pennsylvania, Fisk University, Brown University, and the New York Public Library.

SECONDARY SOURCES

Biography

There is not yet an authoritative life, and the autobiographies *The Big Sea* and *I Wonder as I Wander* are the main sources of biographical information. Milton Meltzer, *Langston Hughes: A Biography* (New York: Crowell, 1968) and Charlemae H. Rollins, *Black Troubadour: Langston Hughes* (Chicago: Rand McNally, 1970) are useful accounts, intended primarily for children and young adults. A useful short biographical treatment is in Donald C. Dickinson, *A Bio-Bibliography of Langston Hughes* (*see* Bibliographies).

Criticism

James A. Emanuel, *Langston Hughes* (New York: Twayne, 1967) contains reliable biographical information and treats themes in the poetry and short prose fiction. Onwuchekwa Jemie, *Langston Hughes: An Introduction to the Poetry* (New York: Columbia Univ. Press, 1976) studies themes and techniques from the stance of oral tradition, struggle, and protest; and Richard K. Barksdale, *Langston Hughes: The Poet and His Critics* (Chicago: American Library Association, 1977) evaluates forty-seven years of criticism. Lengthy and perceptive approaches to the poetry are in two general studies of major black American poets, Jean Wagner, *Black Poets of the United States: From Paul Laurence Dunbar to Langston Hughes* (Urbana: Univ. of Illinois Press, 1973); and Blyden Jackson and Louis D. Rubin, Jr., *Black Poetry in America* (Baton Rouge: Louisiana State Univ. Press, 1974). An outstanding collection which contains a biography, bibliography, and essays on Hughes' literary contribution is *Langston Hughes, Black Genius: A Critical Evaluation*, ed. Therman B. O'Daniel (New York: Morrow, 1971).

Bibliographies

The essay by Blyden Jackson, "Langston Hughes," in *Black American Writers: Bibliographical Essays*, eds. M. Thomas Inge, Maurice Duke, Jackson R. Bryer, 2v. (New York: St. Martin's Press, 1978), v.1, pp.187-206, provides a thorough bibliographic overview. The fullest bibliography of primary and secondary sources is Donald C. Dickinson, *A Bio-Bibliography of Langston Hughes, 1902-1967*, 2nd ed., rev. (Hamden, CT: Archon Books, 1972), but it does not include his radio and television scripts, his song lyrics, or the writing subsequently published in *Good Morning Revolution* (*see* Collected Works). Another valuable bibliography is Therman B. O'Daniel, "Langston Hughes: A Selected Classified Bibliography," in *Langston Hughes, Black Genius* (*see* Criticism), which covers categories of primary contribution omitted by Dickinson, as well as a representative sampling of criticism. R. Baxter Miller, *Langston Hughes and Gwendolyn Brooks: A Reference Guide* (Boston: G. K. Hall, 1978) provides an annotated chronological listing of writings about Hughes, 1924-1977.

Reference Works

Peter Mandelik and Stanley Schatt, *A Concordance to the Poetry of Langston Hughes* (Detroit: Gale, 1975) provides access to the poems.

WASHINGTON IRVING, 1783-1859

PRIMARY SOURCES

Separate Works

Letters of Jonathan Oldstyle, Gent. (1802-03); *Salmagundi; Or, The Whim-Whams and Opinions of Launcelot Langstaff, Esq., and Others* [with J. K. Paulding and William Irving] (1807-08); *A History of New York from the Beginning of the World to the End of the Dutch Dynasty* (1809); biographical sketch of Thomas Campbell in *The Poetical Works of Thomas Campbell* (1810); contributions to the *Alalectic Magazine* (1813-15); *The Sketch Book of Geoffrey Crayon, Gent* (1819-20); *Bracebridge Hall; Or, The Humorists* (1822); *Tales of a Traveller* (1824); *A History of the Life and Voyages of Christopher Columbus* (1828); *A Chronicle of the Conquest of Granada* (1829); *Voyages and Discoveries of the Companions of Columbus* (1831); *The Alhambra* (1832); *The Crayon Miscellany: A Tour on the Prairies, Abbotsford and Newstead Abbey, Legends of the Conquest of Spain* (1835); *Astoria* (1836); *The Rocky Mountains* (1837); *The Life of Oliver Goldsmith with Selections from His Writings* (1840); *Biography and Poetical Remains of the Late Margaret Miller Davidson* (1841); *Mahomet and His Successors* (1850); *The Life of George Washington* (1855-59); *Wolfert's Roost and Other Papers* (1855); *Spanish Papers and Other Miscellanies* (1866); *Abu Hassan* (1924); *The Wild Huntsman* (1924).

Collected Works and Edited Texts

An edition following standards of the Center for Editions of American Authors was begun at the University of Wisconsin, *The Complete Works of Washington Irving*, ed. Henry A. Pochmann (Madison: Univ. of Wisconsin Press, 1969-) and is continuing under the editorship of Richard Dilworth Rust (Boston: Twayne, 1976-). It will include all works published during Irving's life, his letters, of which those written 1802-1823 are available, and *The Journals and Note Books*, eds. Nathalia Wright and Walter A. Reichart (Madison: Univ. of Wisconsin Press, 1969-70). Until its completion, the most reliable edition continues to be *The Works of Washington Irving*, new ed., rev. 15v. (New York: G. P. Putnam, 1848-51).

SECONDARY SOURCES

Biography

An undocumented life, by Irving's nephew, is Pierre M. Irving, *The Life and Letters of Washington Irving*, 4v. (New York: G. P. Putnam, 1862-64). It should be accompanied by Wayne R. Kime, *Pierre M. Irving and Washington Irving: A Collaboration in Life and Letters* (Waterloo, Ontario: Wilfrid Laurier Univ. Press, 1977). The standard biography is Stanley T. Williams, *The Life of Washington Irving*, 2v. (New York: Oxford Univ. Press, 1935). Two other views are Edward Wagenknecht, *Washington Irving: Moderation Displayed* (Oxford Univ. Press, 1962); and Philip McFarland, *Sojourners* (New York: Atheneum, 1979), which is based on primary sources.

Criticism

A brief introductory pamphlet is Lewis Leary, *Washington Irving* (Minneapolis: Univ. of Minnesota Press, 1963). By using selections and notes of Irving, an understanding of the writer within his milieu is gained in *Washington Irving: Representative Selections* (New York: American Book Co., 1934). A more complex view of the influences on Irving's development is in William L. Hedges, *Washington Irving: An American Study, 1802-1832* (Baltimore: Johns Hopkins Press, 1965). Walter A. Reichart, *Washington Irving and Germany* (Ann Arbor: Univ. of Michigan Press, 1957) traces German sources in Irving's writing, while Ben Harris McClary, *Washington Irving and the House of Murray* (Knoxville: Univ. of Tennessee Press, 1969) documents the relation with his English publisher.

Three collections of criticism are *Washington Irving Reconsidered*, ed. Ralph Aderman (Hartford, CT: Transcendental Books, 1969); *Washington Irving: A Tribute* (Tarrytown, NY: Sleepy Hollow Restorations, 1972); and *A Century of Commentary on the Works of Washington Irving*, ed. Andrew B. Myers (Tarrytown, NY: Sleepy Hollow Restorations, 1976), which reprints many of the most important critical statements made between 1860 and 1974.

Bibliographies

An essential bibliographic essay is Henry A. Pochmann, "Washington Irving," in *Fifteen American Authors before 1900*, eds. Robert A. Rees and Earl N. Harbert (Madison: Univ. of Wisconsin Press, 1971), pp.245-61. Jacob N. Blanck, *Bibliography of American Literature* (New Haven, CT: Yale Univ. Press, 1955-) v.5, pp.1-96, provides complete bibliographical descriptions of first and significant later editions. Haskell Springer, *Washington Irving: A Reference Guide* (Boston: G. K. Hall, 1976) is a reliable, annotated, chronological listing of writings about Irving, 1807-1974.

HENRY JAMES, 1843-1916

PRIMARY SOURCES

Separate Works

A Passionate Pilgrim and Other Tales (1875); *Transatlantic Sketches* (1875); *Roderick Hudson* (1876); *The American* (1877); *Watch and Ward* (1878, James' first novel that had been serialized in 1871); *French Poets and Novelists* (1878); *The Europeans* (1878); *Daisy Miller* (1879); *An International Episode* (1879); *The Madonna of the Future and Other Tales* (1879); *Hawthorne* (1879); *The Diary of a Man of Fifty*, and *A Bundle of Letters* (1880); *Confidence* (1880); *Washington Square* (1881); *The Portrait of a Lady* (1881); *The Siege of London, The Pension Beaurepas, and The Point of View* (1883); *Portraits of Places* (1883); *Tales of Three Cities* (1884); *A Little Tour in France* (1885); *Stories Revived* (1885); *The Bostonians* (1886); *The Princess Casamassima* (1886); *Partial Portraits* (1888); *The Aspern Papers, Louisa Pallant*, and *The Modern Warning* (1888); *The Reverberator* (1888); *A London Life, The Patagonia, The Liar*, and *Mrs. Temperley* (1889); *The Tragic Muse* (1890); *The Lesson of the Master, the Marriages, Etc.* (1892); *The Private Life, Etc.* (1893); *The Wheel of Time, Etc.* (1893); *The Real Thing and Other Tales* (1893); *Picture and Text* (1893); *Essays in London and Elsewhere* (1893); *Theatricals: Two Comedies—Tenants, and Disengaged* (1894); *Theatricals, Second Series* (1895); *Terminations, the Death of the Lion, Etc.* (1895); *Embarrassments* (1896); *The Other House* (1896); *The Spoils of Poynton* (1897); *What Maisie Knew* (1897); *The Two Magics, The Turn of the Screw*, and *Covering End* (1898); *In the Cage* (1898); *The Awkward Age*

(1899); *The Soft Side* (1900); *The Sacred Fount* (1901); *The Wings of the Dove* (1902); *William Wetmore Story and His Friends* (1903); *The Better Sort* (1903); *The Ambassadors* (1903); *The Golden Bowl* (1904); *The Question of Our Speech*, and *The Lesson of Balzac* (1905); *English Hours* (1905); *The American Scene* (1907); *Views and Reviews* (1908); *Julia Bride* (1909); *Italian Hours* (1909); *The Finer Grain* (1910); *The Outcry* (1911); *A Small Boy and Others* (1913); *Notes on Novelists* (1914); *Notes of a Son and Brother* (1914); *The Ivory Tower* (1917); *The Middle Years* (1917); *The Sense of the Past* (1917); *Within the Rim and Other Essays, 1914-1915* (1918); *Gabrielle de Bergerac* (1918); *Travelling Companions* (1919).

Collected Works and Edited Texts

There is no standard edition of James' collected works, though many individual editions are available (*see* Bibliographies for Gale's comments). *The Novels and Tales of Henry James*, 26v. (New York: Scribner, 1907-17), planned and edited by James and containing his critical prefaces, was reissued in 1962-65. *The Complete Tales of Henry James*, ed. Leon Edel. 12v. (Philadelphia: Lippincott, 1962-65) reprints novelettes and short stories; and *The Complete Plays of Henry James*, ed. Leon Edel (Lippincott, 1949) is the most comprehensive dramatic collection. James' travel writings are gathered in *The Art of Travel*, ed. Morton D. Zabel (Garden City, NY: Doubleday, 1958). *The Art of the Novel*, ed. Richard P. Blackmur (New York: Scribner, 1934) comprises prefaces from the New York Edition. Two editions of James' correspondence are *The Letters of Henry James*, ed. Percy Lubbock. 2v. (New York: Scribner, 1920); and *The Letters of Henry James*, ed. Leon Edel (Cambridge: Harvard Univ. Press, 1974-), which are not yet complete. Also valuable as sources are *The Notebooks of Henry James*, eds. F. O. Matthiessen and Kenneth B. Murdock (New York: Oxford Univ. Press, 1947); and *Henry James: Autobiography*, ed. Frederick W. Dupee (New York: Criterion, 1956), which contains James' *A Small Boy and Others*, *Notes of a Son and Brother*, and *The Middle Years*. Unfortunately, there is no definitive edition of James' criticism, although *Theory of Fiction: Henry James*, ed. James E. Miller, Jr. (Lincoln: Univ. of Nebraska Press, 1972) is a valuable topical collection of James' statements.

Other Source Materials

The most important sources of James' papers and manuscripts are the libraries of Harvard University and Yale University.

SECONDARY SOURCES

Biography

The standard biography is a psychological analysis by Leon Edel, *Henry James*, 5v. (New York: Lippincott, 1953-72; p.bk. New York: Avon, 1978), which is not unanimously endorsed. F. O. Matthiessen, *The James Family* (New York: Knopf, 1947) includes selections from writings of other members of the James family; and a pictorial biography, Harry T. Moore, *Henry James and His World* (New York: Viking, 1974) contains high-quality illustrations.

Criticism

F. W. Dupee, *Henry James* (New York: Sloane, 1951) and Leon Edel, *Henry James* (Minneapolis: Univ. of Minnesota Press, 1960) are the best introductions, combining biography and criticism. Other reliable introductions are Bruce R. McElderry, Jr., *Henry James* (New York: Twayne, 1965); Lyall H. Powers, *Henry James: An Introduction and Interpretation* (New York: Holt, Rinehart & Winston, 1967); and a lucid account of Darshan Singh Maini, *Henry James: The Indirect Vision: Studies in Themes and Techniques* (Bombay-New Delhi: Tata, McGraw-Hill, 1973). Longer critical works abound, but among the landmarks are Joseph W. Beach, *The Method of Henry James*, enl. ed. (Philadelphia: Saifer, 1954); F. O. Matthiessen, *Henry James: The Major Phase* (New York: Oxford Univ. Press, 1944), which deals with James' last three novels; and Oscar Cargill, *The Novels of Henry James* (New York: Macmillan, 1961), which is a remarkable evaluative summary of criticism and scholarship to that date. Seven of James' works are interpreted in Kenneth Graham, *The Drama of Fulfilment* (New York: Oxford Univ. Press, 1975).

There are several collections of criticism, such as *The Question of Henry James*, ed. Frederick W. Dupee (New York: H. Holt, 1945); *Discussions of Henry James*, ed. Naomi Lebowitz (Boston: Heath, 1962); *Henry James: A Collection of Critical Essays*, ed. Leon Edel (Englewood Cliffs, NJ: Prentice-Hall, 1963); *Henry James: The Critical Heritage*, ed. Roger Gard (New York: Barnes & Noble, 1968); *Henry James: Modern Judgements*, ed. Tony Tanner (Nashville: Aurora, 1970); and *Henry James's Major Novels: Essays in Criticism*, ed. Lyall H. Powers (East Lansing: Michigan State Univ. Press, 1973).

Bibliographies

For a helpful introductory bibliographical essay, see Robert L. Gale, "Henry James," in *Eight American Authors*, rev. ed., ed. James Woodress (New York: Norton, 1971), pp.321-75. The definitive primary bibliography is Leon Edel and Dan H. Laurence, *A Bibliography of Henry James*, 2nd ed. rev. (London: R. Hart-Davis, 1961). The best bibliography of secondary sources, which is arranged by year of publication, is Kristin Pruitt McColgan, *Henry James, 1917-1959: A Reference Guide* (Boston: G. K. Hall, 1979); and its companion volume, Dorothy McInnis Scura, *Henry James, 1960-1974: A Reference Guide* (G. K. Hall, 1979). Less accurate is an approach by literary forms, Beatrice Ricks, *Henry James: A Bibliography of Secondary Works* (Metuchen, NJ: Scarecrow, 1975). A more specialized focus is Thaddeo K. Babiiha, *The James-Hawthorne Relation: Bibliographical Essays* (G. K. Hall, 1980), which contains six overviews on aspects of Hawthorne's influence.

Reference Works

Henry James Review, 1979- is a triquarterly newsletter for communicating research in progress, letters, reviews, and bibliographic contributions. The best dictionary of James' characters is Robert L. Gale, *Plots and Characters in the Fiction of Henry James* (Hamden, CT: Archon Books, 1965). William T. Stafford, *A Name, Title and Place Index to the Critical Writings of Henry James* (Englewood, CO: Microcard Edition Books, 1975) is helpful for finding what James said in his nonfictional work, excluding letters about persons, works, or places, and is keyed to the Edel and Laurence bibliography.

SARAH ORNE JEWETT, 1849-1909
Pseud: Alice C. Eliot

PRIMARY SOURCES

Separate Works

Deephaven (1877); Play Days [children's book] (1878); Old Friends and New (1879); Country By-Ways (1881); The Mate of the Daylight and Friends Ashore (1883); A Country Doctor (1884); A Marsh Island (1885); A White Heron and Other Stories (1886); The Story of the Normans [children's book] (1887); The King of Folly Island, and Other People (1888); Strangers and Wayfarers (1890); Betty Leicester [children's book] (1890); A Native of Winby and Other Tales (1893); Betty Leicester's English Xmas [children's book] (privately printed, 1894; published as Betty Leicester's Christmas, 1899); The Life of Nancy (1895); The Country of the Pointed Firs (1896); The Queen's Twin and Other Stories (1899); The Tory Lover (1901); Verses (1916).

Collected Works and Edited Texts

No authoritatively edited collection exists. The most widely used collections of Jewett's stories for teaching are *The Country of the Pointed Firs and Other Stories*, selected and arranged with a preface by Willa Cather (Garden City, NY: Doubleday, 1956); and *Deephaven and Other Stories*, ed. Richard Cary (New Haven, CT: College and Univ. Press, 1966). *The World of Dunnett Landing: A Sarah Orne Jewett Collection*, ed. David Bonnell Green (Lincoln: Univ. of Nebraska Press, 1962) made available several previously unpublished works and reprinted five critical essays which had appeared elsewhere. Another collection is *Short Fiction of Sarah Orne Jewett and Mary Wilkins Freeman, Including the Country of the Pointed Firs*, ed. Barbara H. Solomon (New York: New American Library, 1979). *The Tory Lover* (South Berwick, ME: Old Berwick Historical Society, 1975) features illustrations reproduced from the original edition. *The Uncollected Short Stories of Sarah Orne Jewett*, ed. Richard Cary (Waterville, ME: Colby College Press, 1971) contains forty-four previously uncollected stories and a scholarly review of criticism.

Although there is no definitive edition of Jewett's letters, there are several good collections. *Letters of Sarah Orne Jewett*, ed. Annie Fields (Boston: Houghton Mifflin, 1911) is not a scholarly compilation, and dates and details are often inaccurate and undocumented. *Letters of Sarah Orne Jewett Now in the Colby College Library*, eds. Carl J. Weber and Clara Weber (Waterville, ME: Colby College Press, 1947) is a professional editing, as is the standard edition, *Letters*, enl. and rev. ed., ed. Richard Cary (Colby College, 1967), which contains 142 letters written between 1869 and 1908, of which 125 are at Colby College. Cary has supplemented this collection with "Jewett to Dresel: 33 Letters," *Colby Library Quarterly* 11 (1975): 13-19.

Other Source Materials

Jewett's manuscripts and papers are collected in the Houghton Library, Harvard University, at Colby College Library, and in the Society for the Preservation of New England Antiquities.

SECONDARY SOURCES

Biography

Book-length biographies and several essays provide details of Jewett's life. F. O. Matthiessen, *Sarah Orne Jewett* (Boston: Houghton Mifflin, 1929) lacks scholarly documentation but is important as the first organization of dispersed information and for its reproductions of photographs. John Eldridge Frost, *Sarah Orne Jewett* (Kittery Point, ME: Gundalow Club, 1960) provides documentation and critical judgement, but is not definitive. Josephine Donovan, *Sarah Orne Jewett* (New York: Ungar, 1980) draws on diaries and letters to show Jewett's emotional bonds with other women, including Annie Fields.

Criticism

A pamphlet by Margaret Farrand Thorp, *Sarah Orne Jewett* (Minneapolis: Univ. of Minnesota Press, 1966), briefly introduces Jewett's life and works. A. M. Buchan, *"Our Dear Sarah": An Essay on Sarah Orne Jewett* (St. Louis: Washington Univ. Press, 1953) explores Jewett's personality and theories of literary creation. The major scholarly work is Richard Cary, *Sarah Orne Jewett* (New York: Twayne, 1962), which gives thorough coverage to her work and provides thoughtful comment as well as a reliable short biographical account. In addition, *Appreciation of Sarah Orne Jewett*, ed. Richard Cary (Waterville, ME: Colby College Press, 1973) provides a comprehensive cross-section of Jewett criticism from 1885 to 1972, including important insights on structure and symbolism by Warner Berthoff and Hyatt H. Waggoner.

Bibliographies

The most inclusive bibliography is Gwen L. Nagel and James Nagel, *Sarah Orne Jewett: A Reference Guide* (Boston: G. K. Hall, 1978), which annotates criticism of Jewett written between 1873 and 1976.

Reference Works

Regionalism and the Female Imagination, a newsletter from the Department of English, University of North Dakota, Grand Forks, includes items on Jewett. The important scholarly activity at Colby College has resulted in notes and articles being published in the *Colby Library Quarterly*.

DENISE LEVERTOV, 1923-

PRIMARY SOURCES

Separate Works

The Double Image (1946); *Here and Now* (1956); *5 Poems* (1958); *Overland to the Islands* (1958); *With Eyes at the Back of Our Heads* (1960); *The Jacob's Ladder* (1961); *O Taste and See* (1964); *The Sorrow Dance* (1967); *In Praise of Krishna: Songs from the Bengali* [translations with Edward C. Dimock, Jr.] (1967); *A Tree Telling of Orpheus* (1968); *In the Night* (1968); *Three Poems* (1968); *The Cold Spring & Other Poems* (1968); *A Marigold from North Viet Nam* (1968); *Eugene Guillevic Selected Poems* [translation] (1969); *Embroideries* (1969); *Summer Poems*

(1969); *Relearning the Alphabet* (1970); *A New Year's Garland for My Students* (1970); *To Stay Alive* (1971); *Footprints* (1972); *The Poet in the World* [essays] (1973); *Conversation in Moscow* (1973); *The Freeing of the Dust* (1975); *Chekhov on the West Heath* (1977); *Life in the Forest* (1978).

Collected Works

Collected Earlier Poems, 1940-1960 (New York: New Directions, 1979) is a major collection.

SECONDARY SOURCES

Biography and Criticism

A book-length study is Linda Welshimer Wagner, *Denise Levertov* (New York: Twayne, 1967).

Bibliographies

Robert A. Wilson, *A Bibliography of Denise Levertov* (New York: Phoenix Book Shop, 1972).

JACK (JOHN GRIFFITH) LONDON, 1876-1916

PRIMARY SOURCES

Separate Works

The Son of the Wolf: Tales of the Far North (1900); *The God of His Fathers and Other Stories* (1901); *A Daughter of the Snows* (1902); *The Cruise of the Dazzler* (1902); *Children of the Frost* (1902); *The People of the Abyss* (1903); *The Call of the Wild* (1903); *The Kempton-Wace Letters* [with Anna Strunsky] (1903); *The Faith of Men and Other Stories* (1904); *The Sea-Wolf* (1904); *War of the Classes* (1905); *The Game* (1905); *Tales of the Fish Patrol* (1905); *Scorn of Women* [play] (1906); *Moon-Face and Other Stories* (1906); *White Fang* (1906); *Before Adam* (1907); *Love of Life and Other Stories* (1907); *The Road* (1907); *The Iron Heel* (1908); *Martin Eden* (1909); *Lost Face* (1910); *Theft* [play] (1910); *Burning Daylight* (1910); *Revolution and Other Essays* (1910); *When God Laughs and Other Stories* (1911); *Adventure* (1911); *The Cruise of the Snark* (1911); *South Sea Tales* (1911); *The House of Pride and Other Tales of Hawaii* (1912); *Smoke Bellew* (1912); *A Son of the Sun* (1912); *The Night-Born* (1913); *The Abysmal Brute* (1913); *John Barleycorn* [autobiography] (1913); *The Valley of the Moon* (1913); *The Strength of the Strong* (1914); *The Mutiny of the Elsinore* (1914); *The Scarlet Plague* (1915); *The Star Rover* (1915); *The Little Lady of the Big House* (1916); *The Acorn-Planter: A California Forest Play* (1916); *The Turtles of Tasman* (1916); *Jerry of the Islands* (1917); *The Human Drift* (1917); *Michael, Brother of Jerry* (1917); *The Red One* (1918): *On the Makaloa Mat* (1919); *Hearts of Three* (1918); *Dutch Courage and Other Stories* (1922); *The Assassination Bureau, Ltd.* [finished by Robert L. Fish, 1963] ; *Daughters of the Rich* [edited by James E. Sisson] (1971); *Gold* [play written with Herbert Heron, ed. James E. Sisson] (1972).

Collected Works and Edited Texts

There is no standard edition of collected works. Macmillan's Sonoma edition, 1919, printed twenty-eight titles, but no definitive canon exists in English and many titles are not in print. A collection of correspondence between London and Sinclair Lewis is *Letters from Jack London*, eds. King Hendricks and Irving Shepard (New York: Odyssey, 1965). *Jack London: No Mentor but Myself*, ed. Dale L. Walker (Port Washington: Kenniket, 1979) is a compilation of London's own observations on the craft of writing. *Jack London on the Road*, ed. Richard W. Etulain (Logan: Utah State Univ. Press, 1979) is a diary that London kept in spring 1894. *Jack London Reports*, eds. King Hendricks and Irving Shepard (New York: Doubleday, 1970) is a collection of war correspondence; and *The Call of the Wild: A Casebook*, ed. Earl J. Wilcox (Chicago: Nelson-Hall, 1980) contains text, early reviews, and critical essays.

Other Source Materials

Substantial collections of London's manuscripts and correspondence are in the Barrett Library of the University of Virginia, the Huntington Library, the New York Public Library, and many other collections, which are described in Sherman's bibliography (*see* Bibliographies).

SECONDARY SOURCES

Biography

An early biography is by London's daughter, Joan London, *Jack London and His Times: An Unconventional Biography* (New York: Doubleday, 1939), while John Perry, *Jack London: An American Myth* (Chicago: Nelson-Hall, 1981) is more recent, and an interesting photographic record is Russ Kingman, *A Pictorial Life of Jack London* (New York: Crown, 1979). Earle Labor, *Jack London* (New York: Twayne, 1974) integrates criticism and biography for a reliable overview, and a scholarly biography based on London's papers is Andrew Sinclair, *Jack: A Biography of Jack London* (New York: Harper & Row, 1977).

Criticism

An excellent short introduction is Charles C. Walcutt, *Jack London* (Minneapolis: Univ. of Minnesota Press, 1966). In addition, see Philip S. Foner, *Jack London: American Rebel* (New York: Citadel, 1947), which provides a collection of London's social writings, as well as biographical and critical comment; and Franklin Walker, *Jack London and the Klondike* (San Marino, CA: Huntington Library, 1966), which documents London's Alaskan experience and relates it to his work. James I. McClintock, *White Logic* (Grand Rapids, MI: Wolf House Books, 1975) is a study of London's short stories. *Jack London: Essays in Criticism*, ed. Ray Wilson Ownbey (Santa Barbara, CA: Peregrine Smith, 1978) is a collection of the most important criticism.

Bibliographies

A major bibliography of primary and secondary material in English and foreign languages is Hensley C. Woodbridge, John London, and George H. Tweney, *Jack London: A Bibliography* (Georgetown, CA: Talisman Press, 1966). Joan R. Sherman, *Jack London: A Reference Guide* (Boston: G. K. Hall, 1977) is an annotated chronological compilation of secondary sources; and James E. Sisson, III, and Robert W. Martens, *Jack London First Editions* (Oakland, CA: Star Rover House, 1979) is an illustrated chronological guide to first editions.

Reference Works

Jack London Newsletter, 1967- is a clearinghouse for current bibliography, reviews, and research. The private press, Wolf House Books, Grand Rapids, Michigan, publishes reprints, collections, and criticism on London.

HENRY WADSWORTH LONGFELLOW, 1807-1882

PRIMARY SOURCES

Separate Works

Elements of French Grammar (1830); *French Exercises* (1830); *Novelas Españolas* (1830); *Manuel de proverbes dramatiques* (1830); *Syllabus de la grammaire Italienne* (1832); *Saggi De' Novellieri Italiani* (1832); *Coplas de Don Jorge Manrique* (1833); *Outre-Mer; A Pilgrimage beyond the Sea* (1833-34); *Hyperion: A Romance* (1839); *Voices of the Night* (1839); *Ballads and Other Poems* (1842); *Poems on Slavery* (1842); *The Spanish Student: A Play in Three Acts* (1843); *Poems* (1845); *The Belfry of Bruges* (1846); *Evangeline: A Tale of Acadie* (1847); *Kavanagh: A Tale* (1849); *The Seaside and the Fireside* (1850); *The Golden Legend* (1851); *The Song of Hiawatha* (1855); *The Courtship of Miles Standish and Other Poems* (1858); *The New England Tragedy* (1860); *Tales of a Wayside Inn* (1863); *Noel* (1864); *The Divine Comedy of Dante Alighieri* (1865-67); *Household Poems* (1865); *Flower-De-Luce* (1867); *The New England Tragedies* (1868); *The Alarm-Bell of Atri* (1871); *The Divine Tragedy* (1871); *Three Books of Song* (1872); *Christus: A Mystery* (1872); *Aftermath* (1873); *The Hanging of the Crane* (1874); *The Masque of Pandora and Other Poems* (1875); *Kéramos* (1877); *Kéramos and Other Poems* (1878); *Bayard Taylor* (1879); *From My Arm-Chair* (1879); *Ultima Thule* (1880); *In the Harbor: Ultima Thule–Part II* (1882); *Michael Angelo* (1882-83); *There Was a Little Girl* (1883).

Collected Works and Edited Texts

There is no scholarly edition of Longfellow's works, although *The Works of Henry Wadsworth Longfellow*, Standard Library Edition, 14v. (Boston: Houghton Mifflin, 1886-91) remains important. *Longfellow: Selected Poetry*, ed. Howard Nemerov (New York: Dell, 1959); and *The Essential Longfellow*, ed. Lewis Leary (New York: Collier, 1963) are more convenient volumes of selections. Correspondence is collected in *The Letters of Henry Wadsworth Longfellow*, ed. Andrew Hilen. 4v. (Cambridge: Harvard Univ. Press, 1966-72).

Other Source Materials

The largest deposits of manuscripts are at the Houghton Library, Harvard University. A guide to an exhibit of Bowdoin College's extensive holdings is Richard Harwell, *Hawthorne and Longfellow* (Brunswick, ME: Bowdoin College, 1966).

SECONDARY SOURCES

Biography

Two biographies are Samuel Longfellow, *Life of Henry Wadsworth Longfellow with Extracts from His Journals and Correspondence*, 2v. (Boston: Ticknor, 1886); and his *Final Memorials* (Ticknor, 1887) which have suppressed some facts, as Hilen's edition of the letters reveals. Well-documented lives are Lawrance R. Thompson, *Young Longfellow, 1807-1843* (New York: Macmillan, 1938; repr. New York: Octagon Books, 1969); and Edward Wagenknecht, *Longfellow: A Full-Length Portrait* (New York: Longmans, Green, 1955), which Wagenknecht also shortened as *Henry Wadsworth Longfellow: Portrait of an American Humanist* (New York: Oxford Univ. Press, 1966). Kenneth W. Cameron, *Longfellow's Reading in Libraries* (Hartford, CT: Transcendental Books, 1973) is based on Longfellow's bookcharging records.

Criticism

The best study of Longfellow is a critical biography, Newton Arvin, *Longfellow: His Life and Work* (Boston: Little, Brown, 1963). In addition, useful introductions are Edward Hirsch, *Henry Wadsworth Longfellow* (Minneapolis: Univ. of Minnesota Press, 1964); and Cecil B. Williams, *Henry Wadsworth Longfellow* (New York: Twayne, 1964). A sympathetic discussion of Longfellow and other Schoolroom poets, together with a selection of their poems, is in Goerge Arms, *The Fields Were Green: A New View of Bryant, Whittier, Holmes, Lowell, and Longfellow* (Stanford, CA: Stanford Univ. Press, 1953).

Bibliography

The best bibliographical orientation is Richard Dilworth Rust, "Henry Wadsworth Longfellow," in *Fifteen American Authors before 1900*, eds. Robert A. Rees and Earl N. Harbert (Madison: Univ. of Wisconsin Press, 1971), pp.263-83. A bibliography of primary sources is in Jacob Blanck, *Bibliography of American Literature* (New Haven, CT: Yale Univ. Press, 1955-73), v.5, pp.468-640.

AMY LOWELL, 1874-1925

PRIMARY SOURCES

Separate Works

Dream Drops; Or, Stories from Fairy Land (1887); *A Dome of Many-Coloured Glass* (1912); *Sword Blades and Poppy Seed* (1914); *Six French Poets* [translation from French] (1915); *Men, Women, and Ghosts* (1916); *Tendencies in Modern American Poetry* (1917); *Can Grande's Castle* (1918); *Pictures of the Floating World* (1919); *Legends* (1921); *Fir-Flower Tablets* [translation from Chinese with Florence Ayscough] (1921); *A Critical Fable* (1922); *John Keats* (1925); *What's O'Clock* (1925); *East Wind* (1926); *Ballads for Sale* (1927); *The Madonna of Carthagena* (1927); *Fool O' the Moon* (1927); *Poetry and Poets: Essays* (1930).

Collected Works and Edited Texts

Poetry is gathered in *The Complete Poetical Works*, ed. Louis Untermeyer (Boston: Houghton Mifflin, 1955); *Selected Poems of Amy Lowell*, ed. John Livingston Lowes (Houghton Mifflin, 1928); *A Shard of Silence: Selected Poems of Amy Lowell*, ed. G. R. Ruihley (New York: Twayne, 1957); and *The Touch of You: Poems of Love and Beauty*, ed. Peter Seymour (Kansas City: Hallmark, 1972). A collection of her critical writing is in *Poetry and Poets* (Houghton Mifflin, 1930); and letters to a friend are in *Florence Ayscough and Amy Lowell: Correspondence of a Friendship*, ed. Harley F. McNair (Chicago: Univ. of Chicago Press, 1945).

Other Source Materials

Correspondence and papers are in the Houghton Library, Harvard University, and the Harriet Monroe Collection of the University of Chicago.

SECONDARY SOURCES

Biography

C. David Heymann, *American Aristocracy: The Lives and Times of James Russell, Amy, and Robert Lowell* (New York: Dodd, Mead, 1979) places the three family members in the context of their times.

Criticism

All the works listed below contain biography and criticism. For a sound introduction, see the pamphlet F. Cudworth Flint, *Amy Lowell* (Minneapolis: Univ. of Minnesota Press, 1969). The standard work is S. Foster Damon, *Amy Lowell: A Chronicle with Extracts from Her Correspondence* (Boston: Houghton Mifflin, 1935). Other lives are Horace Gregory, *Amy Lowell: Portrait of the Poet in Her Time* (New York: T. Nelson, 1958); the less reliable Glenn Richard Ruihley, *The Thorn of a Rose: Amy Lowell Reconsidered* (Hamden, CT: Archon Books, 1975); and Jean Gould, *Amy: The World of Amy Lowell and the Imagist Movement* (New York: Dodd, Mead, 1975).

Bibliographies

A list of first printings of all the published writings, including letters, articles, and reviews that appeared in periodicals, is in Damon's bibliography (*see* Criticism). All works listed above contain secondary bibliographies.

JAMES RUSSELL LOWELL, 1819-1891
Pseuds: Homer Wilbur, A Wonderful Quiz

PRIMARY SOURCES

Separate Works

Class Poem [pamphlet] (1838); *A Year's Life, and Other Poems* (1841); *Poems* (1844); *Conversations on Some of the Old Poets* (1845); *Poems: Second Series* (1848);

A Fable for Critics (1848); *The Biglow Papers: First Series* (1848); *The Vision of Sir Launfal* (1848); *Fireside Travels* (1864); *Ode Recited at the Commemoration of the Living and Dead Soldiers of Harvard University* (1865); *The Biglow Papers: Second Series* (1867); *Under the Willows, and Other Poems* (1869); *The Cathedral* (1870); *Among My Books* (1870); *My Study Windows* (1871); *Among My Books: Second Series* (1876); *Three Memorial Poems* (1877); *Democracy and Other Addresses* (1887); *The English Poets; Lessing, Rousseau* (1888); *Political Essays* (1888); *Heartease and Rue* (1888); *Books and Libraries, and Other Papers* (1889).

Collected Works and Edited Texts

The standard edition is the Riverside edition, *Writings of James Russell Lowell*, 12v. (Boston: Houghton Mifflin, 1890-92). The Cambridge edition of *The Complete Poetical Works of James Russell Lowell*, ed. Horace E. Scudder (Houghton Mifflin, 1897) is the only comprehensive anthology and includes poetry from the Riverside edition, as well as poems from Charles Eliot Norton's edition of *Last Poems of James Russell Lowell* (Houghton Mifflin, 1895). A good modern anthology which includes poems, letters, and prose is *James Russell Lowell: Representative Selections*, eds. Harry Hayden Clark and Norman Foerster (New York: American Book Co., 1947). Lowell's critical views are in *Literary Criticism of James Russell Lowell*, ed. Herbert F. Smith (Lincoln: Univ. of Nebraska Press, 1969). The only modern scholarly edition of Lowell is *The Biglow Papers: First Series*, Critical ed., ed. Thomas Wortham (Dekalb: Northern Illinois Univ. Press, 1977).

Lowell's letters in a bowdlerized version are in *Letters of James Russell Lowell*, ed. Charles Eliot Norton. 2v. (New York: Harper, 1894). *New Letters of James Russell Lowell*, ed. M. A. de Wolfe Howe (New York: Harper, 1932) contains mostly letters to Howell's daughter, while other important correspondence with friends is in *The Scholar Friends: Letters of Francis James Child and James Russell Lowell*, eds. M. A. de Wolfe Howe and G. W. Cottrell, Jr. (Cambridge: Harvard Univ. Press, 1952); and *Browning to His American Friends: Letters between the Brownings, the Storys and James Russell Lowell, 1841-1890*, ed. Gertrude Reese Hudson (New York: Barnes & Noble, 1965).

Other Source Materials

The Houghton Library at Harvard University contains the largest of the many collections of Lowell's manuscripts.

SECONDARY SOURCES

Biography

The standard life is Horace Elisha Scudder, *James Russell Lowell*, 2v. (Boston: Houghton Mifflin, 1901). Martin Duberman, *James Russell Lowell* (Houghton Mifflin, 1966) is based on manuscript sources; and Edward Wagenknecht, *James Russell Lowell: Portrait of a Many-Sided Man* (New York: Oxford Univ. Press, 1971) is more an assemblage of facts than an interpretation. A brief and well-founded biographical introduction by Harry Hayden Clark is in *James Russell Lowell: Representative Selections* (*see* Collected Works and Edited Texts).

Criticism

Equally valuable for biography, the best critical book-length examination of the literature is Leon Howard, *Victorian Knight-Errant: A Study of the Early Literary Career of James Russell Lowell* (Berkeley: Univ. of California Press, 1952), which focusses on Lowell's life and milieu to 1857.

Bibliographies

The best bibliographical introduction is Robert A. Rees, "James Russell Lowell," in *Fifteen American Authors before 1900*, eds. Robert A. Rees and Earl N. Harbert (Madison: Univ. of Wisconsin Press, 1971), pp.285-305. A bibliography of primary sources is in Jacob Blanck, *Bibliography of American Literature* (New Haven, CT: Yale Univ. Press, 1955-), v.6, pp.21-111.

ROBERT LOWELL, 1917-1977

PRIMARY SOURCES

Separate Works

Land of Unlikeness (1944); *Lord Weary's Castle* (1946); *Poems, 1938-1949* (1950); *The Mills of the Kavanaughs* (1951); *Life Studies* (1959); *Imitations* (1961); *Phaedra* [verse translation of Racine's *Phèdre*] (1961); *For the Union Dead* (1964); *Selected Poems* (1965); *The Old Glory* [play based on versions of Hawthorne and Melville] (1965); *Near the Ocean* (1967); *Notebook, 1967-1968* (1969); *Prometheus Bound* [adaptation of Aeschylus] (1969); *Notebook* (1970); *The Dolphin* (1973); *For Lizzie and Harriet* (1973); *History* (1973); *Selected Poems* (1976); *Day by Day* (1977).

Collected Works and Edited Texts

The Achievement of Robert Lowell, ed. William J. Martz (Glenview, IL: Scott Foresman, 1966) contains a fine selection of Lowell's poems, with a critical introduction.

SECONDARY SOURCES

Biography

Important autobiographical information accompanies Lowell's verse collection, *Life Studies* (New York: Farrar, Straus, & Cudahy, 1959). A critical account of the life, which relies on evidence from Lowell's papers, is Steven Axelrod, *Robert Lowell: Life and Art* (Princeton, NJ: Princeton Univ. Press, 1978). C. David Heymann, *American Aristocracy* (New York: Dodd, Mead, 1979) relates the lives and milieus of James Russell, Amy, and Robert Lowell.

Criticism

Among reliable introductions are a clearly written pamphlet, Jay Martin, *Robert Lowell* (Minneapolis: Univ. of Minnesota Press, 1970); and two book-length accounts of the life and work, John F. Crick, *Robert Lowell* (New York: Barnes & Noble, 1974); and Richard J. Fein, *Robert Lowell*, 2nd ed. (Boston: Twayne, 1979). Two important general criticisms are a careful study of the imagery by Marjorie G. Perloff, *The Poetic Art of Robert Lowell* (Ithaca, NY: Cornell Univ. Press, 1973); and Stephen Yenser, *Circle to Circle* (Berkeley: Univ. of California Press, 1975), which traces recurring themes and imagery. Studies on specific periods are Hugh B. Staples, *Robert Lowell: The First Twenty Years* (New York: Farrar, Straus & Cudahy, 1962); Jerome Mazzaro, *The Poetic Themes of Robert Lowell* (Ann Arbor: Univ. of Michigan Press, 1965); Philip Cooper, *The Autobiographical Myth of Robert Lowell* (Chapel Hill: Univ. of North Carolina Press, 1970), which concentrates on poems since *Life Studies* and demonstrates the unity of Lowell's work; Vivian Smith, *The Poetry of Robert Lowell* (Sydney: Sydney Univ. Press, 1974), which is a lucid treatment of single poems through the 1970 *Notebook*; and Roger K. Meiners, *Everything to Be Endured: An Essay on Robert Lowell and Modern Poetry* (Columbia: Univ. of Missouri Press, 1970). For studies of Lowell as a politically oriented poet, see Patrick Cosgrave, *The Public Poetry of Robert Lowell* (London: Gollancz, 1970); Thomas R. Edwards, *Imagination and Power: A Study of Poetry on Public Themes* (New York: Oxford Univ. Press, 1971), pp.210-26; and the close explications in Alan Williamson, *Pity the Monsters: The Political Vision of Robert Lowell* (New Haven, CT: Yale Univ. Press, 1974).

Several anthologies that collect shorter views are *Robert Lowell: A Collection of Critical Essays*, ed. Thomas Parkinson (Englewood Cliffs, NJ: Prentice-Hall, 1968); *Robert Lowell: A Portrait of the Artist in His Time*, eds. Michael London and Robert Boyers (New York: D. Lewis, 1970), which contains a 1961 interview with Lowell and twenty-five essays; *Profile of Robert Lowell*, ed. Jerome Mazzaro (Columbus, OH: Merrill, 1971), which gathers some less accessible essays; and *Critics on Robert Lowell*, ed. Jonathan Price (Coral Gables: Univ. of Miami Press, 1972).

Bibliographies

Jerome Mazzaro, *The Achievement of Robert Lowell, 1939-1959* (Detroit: Univ. of Detroit Press, 1960) is a preliminary checklist of Lowell's books and individual poems and works about him. It is supplemented by Mazzaro's "A Checklist of Materials on Robert Lowell, 1939-1968," in *Robert Lowell a Portrait of the Artist in His Time* (*see* Criticism). A fine selective bibliography of Lowell's poetry, drama, critical essays, and interviews, as well as books and articles about him, is in Stephen Yenser, *Circle to Circle* (*see* Criticism).

ARCHIBALD MacLEISH, 1892-1982

PRIMARY SOURCES

Separate Works

Songs for a Summer's Day (1915); *Tower of Ivory* (1917); *The Happy Marriage and Other Poems* (1924); *The Pot of Earth* (1925); *Nobodaddy* [play] (1926); *Streets in the Moon* (1926); *The Hamlet of A. MacLeish* (1928); *Einstein* (1929); *New Found Land* (1930); *Conquistador* (1932); *Frescoes for Mr. Rockefeller's City* (1933); *Poems, 1924-1933* (1933); *Panic* [play] (1935); *Public Speech* (1936); *The Fall of the City* [play] (1936); *Air Raid* [play] (1938); *Land of the Free* (1938); *America Was*

Promises (1939); *Union Pacific: A Ballet* (produced 1934; published 1939); *The Irresponsibles: A Declaration* [prose] (1940); *The American Cause* [prose] (1941); *A Time to Speak* [prose] (1941); *The States Talking* [play] (1941); *Actfive and Other Poems* (1948); *Poetry and Opinion: The Pisan Cantos of Ezra Pound: A Dialogue on the Role of Poetry* [prose] (1950); *Freedom Is the Right to Choose: An Inquiry into the Battle for the American Future* [prose] (1951); *The Trojan Horse* [play] (1952); *This Music Crept by Me upon the Waters* [play] (1953); *Songs for Eve* (1954); *J. B.* [dramatization of the book of Job] (1958); *Poetry and Experience* [prose] (1961); *The Eleanor Roosevelt Story* [prose] (1965); *A Continuing Journey* [prose] (1967); *An Evening's Journey to Conway, Massachusetts: An Outdoor Play* (1967); *The Wild Old Wicked Man and Other Poems* (1968); *Scratch* [play] (1971); *Champion of a Cause: Essays and Addresses on Librarianship* (1971); *The Great American Fourth of July Parade* [play] (1975); *Riders on the Earth* (1978).

Collected Works and Edited Texts

The most complete collection of poetry is *New and Collected Poems, 1917-1976* (Boston: Houghton Mifflin, 1976). Two earlier collections are *Collected Poems, 1917-1952* (Houghton Mifflin, 1952; rev. ed., 1962) and *The Human Season: Selected Poems, 1926-1972* (Houghton Mifflin, 1972). A collection of his plays is *Six Plays* (Houghton Mifflin, 1980). Collections of his essays and addresses are *A Time to Speak: The Selected Prose of Archibald MacLeish* (Houghton Mifflin, 1941); *A Time to Act: Selected Addresses* (Houghton Mifflin, 1943); and *The American Story: Ten Broadcasts* (New York: Duell, 1944).

SECONDARY SOURCES

Biography

There has been little formal biographical or critical attention to MacLeish, and information must be found in periodical articles.

Criticism

Grover Smith, *Archibald MacLeish* (Minneapolis: Univ. of Minnesota Press, 1971) is a brief pamphlet that gives little attention to the plays. A longer, book-length introduction to the life and work is Signi Lenea Falk, *Archibald MacLeish* (New York: Twayne, 1965).

Bibliographies

Arthur Mizener, *A Catalogue of the First Editions of Archibald MacLeish* (New Haven, CT: Yale Univ. Press, 1938) is a detailed descriptive bibliography of MacLeish's works that were in a 1938 exhibition at Yale. The most recent bibliography of primary and secondary sources is Edward J. Mullaly, *Archibald MacLeish: A Checklist* (Kent, OH: Kent State Univ. Press, 1973), which lists MacLeish's books, pamphlets, appearances of poetry in periodicals and newspapers, and an annotative checklist of criticism, through 1972.

BERNARD MALAMUD, 1914-

PRIMARY SOURCES

Separate Works

The Natural (1952); *The Assistant* (1957); *The Magic Barrel* [short stories] (1958); *A New Life* (1961); *Idiots First* [short stories] (1963); *The Fixer* (1966); *Pictures of Fidelman: An Exhibition* [fiction] (1969); *The Tenants* (1971); *Rembrandt's Hat* [short stories] (1973); *Dubin's Lives* (1979); *God's Grace* (1982).

SECONDARY SOURCES

Biography

There is no biography of Malamud.

Criticism

An early treatment of Malamud and his work is Sidney Richman, *Bernard Malamud* (New York: Twayne, 1966). Robert Ducharme, *Art and Idea in the Novels of Bernard Malamud: Toward the Fixer* (The Hague: Mouton, 1974) traces shifts in authorial stance and examines Malamud's use of myth, especially the wasteland motif; Robert Kegan, *The Sweeter Welcome: Voices for a Vision of Affirmation: Bellow, Malamud, and Martin Buber* (Needham Heights, MA: Humanities Press, 1976) discusses the relation between the works and their readers; Evelyn Gross Avery, *Rebels and Victims: The Fiction of Richard Wright and Bernard Malamud* (Port Washington, NY: Kennikat Press, 1979) examines ways in which Malamud's heroes respond to the indifference of modern society; and Sheldon J. Hershinow, *Bernard Malamud* (New York: Ungar, 1980) examines the works through *Dubin's Lives*. Shorter criticism is gathered in the collections *Bernard Malamud and the Critics*, eds. Leslie A. Field and Joyce W. Field (New York: New York Univ. Press, 1970); *Bernard Malamud: A Collection of Critical Essays*, eds. Leslie A. Field and Joyce W. Field (Englewood Cliffs, NJ: Prentice-Hall, 1975), which includes an interview and several new essays; *The Fiction of Bernard Malamud*, eds. Richard Astro and Jackson Benton (Corvallis: Oregon State Univ. Press, 1977); and "Bernard Malamud: Reinterpretations," which comprised the issue of *Studies in American Jewish Literature* 4 (Spring 1978).

Bibliographies

Bibliographies include Rita Nathalie Kosofsky, *Bernard Malamud: An Annotated Checklist* (Kent, OH: Kent State Univ. Press, 1969); Robert D. Habich, "Bernard Malamud: A Bibliographic Survey," *Studies in American Jewish Literature* 4 (1978): 78-84; and Ira Bruce Nadel, *Jewish Writers of North America: A Guide to Information Sources* (Detroit: Gale, 1981), pp.259-61, which lists journal criticism selectively.

HERMAN MELVILLE, 1819-1891

PRIMARY SOURCES

Separate Works

Typee (1846); *Omoo* (1847); *Mardi* (1849); *Redburn* (1849); *White-Jacket* (1850); *Moby-Dick* (1851); *Pierre* (1852); *Israel Potter* (1855); *The Piazza Tales* (1856); *The Confidence-Man* (1857); *Battle-Pieces* (1866); *Clarel* (1876); *John Marr and Other Sailors* (1888); *Timoleon* (1891); *Billy Budd and Other Prose Pieces* (1924); *Poems* (1924); *Journal up the Straits* (1935).

Collected Works and Edited Texts

When complete, the standard edition, which is also available in paperback, will be *The Writings of Herman Melville*, eds. Harrison Hayford, Herschel Parker, and G. Thomas Tanselle (Evanston, IL: Northwestern Univ. Press, 1968-). *The Works of Herman Melville*, 16v. (London: Constable, 1922-24), though complete, is not a scholarly edition, and *Complete Works of Herman Melville*, ed. H. P. Vincent (Chicago: Hendricks House, 1947-), though never completed and uneven, remains useful for interpretative introductions and notes.

Some important editions will be revised for inclusion in the Newberry-Northwestern *Writings*. Among them are texts of Melville's public lectures, contained in the appendix of Merton M. Sealts, Jr. *Melville as Lecturer* (Cambridge: Harvard Univ. Press, 1957); *The Letters of Herman Melville*, eds. Merrell R. Davis and William H. Gilman (New Haven, CT: Yale Univ. Press, 1960); *Billy Budd, Sailor*, eds. Harrison Hayford and Merton M. Sealts, Jr. (Chicago: Univ. of Chicago Press, 1962); and *Moby-Dick*, eds. Harrison Hayford and Herschel Parker (New York: Norton, 1976). An edition of the poems which has an excellent introductory essay is *Selected Poems of Herman Melville: A Reader's Edition*, ed. Robert Penn Warren (New York: Random House, 1970). *Herman Melville*, v.1. *Typee, Omoo, Mardi*, ed. G. Thomas Tanselle (New York: Viking, 1982) has recently appeared in the series The Library of America.

SECONDARY SOURCES

Biography

Jay Leyda, *The Melville Log: A Documentary Life of Herman Melville, 1819-1891*, 2v. (New York: Harcourt Brace, 1951; repr. with a supplement, New York: Gordian Press, 1969) provides documentation by collecting extracts from letters, ship logs, and newspapers. Leon Howard, *Herman Melville: A Biography* (Berkeley: Univ. of California Press, 1951), the standard biography, draws on Leyda's materials. Merton M. Sealts, Jr., *The Early Lives of Melville* (Madison: Univ. of Wisconsin Press, 1974) reprints and comments on nineteenth-century interpretations; and Edward H. Rosenberry, *Melville* (Boston: Routledge & Kegan Paul, 1979) reliably combines biography and criticism. For useful comment, see Tyrus Hillway, *Herman Melville* (New York: Twayne, 1963); and Herschel Parker's brief introduction in *The Norton Anthology of American Literature*, v.1, ed. Ronald Gottesmann, et al. (New York: Norton, 1979), pp.2032-44, which takes into account recent discoveries.

Criticism

For critical introductions, see James E. Miller, Jr., *A Reader's Guide to Herman Melville* (New York: Farrar, Straus & Cudahy, 1962); and Howard P. Vincent, *The Merrill Guide to Herman Melville* (Columbus, OH: Merrill, 1969). Newton Arvin, *Herman Melville* (New York: Sloane, 1950) is especially penetrating on *Moby-Dick*; and Richard Chase, *Herman Melville, a Critical Study* (New York: Macmillan, 1949) is another among the many important studies. Collections of criticism which should be consulted are *Melville: A Collection of Critical Essays*, ed. Richard Chase (Englewood Cliffs, NJ: Prentice-Hall, 1962); *The Recognition of Herman Melville: Selected Criticism since 1846*, ed. Herschel Parker (Ann Arbor: Univ. of Michigan Press, 1967); and *Melville: The Critical Heritage*, ed. Watson G. Branch (Boston: Routledge & Kegan Paul, 1974). Collections devoted to criticism of specific works are *Moby-Dick Centennial Essays*, eds. Tyrus Hillway and Luther S. Mansfield (Dallas: Southern Methodist Univ. Press, 1953); *Moby-Dick as Doubloon: Essays and Extracts, 1851-1970*, eds. Herschel Parker and Harrison Hayford (New York: Norton, 1970); *The Merrill Studies in Billy Budd*, ed. Haskell S. Springer (Columbus, OH: Merrill, 1970); *Bartleby the Scrivener: A Symposium*, ed. Howard P. Vincent (Kent, OH: Kent State Univ. Press, 1960); and *Bartelby the Inscrutable*, ed. M. Thomas Inge (Hamden, CT: Archon Books, 1979).

Bibliographies

The best general bibliographical orientations are the essays of Stanley Williams, "Herman Melville," in *Eight American Authors*, ed. Floyd Stovall (New York: Modern Language Association of America, 1956), pp.207-270, and Nathalia Wright, "Herman Melville," in *Eight American Authors*, rev. ed., ed. James Woodress (New York: Norton, 1971). A descriptive bibliography by G. T. Tanselle will be included as volume 16 of the Newberry-Northwestern edition. Jeanetta Boswell, *Herman Melville and the Critics* (Metuchen, NJ: Scarecrow, 1981) is a checklist of criticism written 1900-1978 and arranged by author, while Brian Higgins, *Herman Melville: An Annotated Bibliography* (Boston: G. K. Hall, 1979), v.1, is a chronological coverage of criticism and reviews that appeared 1846-1930. Other bibliographies are Theodore L. Gross and Stanley Wertheim, *Hawthorne, Melville, Stephen Crane: A Critical Bibliography* (New York: Free Press, 1971); Steven Mailloux and Herschel Parker, *Checklist of Melville Reviews* (Los Angeles: Melville Society, 1975) which lists accurate texts; and Beatrice Ricks and Joseph D. Adams, *Herman Melville: A Reference Bibliography, 1900-1972, with Selected Nineteenth Century Materials* (G. K. Hall, 1973), which is unreliable. A fine descriptive bibliography of *Moby-Dick*, issued for an exhibition at the Newberry Library, is G. Thomas Tanselle, *A Checklist of Editions of Moby Dick, 1851-1976* (Evanston, IL: Northwestern Univ. Press and The Newberry Library, 1976). An important survey of biographies published between 1852 and 1975 is the critical review Robert Wilder, "Melville and His Biographers," *Emerson Society Quarterly* 22 (3rd Quarter, 1976): 169-82.

Reference Works

Melville Society Newsletter (formerly *Extracts: An Occasional Newsletter*) is the best source of current bibliography and scholarly activity. Robert L. Gale, *Plots and Characters in the Fiction and Narrative Poetry of Herman Melville* (Cambridge: MIT Press, 1969) gives convenient summaries. Merton M. Sealts, Jr., *Melville's Reading* (Madison: Univ. of Wisconsin Press, 1966) lists books Melville owned or used. *A Concordance to Herman Melville's Clarel*, ed. Larry Edward Wegener. 3v. (Melville

Society, 1979; available from Univ. Microfilms International, Ann Arbor, MI) provides access to the first American edition of *Clarel* (New York: G. P. Putnam, 1876).

EDNA ST. VINCENT MILLAY, 1892-1950
Pseud: Nancy Boyd

PRIMARY SOURCES

Separate Works

Renascence and Other Poems (1917); *A Few Figs from Thistles* (1920); *The Lamp and the Bell* (1921); *Aria da Capo* (1921); *Second April* (1921); *Two Slatterns and a King* (1921); *The Ballad of the Harp-Weaver* (1922); *The Harp-Weaver and Other Poems* (1923); *Distressing Dialogues* [prose sketches] (1924); *The King's Henchman* [libretto] (1927); *The Buck in the Snow and Other Poems* (1928); *Fatal Interview* (1931); *The Princess Marries the Page* (1932); *Wine from These Grapes* (1934) *Flowers of Evil* [translation of Baudelaire's work, with George Dillon] (1936); *Conversation at Midnight* (1937); *Huntsman, What Quarry?* (1939); *There Are No Islands Any More* (1940); *Make Bright the Arrows: 1940 Notebook* (1940); *Invocation to the Muses* (1940); *Collected Sonnets* (1941); *The Murder of the Lidice* (1942); *Collected Lyrics* (1943); *Poem and Prayer for an Invading Army* (1944); *Mine the Harvest* (1954); *Collected Poems* (1956).

Collected Works and Edited Texts

There is no definitive edition of Millay's work, but most is gathered in *Collected Sonnets* (New York: Harper, 1941); *Collected Lyrics* (Harper, 1943); and *Collected Poems*, ed. Norma Millay (Harper, 1956). Correspondence is available in *Letters of Edna St. Vincent Millay*, ed. Allan Ross Macdougall (Harper, 1952).

SECONDARY SOURCES

Biography

Some of the biographical and critical work is uneven, but among the more reliable biographies are Vincent Sheean, *The Indigo Bunting* (New York: Harper, 1951), which is a memoir that associates Millay's personality with birds; Jean Gould, *The Poet and Her Book* (New York: Dodd, Mead, 1969); and Joan Dash, *A Life of One's Own* (New York: Harper & Row, 1973), which is a psychological study of the relationships of Margaret Sanger, Maria Goeppert Mayer, and Millay with their husbands.

Criticism

A short contribution concentrating on the theme of integrity is James Gray, *Edna St. Vincent Millay* (Minneapolis: Univ. of Minnesota Press, 1967). An early full-scale, somewhat laudatory study is Elizabeth Atkins, *Edna St. Vincent Millay and Her Times* (Chicago: Univ. of Chicago Press, 1936). The best full-scale study of both life and work is Norman A. Brittin, *Edna St. Vincent Millay* (New York: Twayne, 1967).

Bibliographies

Karl Yost, *A Bibliography of the Works of Edna St. Vincent Millay* (New York: Harper, 1937) is useful for its primary bibliography; and Judith Nierman, *Edna St.*

Vincent Millay: A Reference Guide (Boston: G. K. Hall, 1977) is an excellent annotated chronological guide to the criticism.

ARTHUR MILLER, 1915-

PRIMARY SOURCES

Separate Works

Focus [fiction] (1945); *Situation Normal* [journal] (1944); *That They May Win* (1943 production; 1945 publication); *The Man Who Had All the Luck* (1944 performance; 1945 publication); *All My Sons* (1947); *Death of a Salesman* (1949); *An Enemy of the People* [adaptation of Ibsen's play] (performance 1950; publication 1951); *The Crucible* (1953); *A View from the Bridge: Two One Act Plays* [second play is *A Memory of Two Mondays*] (1955; rev. 1957); *Collected Plays* (1957); *The Misfits* [screenplay] (1961); *Jane's Blanket* [for children] (1963); *After the Fall* (1964); *Incident at Vichy* (1964 performance; 1965 publication); *I Don't Need You Any More* [short stories] (1967); *The Price* (1967 performance; 1968 publication); *In Russia* [journal, with Inge Morath] (1969); *The Creation of the World and Other Business* (1973); *In the Country* [prose, with Inge Morath] (1977); *The Theatre Essays* (1978); *Chinese Encounters* [prose, with Inge Morath] (1979).

SECONDARY SOURCES

Biography

Several of the critical studies, below, incorporate biographical materials.

Criticism

A brief introduction to the life and work is the pamphlet Robert Hogan, *Arthur Miller* (Minneapolis: Univ. of Minnesota Press, 1964). Two critical appraisals of the work through *Incident at Vichy* are Sheila Huftel, *Arthur Miller: The Burning Glass* (New York: Citadel, 1965), which carefully examines Miller's dramatic theory; and Edward Murray, *Arthur Miller, Dramatist* (New York: Ungar, 1967), which provides explications and analyses of structure. Two works which cover the plays through *The Price* are Ronald Hayman, *Arthur Miller* (Ungar, 1972); and Benjamin Nelson, *Arthur Miller: Portrait of a Playwright* (New York: McKay, 1970). Leonard Moss, *Arthur Miller*, rev. ed. (New York: Twayne, 1980) examines the dramatic principles underlying Miller's study of the consequences of self-assertion. Miller's *Theatre Essays* (New York: Viking, 1978) clarify his own work and that of other playwrights. Two critical anthologies are *Arthur Miller: A Collection of Critical Essays*, ed. Robert W. Corrigan (Englewood Cliffs, NJ: Prentice-Hall, 1969), which covers work through *The Price*; and *Critical Essays on Arthur Miller*, ed. James J. Martine (Boston: G. K. Hall, 1979), which collects critical reviews and essays of thirty-five years.

Bibliographies

A scholarly publishing history of all Miller's articles, speeches, interviews, and books, with copies of title pages, is George H. Jensen, *Arthur Miller: A Bibliographical*

Checklist (Columbia, SC: J. Faust, 1976). Two bibliographies of secondary sources are Tetsumaro Hayashi, *An Index to Arthur Miller Criticism*, 2nd ed. (Metuchen, NJ: Scarecrow, 1976); and John H. Ferres, *Arthur Miller: A Reference Guide* (Boston: G. K. Hall, 1979), which is an annotated chronological bibliography for works written about Miller between 1944 and 1978.

MARIANNE (CRAIG) MOORE, 1887-1972

PRIMARY SOURCES

Separate Works

Poems (1921); *Marriage* (1923); *Observations* (1924); *Selected Poems* (1935); *The Pangolin and Other Verse* (1936); *What Are Years?* (1941); *Nevertheless* (1944); *Rock Crystal: A Christmas Tale* by Adalbert Stifler [translation with Elizabeth Mayer] (1945); *Collected Poems* (1951); *The Fables of La Fontaine* [translation] (1954); *Predilections* [critical essays] (1955); *Like a Bulwark* (1956); *Idiosyncrasy & Technique* [two lectures] (1958); *Letters from and to the Ford Motor Company* [with David Wallace] (1958); *O to Be a Dragon* (1959); *A Marianne Moore Reader* (1961); *The Absentee: A Comedy in Four Acts* (1962); *Puss in Boots, The Sleeping Beauty & Cinderella* [a retelling of Charles Perrault's *Fairy Tales*] (1963); *The Arctic Ox* (1964); *Poetry and Criticism* (1965); *Dress and Kindred Subjects* (1965); *A Talisman* (1965); *Tell Me, Tell Me* (1966); *Tipoo's Tiger* (1967); *The Complete Poems* (1967); *The Complete Poems* (1981).

Collected Works and Edited Texts

The Complete Poems, ed. Clive Driver (New York: Viking, 1981) presents all of Moore's final emendations and notes revised after publication of the 1967 edition. In addition, five poems written between 1967 and 1972 are included.

Other Source Materials

Moore's papers are at the Rosenbach Foundation in Philadelphia.

SECONDARY SOURCES

Biography

There is no biography of Moore, and her life must be reconstructed from many sources such as her obituary, by Alden Whitman, "Shaper of Subtle Images," *New York Times* 6 (February 1972) and Winthrop Sargeant, "Profiles: Humility, Concentration, and Gusto," *The New Yorker* 32 (February 16, 1957).

Criticism

An excellent introductory pamphlet is by fellow poet Jean Garrigue, *Marianne Moore* (Minneapolis: Univ. of Minnesota Press, 1965). Full-length studies are Bernard F. Engel, *Marianne Moore* (New York: Twayne, 1964); George W. Nitchie, *Marianne Moore: An Introduction to the Poetry* (New York: Columbia Univ. Press, 1969); Donald Hall, *Marianne Moore: The Cage and the Animal* (New York: Pegasus,

1970), which combines biography and criticism; and Pamela W. Hadas, *Marianne Moore: Poet of Affection* (Syracuse: Syracuse Univ. Press, 1977), which contains some useful analyses of specific poems. Two studies that draw on Moore's papers and notebooks for evidence of her structural method and imagery are Laurence Stapleton, *Marianne Moore: The Poet's Advance* (Princeton, NJ: Princeton Univ. Press, 1978); and Bonnie Costello, *Marianne Moore: Imaginary Possessions* (Cambridge: Harvard Univ. Press, 1981). Other works that contain substantial sections on Moore are A. K. Weatherhead, *The Edge of the Image* (Seattle: Univ. of Washington Press, 1967), which is a study of William Carlos Williams, R. P. Blackmur, and Moore; and Marie Boroff, *Language and the Poet: Verbal Artistry in Frost, Stevens and Moore* Chicago: Univ. of Chicago Press, 1979).

Collections of criticism are in the "Marianne Moore Issue," *Quarterly Review of Literature* 4 (1948): 121-223, ed. Jose Garcia Villa, which contains material by Elizabeth Bishop, Cleanth Brooks, and others; *Festschrift for Marianne Moore's Seventy-Seventh Birthday*, ed. Thurairajah Tambimuttu (New York: Tambimuttu & Mass, 1964); and *Marianne Moore: A Collection of Critical Essays*, ed. Charles Tomlinson (Englewood Cliffs, NJ: Prentice-Hall, 1969), which includes important insights by other poets such as T. S. Eliot, Randall Jarrell, Ezra Pound, and William Carlos Williams.

Bibliographies

Important bibliographies are Eugene P. Sheehy and Kenneth A. Lohf, *The Achievement of Marianne Moore: A Bibliography, 1907-1957* (New York: New York Public Library, 1958); and the more recent Craig S. Abbott, *Marianne Moore: A Descriptive Bibliography* (Pittsburgh: Univ. of Pittsburgh Press, 1977), which describes primary sources including those in periodicals and anthologies, and contains a selected bibliography of principal works about Moore. In addition, Abbott has compiled *Marianne Moore: A Reference Guide* (Boston: G. K. Hall, 1978), which is a thorough chronological annotated guide to criticism 1916 through 1976.

Reference Works

Gary Lane, *A Concordance to the Poems of Marianne Moore* (New York: Haskell House, 1972) is correlated with *The Complete Poems* (New York: Viking, 1967). The Rosenbach Foundation, Philadelphia, serves scholars through *Marianne Moore Newsletter*, Spring 1977- , a semiannual compilation of short items and bibliography.

WRIGHT MORRIS, 1910-

PRIMARY SOURCES

Separate Works

My Uncle Dudley (1942); *The Man Who Was There* (1945); *The Inhabitants* [photos and text] (1946); *The Home Place* [photos and text] (1948); *The World in the Attic* (1949); *Man and Boy* (1951); *The Work of Love* (1952); *The Deep Sleep* (1953); *The Huge Season* (1954); *The Field of Vision* (1956); *Love among the Cannibals* (1957); *The Territory Ahead* [essays] (1958); *Ceremony in Lone Tree* (1960); *What a Way to Go* (1962); *Cause for Wonder* (1963); *One Day* (1965);

In Orbit (1967); *A Bill of Rights, a Bill of Wrongs, a Bill of Goods* (1968); *God's Country and My People* [photos and text] (1968); *Green Grass, Blue Sky, White House* (1970); *Fire Sermon* (1971); *War Games* (1972); *Love Affair: A Venetian Journal* [photos and text] (1972); *Here Is Ein Baum* (1973); *A Life* (1973); *About Fiction* (1975); *The Cat's Meow* (1975); *The Fork River Space Project: A Novel* (1977); *Earthly Delights, Unearthly Adornments* (1978); *Plains Song, for Female Voices* [novel, illustrated with photographs] (1980); *Will's Boy: A Memoir* (1981).

Collected Works and Edited Texts

The University of Nebraska is publishing Morris' novels in paperback. *Wright Morris: A Reader*, ed. Granville Hicks (New York: Harper & Row, 1970) is an anthology which contains a useful introduction. *Real Losses, Imaginary Gains* (Harper & Row, 1976) gathers thirteen short stories published 1948-1975. *Wright Morris: Structures and Artifacts* (Lincoln: Univ. of Nebraska Press, 1975) is the catalog of a retrospective exhibition of Morris' photographs taken between 1933 and 1954.

SECONDARY SOURCES

Biography

There is no biography of Morris. His own memoir, *Will's Boy* (New York: Harper & Row, 1981) is an account of his boyhood from 1910 to 1930 spent with his father in Nebraska and Chicago.

Criticism

For an introductory pamphlet, see Leon Howard, *Wright Morris* (Minnesota: Univ. of Minnesota Press, 1968). Book-length studies are David Madden, *Wright Morris* (New York: Twayne, 1964); and G. B. Crump, *The Novels of Wright Morris: A Critical Interpretation* (Lincoln: Univ. of Nebraska Press, 1978). *Conversations with Wright Morris*, ed. Robert E. Kroll (Univ. of Nebraska Press, 1976) contains lectures on Morris and conversations with him on the theme "the artist as American."

Bibliographies

A chronological bibliography of primary and secondary sources is Robert L. Boyce, "A Wright Morris Bibliography," in *Conversations with Wright Morris*, pp.169-206 (*see* Criticism). An alphabetical bibliography is in Crump (*see* Criticism).

VLADIMIR (VLADIMIROVICH) NABOKOV, 1899-1977
Pseud: V. Sirin

PRIMARY SOURCES

Separate Works

Mary (1926; English translation *of Mashen'ka*, 1970); *King, Queen, Knave* (1928; English translation of *Korol', Dama, Valet*, 1968); *The Defense* (1930; English translation of *Zashchita Luzhina*, 1964); *The Eye* (1930; English translation of *Soglya Datay*, 1965); *Glory* (1932; English translation of *Podvig*, 1971); *Camera Obscura* (1932-33; English translation of *Kamera Obskura*, 1936; American ed. with Nabokov's changes titled *Laughter in the Dark*, 1938); *Nikolai Gogol* [criticism] (1944); *Despair* (1936; English translation of *Ot Chayanie*, 1966); *Invitation to a Beheading* (1938;

English translation of *Priglashenie Na Kazn'*, 1959); *The Gift* (1937-38; with chapter 4, 1952); English translation of *Dar* (1963); *The Real Life of Sebastian Knight* (1941); *Three Russian Poets: Translations of Pushkin, Lermontov and Tiutchev* (1944); *Bend Sinister* (1947); *Conclusive Evidence* [memoirs] (1951; later retitled *Speak Memory*, rev. and expanded, 1966); *Drugiye Berega* [memoirs] (1954); *Pnin* (1957); *Nabokov's Dozen* [13 short stories] (1958); *Poems* (1959); *The Song of Igor's Campaign* [translation] (1960); *Pale Fire* (1962); *Eugene Onegin*, by Alexander Pushkin [translation] (1964); *Nabokov's Quarter* [short stories] (1966); *Ada, or Ardor: A Family Chronicle* (1969); *Poems and Problems* (1970); *Transparent Things* (1972); *Strong Opinions* [essays and interviews] (1973); *Look at the Harlequins!* (1974); *Tyrants Destroyed and Other Stories* [short stories] (1975).

Collected Works and Edited Texts

The Viking Portable Nabokov, ed. Page Stegner (New York: Penguin, 1971) contains selections from Nabokov's works. *The Nabokov-Wilson Letters: Correspondence between Vladimir Nabokov and Edmund Wilson, 1940-1971*, ed. Simon Karlinsky (New York: Harper, 1979) is a collection of 264 letters, most of which were exchanged before Wilson's attack on the translation of *Eugene Onegin*.

SECONDARY SOURCES

Biography

There is no definitive biography. Nabokov's memoir, *Speak Memory: An Autobiography Revisited* (New York: G. P. Putnam, 1966) is a crucial source; and Andrew Field, *Nabokov, His Life in Part* (New York: Viking, 1977) is useful for the early years, but distinctions between fact and fiction are often blurred by Field's style. Two useful short accounts include the introduction to Schuman's bibliography (*see* Bibliographies) and an account by his former student, Alfred Appel, Jr., "Memoirs of Nabokov," *Times Literary Supplement* 7 (October 1977): 1138-42.

Criticism

Among several introductions are a pamphlet, Julian Moynahan, *Vladimir Nabokov* (Minneapolis: Univ. of Minnesota Press, 1971); Donald E. Morton, *Vladimir Nabokov* (New York: Ungar, 1974), which surveys all the novels including the early Russian works, and contains a short life and bibliographies of primary and secondary sources; Douglas Fowler, *Reading Nabokov* (Ithaca, NY: Cornell Univ. Press, 1974), which concentrates on five novels and three short stories; and L. L. Lee, *Vladimir Nabokov* (Boston: Twayne, 1976), which includes substantial treatment of the early Russian writing. Karl Proffer, *Keys to Lolita* (Bloomington: Indiana Univ. Press, 1968) is a guide to literary allusions and contains a calendar of narrative events. Two general studies of Nabokov's literary art are Page Stegner, *Escape into Aesthetics: The Art of Vladimir Nabokov* (New York: Dial, 1966); and Andrew Field, *Nabokov: His Life in Art* (Boston: Little, Brown, 1967). A study showing how the early stories prefigured later work is Marina Turkevich Naumann, *Blue Evenings in Berlin: Nabokov's Short Stories of the 1920's* (New York: New York Univ. Press, 1978). For analyses of the influence of the Russian language, see William Woodin Rowe, *Nabokov's Deceptive World* (New York: New York Univ. Press, 1971); and Jane Grayson, *Nabokov Translated: A Comparison of Nabokov's Russian and English Prose* (New York: Oxford Univ. Press, 1977). Alfred Appel, Jr., *Nabokov's Dark*

Cinema (New York: Oxford Univ. Press, 1974) shows how American cinema in the 1940s and 1950s was a source for many obscure references. A study of autobiographical techniques that contains much on Nabokov's *Speak Memory* and his "burlesque of autobiography" in *Lolita*, is Elizabeth W. Bruss, *Autobiographical Acts: The Changing Situation of a Literary Genre* (Baltimore: Johns Hopkins Univ. Press, 1976).

Collections of criticism include *Nabokov the Man and His Work: Studies*, ed. L. S. Dembo (Madison: Univ. of Wisconsin Press, 1967); *Nabokov: Criticism, Reminiscences, Translations and Tributes*, eds. Alfred Appel and Charles Newman (Evanston, IL: Northwestern Univ. Press, 1970); *A Book of Things about Vladimir Nabokov*, ed. Carl R. Proffer (Ann Arbor, MI: Ardis, 1974); and *Vladimir Nabokov: His Life, His Work, His World*, ed. Peter Quennell (New York: Morrow, 1980).

Bibliographies

Andrew Field, *Nabokov: A Bibliography* (New York: McGraw-Hill, 1973) is an important primary bibliography which lists all writing by Nabokov, including translations, epigrams, and interviews, and has a bibliography of reviews about him that were in the emigré press. For works about Nabokov through 1977, see Samuel Schuman, *Vladimir Nabokov: A Reference Guide* (Boston: G. K. Hall, 1979), which contains a list of his major works and an annotated chronological bibliography of secondary sources.

(BENJAMIN) FRANK(LIN) NORRIS, 1870-1902

PRIMARY SOURCES

Separate Works

Yvernelle (1891); *Moran of the Lady Letty* (1898); *McTeague* (1899); *Blix* (1899); *A Man's Woman* (1900); *The Octopus* (1901); *The Pit* (1903); *The Responsibilities of the Novelist* (1903); *A Deal in Wheat* (1903); *The Joyouse Miracle* (1906); *The Third Circle* (1909); *Vandover and the Brute* (1914); *The Surrender of Santiago* (1917); *Frank Norris of "The Wave": Stories and Sketches from the San Francisco Weekly, 1893-1897* (1931).

Collected Works and Edited Texts

The Complete Edition of Frank Norris (Garden City, NY: Doubleday, Doran, 1928), though the best edition, is not complete. *The Literary Criticism of Frank Norris*, ed. Donald Pizer (Austin: Univ. of Texas Press, 1964) is a collection of Norris' essays. *The Letters of Frank Norris*, ed. Franklin Walker (San Francisco: Book Club of California, 1956) is a selection of correspondence. *McTeague*, ed. Donald Pizer (New York: Norton, 1977) is a useful Norton Critical Edition that contains essays in addition to the text.

Other Source Materials

The most important collection of manuscripts is at the University of California, Berkeley, Bancroft Library.

SECONDARY SOURCES

Biography

The only full-length biography so far is Franklin Walker, *Frank Norris: A Biography* (Garden City, NY: Doubleday, Doran, 1932).

Criticism

A good introduction that places Norris in transcendentalist tradition is Warren French, *Frank Norris* (New York: Twayne, 1962). Lars Åhnebrink, *The Beginnings of Naturalism in American Fiction* (Cambridge: Harvard Univ. Press, 1950) also treats Hamlin Garland and Stephen Crane. Donald Pizer, *The Novels of Frank Norris* (Bloomington: Indiana Univ. Press, 1966) examines value systems in Norris. William B. Dillingham, *Frank Norris: Instinct and Art* (Lincoln: Univ. of Nebraska Press, 1969) has two fine biographical chapters in addition to critical analysis; and Don Graham, *The Fiction of Frank Norris* (Columbia: Univ. of Missouri Press, 1978) examines the aesthetic references in Norris' fiction. A collection of important early reviews and contemporary critical essays is in *Critical Essays on Frank Norris*, ed. Don Graham (Boston: G. K. Hall, 1980).

Bibliographies

An excellent bibliographic essay is William B. Dillingham, "Frank Norris," in *Fifteen American Authors before 1900*, eds. Robert A. Rees and Earl N. Harbert (Madison: Univ. of Wisconsin Press, 1971). Kenneth A. Lohf and Eugene P. Sheehy, *Frank Norris: A Bibliography* (Los Gatos, CA: Talisman Press, 1959) is a listing of primary sources; and William B. Dillingham, *Frank Norris: Instinct and Art* (Lincoln: Univ. of Nebraska Press, 1969) contains an annotated listing of criticism. Jesse E. Crisler and Joseph R. McElrath Jr., *Frank Norris: A Reference Guide* (Boston: G. K. Hall, 1974) is an annotated chronological list of studies about Norris through 1972.

JOYCE CAROL OATES, 1938-

PRIMARY SOURCES

Separate Works

By the North Gate [stories] (1963); *With Shuddering Fall* (1964); *Upon the Sweeping Flood* [stories] (1966); *A Garden of Earthly Delights* (1967); *Expensive People* (1968); *Women in Love* [poems] (1968); *them* (1969); *Anonymous Sins* [poems] (1969); *The Wheel of Love and Other Stories* (1970); *Love and Its Derangements* [poems] (1970); *Wonderland* (1971); *Marriages and Infidelities* [stories] (1972); *The Edge of Impossibility: Tragic Forms in Literature* [essays] (1972); *Do with Me What You Will* (1973); *Angel Fire* [poems] (1973); *Dreaming America and Other Poems* (1973); *The Goddess and Other Women* (1974); *The Hungry Ghosts: Seven Allusive Comedies* (1974); *Where Are You Going? Where Have You Been? Stories of Young America* (1974); *Miracle Play* (1974); *New Heaven, New Earth: The Visionary Experience in Literature* (1974); *The Goddess and Other Women* (1974); *The Assassins: A Book of Hours* (1975); *The Poisoned Kiss and Other Stories from the Portuguese* (1975); *The Seduction and Other Stories* (1975); *Fabulous Beasts* [poems]

(1975); *Childwold* (1976); *The Triumph of the Spider Monkey* (1976); *Crossing the Border* [stories] (1976); *Night-Side* [stories] (1977); *Season of Peril* [poems] (1977); *Son of the Morning* (1978); *All the Good People I've Left Behind* [short stories] (1978); *Women Whose Lives Are Food, Men Whose Lives Are Money* [poems] (1978); *Cybele* (1979); *Unholy Lovers* (1979); *Bellefleur* (1980); *A Sentimental Education* [stories] (1980); *Three Plays* (1980); *Contraries* [essays] (1981); *Angel of Light* (1981); *A Bloodsmoor Romance* (1982).

Collected Works and Edited Texts

Three Plays (Princeton, NJ: Ontario Review Press, 1980) includes "Ontological Proof of My Existence," first published in *Partisan Review* 37 (October 1970), "Miracle Play," and "Triumph of the Spider Monkey."

SECONDARY SOURCES

Biography and Criticism

There is no full-length biography although facts may be gleaned from critical works and interviews. Two useful introductions to the novels are Joanne V. Creighton, *Joyce Carol Oates* (Boston: Twayne, 1979), which concentrates on Oates' themes of search for meaning in fragmentary human experience and liberation through love; and Ellen G. Friedman, *Joyce Carol Oates* (New York: Ungar, 1980), which places the novels in the American literary tradition and cultural milieu. Other important studies are Mary Kathryn Grant, *The Tragic Vision of Joyce Carol Oates* (Durham, NC: Duke Univ. Press, 1978), which shows Oates transcending the nightmarish problems of violence and human fragmentation; and G. F. Waller, *Dreaming America: Obsession and Transcendance in the Fiction of Joyce Carol Oates* (Baton Rouge: Louisiana State Univ. Press, 1979), which examines the affinities of Oates' fiction to that of D. H. Lawrence. A useful collection of reviews and essays, including some which are new, is *Critical Essays on Joyce Carol Oates*, ed. Linda W. Wagner (Boston: G. K. Hall, 1979).

Bibliographies

A list of primary sources is Donald C. Dickinson, "Joyce Carol Oates: A Bibliographical Checklist," *American Book Collector* (November-December 1981): 26-39. Ellen G. Friedman, *Joyce Carol Oates*, and Joanne V. Creighton, *Joyce Carol Oates* (*see* Criticism) contain primary and secondary bibliographies that include articles in periodicals.

FLANNERY O'CONNOR, 1925-1964

PRIMARY SOURCES

Separate Works

Wise Blood (1952); *A Good Man Is Hard to Find and Other Stories* (1955); *The Violent Bear It Away* (1960); *Three* (1964); *Everything That Rises Must Converge* (1965); *Mystery and Manners: Occasional Prose* (1969); *Flannery O'Connor: The Complete Stories* (1971).

Collected Works and Edited Texts

Flannery O'Connor: The Complete Stories (New York: Farrar, Straus & Giroux, 1971) collects thirty-one stories. O'Connor's letters are gathered in *The Habit of Being: The Letters of Flannery O'Connor*, ed. Sally Fitzgerald (Farrar, Straus & Giroux, 1978). A collection of essays is *Mystery and Manners: Occasional Prose*, eds. Sally Fitzgerald and Robert Fitzgerald (Farrar, Straus & Giroux, 1969).

Other Source Materials

The most extensive collection of O'Connor's papers is at Georgia College, Milledgeville.

SECONDARY SOURCES

Biography and Criticism

There is no full-length biography. Critical introductions to O'Connor are Stanley Edgar Hyman, *Flannery O'Connor* (Minneapolis: Univ. of Minnesota Press, 1966); Robert Drake, *Flannery O'Connor: A Critical Essay* (Grand Rapids: W. B. Eerdmans, 1966); Dorothy Walters, *Flannery O'Connor* (New York: Twayne, 1973); and Dorothy Tuck McFarland, *Flannery O'Connor* (New York: Ungar, 1976). Carter W. Martin, *The True Country: Themes in the Fiction of Flannery O'Connor* (Nashville: Vanderbilt Univ. Press, 1969) is an orthodox Christian study of elements of Roman Catholicism in the fiction; Josephine Hendin, *The World of Flannery O'Connor* (Bloomington: Indiana Univ. Press, 1970) sees O'Connor denying a universe with meaning and working with an art of the grotesque to reduce the dimensions of reality; Leon V. Driskell and Joan T. Brittain, *The Eternal Crossroads: The Art of Flannery O'Connor* (Lexington: Univ. Press of Kentucky, 1971) shows O'Connor focussing on the points at which life on earth meets eternity; Miles Orvell, *Invisible Parade: The Fiction of Flannery O'Connor* (Philadelphia: Temple Univ. Press, 1972) sees the pull between "surface and depth" and also gives attention to O'Connor's book reviews for a Catholic journal; Kathleen Feely, *Flannery O'Connor: Voice of the Peacock* (New Brunswick, NJ: Rutgers Univ. Press, 1972) examines theological foundations; Gilbert H. Muller, *Nightmares and Visions: Flannery O'Connor and the Catholic Grotesque* (Athens: Univ. of Georgia Press, 1972) sees O'Connor seeking to overcome the meaningless world with grace; Martha Stephens, *The Question of Flannery O'Connor* (Baton Rouge: Louisiana State Univ. Press, 1973) traces the theme of a Christian journey toward achievement of holiness; Preston M. Browning, Jr., *Flannery O'Connor* (Carbondale: Southern Illinois Univ. Press, 1973) examines the relation of the "holy and the demonic"; John R. May, *The Pruning Word: The Parables of Flannery O'Connor* (Notre Dame, IN: Notre Dame Univ. Press, 1976) concentrates on the power of language; Carol Schloss, *Flannery O'Connor's Dark Comedies, the Limits of Inference* (Louisiana State Univ. Press, 1980) evaluates O'Connor's writing of anagogical fiction for the secular reader; and Robert Coles, *Flannery O'Connor's South* (Louisiana State Univ. Press, 1980) places her work in Georgia's religious, social, and intellectual milieu.

Ten critical essays and some of O'Connor's own correspondence are collected in *The Added Dimension: The Art and Mind of Flannery O'Connor*, eds. Melvin J. Friedman and Lewis A. Lawson (New York: Fordham Univ. Press, 1966).

Bibliographies

Robert E. Golden and Mary C. Sullivan, *Flannery O'Connor and Caroline Gordon: A Reference Guide* (Boston: G. K. Hall, 1977) is a chronologically arranged annotated bibliography of books and articles about O'Connor written between 1952 and 1976. David Farmer, *Flannery O'Connor: A Descriptive Bibliography* (New York: Garland, 1981) covers all first appearances of O'Connor's works through *Habit of Being*, including articles, reviews, translations, and film and television adaptations. Publishing history is given for each item, and illustrations of book jackets and O'Connor's art work are included.

Reference Works

Flannery O'Connor Bulletin, 1972- is a clearinghouse for bibliographical and critical contributions published from the collection at Georgia College.

EUGENE (GLADSTONE) O'NEILL, 1888-1953

PRIMARY SOURCES

Separate Works

Thirst and Other One Act Plays (1914); *Bound East for Cardiff* (1916); *Before Breakfast* (1916); *The Moon of the Caribees, and Six Other Plays of the Sea* (1919); *Beyond the Horizon* (1920); *Gold* (1920); *The Emperor Jones, Diff'rent, and The Straw* (1921); *The Hairy Ape, Anna Christie,* and *The First Man* (1922); *The Dreamy Kid* (1922); *All God's Chillun Got Wings* (1924); *Welded* (1924); *Desire under the Elms* (1925); *The Great God Brown, The Fountain,* and *The Moon of the Caribbees, and Other Plays* (1926); *Marco Millions* (1927); *Lazarus Laughed* (1927); *Strange Interlude* (1928); *Dynamo* (1929); *Mourning Becomes Electra* (1931); *Ah! Wilderness* (1933); *Days without End* (1934); *The Iceman Cometh* (1946); *A Moon for the Misbegotten* (performance 1947; publication 1952); *Long Day's Journey into Night* (1956); *A Touch of the Poet* (1957); *Hughie* (1959); *More Stately Mansions* (1964).

Collected Works and Edited Texts

The Plays of Eugene O'Neill, 3v. (New York: Random House, 1951) is the most complete edition of O'Neill's work, but must be supplemented by later, individually published plays: *A Moon for the Misbegotten* (Random House, 1952); and titles published by Yale University Press between 1956 and 1964, *A Long Day's Journey into Night*; *A Touch of the Poet, Hughie,* and *More Stately Mansions*. Early one-act plays are collected in *Thirst and Other One-Act Plays* (Boston: Gorham Press, 1914); *The Lost Plays* (New York: New Fathoms, 1950); and *Children of the Sea* (Washington: NCR Microcard Editions, 1972). *Poems, 1912-1944*, ed. Donald Gallup (New Haven, CT: Ticknor & Fields, 1980) includes all the known published poems and many more that are unpublished. *Eugene O'Neill at Work*, ed. Virginia Floyd (New York: Ungar, 1981) is a series of O'Neill's notebooks that traces ideas, notes, and drafts for the plays.

Other Source Materials

The major manuscript collections are in the New York Public Library, Dartmouth Library, Princeton University Library, and Yale University Library.

SECONDARY SOURCES

Biography

The best available biography to date is Arthur Gelb and Barbara Gelb, *O'Neill*, 2nd ed. (New York: Harper, 1973). Doris Alexander, *The Tempering of Eugene O'Neill*, (New York: Harcourt Brace, 1962) deals with O'Neill until 1920; Louis Sheaffer, *O'Neill: Son and Playwright* (Boston: Little, Brown, 1968) and his continuation, *O'Neill: Son and Artist* (Little, Brown, 1973), present O'Neill's life and work as well as important criticism of his plays.

Criticism

Dependable introductions to the biography and criticism are Clifford Leech, *Eugene O'Neill* (New York: Barnes & Noble, 1963); Frederick I. Carpenter, *Eugene O'Neill*, rev. ed. (New York: Twayne, 1979); and a pamphlet by John Gassner, *Eugene O'Neill* (Minneapolis: Univ. of Minnesota Press, 1965). For a literary, rather than a dramatic, view, see John Henry Raleigh, *The Plays of Eugene O'Neill* (Carbondale: Southern Illinois Univ. Press, 1965). More specialized studies of importance are Doris V. Falk, *Eugene O'Neill and the Tragic Tension* (New Brunswick, NJ: Rutgers Univ. Press, 1958), which examines psychological patterns in the plays; Timo Tiusanen, *O'Neill's Scenic Images* (Princeton, NJ: Princeton Univ. Press, 1968), which analyzes scenic means of expression; Egil Tornqvist, *A Drama of Souls: Studies in O'Neill's Super-Naturalistic Technique* (New Haven, CT: Yale Univ. Press, 1969), which indicates how the plays transcend realism and reveal values; Travis Bogard, *Contour in Time* (New York: Oxford Univ. Press, 1972), which sees the dramas as autobiography and recounts much of the American theatre scene in the early twentieth century; Winifred Frazer, *E. G. and E. G. O.: Emma Goldman and the Iceman Cometh* (Gainesville: Univ. of Florida Press, 1974), which tells how Goldman's career directly influenced O'Neill; and Jean Chothia, *Forging a Language* (New York: Cambridge Univ. Press, 1979), which concerns itself with O'Neill's use of dialogue.

Important collections of reviews and essays are in *O'Neill and His Plays: Four Decades of Criticism*, eds. Oscar Cargill, N. Bryllion Fagin, and William J. Fisher (New York: New York Univ. Press, 1961); *O'Neill: A Collection of Critical Essays*, ed. John Gassner (Englewood Cliffs, NJ: Prentice-Hall, 1964); *Playwright's Progress: O'Neill and the Critics*, ed. Jordan Y. Miller (Chicago: Scott Foresman, 1965); *Twentieth Century Interpretations of the Iceman Cometh: A Collection of Critical Essays*, ed. John Henry Raleigh (Prentice-Hall, 1968); *Eugene O'Neill: A Collection of Criticism*, ed. Ernest G. Griffin (New York: McGraw-Hill, 1976); and *Eugene O'Neill: A World View*, ed. Virginia Floyd (New York: Ungar, 1979).

Bibliographies

For a bibliographic survey, begin with John H. Raleigh, "Eugene O'Neill," in *Sixteen Modern American Authors*, ed. Jackson R. Bryer (Durham, NC: Duke Univ. Press, 1971). pp.417-43. Primary sources are in Jennifer M. Atkinson, *Eugene O'Neill: A Descriptive Bibliography* (Pittsburgh: Univ. of Pittsburgh Press, 1974), which is a definitive scholarly compilation. Among the several bibliographies of criticism, Jordan Y. Miller, *Eugene O'Neill and the American Critic: A Bibliographical Checklist*, 2nd ed., rev. (Hamden, CT: Archon Books, 1973) is the most complete and includes a chronology and synopsis of each play and its reception up to 1973.

Reference Books

J. Russell Reaver, *An O'Neill Concordance*, 3v. (Detroit: Gale, 1969), which covers twenty-eight of O'Neill's plays, is based on the three-volume Random House edition and other individual plays. *The Eugene O'Neill Newsletter, 1977-* is published tri-yearly to carry items on current stage productions, conferences, book reviews, articles, and bibliographies.

SYLVIA PLATH, 1932-1963
Pseud: Victoria Lucas

PRIMARY SOURCES

Separate Works

A Winter Ship (1960); *The Colossus & Other Poems* (1960); *The Bell Jar* (1963); *Uncollected Poems* (1965); *Ariel* (1965); *Three Women: A Monologue for Three Voices* (1968); *Wreath for a Bridal* (1970); *Million Dollar Month* (1971); *Child* (1971); *Fiesta Melons* (1971); *Crystal Gazer* (1971); *Lyonnesse* (1971); *Crossing the Water* (1971); *Winter Trees* (1971); *Pursuit* (1973); *The Bed Book* [for children] (1976); *Johnny Panic and the Bible of Dreams and Other Prose Writings* (1977).

Collected Works and Edited Texts

There is no authoritative collection of Plath's works, and *The Collected Poems*, ed. Ted Hughes (New York: Harper & Row, 1981), though the most encompassing, is not complete. The collections of poems, *Colossus, Crossing the Water*, and *Winter Trees*, are not identical in the English and American editions, although the overall contents of all the editions are the same, except for three poems which were not printed in Britain: "The Detective," "Amnesiac," and "Eavesdropper," cf. Lane, p.128 (*see* Bibliographies). *Letters Home: Correspondence, 1950-1963*, selected and edited with commentary by Aurelia Schober Plath (London: Faber & Faber, 1978) is controversial, as the mother edited out periods of the life so that there are only 391 out of 696 letters; *The Journals of Sylvia Plath*, ed. Ted Hughes (New York: Dial, 1982) are a truncated version of Plath's diaries from childhood to 1963.

Other Source Materials

Several interviews, many at the BBC, are listed in the Lane bibliography. With the exception of the following, Plath's manuscripts are not yet available to scholars. The English Faculty Library at Cambridge University, England, has a collection of her poetry, and the Lilly Library of Indiana University, Bloomington, contains unpublished letters to and from Plath, as well as 200 early poems, fifty-seven short stories, and fifteen nonfiction prose manuscripts, almost all unpublished.

SECONDARY SOURCES

Biography

There is no definitive biography. Nancy Hunter Steiner, *A Closer Look at Ariel* (New York: Harper's Magazine Press, 1973) is a memoir of the author's friendship during one summer at Harvard. Edward Butscher, *Sylvia Plath: Method and Madness* (New York: Seabury Press, 1976) draws on reminiscences of friends and other biographical information to produce a gossipy and indiscriminating biography that traces the interdependence of Plath's life and art, equating the personna of the poems with the poet.

Criticism

An introduction to both the life and work that has a useful bibliography is Caroline King Barnard, *Sylvia Plath* (Boston: Twayne, 1978). Judith Kroll, *Chapters in a Mythology: The Poetry of Sylvia Plath* (New York: Harper & Row, 1976) rejects the biographical view of Plath as a confessional poet and focusses on the concern with problems of rebirth and transcendancy, indicating the influence of Plath's own reading. Margaret Dickie Uroff, *Sylvia Plath and Ted Hughes* (Urbana: Univ. of Illinois Press, 1979) examines the poetic association of husband and wife. Jon Rosenblatt, *Sylvia Plath: The Poetry of Initiation* (Chapel Hill: Univ. of North Carolina Press, 1979) emphasizes patterns in the art rather than biographical influences. The earliest collection of critical and biographical essays was *The Art of Sylvia Plath: A Symposium*, ed. Charles Newman (Bloomington: Indiana Univ. Press, 1970). *Sylvia Plath: The Woman and the Work*, ed. Edward Butscher (New York: Dodd, Mead, 1977) contains gossipy and anecdotal reminiscences, but is useful for a few of the critical essays it reprints. More recently, *Sylvia Plath: New Views on the Poetry*, ed. Gary Lane (Baltimore: Johns Hopkins Univ. Press, 1979) brings together thirteen critical and biographical essays that give a well-balanced view.

Bibliographies

A checklist of Plath's many periodical articles is Eric Homberger, *A Chronological Checklist of the Periodical Publications of Sylvia Plath* (Exeter: Univ. of Exeter, 1970). Cameron Northouse and Thomas P. Walsh, *Sylvia Plath and Anne Sexton: A Reference Guide* (Boston: G. K. Hall, 1974) lists all Plath's works in chronological order and major writings about her that appeared through 1972. Gary Lane and Marion Stevens, *Sylvia Plath: A Bibliography* (Metuchen, NJ: Scarecrow, 1978) list Plath's works chronologically by type of material as well as works about her. An appendix includes a chronology of all Plath's publications and differentiates the contents of the American and British editions that bear the same titles.

EDGAR ALLAN POE, 1809-1849

PRIMARY SOURCES

Separate Works

Tamerlane and Other Poems (1827); *Al Aaraaf, Tamerlane and Minor Poems* (1829); *Poems* (1831); *The Narrative of Arthur Gordon Pym* (1838); *The*

Conchologist's First Book (1839); *Tales of the Grotesque and Arabesque* (1840); *The Murders in the Rue Morgue, and the Man That Was Used Up* (1843); *The Raven and Other Poems* (1845); *Tales* (1845); *Eureka: A Prose Poem* (1848); *The Literati* (1850); *Politian: An Unfinished Tragedy* (1923).

Collected Works and Edited Texts

The standard text is *Collected Works of Edgar Allan Poe*, ed. T. O. Mabbott. 3v. (Cambridge: Harvard Univ. Press, 1969-78). It reflects scholarship of recent years, superseding *Complete Works*, ed. James A. Harrison, 17v. (New York: Crowell, 1902; repr. New York: AMS Press, 1965). Important editions of the poems are *The Poems of Edgar Allan Poe*, ed. Killis Campbell (Boston: Ginn, 1917; repr. New York: Russell & Russell, 1962); and *The Poems of Edgar Allan Poe*, ed. Floyd Stovall (Charlottesville: Univ. Press of Virginia, 1965). Correspondence is available as *The Letters of Edgar Allan Poe*, ed. John Ward Ostrom. 2v. (New York: Gordian Press, 1966).

Other Source Materials

The largest collection of Poe sources is at the University of Virginia.

SECONDARY SOURCES

Biography

John Carl Miller, *Building Poe Biography* (Baton Rouge: Louisiana State Univ. Press, 1977) is a clear orientation to the problems of amassing biographical evidence. The most reliable biography is Arthur Hobson Quinn, *Edgar Allan Poe* (New York: Appleton-Century-Crofts, 1941). Sarah Helen Whitman, *Poe's Helen Remembers*, ed. John Carl Miller (Charlottesville: Univ. Press of Virginia, 1979) records correspondence, 1873-1878, between Poe's collector, John Ingram, and Sarah Helen Whitman, who had been engaged to Poe in 1848. Two reliable and readable biographies are N. Bryllion Fagin, *The Histrionic Mr. Poe* (Baltimore: Johns Hopkins Press, 1949); and Julian Symons, *The Tell-Tale Heart* (New York: Harper, 1978).

Criticism

Among important book-length studies are Killis Campbell, *The Mind of Poe* (Cambridge: Harvard Univ. Press, 1933; repr. New York: Russell & Russell, 1962); and Edward H. Davidson, *Poe: A Critical Study* (Cambridge: Harvard Univ. Press, 1957). For the French reaction to Poe, see Patrick F. Quinn, *The French Face of Edgar Poe* (Carbondale: Southern Illinois Univ. Press, 1957). Poetry is the focus of Floyd Stovall, *Edgar Allan Poe the Poet* (Charlottesville: Univ. Press of Virginia, 1969). Poe as critic, literary theorist, and magazine writer is treated in Sidney P. Moss, *Poe's Literary Battles: The Critic in the Context of His Literary Milieu* (Durham, NC: Univ. of North Carolina Press, 1963); *Poe's Major Crisis: His Libel Suit and New York's Literary World* (Durham, NC: Duke Univ. Press, 1970); Edd Winfield Parks, *Edgar Allan Poe as Literary Critic* (Athens: Univ. of Georgia Press, 1964); Michael Allen, *Poe and the British Magazine Tradition* (New York: Oxford Univ. Press, 1969); and Robert D. Jacobs, *Poe: Journalist and Critic* (Baton Rouge: Louisiana State Univ. Press, 1969). More unconventional is Daniel Hoffman, *Poe, Poe, Poe, Poe, Poe, Poe, Poe* (New York: Doubleday, 1972), while other thought-provoking accounts are David Halliburton, *Edgar Allan Poe: A Phenomenological View*

(Princeton, NJ: Princeton Univ. Press, 1973); Stuart Levine, *Edgar Allan Poe: Seer and Craftsman* (Deland, FL: Everett/Edwards, 1972); and G. R. Thompson, *Poe's Fiction: Romantic Irony in the Gothic Tales* (Madison: Univ. of Wisconsin Press, 1973).

Important collections of Poe criticism are *The Recognition of Edgar Allan Poe: Selected Criticism since 1829*, ed. Eric W. Carlson (Ann Arbor: Univ. of Michigan Press, 1966), which contains essays by Baudelaire, Dostoevski, D. H. Lawrence, Marie Bonaparte, T. S. Eliot, and others; *Poe: A Collection of Critical Essays*, ed. Robert Regan (Englewood Cliffs, NJ: Prentice-Hall, 1967); and *Twentieth Century Interpretations of Poe's Tales*, ed. William L. Howarth (Prentice-Hall, 1971). The last two collections reprint Richard Wilbur's lecture "The House of Poe." Wilbur's useful introductions are in the Laurel Poetry Series edition of complete poems, *Poe* (New York: Dell, 1959) and in *Major Writers of America*, ed. Perry Miller. 2v. (New York: Harcourt, Brace & World, 1962), v.1, pp.369-82. Further criticism is collected in *Papers on Poe: Essays in Honor of John Ward Ostrom*, ed. Richard P. Veler (Springfield, OH: Chantry Music Press, 1972).

Bibliographies

For a fine review of research and criticism, see Jay B. Hubbell, "Edgar Allan Poe," in *Eight American Authors*, rev. ed., ed. James Woodress (New York: Norton, 1971), pp.3-36. In addition, see the "Selected Bibliography," in *Edgar Allan Poe: A Thematic Reader*, ed. Eric W. Carlson (Glenview, IL: Scott Foresman, 1967), pp. xxxvi-xxxix; J. Lasley Dameron and Irby B. Cauthen, Jr., *Edgar Allan Poe: A Bibliography of Criticism, 1827-1967* (Charlottesville: Univ. Press of Virginia, 1974); and J. Albert Robbins, *The Merrill Checklist of Edgar Allan Poe* (Columbus, OH: Merrill, 1969). Esther F. Hyneman, *Edgar Allan Poe: An Annotated Bibliography of Books and Articles in English, 1827-1973* (Boston: G. K. Hall, 1974) is a chronological listing of secondary materials.

Reference Works

Poe Studies, formerly, *Poe Newsletter*, is published twice yearly since 1968 and acts as a clearinghouse for short critical notes, reviews, and current Poe bibliography. Other useful tools are Burton R. Pollin, *Dictionary of Names and Titles in Poe's Collected Works* (New York: Da Capo Press, 1968), which is based on *Works*, ed. James A. Harrison; J. Lasley Dameron and Louis Charles Stagg, *An Index to Poe's Critical Vocabulary* (Hartford, CT: Transcendental Books, 1966); Bradford A. Booth and Claude E. Jones, *A Concordance of the Poetical Works of Edgar Allan Poe* (Baltimore: Johns Hopkins Press, 1941), which gives access to Campbell's 1917 edition of *The Poems*; and Robert L. Gale, *Plots and Characters in the Fiction and Poetry of Edgar Allan Poe* (Hamden, CT: Archon Books, 1970).

KATHERINE ANNE PORTER, 1890-1980

PRIMARY SOURCES

Separate Works

Flowering Judas and Other Stories (1930); *Pale Horse, Pale Rider: Three Short Novels* (1939); *The Leaning Tower and Other Stories* (1944); *The Days Before* [criticism] (1952); *Ship of Fools* (1962); *Collected Stories* (1965); *Collected Essays* (1970); *The Never Ending Wrong* [reminiscence] (1977).

Collected Works and Edited Texts

There is no standard edition of Porter's works. *The Collected Stories* (New York: A Harvest HBJ Book, 1979) contains short fiction through 1944, together with four stories not previously published in book form.

Other Source Materials

Several interviews that provide Porter's comments on the influence of family and other writers, as well as interpretation of her work, are cited in Kiernan's listing (*see* Bibliographies). Among interviews are Barbara Thompson, "Katherine Anne Porter: An Interview," *Paris Review* 29 (1963): 87-114; and Enrique Hank Lopez, *Conversations with Katherine Anne Porter: Refugee from Indian Creek* (Boston: Little, Brown, 1981), which is invaluable for its record of autobiographical conversations taped over several weeks. *The Never Ending Wrong* (Little, Brown, 1977) is a personal reminiscence of the Sacco Vanzetti case. Porter's literary collections, including letters, are in the University of Maryland's McKeldin Library, College Park.

SECONDARY SOURCES

Biography

There is no standard biography, but the interviews of Thompson, Lopez (*see* Other Source Materials), and Glenway Wescott, "Katherine Anne Porter Personally," in *Images of Truth: Remembrances and Criticism* (New York: Harper & Row, 1962), are especially illuminating.

Criticism

Useful introductions are Ray B. West, *Katherine Anne Porter* (Minneapolis: Univ. of Minnesota Press, 1963); and George Hendrick, *Katherine Anne Porter* (New York: Twayne, 1965). Winifred S. Emmons, *Katherine Anne Porter: The Regional Stories* (Austin, TX: Steck-Vaughn, 1967) explores the role of place; William L. Nance, *Katherine Anne Porter and the Art of Rejection* (Chapel Hill: Univ. of North Carolina Press, 1964) sees oppression and rejection as a unifying theme. In-depth surveys of the life and writings are Harry J. Mooney, *The Fiction and Criticism of Katherine Anne Porter*, rev. ed. (Pittsburgh: Univ. of Pittsburgh Press, 1962); John Edward Hardy, *Katherine Anne Porter* (New York: Ungar, 1973); and M. M. Liberman, *Katherine Anne Porter's Fiction* (Detroit: Wayne State Univ. Press, 1971). Two collections that are useful for critical and biographical contributions are *Katherine Anne Porter: A Critical Symposium*, eds. Lodwick Hartley and George Core (Athens: Univ. of Georgia Press, 1969); and *Katherine Anne Porter: A Collection of Critical Essays*, ed. Robert Penn Warren (Englewood Cliffs, NJ: Prentice-Hall, 1978).

Bibliographies

There are three important bibliographies. Edward Schwartz, "Katherine Anne Porter: A Critical Bibliography," *Bulletin of the New York Public Library* 57 (May 1953): 211-47 is an important guide to Porter's work and criticism of her until 1952. Louise Waldrip and Shirley Ann Bauer, *A Bibliography of the Works of Katherine*

Anne Porter and a Bibliography of the Criticism of the Works of Katherine Anne Porter (Metuchen, NJ: Scarecrow, 1969) contains a descriptive bibliography of all Porter's writings until 1968, with dates of their first appearance and a comprehensive listing of criticism about Porter based on her own clipping file. Robert F. Kiernan's *Katherine Anne Porter and Carson McCullers: A Reference Guide* (Boston: G. K. Hall, 1976) is a chronological, annotated checklist of criticism through 1973.

EZRA (LOOMIS) POUND, 1885-1972
Pseud: William Atheling

PRIMARY SOURCES

Separate Works

A Lume Spento (1908); *Personae* (1909); *Exultations* (1909); *Provença* (1910); *The Spirit of Romance* [prose] (1910); *Canzoni* (1911); *Riposes* (1912); *Lustra* (1916); *Gaudier-Brezeska* [biography] (1916); *Pavannes and Divisions* [prose] (1918); *Quia Pauper Amavi* (1919); *Instigations* [prose] (1920); *Umbra* (1920); *Hugh Selwyn Mauberley* (1920); *Poems, 1918-21* (1921); *Indiscretions* [prose] (1923); *A Draft of XVI. Cantos* (1925); *Antheil and the Treatise on Harmony* [prose] (1924); *A Draft of Cantos 17-27* (1928); *A Draft of XXX Cantos* (1930); *Imaginary Letters* [prose] (1930); *How to Read* [prose] (1931); *ABC of Economics* [prose] (1933); *Eleven New Cantos: XXXI-XLI* (1934); *ABC of Reading* [prose] (1934); *Homage to Sextus Propertius* (1934); *Make It New* [prose] (1934); *Jefferson and/or Mussolini* [prose] (1935); *The Fifth Decad of Cantos* (1937); *Polite Essays* [prose] (1937); *Culture* [prose] (1938); *Cantos LII-LXXI* (1940); *The Pisan Cantos, 74-84* (1948); *The Cantos of Ezra Pound, 1-84* (1948); *Money Pamphlets* [prose] (1950-52); *Section: Rock-Drill, 85-95 de Los Cantares* (1956); *Thrones: 96-109 de Los Cantares* (1959); *Impact: Essays on Ignorance and the Decline of American Civilization* [prose] (1960); *The Cantos* [1-109] (1964); *Drafts and Fragments of Cantos CX-CXVII* (1969); *Selected Cantos* (1970).

Collected Works and Edited Texts

There is no definitive collection of Pound's works. Important editions are *Personae: The Collected Poems* (New York: New Directions, 1949); *Selected Poems of Ezra Pound* (New Directions, 1949); and Pound's own selection, *Selected Cantos* (London: Faber, 1967; New York: New Directions, 1970), which differs in some respects from the Faber edition. *The Cantos, I-CXX* (New Directions, 1972) excludes *LXXII* and *LXXIII*, which have never been published; and *Collected Early Poems of Ezra Pound*, ed. Michael King (New Directions, 1976) is an accurate edition, containing notes on textual variants. Pound's criticism is gathered in *The Literary Essays of Ezra Pound*, ed. T. S. Eliot (Norfolk, CT: New Directions, 1954); and *Selected Prose, 1909-1965*, ed. William Cookson (New York: New Directions, 1973). Correspondence is available in *The Letters of Ezra Pound, 1907-1941*, ed. D. D. Paige (New York: Harcourt Brace, 1950) and reissued as *The Selected Letters of Ezra Pound, 1907-1941* (New York: New Directions, 1971). Pound's World War II radio talks are in *Ezra Pound Speaking*, ed. Leonard W. Doob (Westport, CT: Greenwood, 1978); and his musical criticism is collected in *Ezra Pound and Music*, ed. R. Murray Schafer (New Directions, 1977).

Other Source Materials

The largest collection of Pound's papers is at Yale University. Pound's own account of his early life, *Indiscretions* (Paris: Three Mountains Press, 1923), also in *Quarterly Review of Literature* (1949): 105-135, is an important autobiographical source.

SECONDARY SOURCES

Biography

Mary de Rachewiltz, *Discretions* (Boston: Little, Brown, 1971) is an intimate biography and a commentary on the *Pisan Cantos* by Pound's daughter. The first full-length biography was Charles Norman, *Ezra Pound* (New York: Macmillan, 1960). Noel Stock, *The Life of Ezra Pound* (New York: Pantheon, 1970) reports on day-to-day details; and C. David Heymann, *Ezra Pound: The Last Rower* (New York: Viking, 1976) includes facts unearthed from FBI files that illuminate the later years. Hilda Doolittle, *End to Torment: A Memoir of Ezra Pound*, eds. Norman Holmes Pearson and Michael King (New York: New Directions, 1979) is not only a journal memoir of H. D.'s relationship with Pound, but also contains poems previously unpublished, from "Hilda's Book." Peter Ackroyd, *Ezra Pound and His World* (New York: Scribner, 1981) is a fine, brief biography, illustrated with photographs.

Criticism

Helpful introductions to Pound are M. L. Rosenthal, *A Primer of Ezra Pound* (New York: Macmillan, 1960); and Christine Brooke-Rose, *A ZBC of Ezra Pound* (Berkeley: Univ. of California Press, 1971), which is a chronological exploration of growth and development. Donald Davie, *Ezra Pound* (New York: Viking, 1976) is a stimulating account of the life and work that is helpful on the *Cantos*; Michael Alexander, *The Poetic Achievement of Ezra Pound* (Berkeley: Univ. of California Press, 1979) contains helpful explication on the *Cantos*; and James Knapp, *Ezra Pound* (Boston: Twayne, 1979) is an illuminating guide to the poems.

For full critical studies, see Donald Davie, *Poet as Sculptor* (New York: Oxford Univ. Press, 1964), which discusses Pound as a translator; Hugh Kenner, *The Pound Era* (Berkeley: Univ. of California Press, 1971), which explores Pound's perception of design amid chaotic change; and M. L. Rosenthal, *Sailing into the Unknown: Yeats, Pound and Eliot* (New York: Oxford Univ. Press, 1978), which contains two important chapters on Pound.

Among useful collections of essays on Pound are *New Approaches to Ezra Pound*, ed. Eva Hesse (Berkeley: Univ. of California Press, 1969); *Ezra Pound: The Critical Heritage*, ed. Eric Homberger (London: Routledge & Kegan Paul, 1972), which collects notable reviews and essays, 1904-1970; and *Ezra Pound: The London Years, 1908-1920*, ed. Philip Grover (New York: AMS Press, 1978), which is the proceedings of the Ezra Pound Conference at Sheffield University, 1976.

For specialized criticism, see John J. Espey, *Ezra Pound's Mauberley: A Study in Composition* (Berkeley: Univ. of California Press, 1955); L. S. Dembo, *The Confucian Odes of Ezra Pound* (Univ. of California Press, 1963); and K. K. Ruthven, *A Guide to Ezra Pound's Personae, 1926* (Univ. of California Press, 1969), which provides useful explication for the early verse. Among the most helpful criticism of *The Cantos* are Clark Emery, *Ideas into Action* (Coral Gables: Univ. of Miami Press, 1958); George Dekker, *The Cantos of Ezra Pound: A Critical Study* (New York: Barnes & Noble, 1963); Daniel D. Pearlman, *The Barb of Time: On the Unity of Ezra Pound's Cantos* (New York: Oxford Univ. Press, 1969), which is an influential discussion that stops at the *Pisan Cantos*; Ronald Bush, *The Genesis of Ezra Pound's Cantos* (Princeton, NJ: Princeton Univ. Press, 1976); James J. Wilhelm, *The Later Cantos of Ezra Pound* (New York: Walker, 1977); Barbara Eastman, *Ezra Pound's Cantos: The Story of the Text* (Orono, ME: National Poetry Foundation & Univ. of Maine Press, 1979), which recounts development of the text and collates its variants; Leon Surette, *A Light from Eleusis: A Study of Ezra Pound's Cantos* (New York: Oxford Univ. Press, 1979), which is a structural examination; Wendy Stallard Flory, *Ezra Pound and "The Cantos": A Record of Struggle* (New Haven, CT: Yale Univ. Press, 1980); and George Kearns, *Guide to Ezra Pound's "Selected Cantos"* (New Brunswick, NJ: Rutgers Univ. Press, 1980), which explicates Pound's selection of the *Cantos* using the 1970 New Direction's edition.

Bibliographies

John J. Espey, "Ezra Pound," in *Sixteen Modern American Authors*, ed. Jackson R. Bryer (Durham, NC: Duke Univ. Press, 1974), pp.445-71, is a helpful bibliographical essay. Donald C. Gallup, *A Bibliography of Ezra Pound*, 2nd imp., corr. (London: Rupert Hart-Davis, 1969) contains an authoritative listing of primary sources; and for a comprehensive secondary bibliography, see Robert A. Corrigan, "The First Quarter Century of Ezra Pound Criticism: An Annotated Checklist," *Resources for American Literary Study* (Autumn 1972).

Reference Works

Paideluma, 1972- is an indispensable journal devoted to Pound scholarship, which includes full-length critical articles, explication, reviews, photographs, bibliographical updates, notes, and queries.

Among helpful indexes and concordances are Gary Lane, *A Concordance to Personae: The Shorter Poems of Ezra Pound* (New York: Haskell House, 1972); and for the *Cantos*, see John Hamilton Edwards and William W. Vasse, *Annotated Index to the Cantos* (Berkeley: Univ. of California Press, 1957; 2nd print, with additions and corr., 1959); and Robert J. Dilligan, James W. Parins, and Todd K. Bender, *A Concordance to Ezra Pound's Cantos* (New York: Garland, 1981), which is keyed to the 1975 New Directions edition.

ISHMAEL REED, 1938-

PRIMARY SOURCES

Separate Works

The Free-Lance Pallbearers (1967); *Yellow Back Radio Broke-Down* (1969); *catechism of D Neoamerican Hoodoo Church* [poetry] (1969); *19 Necromancers from Now* (1970); *Conjure: Selected Poems, 1963-1970* (1972); *Mumbo Jumbo* (1972); *Chattanooga: Poems* (1973); *The Last Days of Louisiana Red* (1974); *A*

Secretary to the Spirits (1975); *Flight to Canada* (1976); *Shrovetide in Old New Orleans* (1978).

Other Source Materials

This One's on Me was an autobiographical account announced for publication by Doubleday in 1973, but never published, cf. *Library Journal* 98 (April 1, 1973): 1198.

SECONDARY SOURCES

Biography and Criticism

There is no book-length study of Reed, and the best sources of biography and criticism are articles listed in Bibliographies, below.

Bibliographies

Elizabeth A. Settle and Thomas A. Settle, *Ishmael Reed: An Annotated Checklist* (Dominguez Hills: California State College, 1977) is an annotated "working" bibliography of all known works by and about Reed through March 1977. Primary sources include poems by Reed appearing in collections or separately published, his articles, interviews, recordings, video tapes, and titles of the works he has edited. For subsequent bibliography, see annual volumes of *American Literary Scholarship.*

ADRIENNE (CECILE) RICH, 1929-

PRIMARY SOURCES

Separate Works

A Change of World (1951); *The Diamond Cutters* (1955); *Snapshots of a Daughter-in-Law: Poems, 1954-1962* (1963); *Necessities of Life* (1966); *Leaflets* (1969); *The Will to Change: Poems, 1968-1970* (1971); *Diving into the Wreck* (1973); *Of Woman Born: Motherhood as Experience and Institution* (1976); *The Dream of a Common Language: Poems, 1974-1977* (1978); *On Lies, Secrets, and Silence* (1979); *A Wild Patience Has Taken Me This Far: Poems, 1978-1981* (1981).

Collected Works and Edited Texts

Important collections are *Poems Selected and New, 1950-1974* (New York: Norton, 1974); and *Adrienne Rich's Poetry*, eds. Barbara Charlesworth Gelpi and Albert Gelpi (Norton, 1975), which is a Norton critical edition that includes texts of the poems, Rich on her work, and reviews and criticism. *On Lies, Secrets, and Silence: Selected Prose, 1966-1978* (Norton, 1979) is a collection of her essays, speeches, and lectures.

SECONDARY SOURCES

Biography

There is no full account of Rich, but a short biographical sketch precedes the selection of Rich's poems in *The Norton Anthology of American Literature*, ed. R. Gottesman, et al. (New York: Norton, 1979), v.2, pp.2516-18.

Criticism

There are no full-length studies of Rich, but a selection of reviews and criticism is gathered in *Adrienne Rich's Poetry* (*see* Collected Works).

Bibliographies

The bibliography in *Adrienne Rich's Poetry* contains listings of essays, reviews, interviews, and recordings.

EDWIN ARLINGTON ROBINSON, 1869-1935

PRIMARY SOURCES

Separate Works

The Torrent and the Night Before (1896); *The Children of the Night* (1897); *Captain Craig* (1902; rev. with additional poems, 1915); *The Town Down the River* (1910); *Van Zorn* (1914); *The Porcupine* (1915); *The Man against the Sky* (1916); *Merlin* (1917); *The Three Taverns* (1920); *Lancelot* (1920); *Avon's Harvest* (1921); *Collected Poems* (1921); *Roman Bartholomew* (1923); *The Man Who Died Twice* (1924); *Dionysus in Doubt* (1925); *Tristram* (1927); *Sonnets, 1889-1927* (1928); *Three Poems* (1928); *Fortunatas* (1928); *Modred: A Fragment* (1929); *The Prodigal Son* (1929); *Cavender's House* (1929); *Collected Poems* (1929); *The Glory of the Nightingales* (1930); *Matthias at the Door* (1931); *Nicodemus* (1932); *Talifer* (1933); *Amaranth* (1934); *King Jasper* (1935); *Hannibal Brown: Posthumous Poem* (1936).

Collected Works and Edited Texts

Although *Collected Poems of Edwin Arlington Robinson* (New York: Macmillan, 1937) is the most complete collection available, it omits several of his earliest poems as well as the later *Modred: A Fragment* (New York: Hackett, 1929); and *Fortunatus* (Reno, NV: Slide Mountain Press, 1929). Other important collections are *Selected Early Poems and Letters*, ed. Charles T. Davis (New York: Holt, Rinehart & Winston, 1960); and *Selected Poems of Edwin Arlington Robinson*, ed. Morton D. Zabel (Macmillan, 1965). Important collections of correspondence are *Selected Letters of Edwin Arlington Robinson*, ed. Ridgely Torrence (Macmillan, 1940); *Untriangulated Stars*, ed. Denham Sutcliffe (Cambridge: Harvard Univ. Press, 1947), which contains letters written to his friend, Harry de Forest Smith, 1890-1905; and *Edwin Arlington Robinson's Letters to Edith Brower*, ed. Richard Cary (Harvard Univ. Press, 1968). An edition of all extant letters is being prepared by Wallace Anderson.

Other Source Materials

The most important collections of Robinson's primary sources are at Colby College, Maine, the Boston Public Library, New York Public Library, Yale University Library, the Library of Congress, Duke University Library, and the University of North Carolina.

SECONDARY SOURCES

Biography

There is no standard biography, and the most reliable accounts are Hermann Hagedorn, *Edwin Arlington Robinson: A Biography* (New York: Macmillan, 1938); and Emery Neff, *Edwin Arlington Robinson* (New York: Sloane, 1948).

Criticism

Useful introductions to Robinson are Ellsworth Barnard, *Edwin Arlington Robinson: A Critical Study* (New York: Macmillan, 1952); Louis O. Coxe, *Edwin Arlington Robinson* (Minneapolis: Univ. of Minnesota Press, 1962); and Hoyt C. Franchere, *Edwin Arlington Robinson* (New York: Twayne, 1968). Important full-length studies are Edwin S. Fussell, *Edwin Arlington Robinson: The Literary Background of a Traditional Poet* (Berkeley: Univ. of California Press, 1954); W. R. Robinson, *Edwin Arlington Robinson: A Poetry of the Act* (Cleveland, OH: Press of Western Reserve Univ., 1967); Wallace L. Anderson, *Edwin Arlington Robinson: A Critical Introduction* (Cambridge: Harvard Univ. Press, 1968); Louis O. Coxe, *Edwin Arlington Robinson: The Life of Poetry* (New York: Pegasus, 1969); and Yvor Winter, *Edwin Arlington Robinson*, rev. ed. (New York: New Directions, 1971).

Several collections which provide a range of critical essays are *Edwin Arlington Robinson: Centenary Essays*, ed. Ellsworth Barnard (Athens: Univ. of Georgia Press, 1969); *Appreciation of Edwin Arlington Robinson*, ed. Richard Cary (Waterville, ME: Colby College Press, 1969); and *Edwin Arlington Robinson*, ed. Francis Murphy (Englewood Cliffs, NJ: Prentice-Hall, 1970). Richard Cary, *Early Reception of Edwin Arlington Robinson: The First Twenty Years* (Colby College Press, 1974) provides the context for each of the volumes of poetry published by 1916, including a reprint of every notice and annotations of reviews.

Bibliographies

For a helpful bibliographical essay, see Ellsworth Barnard, "Edwin Arlington Robinson," in *Sixteen Modern American Authors*, ed. Jackson R. Bryer (Durham, NC: Duke Univ. Press, 1974), pp.473-98. The standard bibliography, which includes both primary and secondary sources, is Charles Beecher Hogan, *A Bibliography of Edwin Arlington Robinson* (New Haven, CT: Yale Univ. Press, 1936). It is updated through 1970 by William White, *Edwin Arlington Robinson: A Supplementary Bibliography* (Kent, OH: Kent State Univ. Press, 1971). For a chronologically arranged, annotated list of criticism, 1894-1976, see Nancy Carol Joyner, *Edwin Arlington Robinson: A Reference Guide* (Boston: G. K. Hall, 1978).

THEODORE ROETHKE, 1908-1963

PRIMARY SOURCES

Separate Works

Open House (1941); *The Lost Son and Other Poems* (1948); *Praise to the End!* (1951); *The Waking: Poems 1933-1953* (1953); *The Exorcism* (1957); *Words for the Wind: Collected Verse* (1958); *I Am! Says the Lamb* (1961); *Sequence, Sometimes Metaphysical* (1963); *The Far Field* (1964); *The Collected Poems* (1966); *Party at the Zoo* [for children] (1963); *Dirty Dinky and Other Creatures* (1973).

Collected Works and Edited Texts

The Collected Poems (Garden City, NY: Doubleday, 1966) is a complete edition. *On the Poet and His Craft: Selected Prose of Theodore Roethke*, ed. Ralph J. Mills, Jr. (Seattle: Univ. of Washington Press, 1965); and *Selected Letters*, ed. Ralph J. Mills, Jr., with the assistance of Beatrice Roethke (Univ. of Washington Press, 1968) are invaluable for Roethke's own views on the poetic craft. *Straw for the Fire: From the Notebooks of Theodore Roethke, 1948-63*, ed. David Wagoner (New York: Doubleday, 1972) is a collection of Roethke's unpublished poems and fragments, lecture notes, essays, and prose from 277 notebooks, and over 8,000 loose sheets from which Wagoner pieced together several versions of an image or idea.

Theodore Roethke: Selected Poems, selected by Beatrice Roethke (London: Faber & Faber, 1969); and *The Achievement of Theodore Roethke: A Comprehensive Selection of His Poems*, with a critical introduction by William J. Martz (Glenview, IL: Scott Foresman, 1966), are important editions.

Other Source Materials

Roethke's papers, including letters and notebooks, are at the University of Washington, Seattle, and a number of other institutions. A guide to location of the manuscripts is McLeod's checklist (*see* Bibliographies). A visual interview which includes some readings is the film *In a Dark Time*, an interview with David Myers in spring 1973 (distributed by Contemporary Films, Inc.).

SECONDARY SOURCES

Biography

Allan Seager, *The Glass House: The Life of Theodore Roethke* (New York: McGraw-Hill, 1968) is the first full-length biography based on the Roethke papers.

Criticism

A short introductory pamphlet is Ralph J. Mills, Jr., *Theodore Roethke* (Minneapolis: Univ. of Minnesota Press, 1963). The first comprehensive survey of Roethke's work was Karl Malkoff, *Theodore Roethke: An Introduction to the Poetry* (New York: Columbia Univ. Press, 1966), which explicated the key themes from a psychoanalytical point of view. An overview which analyzes Roethke's aesthetic of motion is Richard A. Blessing, *Theodore Roethke's Dynamic Vision* (Bloomington: Indiana Univ. Press, 1974). Rosemary Sullivan, *Theodore Roethke: The Garden Master* (Seattle: Univ. of Washington Press, 1975) uses material from Seager's biography and

Roethke's letters and notebooks in a chronological development which stresses the continuity of Roethke's major themes. Jenijoy La Belle, *The Echoing Wood of Theodore Roethke* (Princeton, NJ: Princeton Univ. Press, 1976) shows that Roethke's poetic innovation was based on a wide knowledge of earlier poetry. A study of the influence of Roethke on James Wright, Robert Bly, James Dickey, Sylvia Plath, and Ted Hughes is by Harry Williams, *"The Edge is What I Have": Theodore Roethke and After* (Lewisburg, PA: Bucknell Univ. Press, 1977); and Jay Parini, *Theodore Roethke: An American Romantic* (Amherst: Univ. of Massachusetts Press, 1979) relates poetic themes to romantic tradition.

Two collections of criticism are *Profile of Theodore Roethke*, ed. William Heyen (Columbus, OH: Merrill, 1971), which contains ten contributions, nine of them by poets; and *Theodore Roethke: Essays on the Poetry*, ed. Arnold Stein (Seattle: Univ. of Washington Press, 1965), which contains explications by Stephen Spender, Louis L. Martz, Ralph J. Mills, and others.

Bibliographies

The manuscript locations of Roethke's published and unpublished poems, prose works, letters to and from Roethke, as well as his notebooks, are indicated for twenty repository libraries in James Richard McLeod, *Theodore Roethke: A Manuscript Checklist* (Kent, OH: Kent State Univ. Press, 1971). A complete listing of Roethke's prose and poetic works and criticism, together with locations in special collections and repositories, is James R. McLeod, *Theodore Roethke: A Bibliography* (Kent State Univ. Press, 1973). The most recent bibliography is Keith R. Moul, *Theodore Roethke's Career: An Annotated Bibliography* (Boston: G. K. Hall, 1977). It lists chronologically all works by Roethke and works about him which appeared between 1922 and 1973, with concise annotations.

Reference Works

A list of each significant word and line in which it occurs in the edition, *Collected Poems, 1966*, is in Gary Lane, ed., *A Concordance to the Poems of Theodore Roethke*, programmed by Roland Dedekind (Metuchen, NJ: Scarecrow, 1972).

PHILIP (MILTON) ROTH, 1933-

PRIMARY SOURCES

Separate Works

Goodbye Columbus and Five Short Stories (1959); *Letting Go* (1962); *When She Was Good* (1964); *Portnoy's Complaint* (1969); *Our Gang* (1971); *The Breast* (1972); *The Great American Novel* (1973); *My Life as a Man* (1974); *Reading Myself and Others* [essays and interviews] (1975); *The Professor of Desire* (1977); *The Ghost Writer* (1979); *Zuckerman Unbound* (1981).

Collected Works and Edited Texts

A Philip Roth Reader (New York: Farrar, Straus & Giroux, 1980) selects and groups extracts from the works.

SECONDARY SOURCES

Biography

There is no full-length biography of Roth and interviews such as those listed in Nadel (*see* Bibliographies) should be consulted.

Criticism

Two useful introductions are Sanford Pinsker, *The Comedy That "Hoits":* *An Essay on the Fiction of Philip Roth* (Columbia: Univ. of Missouri Press, 1975); and the first substantial study, Bernard F. Rodgers, Jr., *Philip Roth* (Boston: Twayne, 1978).

Bibliographies

Two published bibliographies which need updating are John N. McDaniel, "Philip Roth: A Checklist, 1954-1973," *Bulletin of Bibliography* 31 (1974): 51-53, which also covers criticism and reviews; and Bernard F. Rodgers, Jr., *Philip Roth: A Bibliography* (Metuchen, NJ: Scarecrow, 1974), which is an annotated list that includes dissertations, interviews, and criticism. Interviews and criticism are also listed in Ira Bruce Nadel, *Jewish Writers of North America: A Guide to Information Sources* (Detroit: Gale, 1981), pp.283-86.

CARL (CHARLES AUGUST) SANDBURG, 1878-1967

PRIMARY SOURCES

Separate Works

In Reckless Ecstasy (1904); *Chicago Poems* (1916); *Cornhuskers* (1918); *Smoke and Steel* (1920); *Slabs of the Sunburnt West* (1922); *Rootabaga Stories* (1922); *Rootabaga Pigeons* (1923); *Abraham Lincoln: The Prairie Years* (1926); *Good Morning America* (1928); *Steichen, the Photographer* (1929); *Potato Face* (1930); *Early Moon* (1930); *Mary Lincoln, Wife and Widow* [with Paul N. Angle] (1932); *The People, Yes* (1936); *A Lincoln and Whitman Miscellany* (1938); *Abraham Lincoln: The War Years* (1939); *The Photographs of Abraham Lincoln* [with Frederick Hill Meserve] (1944); *Remembrance Rock* (1948); *Complete Poems* (1950); *Carl Sandburg's New American Songbag* (1950); *Always the Young Strangers* [autobiography] (1953); *Wind Song* (1960); *Honey and Salt* (1963).

Collected Works and Edited Texts

Sandburg's poems are collected as *The Complete Poems*, rev. ed. (New York: Harcourt, Brace & World, 1969); and his correspondence between 1898 and 1962 is available in *The Letters of Carl Sandburg*, ed. Herbert Mitang (Harcourt, Brace & World, 1968).

SECONDARY SOURCES

Biography

There is no authoritative biography, but the following studies should be consulted. Karl Detzer, *Carl Sandburg: A Study in Personality and Background* (New

York: Harcourt Brace, 1941), which contains photographs by Steichen; Harry Golden, *Carl Sandburg* (Cleveland, OH: World, 1961), which is a portrait by a friend; and North Callahan, *Carl Sandburg: Lincoln of Our Literature* (New York: New York Univ. Press, 1970), which is a sound life and critical appraisal. For personal records or relationships, see Helga Sandburg, *A Great and Glorious Romance* (New York: Harcourt Brace Jovanovich, 1978), which his daughter has based on letters between Sandburg and Lillian Steichen until 1926. Lilla S. Perry, *My Friend, Carl Sandburg* (Metuchen, NJ: Scarecrow, 1981) documents the friendship with Perry; and *Carl Sandburg Remembered*, ed. William A. Sutton (Scarecrow, 1979) is a collection of over seventy reminiscences.

Criticism

Among pamphlet-length introductions are Mark Van Doren, *Carl Sandburg: With a Bibliography of Sandburg Materials in the Collection of the Library of Congress* (Washington, DC: Library of Congress, 1969); Gay Wilson Allen, *Carl Sandburg* (Minneapolis: Univ. of Minnesota Press, 1972); and Daniel Hoffman, *Moonlight Dries No Mittens: Carl Sandburg Reconsidered* (Library of Congress, 1978), which celebrates Sandburg's perception of the variety of American life and language. The most useful full-scale critical work is Richard Crowder, *Carl Sandburg* (New York: Twayne, 1964). Hazel Durnell, *The America of Carl Sandburg* (Washington, DC: Univ. Press of Washington, 1965) places Sandburg in American literary tradition; and *The Vision of This Land: Studies of Vachel Lindsay, Edgar Lee Masters and Carl Sandburg*, eds. John E. Hallwas and Dennis J. Reader (Macomb: Western Illinois Univ. Press, 1976) contains essays on the poetry and the Lincoln books.

Bibliographies

The most extensive bibliography which gives access to translations, addresses, and interviews is in Mark Van Doren, *Carl Sandburg* (*see* Criticism). Another useful listing is in Gay Wilson Allen's pamphlet (*see* Criticism).

ANNE SEXTON, 1928-1975

PRIMARY SOURCES

Separate Works

To Bedlam and Part Way Back (1960); *All My Pretty Ones* (1962); *Live or Die* (1966); *Love Poems* (1969); *Transformations* (1971); *The Book of Folly* (1972); *The Death Notebooks* (1974); *The Awful Rowing toward God* (1975); *The Wizard's Tears* [with Maxine Kumin] (1975); *45 Mercy Street* (1976).

Collected Works and Edited Texts

Important collections of poetry are *Complete Poems* (Boston: Houghton Mifflin, 1981), which includes a memoir by M. Kumin and some poems that are collected for the first time; *Selected Poems* (London: Oxford Univ. Press, 1964); and *Words for Dr. Y.: Uncollected Poems with Three Stories*, ed. Linda Gray Sexton (Houghton Mifflin, 1978). A collection of correspondence is *Anne Sexton: A Self-Portrait in Letters*, eds. Linda Gray Sexton and Lois Ames (Houghton Mifflin, 1977).

Other Source Materials

Papers and letters are in the Anne Sexton Archive at Boston University.

SECONDARY SOURCES

Biography

There is no full-length biography.

Criticism

J. D. McClatchy, *Anne Sexton: The Artist and Her Critics* (Bloomington: Indiana Univ. Press, 1978) brings together three interviews, Sexton's worksheets, reminiscences, reviews, and critical essays.

Bibliographies

Cameron Northouse and Thomas P. Walsh, *Sylvia Plath and Anne Sexton: A Reference Guide* (Boston: G. K. Hall, 1974) is a bibliography of secondary sources.

GERTRUDE STEIN, 1874-1946

PRIMARY SOURCES

Separate Works

Three Lives (1909); *Tender Buttons* (1914); *Geography and Plays* (1922); *The Making of Americans* (1925); *Composition as Explanation* (1926); *Useful Knowledge* (1928); *Lucy Church Amiably* (1930); *Before the Flowers of Friendship Faded Friendship Faded* (1931); *How to Write* (1931); *Operas and Plays* (1932); *Matisse, Picasso and Gertrude Stein with Two Shorter Stories* (1933); *The Autobiography of Alice B. Toklas* (1933); *Four Saints in Three Acts* (1934); *Portraits and Prayers* (1934); *Lectures in America* (1935); *Narration* (1935); *The Geographical History of America* (1936); *Everybody's Autobiography* (1937); *Picasso* (1938); *The World Is Round* (1939); *Paris France* (1940); *What Are Masterpieces* (1940); *Ida: A Novel* (1941); *Wars I Have Seen* (1945); *Brewsie and Willie* (1946); *The Gertrude Stein First Reader and Three Plays* (1946); *Four in America* (1947); *Blood on the Dining-Room Floor* (1948); *Last Operas and Plays* (1949); *Things as They Are* (1950).

Collected Works and Edited Texts

There is no complete collection of Stein's works. Important collections are *The Yale Edition of the Unpublished Writings of Gertrude Stein*, ed. Carl Van Vechten. 8v. (New Haven, CT: Yale Univ. Press, 1951-58); and *The Yale Gertrude Stein* (Yale Univ. Press, 1980), which contains selections from the Yale edition. Other collections of note are *Selected Writings*, ed. Carl Van Vechten (New York: Modern Library, 1962); *Gertrude Stein: Writings and Lectures, 1909-1945*, ed. Patricia Meyerowitz (London: P. Owen, 1967); and *Fernhurst, Q.E.D. and Other Early Writings* (New York: Liveright, 1971). Among collections of correspondence useful for biographical details are *The Flowers of Friendship*, ed. Donald C. Gallup (New York: Knopf, 1953); *Sherwood Anderson/Gertrude Stein: Correspondence and Personal*

Essays, ed. Ray Lewis White (Chapel Hill: Univ. of North Carolina Press, 1972); and *Dear Sammy: Letters from Gertrude Stein and Alice B. Toklas, Edited with a Memoir*, ed. Samuel M. Steward (Boston: Houghton Mifflin, 1977).

Other Sources

The most significant collection of Stein materials is at the Beinecke Library, Yale University.

SECONDARY SOURCES

Biography

The best biographies are John Malcolm Brinnin, *The Third Rose: Gertrude Stein and Her World* (Boston: Little, Brown, 1959), which is about Stein and her friends; and James R. Mellow, *Charmed Circle: Gertrude Stein and Company* (New York: Praeger, 1974), which draws on the Stein collection to document the milieu. Three interesting memoirs by Stein's friend are Alice B. Toklas, *The Alice B. Toklas Cook Book* (New York: Doubleday, 1954); *What Is Remembered* (New York: Holt, Rinehart & Winston, 1963); and *Staying on Alone: Letters of Alice B. Toklas*, ed. Edward Burnes (New York: Liveright, 1973). *Gertrude Stein: A Composite Portrait* (New York: Avon, 1974) is a collection of statements about Stein.

Criticism

Two useful introductions are a pamphlet, Frederick John Hoffman, *Gertrude Stein* (Minneapolis: Univ. of Minnesota Press, 1961); and a longer study of the development of Stein's narrative style, Michael J. Hoffman, *Gertrude Stein* (Boston: Twayne, 1976). Full-length studies are Richard Bridgman, *Gertrude Stein in Pieces* (New York: Oxford Univ. Press, 1970), which is a thorough attempt to explain the ambiguities in Stein's work; Bruce F. Kawin, *Telling It Again and Again* (Ithaca, NY: Cornell Univ. Press, 1972), which discusses time and repetition, especially in the plays; Carolyn Faunce Copeland, *Language and Time and Gertrude Stein* (Iowa City: Univ. of Iowa, 1975), which analyzes narrative style over three periods of Stein's career; Wendy Steiner, *Exact Resemblance to Exact Resemblance: The Literary Portraiture of Gertrude Stein* (New Haven, CT: Yale Univ. Press, 1978), which is a perceptive study of the theoretical framework of Stein's literary experiments with portrait genre; and S. C. Neuman, *Gertrude Stein: Autobiography and the Problem of Narration* (Victoria, BC: University of Victoria, 1979), which indicates how Stein implements her theory of literature.

Bibliographies

The best primary bibliography is Robert A. Wilson, *Gertrude Stein: A Bibliography* (New York: Phoenix Bookshop, 1974). For a helpful selective bibliography of criticism, 1909-1978, which includes reviews, see Maureen R. Liston, *Gertrude Stein: An Annotated Critical Bibliography* (Kent, OH: Kent State Univ. Press, 1979).

JOHN (ERNST) STEINBECK, 1902-1968

PRIMARY SOURCES

Separate Works

Cup of Gold (1929); The Pastures of Heaven (1932); To a God Unknown (1933); Tortilla Flat (1935); In Dubious Battle (1936); Saint Katy the Virgin (1936); Of Mice and Men (1937); Of Mice and Men [play] (1937); The Red Pony (1937); Their Blood Is Story [pamphlet] (1938); The Long Valley (1938); The Grapes of Wrath (1939); The Forgotten Village (1941); Sea of Cortez (1941); The Moon Is Down (1942); Bombs Away (1942); The Moon Is Down [play] (1943); Cannery Row (1945); The Pearl (1947); Vanderbilt Clinic [pamphlet] (1947); The Wayward Bus (1947); A Russian Journal [with Robert Capa] (1948); Burning Bright (1950); Burning Bright [play] (1951); The Log from the Sea of Cortez (1951); East of Eden (1952); Sweet Thursday (1954); Pipe Dream [musical comedy based on Sweet Thursday] (1955); The Short Reign of Pippin IV (1957); Once There Was a War (1958); The Winter of Our Discontent (1961); Travels with Charley in Search of America (1962); America and Americans (1966); Journal of a Novel (1969); Viva Zapata! (1975); The Acts of King Arthur and His Noble Knights (1976).

Collected Works and Edited Texts

There is no standard scholarly collection of Steinbeck's writings, and the most reliable texts are those of the Compass series of his publisher, Viking Press. John Steinbeck, "The Grapes of Wrath": Text and Criticism, ed. Peter Lisca (New York: Viking, 1972) is a handy study edition. Collections of Steinbeck's correspondence that provide documentation of his themes and methods of literary composition are Journal of a Novel: The "East of Eden" Letters (Viking, 1969); and Steinbeck and Covici: The Story of a Friendship, ed. Thomas Fensch (Middleburg, VT: Erickson, 1979), which has a commentary on the relationship between Steinbeck and his editor. An account whose connecting comments help to make its collection of 861 letters a useful biographical study is Steinbeck: A Life in Letters, eds. Elaine Steinbeck and Robert Wallsten (Viking, 1975).

Other Source Materials

Steinbeck manuscripts and papers are deposited in the libraries of the University of California, Berkeley, the University of Virginia, the Library of Congress, and the Pierpont Morgan Library, New York. Six essays describing Steinbeck collections in research libraries are in A Handbook for Steinbeck Collectors, Librarians, and Scholars, ed. Tetsumaro Hayashi (Muncie, IN: Steinbeck Society of America, English Dept., Ball State Univ., 1981), pp.29-46.

SECONDARY SOURCES

Biography

The first full-length biography is Thomas Kiernan, The Intricate Music (Boston: Little, Brown, 1979). One of the best accounts is an essay by Peter Lisca, "John Steinbeck: A Literary Biography," in Steinbeck and His Critics (see Criticism), and biographical chapters in other works will be helpful.

Criticism

Reliable introductions are the pamphlet James Gray, *John Steinbeck* (Minneapolis: Univ. of Minnesota Press, 1971); Peter Lisca, *John Steinbeck: Nature and Myth* (New York: Crowell, 1978), which provides a biographical introduction and studies on the novels, short fiction, and nonfiction; and Paul McCarthy, *John Steinbeck* (New York: Ungar, 1980), which intertwines biography and brief explication.

Critical studies of value include Harry T. Moore, *The Novels of John Steinbeck: A First Critical Study* (Chicago: Normandie House, 1939), which deals with earlier novels; Peter Lisca, *The Wide World of John Steinbeck* (New Brunswick, NJ: Rutgers Univ. Press, 1958), which examines novels through *The Short Reign of Pippin IV*; Warren French, *John Steinbeck* (New York: Twayne, 1961), of which the second edition revised, 1975, has greatly changed and expanded the study to cover Steinbeck's whole output; and John Fontenrose, *John Steinbeck: An Introduction and Interpretation* (New York: Barnes & Noble, 1963), which follows Steinbeck's development chronologically. The later novels receive attention in Lester Jay Marks, *Thematic Design in the Novels of John Steinbeck* (The Hague: Mouton, 1969); and Richard Astro, *John Steinbeck and Edward F. Ricketts: The Shaping of a Novelist* (Minneapolis: Univ. of Minnesota Press, 1973), which examines the influence of Steinbeck's friend, Lawrence William Jones, who served as model for principal characters. *John Steinbeck as Fabulist*, ed. Marston LaFrance (Muncie, IN: Ball State Univ., 1973) analyzes reasons for the failure of Steinbeck's later fiction; and Howard Levant, *The Novels of John Steinbeck: A Critical Study* (Columbia: Univ. of Missouri Press, 1974) examines Steinbeck's total career, seeking to understand the reasons for decline in the later work.

A range of critical opinion is collected in *Steinbeck and the Critics: A Record of Twenty-Five Years*, eds. E. W. Tedlock, Jr., and C. V. Wicker (Albuquerque: Univ. of New Mexico Press, 1957); *Steinbeck: The Man and His Work*, eds. R. Astro and T. Hayashi (Corvallis: Oregon State Univ. Press, 1971); *Steinbeck: A Collection of Critical Essays*, ed. Robert Murray Davis (Englewood Cliffs, NJ: Prentice-Hall, 1972); and *A Study Guide to Steinbeck: A Handbook to His Major Works*, ed. Tetsumaro Hayashi (Metuchen, NJ: Scarecrow, Part I, 1974; Part II, 1979), including essays which give background information, plot explication, suggestions for research, and an annotated bibliography. *Steinbeck's Literary Dimension: A Guide to Comparative Studies*, ed. Tetsumaro Hayashi (Scarecrow, 1973) is a collection of essays which compare Steinbeck with other authors. In addition, collections devoted to individual novels are *A Companion to "The Grapes of Wrath,"* ed. Warren French (New York: Viking, 1963), which makes available background material such as newspaper accounts; *A Casebook on "The Grapes of Wrath,"* ed. Agnes M. Donohue (New York: Crowell, 1968); and *A Study Guide to Steinbeck's "The Long Valley"* (Ann Arbor, MI: Pierian Press, 1976).

Bibliographies

Warren French, "John Steinbeck," in *Sixteen Modern American Authors*, ed. Jackson R. Bryer (Durham, NC: Duke Univ. Press, 1974), pp.499-527, is a helpful bibliographic essay on Steinbeck scholarship. Access to primary sources is provided in Tetsumaro Hayashi, *A New Steinbeck Bibliography, 1929-1971* (Metuchen, NJ: Scarecrow, 1973) and to secondary sources through Hayashi's *Steinbeck Criticism: A Review of Book-Length Studies, 1933-1973*, Steinbeck Monograph Series, no. 4 (Muncie, IN: Steinbeck Society, Ball State Univ., 1974).

Reference Works

Steinbeck Quarterly, 1 (1968)- , the organ of the Steinbeck Society, is a comprehensive source of information, reviews, and critical analysis, produced together with the Steinbeck Monograph Series at Ball State University, Muncie Indiana. Tetsumaro Hayashi, *John Steinbeck: A Dictionary of His Fictional Characters* (Metuchen, NJ: Scarecrow, 1976) provides summaries.

WALLACE STEVENS, 1879-1955

PRIMARY SOURCES

Separate Works

Harmonium (1923); *Ideas of Order* (1935); *Owl's Clover* (1936); *The Man with the Blue Guitar and Other Poems* (1937; with rev. version of *Owl's Clover*); *Parts of a World* (1942); *Notes toward a Supreme Fiction* (1942); *Ésthetique du mal* (1945); *Transport to a Summer* (1947); *Three Academic Pieces: The Realm of Resemblance, Someone Puts a Pineapple Together, of Ideal Time and Choice* (1947); *A Primitive Like an Orb* (1948); *The Auroras of Autumn* (1950); *The Relations between Poetry and Painting* (1951); *The Necessary Angel: Essays on Reality and the Imagination* (1951); *Selected Poems* (1953); *Raoul Dufy, a Note* (1953); *Collected Poems* (1954); *Opus Posthumous* (1957).

Collected Works and Edited Texts

The standard edition is *The Collected Poems* (New York: Knopf, 1954), which contains *Harmonium* as revised in 1931, and a dozen other poems. In addition, about a third of *Opus Posthumous*, ed. Samuel French Morse (Knopf, 1957) is collected for the first time and includes poems, plays, and prose, most of which appeared in magazines and anthologies. From over 3,000 available letters written from 1895 on, Stevens' daughter has selected about 1,000 which are chronologically presented in *Letters of Wallace Stevens*, ed. Holly Stevens (Knopf, 1966). This major source emphasizes biographical details as background for the poems and also contains parts of a journal kept between 1898 and 1912. This journal has been presented by Holly Stevens, *Souvenirs and Prophecies: The Young Wallace Stevens* (Knopf, 1977). Here Holly Stevens interweaves passages from her father's journals and correspondence with her own comments and prints some of the early verses for the first time.

Two major editions, apart from those above, are *Poems of Wallace Stevens*, selected and introduced by Samuel French Morse (New York: Vintage Books, 1959). A fuller selection is *The Palm at the End of the Mind: Selected Poems and a Play*, ed. Holly Stevens (Knopf, 1971; New York: Vintage Books, 1972). Included are two previously uncollected poems and some useful notes on textual corrections and variants, as well as "Bowl, Cat and Broomstick," a one-act play presented in 1917 and first published in *Quarterly Review of Literature* 16 (1969): 23-247.

Other Source Materials

Books, papers, and volumes from his private library, many of which are annotated, are in the Huntington Library, San Marino, California. Other important collections are at Harvard University, the State University of New York at Buffalo,

Dartmouth College, the University of Chicago, the University of Manchester, and the Library of Congress.

SECONDARY SOURCES

Biography

Long awaited, but disappointing because it reveals little evidence of original research, was the first critical biography by Samuel French Morse, *Wallace Stevens: Poetry as Life* (New York: Pegasus, 1970). The best biographical sources are in the *Letters*; and *Souvenirs and Prophecies*, edited by his daughter (*see* Collected Works). In honor of Stevens' centenary, an anthology that includes much biographical material is *Wallace Stevens: A Celebration*, eds. Frank Doggett and Robert Buttel (Princeton, NJ: Princeton Univ. Press, 1980).

Criticism

An extended essay by Frank Kermode, *Wallace Stevens* (Edinburgh: Oliver & Boyd, 1960; New York: Grove, 1961) paraphrases the major poems, providing an excellent introduction. Among other introductory studies are a pamphlet focussing on the influence of French symbolism, by William York Tindall, *Wallace Stevens* (Minneapolis: Univ. of Minnesota Press, 1961); and Ronald Sukenick, *Wallace Stevens: Musing the Obscure: Readings, an Interpretation, and a Guide to the Collected Poetry* (New York: New York Univ. Press, 1967). Daniel Fuchs, *The Comic Spirit of Wallace Stevens* (Durham, NC: Duke Univ. Press, 1963) is concerned primarily with the style and themes of *Harmonium* and the cultural milieu in which it was written; a chronological explication of the entire poetry and its theory is in Joseph N. Riddell, *The Clairvoyant Eye: The Poetry and Poetics of Wallace Stevens* (Baton Rouge: Louisiana State Univ. Press, 1965); Frank Doggett, *Stevens' Poetry of Thought* (Baltimore: Johns Hopkins Press, 1966) is a study of the sources and analogues; Robert Buttel, *Wallace Stevens: The Making of "Harmonium"* (Princeton, NJ: Princeton Univ. Press, 1967) traces the influences of music, painting, and poetry of the Pre-Raphaelites, the Harvard Poets, imagism, and symbolism; James Baird, *The Dome and the Rock: Structure in the Poetry of Wallace Stevens* (Baltimore: Johns Hopkins Press, 1968) is a study of the aesthetic value of the poetry, seeing the canon as a structural whole rather than as separate parts; Helen Hennessy Vendler, *On Extended Wings: Wallace Stevens' Longer Poems* (Cambridge: Harvard Univ. Press, 1969) emphasizes Stevens' internal stylistic coherence; and A. Walton Litz, *Introspective Voyager: The Poetic Development of Wallace Stevens* (New York: Oxford Univ. Press, 1972) concentrates on work written 1914-1937, including some uncollected early poems in the appendix. Lucy Beckett's *Wallace Stevens* (New York: Cambridge Univ. Press, 1974); and Adalaide Kirby Morris, *Wallace Stevens: Imagination and Faith* (Princeton, NJ: Princeton Univ. Press, 1974) are studies of Stevens as a contemplative poet, who sought for a belief through poetry. A chronological study which analyzes the poems and sees Stevens' preoccupation with the process of the mind perceiving reality is Susan B. Weston, *Wallace Stevens: An Introduction to the Poetry* (New York: Columbia Univ. Press, 1977); Harold Bloom, *Wallace Stevens: The Poems of Our Climate* (Ithaca, NY: Cornell Univ. Press, 1977) is a complex study that surveys romanticism from Emerson to Stevens and explicates the poems tracing key words throughout the canon; and Frank Doggett, *Wallace Stevens: The Making of the Poem* (Baltimore: Johns Hopkins Press, 1980) considers Stevens' theories of creativity.

Several anthologies that bring together a variety of critical opinion are *The Achievement of Wallace Stevens*, eds. Ashley Brown and Robert S. Haller (Philadelphia: Lippincott, 1962); *Wallace Stevens: A Collection of Critical Essays*, ed. Marie Boroff (Englewood Cliffs, NJ: Prentice-Hall, 1963); *The Act of the Mind: Essays on the Poetry of Wallace Stevens*, eds. Roy Harvey Pearce and J. Hillis Miller (Baltimore: Johns Hopkins Press, 1965); *Critics on Wallace Stevens*, ed. Peter L. McNamara (Coral Gables, FL: Univ. of Miami Press, 1973); and *Wallace Stevens: A Critical Anthology*, ed. Irving Ehrenpreis (Harmondsworth, England: Penguin Books, 1972), which is a chronological presentation of extracts from Stevens' letters and journals with a collection of critical opinions from 1919 to 1971. *Wallace Stevens: A Celebration* (*see* Biography) makes available some previously unpublished *Adagia* items and also provides critical comment by Litz, Martz, Vendler, and others.

Bibliographies

For a scholarly introduction, a bibliographical essay on Stevens criticism to 1972 is provided by Joseph N. Riddell, "Wallace Stevens," in *Sixteen Modern American Authors* (Durham, NC: Duke Univ. Press, 1974), pp.529-71. J. M. Edelstein, *Wallace Stevens: A Descriptive Bibliography* (Pittsburgh: Univ. of Pittsburgh Press, 1973) is the fullest listing of primary sources, including musical settings and recordings. Abbie F. Willard, *Wallace Stevens: The Poet and His Critics* (Chicago: American Library Association, 1978) is a review of critical perspectives.

Reference Works

Wallace Stevens Journal, California State Univ., Northridge, Dept. of English, 1977- is devoted to Stevens' studies. A concordance is Thomas F. Walsh, *Concordance to the Poetry of Wallace Stevens* (University Park: Pennsylvania State Univ. Press, 1963). A leaflet describing and reproducing items from an exhibition at the Huntington Library and Art Gallery is *Thirteen Ways of Looking at Wallace Stevens: A Special Exhibition* (San Marino, CA: Huntington Library, Art Gallery and Botanical Gardens, 1975).

HARRIET (ELIZABETH) BEECHER STOWE, 1811-1896

PRIMARY SOURCES

Separate Works

Prize Tale: A New England Sketch (1834); *An Elementary Geography* (1835); *The Mayflower; Or, Sketches of Scenes and Characters among the Descendants of the Pilgrims* (1843); *Uncle Tom's Cabin* (1852); *A Key to Uncle Tom's Cabin* (1853); *Uncle Tom's Emancipation, Etc.* (1853); *Sunny Memories of Foreign Lands* (1854); *Geography for My Children* (1855); *Dred: A Tale of the Great Dismal Swamp* (1856); *Our Charley and What to Do with Him* (1858); *The Minister's Wooing* (1859); *The Pearl of Orr's Island* (1862); *Agnes of Sorrento* (1862); *A Reply in Behalf of the Women of America, Etc.* (1863); *The Ravages of a Carpet* (1865); *House and Home Papers* (1865); *Little Foxes* (1866); *Stories about Our Dogs* (1865); *Religious Poems* (1867); *Queer Little People* (1867); *Daisy's First Winter and Other Stories* (1867); *The Chimney-Corner* (1868); *Men of Our Times* (1868); *Oldtown Folks* (1869); *The American Woman's Home* (1869); *Lady Byron Vindicated* (1870); *Little Pussy*

Willow (1870); *My Wife and I* (1871); *Pink and White Tyranny* (1871); *Sam Lawson's Oldtown Fireside Stories* (1872); *Palmetto-Leaves* (1873); *Woman in Sacred History* (1873); *We and Our Neighbors* (1875); *Betty's Bright Idea, Etc.* (1876); *Footsteps of the Master* (1876); *Poganuc People* (1878); *A Dog's Mission* (1881); *Our Famous Women* (1884).

Collected Works and Edited Texts

The Writing of Harriet Beecher Stowe (Boston: Houghton Mifflin, 1896-1900) is the best collection to date. Two important reprints are *Uncle Tom's Cabin*, ed. Kenneth S. Lynn (Cambridge: Harvard Univ. Press, 1962); and *Oldtown Folks*, ed. Henry F. May (Harvard Univ. Press, 1966). *Harriet Beecher Stowe: Three Novels: Uncle Tom's Cabin, The Minister's Wooing, and Oldtown Folks*, ed. Kathryn Kish Sklar (New York: Viking, 1982) is available in the Library of America Series. Poetry is available in *Collected Poems*, ed. John M. Moran (Hartford, CT: Stowe-Day Foundation, 1967). The Stowe-Day Foundation has reprinted all Stowe's works. Anne A. Fields, ed. *Life and Letters of Harriet Beecher Stowe* (Boston: Houghton Mifflin, 1898) contains useful biographical source material.

Other Source Materials

Manuscripts are at the Huntington Library, Harvard University, Yale University, the Library of Congress, the Boston Public Library, and the Stowe-Day Foundation, Hartford, Connecticut. A bibliography of manuscripts in the Stowe-Day Library is Margaret Granville Mair, *The Papers of Harriet Beecher Stowe* (Hartford, CT: Stowe-Day Foundation, 1977).

SECONDARY SOURCES

Biography

Forrest Wilson, *Crusader in Crinoline* (Philadelphia: J. B. Lippincott, 1941) is the most dependable biography. In addition are Johanna Johnston, *Runaway to Heaven* (Garden City, NY: Doubleday, 1963); Edward Wagenknecht, *Harriet Beecher Stowe: The Known and the Unknown* (New York: Oxford Univ. Press, 1965); and Noel B. Gerson, *Harriet Beecher Stowe* (New York: Praeger, 1976).

Criticism

John R. Adams, *Harriet Beecher Stowe* (New York: Twayne, 1963); and Alice C. Crozier, *The Novels of Harriet Beecher Stowe* (New York: Oxford Univ. Press, 1969) are good introductions; and Charles H. Foster, *The Rungless Ladder: Harriet Beecher Stowe and New England Puritanism* (Durham, NC: Duke Univ. Press, 1954) relates Stowe's novels to her Calvinist heritage. E. Bruce Kirkham, *The Building of Uncle Tom's Cabin* (Knoxville: Univ. of Tennessee Press, 1977) documents the growth of the novel from a short serial to a full-scale work. Major critical trends of the last 125 years are surveyed in *Critical Essays on Harriet Beecher Stowe*, ed. Elizabeth Ammons (Boston: G. K. Hall, 1980).

Bibliographies

Margaret Holbrook Hildreth, *Harriet Beecher Stowe: A Bibliography* (Hamden, CT: Archon Books, 1976) is a bibliography of editions, chronologically arranged, and a list of writings about Stowe, arranged alphabetically by author. A useful companion is Jean W. Ashton, *Harriet Beecher Stowe: A Reference Guide* (Boston: G. K. Hall, 1977), which annotates Stowe criticism, 1843-1974, providing a chronological perspective.

(JOHN ORLEY) ALLEN TATE, 1899-1979

PRIMARY SOURCES

Separate Works

Mr. Pope and Other Poems (1928); *Stonewall Jackson: The Good Soldier* [biography] (1928); *Jefferson Davis: His Rise and Fall* [biography] (1929); *Three Poems: Ode to the Confederate Dead, Message from Abroad,* and *The Cross* (1930); *Poems, 1928-1931* (1932); *The Mediterranean and Other Poems* (1936); *Reactionary Essays on Poetry and Ideas* (1936); *Selected Poems* (1937); *The Fathers* [fiction] (1938); *Sonnets at Christmas* (1941); *Reason in Madness: Critical Essays* (1941); *The Vigil of Venus* (1943); *The Winter Sea* (1944); *Poems, 1922-1947* (1948); *The Hovering Fly* [essay] (1948); *On the Limits of Poetry* [essay] (1948); *The Forlorn Demon* [essay] (1953); *The Man of Letters in the Modern World* [essay] (1955); *Collected Essays* (1959); *Poems* (1960); *Essays of Four Decades* (1968); *The Swimmers and Other Selected Poems* (1971); *Memoirs and Opinions, 1926-1974* (1975); *Collected Poems, 1919-1976* (1977).

Collected Works and Edited Texts

The most complete collection, arranged in order of first publication, is *Collected Poems, 1919-1976* (New York: Farrar, Straus & Giroux, 1977). An important earlier collection is *The Swimmers and Other Selected Poems* (New York: Scribner, 1971). *Essays of Four Decades* (Chicago: Swallow Press, 1968) contains much of Tate's prose; and *The Literary Correspondence of Donald Davidson and Allen Tate*, eds. John Tyree Fain and Thomas David Young (Athens: Univ. of Georgia Press, 1974) collects letters from Tate's files at Princeton concerned with literary matters and covering the years 1922-1966.

SECONDARY SOURCES

Biography

The first life is Radcliffe Squires, *Allen Tate* (New York: Bobbs Merrill, 1971), which reliably combines biography and criticism. Also important are studies about *The Fugitive*, the literary journal in which Tate's first poems were published, by John M. Bradbury, *The Fugitives: A Critical Account* (New Haven, CT: College & Univ. Press, 1958); and Louise Cowan, *The Fugitive Group: A Literary History* (Baton Rouge: Louisiana State Univ. Press, 1959).

Criticism

Useful introductions are the pamphlets of George Hemphill, *Allen Tate* (Minneapolis: Univ. of Minnesota Press, 1964); and M. E. Bradford, *Rumors of Mortality: An*

Introduction to Allen Tate (Dallas, TX: Argus Academic Press, 1969). Two full-length studies are Roger K. Meiners, *The Last Alternatives: A Study of the Works of Allen Tate* (Denver, CO: A. Swallow, 1963); and Ferman Bishop, *Allen Tate* (New York: Twayne, 1967). A collection of criticism that contains a bibliography of primary and secondary sources is *Allen Tate and His Work*, ed. Radcliffe Squires (Minneapolis: Univ. of Minnesota Press, 1972).

Bibliographies

Marshall Fallwell, Jr., *Allen Tate: A Bibliography* (New York: D. Lewis, 1969) is a checklist of all Tate's important writings and the most significant criticism about him through 1967.

EDWARD TAYLOR, 1645-1729

PRIMARY SOURCES

Separate Works

The poetry of Edward Taylor was not published separately in his lifetime and remained in manuscript until 1937.

Collected Works and Edited Texts

There is no collected edition containing all of Taylor's works. *Poems of Edward Taylor*, ed. Donald E. Stanford (New Haven, CT: Yale Univ. Press, 1960) is the standard edition of poetry, of which an abridged reissue was published as a Yale Paperbound in 1963. An earlier edition, still useful, is *The Poetical Works of Edward Taylor*, ed. Thomas H. Johnson (Princeton, NJ: Princeton Univ. Press, 1939; repr. 1966). Also available is *Edward Taylor's Minor Poetry*, eds. Thomas M. Davis and Virginia L. Davis (Boston: Twayne, 1981). Taylor's sermons delivered between 1701 and 1703 are in *Christographia*, ed. Norman S. Grabo (Yale Univ. Press, 1962); his *Treatise Concerning the Lord's Supper*, ed. Norman S. Grabo (East Lansing: Michigan State Univ. Press, 1966) contains eight further sermons. Two volumes edited by Thomas M. Davis and Virginia L. Davis are available in the series The Unpublished Writings of Edward Taylor, as *Edward Taylor vs. Solomon Stoddard: The Nature of the Lord's Supper* (Twayne, 1981); and *Edward Taylor's Church Records and Related Sermons* (Twayne, 1981).

Other Source Materials

Major collections of manuscripts at Yale University Library, the Massachusetts Historical Society, the Westfield Athenaeum, and the Redwood Library, Newport, Rhode Island are described in Stanford's edition of *The Poems*.

SECONDARY SOURCES

Biography and Criticism

There is no definitive biography of Taylor, and the best biographical and critical introductions are Norman S. Grabo, *Edward Taylor* (New York: Twayne, 1961); and

Donald E. Stanford, *Edward Taylor* (Minneapolis: Univ. of Minnesota Press, 1965). William J. Scheick, *The Will and the Word: The Poetry of Edward Taylor* (Athens: Univ. of Georgia Press, 1974) examines Taylor's intellectual and theological background and his patterns of imagery. Although full-length studies are lacking, helpful critical comment by Louis L. Martz is available in the introduction to Stanford's edition of *The Poems* (*see* Collected Works); in Louis L. Martz, *The Poetry of Meditation: A Study in English Religious Literature of the Seventeenth Century*, rev. ed. (New Haven, CT: Yale Univ. Press, 1962); and "Edward Taylor," in Austin Warren, *Rage for Order* (Chicago: Univ. of Chicago Press, 1948).

Bibliographies

Norman S. Grabo, "Edward Taylor," in *Fifteen American Authors before 1900*, eds. Robert A. Rees and Earl N. Harbert (Madison: Univ. of Wisconsin Press, 1971), pp.333-56, provides a bibliographical overview. Constance J. Gefvert, *Edward Taylor: An Annotated Bibliography, 1668-1970* (Kent, OH: Kent State Univ. Press, 1971) is a comprehensive, annotated compilation of primary and secondary sources.

Reference Works

Gene Russell, *A Concordance to the Poems of Edward Taylor* (Washington, DC: Microcard Editions, 1973) has as referent text, Stanford's edition of *The Poems*.

SARA TEASDALE, 1884-1933

PRIMARY SOURCES

Separate Works

Sonnets to Duse and Other Poems (1907); *Helen of Troy and Other Poems* (1911); *Rivers to the Sea* (1915); *Love Songs* (1917); *Flame and Shadow* (1920); *Dark of the Moon* (1926); *Stars Tonight* (1930); *A Country House* (1932); *Strange Victory* (1933).

Collected Works and Edited Texts

The Collected Poems of Sara Teasdale (New York: Macmillan, 1937).

Other Source Materials

Collections of Teasdale's poems are in the libraries of the University of Buffalo, Harvard University, and Yale University.

SECONDARY SOURCES

Biography

Two important full-length works are Margaret Haley Carpenter, *Sara Teasdale: A Biography* (New York: Schulte, 1960; repr. Norfolk, VA: Pentelic Press, 1977); and William Drake, *Sara Teasdale: Woman & Poet* (New York: Harper & Row, 1979), which closely links the events of Teasdale's life with the content and tone of her poems.

Bibliographies

Drake's biography has useful bibliographical citations.

HENRY DAVID THOREAU, 1817-1862

PRIMARY SOURCES

Separate Works

A Week on the Concord and Merrimack Rivers (1849); Walden; Or, Life in the Woods (1854); Excursions (1863); The Maine Woods (1864); Cape Cod (1865); Letters to Various Persons (1865); A Yankee in Canada, with Antislavery and Reform Papers (1866); Early Spring in Massachusetts (1881); Summer (1884); Winter (1888); Autumn (1892); Miscellanies (1894); Familiar Letters of Henry David Thoreau (1894); Poems of Nature (1895); The Service (1902); Sir Walter Raleigh (1905); Journal (1906); The Moon (1927); The Transmigration of the Seven Brahmans: A Translation (1932).

Collected Works and Edited Texts

The Writings of Henry D. Thoreau, eds. Walter Harding and Carl Bode (Princeton, NJ: Princeton Univ. Press, 1971-), when completed, will be the standard edition, superseding The Writings of Henry David Thoreau, 20v., Manuscript and Walden editions (Boston: Houghton Mifflin, 1906). The Journal, Volume 1: 1837-1844, ed. Elizabeth Hall Witherell, et al. (Princeton Univ. Press, 1981) is available. Thoreau's letters are available in The Correspondence of Henry David Thoreau, eds. Walter Harding and Carl Bode (New York: New York Univ. Press, 1958); and should be read with Kenneth W. Cameron, Companion to Thoreau's Correspondence (Hartford, CT: Transcendental Books, 1964), which annotates and indexes the letters. Collected Poems, enl. ed., ed. Carl Bode (Baltimore: Johns Hopkins Press, 1964) is being reedited for Princeton by Elizabeth Witherell.

Two usefully annotated editions of Walden are The Variorum Walden, ed. Walter Harding (New York: Washington Square Press, 1968); and The Annotated Walden, ed. Philip Van Doren Stern (New York: Crown, 1970), which is a facsimile of the first edition. The Norton Critical Edition of Walden and Civil Disobedience, ed. Owen Thomas (New York: Norton, 1966) also contains important reviews and critical essays.

Other Source Materials

Thoreau's manuscripts are described and located in William L. Howarth, The Literary Manuscripts of Henry David Thoreau (Columbus: Ohio State Univ. Press, 1974).

SECONDARY SOURCES

Biography

Walter Harding, The Days of Henry Thoreau (New York: Knopf, 1965) is the most reliable biography. Recollections of many who knew Thoreau are collected in

Thoreau: Man of Concord, ed. Walter Harding (New York: Holt, Rinehart & Winston, 1960). *A Thoreau Profile*, eds. Milton Meltzer and Walter Harding (New York: Crowell, 1962) is a pictorial biography; and Richard Lebeaux, *Young Man Thoreau* (Amherst: Univ. of Massachusetts Press, 1977) studies Thoreau's development to the 1845 Walden experiment.

Criticism

Among the most important criticisms are F. O. Matthiessen, "From Emerson to Thoreau," in *American Renaissance: Art and Expression in the Age of Emerson and Whitman* (New York: Oxford Univ. Press, 1941), which places Thoreau in American literary tradition; J. Lyndon Shanley, *The Making of Walden with a Text of the First Version* (Chicago: Univ. of Chicago Press, 1957), which examines versions of Walden from 1849 to 1854; Sherman Paul, *The Shores of America: Thoreau's Inward Exploration* (Urbana: Univ. of Illinois Press, 1958); Charles R. Anderson, *The Magic Circle of Walden* (New York: Holt, Rinehart & Winston, 1968); and Frederick Garber, *Thoreau's Redemptive Imagination* (New York: New York Univ. Press, 1977). For Thoreau's political reputation in America, see Michael Meyer, *Several More Lives to Live* (Westport, CT: Greenwood, 1977).

Among the convenient collections providing a critical survey are *Thoreau: A Century of Criticism*, ed. Walter Harding (Dallas, TX: Southern Methodist Univ. Press, 1954); *Thoreau: A Collection of Critical Essays*, ed. Sherman Paul (Englewood Cliffs, NJ: Prentice-Hall, 1962); and *The Recognition of Henry David Thoreau: Selected Criticism since 1848*, ed. Wendell Glick (Ann Arbor: Univ. of Michigan Press, 1969).

Bibliographies

The best bibliographic guides to Thoreau are Lewis Leary, "Henry David Thoreau," in *Eight American Authors*, rev. ed., ed. James Woodress (New York: Norton, 1971); and Walter Harding and Michael Meyer, *The New Thoreau Handbook* (New York: New York Univ. Press, 1980). In addition, Jean C. Advena has cumulated articles from bibliographies in the *Thoreau Society Bulletin* as *A Bibliography of the Thoreau Society Bulletin Bibliographies, 1941-1969*, ed. Walter Harding (Troy, NY: Whitston, 1971). Jeanetta Boswell and Sarah Crouch, *Henry David Thoreau and the Critics: A Checklist of Criticism, 1900-1978* (Metuchen, NJ: Scarecrow, 1981) also contains a subject index. A full bibliographical calendar of all known manuscripts is William L. Howarth, *The Literary Manuscripts of Henry David Thoreau* (Columbus: Ohio State Univ. Press, 1974). Steven J. Mailloux and Michael Meyer are preparing a G. K. Hall Reference Guide.

Reference Works

The Thoreau Society Bulletin has been published four times a year since 1941, and numbers 1-100 are reprinted with an index (New York: Johnson Reprint Corporation, 1970). Walter Harding, *Thoreau's Library* (Charlottesville: Univ. of Virginia Press, 1957) lists the majority of books from Thoreau's library, giving location when known. Kenneth Cameron, *Transcendental Apprenticeship* (Hartford, CT: Transcendental Books, 1976) is a comprehensive sourcebook on Thoreau's reading. Robert F. Stowell, *A Thoreau Gazeteer*, ed. William L. Howarth (Princeton, NJ: Princeton Univ. Press, 1970) provides maps for readers to use in following Thoreau's journeying. Two indexes to Walden are Joseph Jones, *Index to Walden with Notes, Map, and Vocabulary Lists* (Austin, TX: Hemphill, 1955); and J. Stephen Sherwin and Richard C. Reynolds, *A Word Index to Walden with Textual Notes*, a corrected ed. (Hartford, CT: Emerson Society, 1969).

JEAN TOOMER, 1894-1967

PRIMARY SOURCES

Separate Works

Cane (1923); *Essentials* (1931); *Portage Potential* (1932); *The Flavor of Man* [an address] (1949).

Collected Works and Edited Texts

The Wayward and the Seeking: A Collection of Writings by Jean Toomer, ed. Darwin T. Turner (Washington, DC: Howard University, 1980) brings together autobiographical work, three stories, twelve poems, two plays, and many aphorisms in the most representative collection available. *Cane* (New York: Harper & Row, 1969) contains an introduction by Arna Bontemps.

Other Source Materials

Manuscripts and letters of Toomer are in Fisk University Library, Nashville, Tennessee.

SECONDARY SOURCES

Biography

There is no full-length biography, and details must be drawn from such works as Fritz Gysin, *The Grotesque in American Negro Fiction: Jean Toomer, Richard Wright, and Ralph Ellison* (Bern, Switzerland: Francke, 1975); and Darwin T. Turner, *In a Minor Chord: Three Afro-American Writers and Their Search for Identity* (Carbondale: Southern Illinois Univ. Press, 1971).

Criticism

Brian Joseph Benson and Mable Mayle Dillard, *Jean Toomer* (Boston: Twayne, 1980) is a full-length introduction to the life and works; and a collection of criticism is *The Merrill Studies in Cane*, ed. Frank Durham (Columbus, OH: Merrill, 1971). More general works containing useful criticism on *Cane* are Hugh M. Gloster, *Negro Voices in American Fiction* (Chapel Hill: Univ. of North Carolina Press, 1948); Robert A. Bone, *The Negro Novel in America*, rev. ed. (New Haven, CT: Yale Univ. Press, 1965); Arna Bontemps, "Jean Toomer and the Harlem Writers of the 1920's," in *Anger and Beyond: The Negro Writer in the United States*, ed. Herbert Hill (New York: Harper & Row, 1966); and Edward Margolies, *Native Sons: A Critical Study of Twentieth Century Negro American Authors* (Philadelphia: Lippincott, 1968).

Bibliographies

The most helpful bibliographic overview is Ruth Miller and Peter J. Katopes, "The Harlem Renaissance," in *Black American Writers: Bibliographical Essays*, eds. M. Thomas Inge, Maurice Duke, Jackson R. Bryer (New York: St. Martin's Press, 1978), pp.161-86. A chronological bibliography covering the years 1923 to 1973 is John M. Reilly, "Jean Toomer: An Annotated Checklist of Criticism," in *Resources for American Literary Study*, Spring 1974.

MARK TWAIN, *see* SAMUEL LANGHORNE CLEMENS

JOHN UPDIKE, 1932-

PRIMARY SOURCES

Separate Works

The Carpentered Hen and Other Tame Creatures: Poems, English ed. titled *Hoping for a Hoopoe* (1958); *The Poorhouse Fair* (1959); *The Same Door: Short Stories* (1959); *Rabbit Run* (1960); *Pigeon Feathers and Other Stories* (1962); *The Magic Flute*, by Wolfgang Amadeus Mozart [for children, with Warren Chappell] (1962); *The Centaur* (1963); *Telephone Poles and Other Poems* (1963); *Olinger Stories: A Selection* (1964); *The Ring*, by Richard Wagner [for children, with Warren Chappell] (1964); *Of the Farm* (1965); *Assorted Prose* [essays] (1965); *A Child's Calendar* [for children] (1965); *The Music School: Short Stories* (1966); *Couples* (1968); *On Meeting Authors* (1968); *Midpoint and Other Poems* (1969); *Bottom's Dream* [adapted from William Shakespeare's *A Midsummer Night's Dream* [for children] (1969); *Bech: A Book* [short stories] (1970); *The Fisherman and His Wife* [opera adapted for children] (1970); *Rabbit Redux* (1971); *Museums and Women and Other Stories* (1972); *Buchanan Dying: A Play* (1974); *A Month of Sundays* (1975); *Picked-Up Pieces* (1975); *Marry Me* (1976); *Tossing and Turning* [poems] (1977); *The Coup* (1978); *Problems and Other Stories* (1979); *Too Far to Go: The Maples Stories* (1979); *Problems* [short stories] (1979); *Rabbit Is Rich* (1981).

Collected Works and Edited Texts

There is no collection of Updike's works. *Seventy Poems* (Harmondsworth, England: Penguin Books, 1972) is a selection of poetry from *Midpoint* and *Telephone Poles*.

Other Source Materials

Washington University Library, St. Louis, Missouri, has begun a collection of Updike's works.

SECONDARY SOURCES

Biography

Several personal reminiscences are available under "First Person Singular," in *Assorted Prose* (New York: Knopf, 1965); and "The Dogwood Tree: A Boyhood" is reprinted in *The Norton Anthology of American Literature*, 1st ed. (New York: Norton, 1979), v.2, pp.2174-99.

Criticism

Charles Thomas Samuels, *John Updike* (Minneapolis: Univ. of Minnesota Press, 1969) is a brief but reliable introduction, though now somewhat dated. Alice Hamilton and Kenneth Hamilton, *The Elements of John Updike* (Grand Rapids, MI: Eerdmans, 1970) is an interpretation of Christian aspects. Longer studies are Larry E. Taylor, *Pastoral and Anti-Pastoral Patterns in John Updike's Fiction* (Carbondale: Southern Illinois Univ. Press, 1971); Rachel C. Burchard, *John Updike: Yea Sayings* (Southern Illinois Univ. Press, 1971); Robert Detweiler, *John Updike* (New York: Twayne, 1972), which explicates major fiction through *Rabbit Redux*; Joyce B. Markle, *Fighters and Lovers: Theme in the Novels of John Updike* (New York: New York Univ. Press, 1973), which contains useful insights into Updike's fictional techniques; Suzanne Henning Uphaus, *John Updike* (New York: Ungar, 1980), which concentrates on the novels and selected short stories, focussing on the spiritual yearnings of the protagonists in contemporary American life; and Donald J. Greiner, *The Other John Updike* (Columbus: Ohio State Univ. Press, 1981), which considers the range of Updike's poems, short stories, and prose.

Collections of critical essays are in the Updike number of *Modern Fiction Studies* 20 (1974); and *John Updike: A Collection of Critical Essays*, eds. David Thorburn and Howard Eilard (Englewood Cliffs, NJ: Prentice-Hall, 1979).

Bibliographies

The most recent bibliography, Elizabeth A. Gearhart, *John Updike: A Comprehensive Bibliography with Selected Annotations* (Norwood, PA: Norwood Editions, 1978) lists primary sources beginning with Updike's earliest contributions to the *Harvard Lampoon* and secondary sources including reviews. In addition, see Michael A. Olivas, *An Annotated Bibliography of John Updike Criticism, 1967-1973*, and *A Checklist of His Works* (New York: Garland, 1975).

KURT VONNEGUT, JR., 1922-

PRIMARY SOURCES

Separate Works

Player Piano (1952); *The Sirens of Titan* (1959); *Canary in a Cat House* (1961); *Mother Night* (1962); *Cat's Cradle* (1963); *God Bless You Mr. Rosewater* (1965); *Welcome to the Monkey House* (1968); *Slaughterhouse-Five* (1969); *Happy Birthday, Wanda June* [screen play] (1970); *Between Time and Timbuktu* [space fantasy for TV] (1972); *Breakfast of Champions* (1973); *Wampeter, Foma & Granfalloons*

(Opinions) (1974); *Palm Sunday: An Autobiographical Collage* (1981); *Sense of Humor: Who Am I This Time?* [TV adaptation of story] (1982).

Collected Works and Edited Texts

Wampeters, Foma & Granfalloons (Opinions) (New York: Delacorte Press, 1974) is a collection of some of Vonnegut's reviews, essays, and speeches. *Palm Sunday: An Autobiographical Collage* (Delacorte Press, 1981) is a collection of writings by Vonnegut and his relatives that includes reviews, speeches, anecdotes, and reminiscences.

SECONDARY SOURCES

Biography

There have been no book-length biographies, and the most convenient sources of information on Vonnegut's life will be found in critical introductions and through using the Bibliographies listed below.

Criticism

Three introductions to Vonnegut are Peter J. Reed, *Kurt Vonnegut, Jr.* (New York: Warner Paperback Library, 1972), which contains an overview of the novels and dependable comment; Stanley Schatt, *Kurt Vonnegut, Jr.* (Boston: Twayne, 1976), which introduces the novels, short stories, and plays; and James Lundquist, *Kurt Vonnegut* (New York: Ungar, 1977). Richard Giannone, *Vonnegut: A Preface to His Novels* (Port Washington, NY: Kennikat Press, 1977) is a thoughtful study of Vonnegut's narrative craft and the theme of man's place in the universe. Two collections of criticism are *The Vonnegut Statement*, eds. Jerome Klinkowitz and John Somer (New York: Delacorte, 1973), which contains critical essays and reminiscences; and *Vonnegut in America: An Introduction to the Life and Work of Kurt Vonnegut*, eds. Jerome Klinkowitz and Donald L. Lawler (New York: Delacorte Press/ S. Lawrence, 1977), which includes a biographical essay by Klinkowitz as well as an updating of primary and secondary bibliography.

Bibliographies

Betty Lenhardt Hudgens, *Kurt Vonnegut, Jr.: A Checklist* (Detroit: Gale, 1972) includes facsimile title pages of first editions, and lists of all work, including juvenilia, interviews, and magazine stories. All material by and about Vonnegut published between 1950 and 1973, including dissertations, is listed in Asa B. Pieratt and Jerome Klinkowitz, *Kurt Vonnegut, Jr.: A Descriptive Bibliography and Annotated Secondary Checklist* (Hamden, CT: Archon Books, 1974).

EUDORA WELTY, 1909-

PRIMARY SOURCES

Separate Works

A Curtain of Green and Other Stories (1941); *The Robber Bridegroom* (1942); *The Wide Net and Other Stories* (1943); *Delta Wedding* (1946); *Music from Spain* (1948); *The Golden Apples* (1949); *The Ponder Heart* (1954); *The Bride of the Innisfallen* (1955); *A Sweet Devouring* [autobiographical] (1957); *Three Papers on Fiction* (1962); *The Shoe Bird* [for children] (1964); *Losing Battles* (1970); *One Time, One Place: Mississippi in the Depression: A Snapshot Album* (1971); *The Optimist's Daughter* (1972); *The Eye of the Story: Selected Essays and Reviews* (1978); *Women!! Make Turban in Own Home* (1979).

Collected Works and Edited Texts

There is no collected edition of Welty's entire works, and *The Collected Stories of Eudora Welty*, 1st ed. (New York: Harcourt Brace Jovanovich, 1980) is the fullest available. Selections are contained in *Short Stories* (New York: Harcourt Brace, 1949); and *Selected Stories* (New York: Modern Library, 1943), which has an important introduction by Katherine Anne Porter.

Other Source Materials

There are several important articles on her craft by Welty, including "The Reading and Writing of Short Stories,"*Atlantic Monthly* 183 (February 1949): 54-58; "How I Write," *Virginia Quarterly Review* 31 (Spring 1955): 240-51; "Place in Fiction," *South Atlantic Quarterly* 55 (January 1956): 57-72; *Three Papers on Fiction* (Northampton, MA: Smith College, 1962); and her address on the use of history, folklore, and Southern humor, "The Robber Bridegroom," in *Tale of the Natchez Trace: A Paper Read at the Annual Dinner Meeting of the Mississippi Historical Society...* (Jackson: Mississippi Historical Society, 1975).

Two significant collections of manuscripts, letters, and unpublished items are at the State of Mississippi Department of Archives and History, Jackson, and the Humanities Research Center, University of Texas at Austin.

SECONDARY SOURCES

Biography

No full-length biography is available, and the most convenient access to shorter accounts is provided under "Biography" in Thompson's index (*see* Bibliographies).

Criticism

For a reliable short introduction, see Joseph A. Bryant, Jr., *Eudora Welty* (Minneapolis: Univ. of Minnesota Press, 1968). Earlier critical studies that are still important include an essay discussing Welty's vision, Robert Penn Warren, "The Love and Separateness in Miss Welty," *Kenyon Review* 6 (Spring 1944): 246-59; the influential work of Ruth M. Vande Kieft, *Eudora Welty* (New York: Twayne, 1962); and the topical discussion of Alfred Appel, Jr., *A Season of Dreams* (Baton Rouge: Louisiana State Univ. Press, 1965). More recent are Zelma Turner Howard, *The*

Rhetoric of Eudora Welty's Short Stories (Jackson: Univ. and College Press of Mississippi, 1973); and Michael Kreyling, *Eudora Welty's Achievement of Order* (Baton Rouge: Louisiana State Univ. Press, 1980), which seeks to show how Welty, not primarily a regional writer, encompasses "the general consciousness." In addition, many critical essays are collected in *A Still Moment: Essays on the Art of Eudora Welty*, ed. John F. Desmond (Metuchen, NJ: Scarecrow, 1978). *Eudora Welty: A Form of Thanks: Essays*, by Cleanth Brooks, et al., eds. Louis D. Dollarhide and Ann J. Abodie (Jackson: Univ. Press of Mississippi, 1979) contains papers presented at the University of Mississippi in 1979; and *Eudora Welty: Critical Essays*, ed. Peggy Whitman Prenshaw (Univ. Press of Mississippi, 1979) is an important collection of previously unpublished essays.

Bibliographies

Noel Palk, "A Eudora Welty Checklist," *Mississippi Quarterly* 26 (Fall 1973): 663-93, is a primary bibliography which will need updating. Michael Kreyling, *Eudora Welty* (*see* Criticism) contains a convenient listing of books, short stories, and criticism. Victor H. Thompson, *Eudora Welty: A Reference Guide* (Boston: G. K. Hall, 1976) is an annotated chronological listing of biography, criticism, and bibliography published between 1936 and 1975.

Reference Works

Eudora Welty Newsletter, 1977- provides bibliographies and reviews, acting as a clearinghouse for current Welty information.

NATHANAEL WEST, 1903-1940

PRIMARY SOURCES

Separate Works

The Dream Life of Balso Snell (1931); *Miss Lonelyhearts* (1933); *A Cool Million: The Dismantling of Lemuel Pitkin* (1934); *The Day of the Locust* (1939); *The Complete Works* (1957).

Collected Works

The Complete Works of Nathanael West, intro. by Alan Ross (New York: Farrar, Straus & Cudahy, 1957) contains the four novels, but none of West's other works.

Other Sources

West's manuscripts are available at the New York Public Library and the libraries of Princeton University, Yale University, the University of Delaware, Southern Illinois University, and the Lockwood Memorial Library, SUNY, Buffalo.

SECONDARY SOURCES

Biography

The only full-scale biography is Jay Martin, *Nathanael West: The Art of His Life* (New York: Farrar, Straus & Giroux, 1970). This detailed life is based on documents that indicate the range of West's involvement with radical politics, friends, films, and the Dadaist and Surrealist movements.

Criticism

Two introductory pamphlets are Stanley E. Hyman, *Nathanael West* (Minnesota: Univ. of Minnesota Press, 1962); and Nathan A. Scott, Jr., *Nathanael West: A Critical Essay* (Grand Rapids, MI: Eerdmans, 1971). An influential pioneering work of 1961, subsequently updated, is James F. Light, *Nathanael West: An Interpretative Study*, 2nd ed. (Evanston, IL: Northwestern Univ. Press, 1971). Other important criticism is Randall Reid, *The Fiction of Nathanael West: No Redeemer, No Promised Land* (Chicago: Univ. of Chicago Press, 1967), which treats the literary and intellectual milieu of the works; Victor Comerchero, *Nathanael West: The Ironic Prophet* (Syracuse, NY: Syracuse Univ. Press, 1964), which takes a variety of approaches via such paths as Freudian psychology, mythic wastelands, and social dimensions; and Irving Malin, *Nathanael West's Novels* (Carbondale: Southern Illinois Univ. Press, 1972), which explicates the texts to show that West's interest is in "the irrational dreams we share."

Comment by West and others is included in *Nathanael West: A Collection of Critical Essays*, ed. Jay Martin (Englewood Cliffs, NJ: Prentice-Hall, 1971); and *Nathanael West: The Cheaters and the Cheated*, ed. David Madden (Deland, FL: Everett/Edwards, 1973) is an important collection that presents a fine overview of West's contribution through accounts of friends, critics, and other writers who knew him. Essays that focus on West's second novel are reprinted in *Twentieth Century Interpretations of Miss Lonely-Hearts: A Collection of Critical Essays*, ed. Thomas H. Jackson (Prentice-Hall, 1971).

Bibliographies

William White, *Nathanael West: A Comprehensive Bibliography* (Kent, OH: Kent State Univ. Press, 1975) gives full bibliographic descriptions, chronologically arranged, of the editions and translations of West's works, with title pages reproduced from first editions of the novels. Separate chapters include works that first appeared in collections and periodicals. Biographies, criticism, and reviews about West are listed without annotations and followed by an appendix that conveniently contains the texts of West's uncollected poems, essays, and book reviews. In a format which is somewhat difficult to use, Dennis P. Vannatta, *Nathanael West: An Annotated Bibliography of the Scholarship and Works* (New York: Garland, 1976) contains a brief checklist of West's works, including film scripts, plays, and unpublished writings. Secondary sources, however, are annotated, and thus complement White's bibliography, which concentrates on primary sources. Further critical opinion is indexed in Ray Lewis White, "Nathanael West: Additional Reviews of His Work, 1933-57," *Yale University Library Gazette*, vol.51 (1977), pp.218-32.

EDITH (NEWBOLD JONES) WHARTON, 1862-1937
Pseuds: Mr. Olivieri; David Olivieri

PRIMARY SOURCES

Separate Works

Fast and Loose (1876); *Verses* (1878); *The Decoration of Houses* [with Ogden Codman, Jr.] (1897); *The Greater Inclination* (1899); *The Touchstone* (1900); *Crucial Instances* (1901); *The Valley of Decision* (1902); *Sanctuary* (1903); *Italian Villas and Their Gardens* (1904); *The Descent of Man and Other Stories* (1904); *Italian Backgrounds* (1905); *The House of Mirth* (1905); *Madame De Treymes* (1907); *The Fruit of the Tree* (1907); *A Motor-Flight through France* (1908); *The Hermit and the Wild Woman, and Other Stories* (1908); *Artemis to Actaeon and Other Verse* (1909); *Tales of Men and Ghosts* (1910); *Ethan Frome* (1911); *The Reef* (1912); *The Custom of the Country* (1913); *Fighting France: From Dunkerque to Belfort* (1915); *Xingu and Other Stories* (1916); *Summer* (1917); *The Marne* (1918); *French Ways and Their Meaning* (1919); *The Age of Innocence* (1920); *In Morocco* (1920); *The Glimpses of the Moon* (1922); *A Son at the Front* (1923); *Old New York* (1924); *The Mother's Recompense* (1925); *The Writing of Fiction* (1925); *Here and Beyond* (1926); *Twelve Poems* (1926); *Twilight Sleep* (1927); *The Children* (1928); *Hudson River Bracketed* (1929); *Certain People* (1930); *The Gods Arrive* (1932); *Human Nature* (1933); *A Backward Glance* (1934); *The World Over* (1936); *Ghosts* (1937); *The Buccaneers* (1938).

Collected Works and Edited Texts

No uniform edition of Wharton's complete works is yet available. *The Collected Short Stories*, ed. R. W. B. Lewis, 2v. (New York: Scribner, 1968) contains all of the short stories, including those previously uncollected, except for "Bunner Sisters," which is available in *Xingu and Other Stories* (Scribner, 1916); and in *The Norton Anthology of American Literature* (New York: Norton, 1979), v.2, pp.700-64. Other collections are *The Edith Wharton Reader*, ed. Louis Auchincloss (Scribner, 1965); and *An Edith Wharton Treasury*, ed. Arthur H. Quinn (New York: Appleton-Century-Crofts, 1950). Individual novels in useful editions are *Ethan Frome: The Story with Sources and Commentary*, ed. Blake Nevius (Scribner, 1968); and *The House of Mirth*, ed. R. W. B. Lewis (New York: New York Univ. Press, 1977). An edition of a novelette that appeared under the pseudonym David Olivieri is *Fast and Loose*, ed. Viola Hopkins Winner (Charlottesville: Univ. Press of Virginia, 1979).

Other Source Materials

Several statements of Wharton's artistic credo are in *The Decoration of Houses*; "The Criticism of Fiction," *Times Literary Supplement*, May 14, 1914; *The Writing of Fiction* (repr. New York: Octagon Books, 1966); and "The Writing of Ethan Frome," *Colophon*, Pt. 2 (1931): 1-4. Most of the first copies of Wharton's published materials and all unpublished fragments and notebooks are in the Bienecke Library, Yale University. Correspondence between Wharton and her publishers, C. Scribner's Sons, is in the Firestone Library, Princeton University. An appendix listing major sources of correspondence, memoirs, biographies, and other unpublished materials is in the Lewis biography.

In her 1934 autobiography, *A Backward Glance*, Wharton chose carefully what she would reveal. "Life and I," a fragment in the Beinecke Library, provides further material about her early development, while her childhood and adolescence are described in "A Little Girl's Old New York," *Harper's* (August 1938); and impressions of travel are in *A Motor-Flight through France*; *Fighting France*; and *In Morocco*.

SECONDARY SOURCES

Biography

The first important biography, by Percy Lubbock, *Portrait of Edith Wharton* (New York: Appleton-Century-Crofts, 1947), is the discreet memoir of a friend. Millicent Bell, *Edith Wharton and Henry James: The Story of Their Friendship* (New York: G. Braziller, 1965) is based on the correspondence of Wharton and James between 1902 and 1916. The most authoritative biography, by R. W. B. Lewis, *Edith Wharton: A Biography* (New York: Harper & Row, 1976), provides new insights from the papers into Wharton's passionate personality, which had been depicted as aloof and conventional by earlier biographers.

Criticism

Blake Nevius, *Edith Wharton: A Study of Her Fiction* (Berkeley: Univ. of California Press, 1953) is valuable for its comprehensive treatment of the themes of "the trapped spirit" and the meaning of manners. Gary H. Lindberg, *Edith Wharton and the Novel of Manners* (Charlottesville: Univ. Press of Virginia, 1975) explores Wharton's belief that, although it is necessary for the individual to live in society, social structures themselves are destructive of the inner life. Margaret B. McDowell, *Edith Wharton* (Boston: Twayne, 1976) focusses on the major novels and stories, tracing the development of Wharton's literary technique. Wharton's fiction is related to her psychological development in a brilliant study by Cynthia Griffin Wolff, *A Feast of Words: The Triumph of Edith Wharton* (New York: New York Univ. Press, 1977). A diversity of critical judgement is gathered from the best essays before the 1960s in *Edith Wharton: A Collection of Critical Essays*, ed. Irving Howe (Englewood Cliffs, NJ: Prentice-Hall, 1962).

Bibliographies

Vito J. Brenni, *Edith Wharton: A Bibliography* (Morgantown: West Virginia Univ. Library, 1966) is the first attempt to list all of Wharton's works and periodical contributions, as well as writings about her, in one volume. James Tuttleton, "Edith Wharton: An Essay in Bibliography," *Resources for American Literary Study* 3 (1973): 163-202, is a detailed analysis. Marlene Springer, *Edith Wharton and Kate Chopin: A Reference Guide* (Boston: G. K. Hall, 1976) is the fullest secondary bibliography and provides annotated entries for criticism and scholarship on Wharton published between 1897 and 1973. Wolff's *A Feast of Words* (*see* Criticism) contains a list of the published works by category, including citations to Wharton's articles, translations, editions, reviews, and introductions.

PHILLIS WHEATLEY, 1753-1784

PRIMARY SOURCES

Separate Works

Poems on Various Subjects, Religious and Moral (1773).

Collected Works and Edited Texts

Life and Works of Phillis Wheatley, ed. G. Herbert Renfro (Washington, 1916; repr. Plainview, NY: Books for Libraries, 1970) contains a biography and letters. A definitive edition of Wheatley's poetry is *The Poems of Phillis Wheatley*, ed. Julian D. Mason, Jr. (Chapel Hill: Univ. of North Carolina Press, 1966), which includes *Poems on Various Subjects* and also reprints previously uncollected poems. Mason's collection is supplemented by Carl Bridenbaugh, "The Earliest Published Poem of Phillis Wheatley," *New England Quarterly*, December 1969; and Robert C. Kunico, "Some Unpublished Poems of Phillis Wheatley," *New England Quarterly*, June 1970. A description of reprints is available in Jerome Klinkowitz, "Early Writers" essay (*see* Bibliographies). Wheatley's correspondence is in *Letters of Phillis Wheatley*, ed. Charles Deane (Boston: J. Wilson, 1864); *Phillis Wheatley (Phillis Peter): Poems and Letters*, ed. Charles F. Heartman (New York, 1915; repr. Coral Gables, FL: Mnemosyne, 1969).

Other Source Materials

Collections of manuscripts and letters are at Harvard University, Boston Public Library, the Massachusetts Historical Society Library, Boston, the American Antiquarian Society, Worcester, Massachusetts, Bowdoin College, Dartmouth College, and the Historical Society of Pennsylvania, Philadelphia.

SECONDARY SOURCES

Biography

There is no definitive life of Wheatley. For comments on early remains, and brief biographical sketches, see Klinkowitz's essay (*see* Bibliographies).

Criticism

Two critical introductions that emphasize Wheatley's contribution as an early black American woman writer are Merle A. Richmond, *Bid the Vassal Soar: Interpretative Essays on the Life and Poetry of Phillis Wheatley and George Moses Horton* (Washington, DC: Howard Univ. Press, 1974); and William H. Robinson, *Phillis Wheatley in the Black American Beginnings* (Detroit: Broadside Press, 1975).

Bibliographies

For a bibliographic overview, see the essay of Jerome Klinkowitz, "Early Writers: Jupiter Hammon, Phillis Wheatley, and Benjamin Banneker," in *Black American Writers: Bibliographical Essays*, eds. M. Thomas Inge, Maurice Duke, Jackson R. Bryer. 2v. (New York: St. Martin's Press, 1978), v.1, pp.6-15. William H. Robinson, *Phillis Wheatley: A Bio-Bibliography* (Boston: G. K. Hall, 1981) contains an introductory essay and a comprehensive bibliography of writing by and about Wheatley to 1979.

WALT(ER) WHITMAN, 1819-1892

PRIMARY SOURCES

Separate Works

Franklin Evans (1842); *Leaves of Grass* (1855; 1856; 1860-61; 1867; 1871; 1872; 1876; 1881-82; 1882; 1888; 1889; 1891-92); *Drum-Taps* (1865); *Democratic Vistas* (1871); *Passage to India* (1871); *After All, Not to Create Only* (1871); *As a Strong Bird on Pinions Free* (1872); *Memoranda during the War* (1875-76); *Two Rivulets* (1876); *Specimen Days and Collect* (1882-83); *November Boughs* (1888); *Good-Bye My Fancy* (1891); *Autobiographica* (1892); *Notes and Fragments* (1899); *An American Primer* (1904); *Lafayette in Brooklyn* (1905); *Criticism: An Essay* (1913); *Pictures* (1927); *A Child's Reminiscence* (1930).

Collected Works and Edited Texts

The Collected Writings of Walt Whitman, ed. Gay Wilson Allen (New York: New York Univ. Press, 1961-), when complete, will be the most scholarly edition. Included in the edition is *Walt Whitman: The Correspondence*, ed. Edwin H. Miller (New York Univ. Press, 1961-69). *Leaves of Grass: A Textual Variorum of the Printed Poems, 1855-1892*, ed. Sculley Bradley, et al., 3v., will be published with manuscript variants in a fourth volume. *Leaves of Grass: Comprehensive Reader's Edition*, eds. Harold W. Blodgett and Sculley Bradley (New York Univ. Press, 1965) conveniently brings together in a reliable text all Whitman's poems and fragments. Blodgett and Bradley have also edited a Norton Critical Edition, *Leaves of Grass* (New York: Norton, 1973). *Walt Whitman's Blue Book: The 1860-61 Leaves of Grass*, ed. Arthur Golden. 2v. (New York: New York Public Library, 1968) includes a facsimile of Whitman's marked copy of the 1860 edition. *Walt Whitman: Poetry and Prose*, ed. Justin Kaplan (New York: Viking, 1982) is a one-volume edition in the series Library of America which includes *Leaves of Grass 1885*, *Leaves of Grass, 1891-92*, and *Complete Prose Works*.

Other Source Materials

Manuscripts are deposited in the Library of Congress, Duke University, New York Public Library, and several other libraries.

SECONDARY SOURCES

Biography

The standard biography is Gay Wilson Allen, *The Solitary Singer*, reissued with revisions (New York: New York Univ. Press, 1967). Other useful accounts are Frederik Schyberg, *Walt Whitman* (New York: Columbia Univ. Press, 1951); Roger Asselineau, *The Evolution of Walt Whitman*, 2v. (Cambridge: Harvard Univ. Press, 1960); and the more popular Justin Kaplan, *Walt Whitman: A Life* (New York: Simon & Schuster, 1980). Two reliable biographies for the period before 1855 are Joseph Jay Rubin, *The Historic Whitman* (University Park: Pennsylvania State Univ. Press, 1973), which also reprints "Letters from a Travelling Bachelor" from the New York Sunday *Dispatch*, October 14, 1849-January 6, 1850; and Floyd Stovall, *The Foreground of*

Leaves of Grass (Charlottesville: Univ. Press of Virginia, 1974). An accurate, brief introduction is Richard Chase, *Walt Whitman* (Minneapolis: Univ. of Minnesota Press, 1961).

Criticism

Indispensable guides are James E. Miller, Jr., *A Critical Guide to Leaves of Grass* (Chicago: Univ. of Chicago Press, 1957); and two works by Gay Wilson Allen, *A Reader's Guide to Walt Whitman* (New York: Farrar, Straus & Giroux, 1970); and *New Walt Whitman Handbook* (New York: New York Univ. Press, 1975). Newton Arvin, *Whitman* (New York: Macmillan, 1938) examines the influence of Whitman's social and political background; and Richard Chase, *Walt Whitman Reconsidered* (New York: Sloane, 1955) includes consideration of Whitman as a comic poet. Two important works by the editor of Whitman's letters are Edwin H. Miller, *Walt Whitman's Poetry: A Psychological Journey* (Boston: Houghton Mifflin, 1968); and *The American Quest for a Supreme Fiction: Whitman's Legacy in the Personal Epic* (Chicago: Univ. of Chicago Press, 1979).

Convenient collections of criticism are *The Presence of Walt Whitman*, ed. R. W. B. Lewis (New York: Columbia Univ. Press, 1962); *Whitman: A Collection of Critical Essays*, ed. Roy Harvey Pearce (Englewood Cliffs, NJ: Prentice-Hall, 1962); *A Century of Whitman Criticism*, ed. Edwin H. Miller (Bloomington: Indiana Univ. Press, 1969); *Walt Whitman*, ed. Francis Murphy (Harmondsworth, England: Penguin, 1969); *Whitman: The Critical Heritage*, ed. Milton Hindus (New York: Barnes & Noble, 1971); and *Walt Whitman*, ed. Arthur Golden (New York: McGraw-Hill, 1973).

Bibliographies

An essay providing bibliographic guidance to scholarship and criticism is Roger Asselineau, "Walt Whitman," in *Eight American Authors*, rev. ed., ed. James Woodress (New York: Norton, 1971). Gloria A. Francis and Artem Lozynsky, *Whitman at Auction, 1899-1972* (Detroit: Gale, 1978) reproduces descriptive bibliography from 43 auction catalogs and includes notes on Whitman collections and collectors. Jeanetta Boswell, *Walt Whitman and the Critics: A Checklist of Criticism, 1900-1978* (Metuchen, NJ: Scarecrow, 1980) is an alphabetical listing by critic with a subject index.

Reference Works

Walt Whitman Review (formerly *Walt Whitman Newsletter*) was founded in 1955 to publish scholarly articles and quarterly checklists of recent publications. A useful index is *A Concordance of Walt Whitman's Leaves of Grass and Selected Prose Writings*, ed. Edwin H. Eby (Seattle: Univ. of Washington Press, 1949-55).

JOHN GREENLEAF WHITTIER, 1807-1892

PRIMARY SOURCES

Separate Works

Legends of New-England (1831); *Moll Pitcher* (1832); *Justice and Expediency* (1833); *Mogg Megone* (1836); *Poems Written . . . between . . . 1830 and 1838* (1837);

Narrative of James Williams (1838); *Poems* (1838); *Moll Pitcher, and the Minstrel Girl* (1840); *Lays of My Home* (1843); *The Song of the Vermonters* (1843?); *Ballads and Other Poems* (1844); *The Stranger in Lowell* (1845); *Voices of Freedom* (1846); *The Supernaturalism of New England* (1847); *Poems* (1849); *Leaves from Margaret Smith's Journal* (1849); *Old Portraits and Modern Sketches* (1850); *Songs of Labor and Other Poems* (1850); *The Chapel of the Hermits* (1853); *Literary Recreations and Miscellanies* (1854); *The Panorama* (1856); *The Sycamores* (1857); *Home Ballads* (1860); *In War Time* (1864); *National Lyrics* (1865); *Snow-Bound* (1866); *The Tent on the Beach* (1867); *Among the Hills* (1869); *Miriam* (1871); *The Pennsylvania Pilgrim* (1872); *Hazel-Blossoms* (1875); *Mabel Martin* (1876); *The Vision of Echard* (1878); *The King's Missive* (1881); *The Bay of Seven Islands* (1883); *Saint Gregory's Guest* (1886); *At Sundown* (1890); *A Legend of the Lake* (1893); *The Demon Lady* (1894).

Collected Works and Edited Texts

The standard Riverside Edition, which includes poetry and prose, is *The Writings of John Greenleaf Whittier*, ed. Horace E. Scudder with Whittier's assistance. 7v. (Boston: Houghton Mifflin, 1888-89). Single volume editions are the *Complete Poetical Works of John Greenleaf Whittier* (Boston: Houghton Mifflin, 1895); and *The Complete Poetical Works of John Greenleaf Whittier*, Household ed. (Boston: J. R. Osgood, 1884). *The Letters of John Greenleaf Whittier*, ed. John B. Pickard. 3v. (Cambridge: Harvard Univ. Press, 1975) contains all the surviving correspondence to the Civil War and a selection of important later letters.

Other Source Materials

The largest collections of manuscripts are at the Essex Institute, Salem, Massachusetts, the Haverhill Public Library, Massachusetts, and Swathmore College.

SECONDARY SOURCES

Biography

Samuel T. Pickard, *Life and Letters of John Greenleaf Whittier*, 2v. (Boston: Houghton Mifflin, 1894) changed the text of some letters, but the biography remains standard because it covers Whittier's sources most broadly. A good critical biography is Edward Wagenknecht, *John Greenleaf Whittier: A Portrait in Paradox* (New York: Oxford Univ. Press, 1967). John A. Pollard, *John Greenleaf Whittier: Friend of Man* (Houghton Mifflin, 1949) concentrates on Whittier's public life.

Criticism

Among the best critical introductions are John B. Pickard, *John Greenleaf Whittier* (New York: Barnes & Noble, 1961); and Lewis Leary, *John Greenleaf Whittier* (New York: Twayne, 1961). There is an excellent introductory essay in *John Greenleaf Whittier's Poetry: An Appraisal and Selection*, ed. Robert Penn Warren (Minneapolis: Univ. of Minnesota Press, 1971); and *Critical Essays on John Greenleaf Whittier*, ed. Jayne K. Kribbs (Boston; G. K. Hall, 1980) collects reviews and essays that represent both contemporary and modern assessments.

Bibliographies

Karl Keller, "John Greenleaf Whittier," in *Fifteen American Authors before 1900*, eds. Robert A. Rees and Earl N. Harbert (Madison: Univ. of Wisconsin Press, 1971), pp.357-86, is the best bibliographic orientation. Most of Whittier's works have been described thoroughly in Thomas F. Currier, *A Bibliography of John Greenleaf Whittier* (Cambridge: Harvard Univ. Press, 1937). Albert J. von Frank, *Whittier: A Comprehensive Annotated Bibliography* (New York: Garland, 1976) includes editions and works about Whittier in chronological sequence, while *Whittier Newsletter, 1966-* provides current bibliography.

TENNESSEE (THOMAS LANIER) WILLIAMS, 1914-1983

PRIMARY SOURCES

Separate Works

* represents New York production date

Battle of Angels (*1940; 1945); *The Glass Menagerie* (1945); *27 Wagons Full of Cotton and Other One-Act Plays* (1946); *You Touched Me!* [with Donald Windham] (*1945; 1947); *A Streetcar Named Desire* (1947); *One Arm and Other Stories* [fiction] (1948); *Summer and Smoke* (1948); *American Blues: Five Short Plays* (1948); *The Roman Spring of Mrs. Stone* [fiction] (1950); *The Glass Menagerie* [screen play, with Peter Berneis] (1950); *A Streetcar Named Desire* [screenplay, with Oscar Saul] (1951); *The Rose Tattoo* (1951); *I Rise in Flames, Cried the Phoenix* (1951); *Camino Real* (1953); *Hard Candy: A Book of Stories* (1954); *The Rose Tattoo* [screenplay] (1955); *Cat on a Hot Tin Roof* (1955); *Lord Byron's Love Letter* [libretto for an opera by Raffaello de Banfield] (1955); *Baby Doll* [screenplay] (1956); *In the Winter of Cities* [poetry] (1956); *Orpheus Descending* (*1957; 1958); *Garden District: Something Unspoken* (1958); *Suddenly Last Summer* (*1958; 1959); *Sweet Bird of Youth* (1959); *Suddenly Last Summer* [screenplay, with Gore Vidall] (1959); *Period of Adjustment* (1960); *The Fugitive Kind* [screenplay, with Meade Roberts] (1960); *Three Players of a Summer Game and Other Stories* (1960); *The Night of the Iguana* (*1961; 1962); *The Milk Train Doesn't Stop Here Anymore* (*1963; 1964); *The Eccentricities of a Nightingale* (1965); *Slapstick Tragedy: The Mutilated* (1967); *The Gnädiges Fräulein* (*1966; 1967); *The Knightly Quest: A Novella and Four Short Stories* (1967); *The Two Character Play* (*1967; 1969); *Kingdom on Earth (The Seven Descents of Myrtle)* (1968); *In the Bar of a Tokyo Hotel* (1969); *Dragon Country* (1970); *Small Craft Warnings* (1972); *Eight Mortal Ladies Possessed* [stories] (1974); *Moise and the World of Reason* (1975); *Memoirs* (1975).

Collected Works and Edited Texts

The Theatre of Tennessee Williams (New York: New Directions; distr. by Norton, 1971-) collects the plays, with production notes, essays, and lists of casts. *Where I Live: Selected Essays*, eds. Christine R. Day and Bob Woods (New York: New Directions, 1977) collects eight essays published between 1944 and 1978. A selection of Williams' correspondence is *Tennessee Williams Letters to Donald Windham, 1940-65*, ed. Donald Windham (New York: Holt, Rinehart & Winston, 1977).

Other Source Materials

An important collection of papers is at the University of Texas Humanities Research Center. For autobiography, consult Williams' *Memoirs* (Garden City, NY: Doubleday, 1975), which is a stream of consciousness account of his early life; and his semi-autobiographical novel, *Moise and the Worlds of Reason* (New York: Simon & Schuster, 1975).

SECONDARY SOURCES

Biography

Two books of recollections are by his mother, Edwina Dakin Williams, as told to Lucy Freeman, *Remember Me to Tom* (New York: G. P. Putnam, 1963); and Gilbert Maxwell, *Tennessee Williams and Friends* (Cleveland, OH: World Publishing, 1965). A useful, though undocumented, life is Nancy M. Tischler, *Tennessee Williams: Rebellious Puritan* (New York: Citadel Press, 1961). *The World of Tennessee Williams*, ed. Richard F. Leavitt (New York: G. P. Putnam, 1978) is an interesting photographic record of his productions.

Criticism

A reliable introductory pamphlet is Gerald Weales, *Tennessee Williams* (Minneapolis: Univ. of Minnesota Press, 1965). An excellent book-length study is Signi Lenea Falk, *Tennessee Williams*, 2nd ed. (Boston: Twayne, 1978). Earlier studies that interweave the life and work are Benjamin Nelson, *Tennessee Williams: The Man and His Work* (New York: Obolensky, 1961); Nancy M. Tischler, *Tennessee Williams: Rebellious Puritan* (New York: Citadel, 1961); and Francis Donahue, *The Dramatic World of Tennessee Williams* (New York: Ungar, 1964). Esther M. Jackson, *The Broken World of Tennessee Williams* (Madison: Univ. of Wisconsin Press, 1965) is a study of form and ideas in the plays. More specialized is Norman J. Fedder, *The Influence of D. H. Lawrence on Tennessee Williams* (The Hague: Mouton, 1966). For an examination of fifteen of Williams' films, see Maurice Yacowar, *Tennessee Williams and Film* (New York: Ungar, 1977). Felicia Hardison Londre, *Tennessee Williams* (Ungar, 1979) examines all the plays.

Convenient collections of criticism are *Twentieth Century Interpretations of a Streetcar Named Desire*, ed. Jordan Y. Miller (Englewood Cliffs, NJ: Prentice-Hall, 1971); *Tennessee Williams: A Tribute*, ed. Jac Tharpe (Jackson: Univ. Press of Mississippi, 1977), which contains over fifty important essays; and *Tennessee Williams: A Collection of Critical Essays*, ed. Stephen S. Stanton (Prentice-Hall, 1977).

Bibliographies

Drewey Wayne Gunn, *Tennessee Williams: A Bibliography* (Metuchen, NJ: Scarecrow, 1980) lists both primary and secondary sources.

Reference Works

Tennessee Williams Newsletter, 1979- is a clearinghouse for recent scholarship, bibliographies, and reviews of productions.

WILLIAM CARLOS WILLIAMS, 1883-1963

PRIMARY SOURCES

Separate Works

Poems (1909); The Tempers (1913); A Book of Poems, Al Que Quiere! (1917); Kora in Hell: Improvisations (1920); Sour Grapes: A Book of Poems (1921); Spring and All (1923); Go, Go (1923); The Great American Novel (1923); In the American Grain (1925); A Voyage to Pagany (1928); The Knife of the Times and Other Stories (1932); A Novelette, and Other Prose, 1921-1931 (1932); The Cod Head (1932); An Early Martyr, and Other Poems (1935); Adam & Eve & the City (1936); White Mule (1937); Life along the Passaic River (1938); In the Money: White Mule, Part II (1940); The Broken Span (1941); The Wedge (1944); Paterson (1946); Paterson, Book II (1948); A Dream of Love (1948); The Clouds (1948); Paterson, Book III (1949); The Pink Church (1949); Paterson, Book IV (1951); The Autobiography of William Carlos Williams (1951); The Build-Up (1952); The Desert Music, and Other Poems (1954); Journey to Love (1955); John Marin [with Duncan Phillips and others] (1956); Paterson, Book V (1958); Many Loves: A Play (produced 1958); Yes, Mrs. Williams: A Personal Record of My Mother (1959); Many Loves and Other Plays (1961); Pictures from Brueghel and Other Poems (1962); Paterson, Book I-V (1963).

Collected Works and Edited Texts

Collections of Williams' poetry are Collected Earlier Poems (New York: New Directions, 1951); Collected Later Poems (New Directions, 1950); and Pictures from Brueghel and Other Poems (New Directions, 1962). The five separately published books of Paterson are available as Paterson (New Directions, 1963). Short stories are collected in Make Light of It (New York: Random House, 1950); and The Farmer's Daughters (New Directions, 1961). His dramatic works are in Many Loves and Other Plays (New Directions, 1961). Essays are in In the American Grain (New Directions, 1925; reissued 1940); Selected Essays (New Directions, 1954); and Imaginations, ed. Webster Schott (New Directions, 1970). A Recognizable Image: William Carlos Williams on Art and Artists, ed. Bram Dijkstra (New Directions, 1979) collects many previously unpublished writings. Correspondence is gathered in The Selected Letters, ed. John C. Thirlwall (New York: McDowell, Obolensky, 1957). Autobiographical works are The Autobiography of William Carlos Williams (New York: Random House, 1951); I Wanted to Write a Poem, ed. Edith Heal (Boston: Beacon Press, 1958), which is a conversation about his works that has a bibliographical format; and Williams' description of his mother, Yes, Mrs. Williams (McDowell, Obolensky, 1959). The Embodiment of Knowledge, ed. Ron Loewinsohn (New Directions, 1974) is a 1928-30 manuscript of Williams.

Other Source Materials

Important collections of manuscripts and papers are at the libraries of Yale University and the State University of New York, Buffalo, for which a descriptive catalog is available, Neil Baldwin and Steven L. Meyers, The Manuscripts and Letters of William Carlos Williams in the Poetry Collection of the Lockwood Memorial Library (Boston: G. K. Hall, 1978).

SECONDARY SOURCES

Biography

There are two reliable biographies, Michael Weaver, *William Carlos Williams: The American Background* (New York: Cambridge Univ. Press, 1971), which is a far-ranging study of influences and milieu; and Paul Mariani, *William Carlos Williams: A New World Naked* (New York: McGraw-Hill, 1981), a critical biography which demonstrates Williams' attempts "to keep a beleaguered line of understanding" from sinking "decoratively to rest."

Criticism

Introductions combining criticism and biography are John Malcolm Brinnin, *William Carlos Williams* (Minneapolis: Univ. of Minnesota Press, 1963); Thomas R. Whitaker, *William Carlos Williams* (New York: Twayne, 1968), which is a reliable chronological survey of prose and poetry; and Paul Mariani, *William Carlos Williams: The Poet and His Critics* (Chicago: American Library Association, 1975), which is a perceptive review of the critical response to Williams. Other studies to consult are Linda W. Wagner, *The Poems of William Carlos Williams* (Middletown, CT: Wesleyan Univ. Press, 1963); J. Hillis Miller, *Poets of Reality* (Cambridge, MA: Harvard Univ. Press, 1965); Alan B. Ostrom, *The Poetic World of William Carlos Williams* (Carbondale: Southern Illinois Univ. Press, 1966), which is useful for discussion of shorter poems; James Guimond, *The Art of William Carlos Williams: A Discovery and Possession of America* (Urbana: Univ. of Illinois Press, 1968), which focusses on works of the twenties and thirties; Sherman Paul, *The Music of Survival: A Biography of a Poem by William Carlos Williams* (Urbana: Univ. of Illinois Press, 1968), which concentrates on *The Desert Music*; Bram Dijkstra, *The Hieroglyphics of a New Speech: Cubism, Stieglitz, and the Early Poetry of William Carlos Williams* (Princeton, NJ: Princeton Univ. Press, 1969), which identifies many poems described in the early works; and James Breslin, *William Carlos Williams: An American Artist* (New York: Oxford Univ. Press, 1970), which assesses Williams' place in American literary heritage. Discussions devoted to *Paterson* are W. S. Peterson. *An Approach to Paterson* (New Haven, CT: Yale Univ. Press, 1967); Joel Conarroe, *William Carlos Williams' Paterson: Language and Landscape* (Philadelphia: Univ. of Pennsylvania Press, 1970); and Benjamin Sankey, *A Companion to William Carlos Williams's "Paterson"* (Berkeley: Univ. of California Press, 1971). Jerome Mazzaro, *William Carlos Williams: The Later Poems* (Ithaca, NY: Cornell Univ. Press, 1973) shows how Williams continues to enrich his imagist poetics through experimentation. Linda W. Wagner, *The Prose of William Carlos Williams* (Middletown, CT: Wesleyan Univ. Press, 1970) examines interrelationships between the poetry and prose; and Robert Coles, *William Carlos Williams: The Knack of Survival in America* (New Brunswick, NJ: Rutgers Univ. Press, 1975) interprets the fiction as a parable of American contradictions and ambiguities.

Collections of critical essays are *William Carlos Williams*, ed. J. Hillis Miller (Englewood Cliffs, NJ: Prentice-Hall, 1966); *Profile of William Carlos Williams*, ed. Jerome Mazzaro (Columbus, OH: Merrill, 1971); *William Carlos Williams: A Critical Anthology* (London: Penguin, 1972), which contains essays by other poets and critics; and *William Carlos Williams: The Critical Heritage*, ed. Charles Doyle (Boston: Routledge & Kegan Paul, 1980), which contains criticism and reviews of Williams' work from 1909 to 1964 and letters between Williams and other poets.

Bibliographies

A helpful bibliographic overview is Linda W. Wagner, "William Carlos Williams," in *Sixteen Modern American Authors*, ed. Jackson R. Bryer (Durham, NC: Duke Univ. Press, 1974), pp.573-85. For an annotated list of primary sources, see Emily Mitchell Wallace, *A Bibliography of William Carlos Williams* (Middletown, CT: Wesleyan Univ. Press, 1968); and for a chronological guide to secondary sources, see Linda W. Wagner, *William Carlos Williams: A Reference Guide* (Boston: G. K. Hall, 1978).

Reference Works

William Carlos Williams Newsletter, 1975- contains bibliographies, reviews, explication, and previously unpublished material by Williams. It is continued as *William Carlos Williams Review, 1980-* .

THOMAS (CLAYTON) WOLFE, 1900-1938

PRIMARY SOURCES

Separate Works

Look Homeward Angel: A Story of the Buried Life (1929); *Of Time and the River: A Legend of Man's Hunger in His Youth* (1935); *From Death to Morning* (1935); *The Story of a Novel* (1936); *The Web and the Rock* (1939); *A Note on the Experts: Dexter Vespasian Joyner* (1939); *You Can't Go Home Again* (1940); *The Hills Beyond* (1941); *Gentlemen of the Press: A Play* (1942); *Mannerhouse* [play] (1948); *A Western Journal: A Daily Log of the Great Parks Trip . . . 1938* (1951); *The Mountains* [play] (1970).

Collected Works and Edited Texts

Wolfe's novels are still available in editions by their original publishers, and Holman comments on their textual problems in his essay (*see* Bibliographies). *The Face of the Nation*, ed. John Hall Wheelock (New York: Scribner, 1939) is a selection of poetry about America from the novels *The Story of a Novel* and *From Death to Morning*. *The Mountains*, ed. Pat M. Ryan (Chapel Hill: Univ. of North Carolina Press, 1970) brings together the one-act and three-act versions of this play. *The Portable Thomas Wolfe*, ed. Maxwell Geismar (New York: Viking, 1946) contains selections from the novels and short stories; and *The Short Novels of Thomas Wolfe*, ed. C. Hugh Holman (New York: Scribner, 1961) reprints magazine versions of "A Portrait of Bascom Hawke," "The Web of Earth," "I Have a Thing to Tell You," and "The Party at Jack's," and contains a first printing of a short novel version of "No Door." *The Thomas Wolfe Reader* (Scribner, 1962) reprints *The Story of a Novel* and brings together in "self contained units" material that is fragmented throughout the volumes of fiction. Important sources of biographical materials are *Thomas Wolfe's Letters to His Mother, Julia Elizabeth Wolfe*, ed. John Skally Terry (Scribner, 1943); and a more scholarly presentation of the letters from the University of North Carolina Library, *The Letters of Thomas Wolfe to His Mother*, eds. C. Hugh Holman and Sue Fields Ross (Chapel Hill: Univ. of North Carolina Press, 1968). *The Letters of Thomas Wolfe*, ed. Elizabeth Nowell (Scribner, 1956) collects other letters than those to his mother, with narrative connections. It should be supplemented by the letters of Wolfe's editor, Maxwell Perkins, *Editor to Author* (Scribner, 1950; repr. 1979); and

The Correspondence of Thomas Wolfe and Homer Andrew Watt, eds. Oscar Cargill and Thomas Clark Pollock (New York: New York Univ. Press, 1954). The *Notebooks of Thomas Wolfe,* eds. Richard S. Kennedy and Paschal Reeves. 2v. (Chapel Hill: Univ. of North Carolina Press, 1970) are detailed sources, with extracts from letters and manuscripts interwoven.

Other Source Materials

The major collections of Wolfe's books, papers, and manuscripts are at Harvard University and the University of North Carolina.

SECONDARY SOURCES

Biography

In addition to the notebooks and letters, several biographical accounts are important. A full-scale biography by Elizabeth Nowell, *Thomas Wolfe: A Biography* (Garden City, NY: Doubleday, 1960), tends to blur the fiction with fact, yet remains essential for its informational details. The standard biography, Andrew Turnbull, *Thomas Wolfe* (New York: Scribner, 1967) relies on primary sources and interviews. Richard S. Kennedy, *The Window of Memory* (Chapel Hill: Univ. of North Carolina Press, 1962) concentrates on those aspects of the life that are directly related to Wolfe's literary output. Leo Gurko, *Thomas Wolfe: Beyond the Romantic Ego* (New York: Crowell, 1975) is a clear introduction to the life and works, intended for young adults; and Richard Walser, *Thomas Wolfe Undergraduate* (Durham, NC: Duke Univ. Press, 1977) helpfully documents Wolfe's years at the University of North Carolina, Chapel Hill, from 1916 to 1920.

Criticism

Two reliable short introductions to the life and novels are C. Hugh Holman, *Thomas Wolfe* (Minneapolis: Univ. of Minnesota Press, 1960); and Ladell Payne, *Thomas Wolfe* (Austin, TX: Steck-Vaughn, 1969). Richard Walser, *Thomas Wolfe: An Introduction and Interpretation* (New York: Barnes & Noble, 1961) is a bio-critical introduction, with separate chapters on the four major novels and briefer consideration of the other writings. Louis D. Rubin, Jr., *Thomas Wolfe: The Weather of His Youth* (Baton Rouge: Louisiana State Univ. Press, 1955) regards time and its relation to eternity as the organizing force in Wolfe's work. Two studies that provide insights into the transformation of events from Wolfe's life into fiction are Floyd Watkins, *Thomas Wolfe's Characters: Portraits from Life* (Norman: Univ. of Oklahoma Press, 1957); and Bruce R. McElderry Jr., *Thomas Wolfe* (New York: Twayne, 1964). Paschal Reeves, *Thomas Wolfe's Albatross: Race and Nationality in America* (Athens: Univ. of Georgia Press, 1968) is a study of Wolfe's attitudes towards minorities in his fiction. C. Hugh Holman, *The Loneliness at the Core* (Baton Rouge: Louisiana State Univ. Press, 1975) conveniently brings together much of Holman's distinguished criticism.

There are many collections of critical essays on Wolfe, which include *The Enigma of Thomas Wolfe: Biographical and Critical Selections,* ed. Richard Walser (Cambridge: Harvard Univ. Press, 1953); *The World of Thomas Wolfe,* ed. C. Hugh Holman (New York: Scribner, 1962); *Thomas Wolfe: Three Decades of Criticism,* ed. Leslie A. Field (New York: New York Univ. Press, 1968); *Thomas Wolfe and the Glass of Time,* ed. Paschal Reeves (Athens: Univ. of Georgia Press, 1971), which makes available the papers presented by scholars at the 1969 University of Georgia conference on Wolfe; *Thomas Wolfe: A Collection of Critical Essays*, ed. Louis D. Rubin, Jr. (Englewood Cliffs, NJ: Prentice-Hall, 1973); and *Thomas Wolfe: The Critical Reception*, ed. Paschal Reeves (New York: David Lewis, 1974), which contains significant reviews from 1929 on. A more specialized collection of contemporary reviews and later critical essays on a single novel is *Studies in "Look Homeward Angel,"* ed. Paschal Reeves (Columbus, OH: Merrill, 1970).

Bibliographies

A bibliographic overview of primary and secondary sources is the essay by C. Hugh Holman, "Thomas Wolfe," in *Sixteen Modern American Authors*, ed. Jackson R. Bryer (Durham, NC: Duke Univ. Press, 1974), pp. 587-624. The most complete listing of primary sources, which includes many fugitive publications from newspapers and magazines, is Elmer D. Johnson, *Thomas Wolfe: A Checklist* (Kent, OH: Kent State Univ. Press, 1970). John S. Phillipson, *Thomas Wolfe: A Reference Guide* (Boston: G. K. Hall, 1977) is an annotated bibliography of writing about Wolfe from 1929 to 1976, including dissertations and work in foreign languages.

Reference Works

A semiannual clearinghouse of the Thomas Wolfe Society, which published reviews, notes, news, and bibliographies, was *Thomas Wolfe Newsletter*, v.1, Spring 1977-v.4, Fall 1980. From v.5, Spring 1981, it has been renamed *Thomas Wolfe Review*.

RICHARD WRIGHT, 1908-1960

PRIMARY SOURCES

Separate Works

Uncle Tom's Children: Four Novellas (1938; enlarged and reissued as *Uncle Tom's Children: Five Long Stories*, 1940); *Native Son* (1940); *Bright and Morning Star* (1940, c1938); *12 Million Black Voices* (1941); *Black Boy* [autobiography] (1945); *The Outsider* (1953); *Savage Holiday* (1954); *Black Power: A Record of Reactions in a Land of Pathos* (1954); *The Color Curtain: A Report on the Bandung Conference* (1956); *Pagan Spain* (1957); *White Man, Listen!* (1957); *The Long Dream* (1958); *Eight Men* (1961); *Lawd Today* (1963); *American Hunger* [autobiographical fragment on experience in the Communist Party] (1977).

Collected Works and Edited Texts

There is no standard edition of Wright's works. *Uncle Tom's Children* (New York: Harper Perennial Paperback, 1965) contains his essay "The Ethics of Living Jim Crow"; and "How Bigger Was Born" is reprinted in *Native Son* (New York: Harper Perennial Paperback, 1966). *The Richard Wright Reader*, eds. Ellen Wright and Michel Fabre (New York: Harper & Row, 1978) includes some essays and poems that are not readily available, together with a good introduction.

SECONDARY SOURCES

Biography

Constance Webb, *Richard Wright: A Biography* (New York: G. P. Putnam, 1968), though based on Wright's papers, contains much that is conjectural, and a more reliable study of the life and work is Michel Fabre, *The Unfinished Quest of Richard Wright* (New York: Morrow, 1973). John A. Williams, *A Biography of Richard Wright: The Most Native of Sons* (Garden City, NY: Doubleday, 1970) is intended for young adults.

Criticism

Three reliable introductions are Robert A. Bone, *Richard Wright* (Minneapolis: Univ. of Minnesota Press, 1969); Milton Rickels and Patricia Rickels, *Richard Wright* (Austin, TX: Steck-Vaughn, 1970); and David Bakish, *Richard Wright* (New York: Ungar, 1973). Full-length studies are Edward Margolies, *The Art of Richard Wright* (Carbondale, IL: Southern Illinois Univ. Press, 1969), which explores the progression in Wright's life and writing from emotional and political bondage to freedom; Carl Russell Brignano, *Richard Wright: An Introduction to the Man and His Works* (Pittsburgh: Univ. of Pittsburgh Press, 1970), which examines language and themes; Keneth Kinnamon, *The Emergence of Richard Wright* (Urbana: Univ. of Illinois Press, 1972), which traces Wright's literary development in the context of American society; Katherine Fishburn, *Richard Wright's Hero: The Faces of a Rebel-Victim* (Metuchen, NJ: Scarecrow, 1977), which affirms the dignity of Wright's hero; and Evelyn Gross Avery, *Rebels and Victims: The Fiction of Richard Wright and Bernard Malamud* (Port Washington, NY: Kennikat, 1979), which interprets Wright as a naturalist. A chronological presentation of representative reviews and a checklist for further reading is *Richard Wright: The Critical Reception*, ed. John M. Reilly (New York: Burt Franklin, 1978). A useful collection of criticism is *Twentieth Century Interpretations of Native Son*, ed. Houston A. Baker, Jr. (Englewood Cliffs, NJ: Prentice-Hall, 1972).

Bibliographies

A helpful bibliographic essay is John M. Reilly, "Richard Wright," in *Black American Writers: Bibliographical Essays*, eds. M. Thomas Inge, Maurice Duke, and Jackson R. Bryer. 2v. (New York: St. Martin's Press, 1978), v.2, pp.1-46. Michel Fabre, *The Unfinished Quest of Richard Wright* (*see* Criticism) contains a full listing of primary sources. An excellent bibliography of secondary writing is John M. Reilly, "Richard Wright: An Essay in Bibliography," in *Resources for American Literary Study*, Autumn 1971.

ELINOR (HOYT) WYLIE, 1885-1928

PRIMARY SOURCES

Separate Works

Incidental Numbers (1912); *Nets to Catch the Wind* (1921); *Black Armour: A Book of Poems* (1923); *Jennifer Lorn: A Sedate Extravaganza* (1923); *The Venetian*

Glass Nephew (1925); *The Orphan Angel* [English ed. titled *Mortal Image*] (1926); *Mr. Hodge & Mr. Hazard* (1928); *Trivial Breath* (1928); *Angels and Earthly Creatures: A Sequence of Sonnets* (1929).

Collected Works and Edited Texts

The most important editions are *Collected Poems of Elinor Wylie*, ed. William R. Benét (New York: Knopf, 1932); and *Last Poems of Elinor Wylie* (Knopf, 1943), which contains previously uncollected poems, including some from *Incidental Numbers*. Other work is in *Collected Prose* (Knopf, 1933).

Other Source Materials

Collections of Wylie's papers are at the Library of Congress and the Lockwood Memorial Library, University of Buffalo.

SECONDARY SOURCES

Biography

Stanley Olson, *Elinor Wylie: A Life Apart* (New York: Dial Press, 1979) is a book-length study; but the best sources are among memoirs, which include Elizabeth S. Sergeant, *Fire under the Andes: A Group of North American Portraits* (New York: Knopf, 1927); William Rose Benét, *The Prose and Poetry of Elinor Wylie* (Norton, MA: Wheaton College Press, 1934); Nancy Hoyt, *Elinor Wylie: The Portrait of an Unknown Lady* (Indianapolis: Bobbs-Merrill, 1935; repr. Norfolk, VA: Pentelic Press, 1977), which is by her sister; Carl Van Doren, *Three Worlds* (New York: Harper, 1936); Mary Colum, *Life and the Dream* (Garden City, NY: Doubleday, 1947); and Edmund Wilson, *The Shores of Light: A Literary Chronicle of the Twenties and Thirties* (New York: Farrar, Straus, & Young, 1952).

Criticism

A bio-critical study is Thomas Gray, *Elinor Wylie* (New York: Twayne, 1969).

Author/Title/Subject Index to Part I and Subject Index to Part II

This index provides access to authors, editors, titles, and subject entries for part I and to the 100 subject authors of part II (indicated by *).

Abdullah, Omanii, and James V. Hatch, *Black Playwrights*, 47

Abrams, M. H., *Glossary of Literary Terms*, 31

Abstracts of English Studies, 23

Access, 22

Achievement in American Poetry, 1900-1950, Louise Bogan (ed.), 38

Achievement of American Criticism, Clarence Arthur Brown (ed.), 53

Acres of Flint, Perry D. Westbrook, 41

Acronyms, *See* **Periodicals, acronyms**

***Adams, Henry (Brooks), 70-71**

Adelman, Irving, and Rita Dworkin, *Contemporary Novel*, 27; *Modern Drama*, 26

Afro-American Fiction, Edward Margolies and David Bakish, 47

Afro-American Literature, *See* **Black American Literature**

Afro-American Literature and Culture since World War II, Charles D. Peavy, 47

Afro-American Poetry and Drama, William P. French, et al., 46-47

Afro-American Writers, Darwin T. Turner, 47

After the New Criticism, Frank Lentricchia, 53

Age of Energy, Howard Mumford Jones, 37

Ahlstrom, Sydney E., *Religious History of the American People*, 56

Aiiieeeee!, Frank Chin, et al. (eds.), 46

Aims and Methods of Scholarship in Modern Languages and Literature, James Thorpe (ed.), 55

Aims of Phenomenology, Martin Farber, 54

***Alcott, Louisa May, 71-72**

Allen, Gay Wilson (ed.), *American Poetry*, 60

Altick, Richard D., and Andrew Wright, *Selective Bibliography for the Study of English and American Literature*, 17

Altieri, Charles, *Modern Poetry*, 19

American Authors, 1600-1900, Stanley J. Kunitz and Howard Haycraft, 34

American Authors and Books, W. J. Burke and Will D. Howe, 33

American Dialect Dictionary, Harold Wentworth, 59

American Drama, Travis Bogard, Richard Moody, and Walter J. Meserve, 39

American Drama since 1918, Joseph Wood Krutch, 39

American Drama to 1900, Walter J. Meserve, 25, 39

American English, 58-59

  bibliographic guides, 40 (Tanner)

  pronunciation, 59

  slang, 59 (Wentworth)

American English, Albert H. Marckwardt, 59

American English: A Bibliography, Vito J. Brenni, 58

American English Dialects in Literature, Eva M. Burkett, 58

American Fiction, 1774-1850; 1851-1875; 1876-1900, Lyle H. Wright, 27

American Fiction, 1900-1950, James Woodress, 26

American Fiction to 1900, David K. Kirby, 40

American Folklore, Richard M. Dorson, 38

American Humor, Constance M. Rourke, 41

American Humorist, Norris Y. Yates, 41

American Indian and Eskimo Authors, Arlene B. Hirschfelder, 50